Constitutions and the Commons

Constitutions and the Commons looks at a critical but little examined issue of the degree to which the federal constitution of a nation contributes toward or limits the ability of the national government to manage its domestic natural resources. Furthermore it considers how far the constitution facilitates the binding of constituent states, provinces, or subnational units to honor the conditions of international environmental treaties. While the main focus is on the U.S. and Canada, there is also detailed coverage of other nations such as Australia, Brazil, India, and Russia.

After introducing the role of constitutions in establishing the legal framework for environmental management in federal systems, the author presents a continuum of constitutionally driven natural resource management scenarios, from local to national, and then to global governance. These sections describe how subnational governance in federal systems may take on the characteristics of a commons—with all the attendant tragedies—in the absence of sufficient national constitutional authority. In turn, sufficient national constitutional authority over natural resources also allows these nations to more effectively engage in efforts to manage the global commons, as these nations would be unconstrained by subnational units of government during international negotiations.

It is thus shown that national governments in federal systems are at the center of a constitutional "nested governance commons," with lower levels of government potentially acting as rational herders on the national commons and national governments potentially acting as rational herders on the global commons. National governments in federal systems are therefore crucial to establishing sustainable management of resources across scales.

The book concludes by discussing how federal systems without sufficient national constitutional authority over resources may be strengthened by adopting the approach of federal constitutions that facilitate more robust national level inputs into natural resources management, facilitating national minimum standards as a form of "Fail-safe Federalism" that subnational governments may supplement with discretion to preserve important values of federalism.

Blake Hudson is Associate Professor at both the Paul M. Hebert Law Center and the School of the Coast and Environment, Louisiana State University, USA.

About Resources for the Future *and* RFF Press

Resources for the Future (RFF) improves environmental and natural resource policymaking worldwide through independent social science research of the highest caliber. Founded in 1952, RFF pioneered the application of economics as a tool for developing more effective policy about the use and conservation of natural resources. Its scholars continue to employ social science methods to analyze critical issues concerning pollution control, energy policy, land and water use, hazardous waste, climate change, biodiversity, and the environmental challenges of developing countries.

RFF Press supports the mission of RFF by publishing book-length works that present a broad range of approaches to the study of natural resources and the environment. Its authors and editors include RFF staff, researchers from the larger academic and policy communities, and journalists. Audiences for publications by RFF Press include all of the participants in the policymaking process—scholars, the media, advocacy groups, NGOs, professionals in business and government, and the public.

Constitutions and the Commons

The Impact of Federal Governance on Local, National, and Global Resource Management

Blake Hudson

Routledge
Taylor & Francis Group
LONDON AND NEW YORK

First published 2014
by RFF Press

2 Park Square, Milton Park, Abingdon, Oxfordshire OX14 4RN
711 Third Avenue, New York, NY 10017

Routledge is an imprint of the Taylor & Francis Group, an informa business

First issued in paperback 2017

British Library Cataloguing-in-Publication Data
A catalogue record for this book is available from the British Library

Library of Congress Cataloging in Publication Data
Hudson, Blake, author.
Constitutions and the commons : the impact of federal governance on local, national, and global resource management / Blake Hudson.
pages cm
Includes bibliographical references and index.
1. Natural resources–Law and legislation. 2. Federal government. I. Title.
K3478.H835 2014
333.2–dc23
2013035371

ISBN: 978-1-61726-096-4 (hbk)
ISBN: 978-1-138-57479-3 (pbk)

Typeset in Garamond
by Taylor & Francis Books

Contents

List of Illustrations

Figures

Tables

Preface

The inspiration for this book, and indeed for virtually my entire research agenda to this point, arose from the experience of a single hike through my family's forestland in south Alabama (depicted on the cover of this book). Upon stopping at the stream that divided our property from our neighbors' property, I was shocked to see the neighboring land completely devoid of the beautiful forest that had previously stood there. The landowner had clear-cut the trees on the entire parcel, including all the way to the stream bank. This action eventually led to erosion which in turn contributed to both environmental and economic degradation of resources on our property. I remember thinking at the time: "Who is responsible for this? Surely this is not legal?" It was not until law school that I learned what my family's option might have been had we sought recourse against our neighbor. Our only action would have been in tort law, by, for example, claiming in court that our neighbors' actions had constituted a nuisance and that the neighbors had used their property in a way that unlawfully interfered with the use and value of our property.

The first problem with this recourse mechanism, aside from the fact that it is a difficult legal claim to prove, is that my family did not have any information that such a claim was possible. Second, though natural resources were abundant on our land, my family did not have the economic resources to bring such a claim. I learned that other states had regulatory regimes designed to prevent such actions by property owners. These regulations required that forested streamside buffer zones be left along streams, to prevent erosion, water eutrophication, impacts on fisheries due to increased stream temperature, and a number of other ills associated with cutting timber too close to watercourses. But my home state, Alabama, has no such regulations. Indeed, virtually every state in the southeastern United States maintains only voluntary best management practices.

Though I grew up in an area that prides itself on stringent protection of private property rights, this experience made me reevaluate the role of government in balancing not only the interests of private property owners relative to each other, but also balancing the rights of private property owners with the public's interest in a healthy environment. Central governments control most of the world's natural resources, and this is especially so in the case of forests.

Much scholarship is (rightly) focused on the abuses of central governments in not empowering local populations, through property rights and land tenure, to control resources. As a result, those local populations do not have a vested interest in protecting or sustainably managing resources, nor do they receive the benefits of social and economic justice.

Yet, in some federal nations the opposite is true, whereby highly decentralized subnational governments and private property owners control a majority of a nation's resources. These entities often exercise such a degree of exclusive control over those resources that they are free to make decisions that are environmentally destructive over the long term in order to capture short-term economic gains, and they do so with legal protections that prohibit potentially needed centralized inputs into forest management. In other words, so much of the emphasis in forest policy circles today is aimed at addressing overcentralization, but there remains a problem at the other end of that spectrum—a problem of over-*decentralization* of natural resource policy. This over-decentralization is not only driven by political choices in certain federal systems, but manifests as even more problematic when it becomes entrenched by legal institutions, such as those established by national constitutions.

When these legal institutions entrench uncoordinated and individually rational, but collectively deficient, resource policy within a nation, what results is a synergy between constitutions and the commons. This book is an initial attempt to describe some of the more notable attributes of this synergy, and hopefully this endeavor will provide a foundation for future study of the phenomenon.

I would like to thank my primary mentors in legal academia, Jim Salzman and Laura Underkuffler, for encouraging me to explore property and natural resource management issues of genuine interest and for giving me the confidence that I could achieve my goals. I would like to thank Erika Weinthal for introducing me to the nexus between law and political science, and Ben Cashore for mentoring me on that nexus in the forest context. Finally, I would like to thank my friends and colleagues Brigham Daniels and Jonathan Rosenbloom for always being willing to discuss the commons and for expanding my understanding of commons scholarship.

I dedicate this book first to my grandfather, George Campbell, who took me to the woods every day—though he did not have much to say, he taught me the value of sitting by a tree or creek and simply being still in nature. I also dedicate this book to my wife Eliza and to my son, Campbell, whose name represents the legacy of those who have come before to care about the forests and other natural resources of southern Alabama.

Part I

Constitutionalization of the Commons

1 Introduction[1]

What this Book is About

Garrett Hardin's *Tragedy of the Commons*[2] describes the consequences of rational individuals seeking to maximize personal economic benefits within a closed system of natural resources, or "natural capital." Without some coordinating force, arising either internally from the collection of individuals or externally from an outside authority, each individual's exercise of rational self-interest results in overconsumption of natural capital and ultimately its complete and tragic elimination from the system. The *Tragedy of the Commons* is one of the most cited policy articles of our time,[3] has become one of the primary theoretical drivers of environmental policy, and has spawned a growing body of scholarship expanding our understanding of the commons—including the Nobel Prize-worthy work of Elinor Ostrom. The commons theoretical construct has been applied to everything from traditional natural resources to social constructs like the U.S. presidential primary system.[4] Even so, the theory has yet to be applied to the system of government most likely to parallel, and perhaps even *legally entrench*, the natural capital commons described by Hardin and others—the federal system of government. This book seeks to act as a genesis for that endeavor.

Within federal systems of government numerous subnational governments and private entities seek to maximize individual benefits, such as economic growth through land development and resource extraction, within closed systems of natural capital defined by artificial governmental boundaries—boundaries that bear little to no relationship with the natural environment over which they are layered. Some subnational governments and private entities may succeed in gaining the benefits of economic growth *while avoiding* natural capital overuse and degradation by acting "irrationally" as that term is understood under the Hardin paradigm. They may even do so in the presence of free-riding by others who would reap the benefits of their actions without contributing to the sustainable management regime. In addition, groups of subnational governments or private entities may come together to successfully sustain natural capital by overcoming the collective action problems that might typically plague commons management.

But what if subnational governments or private entities refuse to act individually irrational or to self-coordinate as a group to sustainably manage the natural capital over which they maintain control? Assuming that the requisite amount of political will exists, a higher level of government might step in to incentivize or coerce better management of those resources. What if, however, a higher level of government does not maintain the *legal authority* under the national constitution to coordinate subnational action? Or, what if a higher level of government acts under its constitutional authority to legally preempt subnational action seeking to resolve the commons dilemma? In these cases, each subnational government's individualized, legally defensible, or coerced, rationality may result in overconsumption of natural capital within its jurisdiction and ultimately its complete and tragic elimination from both subnational resource systems and the aggregate of subnational systems constituting national and global natural capital systems. The commons and the associated resource tragedies that might occur upon it have become constitutionalized.

Take a scenario from the United States, where the U.S. federal government has never claimed, nor does it currently[5] maintain, recognized constitutional authority over a variety of direct land use planning activities in the nearly 88,000 subnational governments within its borders.[6] Meanwhile, state governments in the U.S. often decline to coordinate land use activities of local governments and private property owners despite maintaining the constitutional authority to do so. States may also exercise their constitutional authority over land use to preempt local government attempts to address natural capital commons issues. Thus state and local governments often maintain lax land use standards with a view toward promoting economic development and the replacement of natural capital with human-made capital[7]—a phenomena commonly known as a "race to the bottom." Ultimately, the U.S. federal government currently lacks recognized constitutional authority to coordinate this vast abundance of potential individualized subnational rationality in the context of private land development and certain landed resource extraction activities (private forest management, for example). To the extent that scholars believe U.S. constitutional law could certainly facilitate federal regulatory inputs into direct land use planning should Congress choose to act, notwithstanding a current lack of resolution of that constitutional question, other federal nations present more compelling examples of the federally entrenched commons phenomena. In Canada, for example, there remains no doubt that the federal government currently may not prescriptively regulate the 84 percent of the nation's forests under provincial control, as the provinces receive exclusive regulatory control over those resources from the explicit text of the Canadian Constitution. Putting aside prescriptive regulatory inputs, the Canadian federal government has even had a difficult time incentivizing provinces to *voluntarily* adopt federal standards or targets.

Though this scenario is but one of the many ways in which the commons dynamic can play out in federal systems, the lack of coordinating legal authority at the national level within a federal system of government has the potential to legally entrench a natural capital commons within national and subnational jurisdictional boundaries. In addition, these domestic constitutional constraints also may contribute to a natural capital commons at the global level, at a time when some of the most important commons problems, such as climate change, have expanded to the global scale.[8] Federal constitutions that grant subnational governments exclusive regulatory authority over certain subject matters may constrain national governments during international negotiations—a national government that cannot legally bind subnational governments to an international agreement cannot fully and freely arrange its international obligations. In fact, the international governance system itself operates like a federal nation in which exclusive regulatory authority resides in subnational units, because no hegemonic, higher level authority exists to prescribe and enforce rules upon nations. As a result, global governance depends entirely upon internal rules of operation established by altruistically cooperating nations. Those internal rules may not materialize—at least in their most robust form—if national governments in federal systems cannot bind subnational governments to ensure international treaties are enforced on domestic scales.

The case of subnational forest management in the U.S. and Canada provides a more tangible example of how a single federal constitution may entrench a natural capital commons on local, national, and global scales. Forests are perhaps the quintessential scalar resource. On local scales forests provide timber resources, watershed protection, flood control services, air quality benefits, gains in energy efficiency, regulation of local ambient air temperatures, species habitat, and cultural and recreational values, while on global scales they provide a renewable fuel source and sequester large amounts of greenhouse gases that would otherwise exacerbate climate change. Pursuant to their reserved constitutional power over land use regulation, states currently maintain virtually exclusive regulatory authority over the 65 percent of U.S. forests in subnational ownership,[9] while, as noted above, Canadian provinces maintain exclusive constitutional authority over the 84 percent of Canadian forests in subnational ownership.[10] In the U.S., some states maintain robust standards to achieve sustainable forest management protections, while a number of other states, particularly in the southeast, maintain only voluntary forest management standards that are some of the least rigorous in the world—even less stringent than many developing countries.[11] These poor standards can lead to a variety of environmental harms, and even the baseline forest management standards in states with prescriptive regulations may be far from what is needed to ensure a substantial role for forests in sequestering carbon to combat climate change. In Canada, meanwhile, the provinces maintain better baseline forest management standards across the board than do many U.S. states, yet the Canadian federal government is even more limited by its constitution than is the U.S. federal government in gaining regulatory inputs into subnational forest policy. This severe limitation is due to the aforementioned fact that Canada's constitution contains an *explicit* textual grant of exclusive subnational forest regulatory authority to the provinces. As a result, if the Canadian federal government sought to bind the provinces to forest management prescriptions, it would have even fewer options available to it than would the U.S. federal government.

The same constitution that allows southeastern U.S. states to exercise "rationality" in maintaining poor forest management standards on local scales, and the Canadian federal government's inability to gain virtually any direct (or even indirect) inputs into provincial forest policy, also limits these federal systems' ability to effectively engage in certain types of international negotiations, such as a climate change agreement dictating certain types of forest management activities globally. The inability to implement such a treaty regarding a majority of forests within these federal systems' borders would render their participation, at least in a prescriptive arrangement, virtually meaningless. Thus, constitutional constraints allow rational private foresters to freely appropriate forest resources from local, state, or provincial natural capital commons, rational states and provinces to facilitate unchecked forest capital appropriation from the national natural capital commons, and leave rational nations unable to intervene in unchecked appropriation of forest capital from the global natural capital commons.

In the end, the constitutional rules guiding a federal nation's governance structure are crucial to determining whether subnational, national, or global natural capital commons will be legally entrenched across geopolitical scales for certain resources. In this way, federal constitutions act as a keystone for connecting these commons, "nested" one within another, and for supporting effective natural capital management across scales. This book analyzes the implications of constitutionally entrenched nested natural capital commons in order to better understand how federal systems of government can avoid rushing toward tragic overconsumption of natural resources on local and national scales, and also how they can avoid doing so on a global scale within the ultimate federal system—the international community. This novel examination of federal nested commons is only an introduction to some of the more notable features of federal constitutional impacts on resource governance across scales. Hopefully the examination will lead to further research into the nuances of federal nested commons, their implications for resource governance across scales, and better overall management of natural capital within federal systems.

Chapter 2 will define "commons" and "commons resources" both as traditionally understood and as understood given recent scholarship on the types of resources considered commons resources, including natural capital subject to both privatization and government regulatory authority. Chapter 2 will further explain how federal systems of government may entrench a legally protected natural capital commons and how that commons is actually a nested set of commons at different governmental scales—subnational commons within national commons within the global commons. In addition, the chapter will describe how a federal nation's constitutional structure is crucial to avoiding natural capital commons tragedies driven by legal entrenchment not only within federal nations on both local and national scales, but also globally as nations attempt to negotiate rules guiding the global governance of natural capital. In this way, we might say that the commons has been "constitutionalized," as federal constitutions establish rules for resource management across the scales of federal systems of government.

Chapter 3 takes us into an examination of decentralization within the nested governance commons described in Chapter 2. This chapter makes clear how federal constitutionalization has led to decentralization that, while certainly resulting in many benefits for resource management and resource managers, also may result in a variety of resource management ills—ills tracking a classic commons tragedy. While a great deal of institutional scholarship has focused on over-centralization of resource management, "over-decentralization" of resource management, at least from a legal and institutional perspective, is not sufficiently understood. This chapter lays a foundation for those efforts. Chapter 3 undertakes an analysis of the four nested natural capital commons that arise as a result of federal constitutional structure. These nested commons need not necessarily result in tragedy for the natural capital within a federal system, but in reality the tragedy remains a distinct, legally defensible possibility—and indeed, a variety of examples across natural capital management scales demonstrate that legal "over-decentralization" in federal systems creates the same collective action, over-exploitation and other commons problems as traditionally understood commons resources do.

Chapter 4 begins our review of the federalization of the commons by examining case studies from the U.S. regarding the ability (or the lack thereof) of the federal government to aggregate authority back to the federal level when over-decentralization would result in poor management of the nation's resources. The legal authority to do so in the U.S., primarily the Commerce Clause, is very much unclear under some circumstances and for certain resources. Indeed, as discussed in Chapter 5, certain federal systems, like the U.S. and Canada, maintain federal structures that contain elements of both "dynamic" and "dual" federalism. Dynamic federalism allows regulatory inputs at both decentralized and federal levels, whereas dual reserves certain regulatory authority to *either* the federal or subnational governments, creating stark problems for resource management, especially if the federal government would like to resolve a commons dilemma occurring on subnational scales.

Chapter 6 takes us into a discussion of the internationalization of the commons, and how dual federalism on domestic scales can impact global resource management—primarily through the lens of a U.S. forest management case study. Chapter 7 broadens the inquiry by assessing other federal systems containing important forest resources in order to determine which systems might be *legally sufficient* in facilitating dynamic federalism structures whereby neither over-centralization nor over-decentralization of resource management occurs. Chapter 8 takes the results of Chapter 7's review and focuses on two federal systems in particular, the U.S. and Canada, which maintain, at least to a degree, the type of legal *deficiencies* in constitutional structure that can lead to nested commons tragedies in federal systems. Chapter 9 concludes by introducing how keystone constitutions in federal systems might be "fortified"—that is, how they can all be similarly strengthened to facilitate more effective natural capital resource governance by rebalancing regulatory authority between central and decentralized governments.

Before diving fully into the details of this book, however, it is important to also detail what this book does not set out to achieve, which will allow a more precise focus on the thesis here presented.

What this Book is Not About

First, this book is not arguing that federal systems of government are inherently ineffective or necessarily a poor form of governance for the effective management of natural capital. Indeed, later chapters describe the important natural resource management benefits that decentralized systems of government provide. Nor does this book argue that high degrees of centralization of governance authority are necessarily appropriate. Ostrom and others have provided important empirical evidence that over-centralization can lead to a variety of governance and resource management ills. Rather, this book is concerned with the opposite problem—that of *over-decentralization*—and seeks to highlight a form of federal governance that strikes the appropriate balance of centralized and decentralized natural capital governance inputs.

Second, this book also does not intend to paint federal systems of government with too broad of a brush. As the text will demonstrate, federal systems vary greatly with regard to their likelihood to legally entrench natural capital commons. For example, as described in Part IV., the constitutional allocation of subnational forest governance authority in federal systems lies along a broad spectrum. On one end of the spectrum is Canada, which has a constitution that contains explicit text granting constitutional authority to the *provinces* to formulate subnational forest policy. The U.S. is a bit further along the spectrum, maintaining a constitution that does not contain any explicit text related to forestry, but whose courts as a matter of constitutional interpretation have to date recognized subnational forest governance authority as residing almost exclusively in the states—a situation always subject to change as controversies arise and new legal arguments are potentially put forth and adopted by courts. A bit further along the spectrum is Australia, whose constitution also contains no explicit text related to subnational forestry, but whose courts as a matter of constitutional interpretation *have* recognized the authority of the national government to engage in subnational forest policy-making to fulfill a wide range of international obligations. Finally, on the opposite end of the spectrum are federal nations like Brazil, whose constitution contains explicit provisions granting legal authority to the *national* government to formulate subnational forest policy.

Third, this book does not engage all of the potential arguments to which the constitutional debate within a given federal system might lend itself. For example, the constitutional question regarding federal versus subnational regulatory authority over a given subject may be due almost entirely to federal government regulatory inaction, rather than definitive jurisprudential treatment whereby courts make final judgments regarding the constitutional allocation of governance authority. Many might argue this is the case in the U.S. regarding land use planning or subnational forest management—arguing that the federal government maintains the legal authority to regulate, but has simply not yet acted, which in turn prohibits the judiciary from considering the constitutionality of federal action. Others may disagree, arguing that the federal government in the U.S. is constitutionally bound from, for example, establishing limits lines within a municipality beyond which certain forms or a certain density of land development are prohibited. Nonetheless, legal questions of relative federal/subnational regulatory authority all too often remain open, regardless of good constitutional arguments on either side. Until these questions are resolved, we need to better understand the impacts that potential legal constraints can have on adequate resource management in federal systems.

Fourth, this book does not argue that commons tragedies will *inevitably* flow out of federal constitutional structures—even out of ones that legally entrench certain types of natural capital commons. Even when a constitution does not allow higher level governance inputs into resource management, subnational governments and private individuals remain free to act individually "irrationally," as Hardin would use the term, against their perceived individual short-term economic interest and for the benefit of broader society through political action (unless they are preempted by higher level governments from doing so, of course). Theoretically, every subnational government or private individual may choose to act irrationally—every herder is capable of refraining from adding more cattle to the heard in a way that degrades the resource. They may also act irrationally not in an incidental, individual manner, but by coordinating with each other through successful collective action arrangements. As demonstrated by the evidence presented in this book, however, widespread "irrational" political action instituting responsible natural capital management is largely lacking, with rationality instead manifesting on large scales. The term "rational" is here used to simply describe governments or individuals who make policy and natural capital appropriation decisions based primarily on short-term economic costs and benefits within their own jurisdictional or property boundaries, much like Hardin's herders with respect to the natural capital immediately available to them on the commons. The term is not used to debate or explore the nuances of behavioral economics or whether under all circumstances individuals or governments necessarily behave "rationally." Ultimately, this book focuses on the circumstances in which individuals or governments do behave in this manner, rather than normatively arguing that they always do so.

Along these same lines, the type of rationality explored in this book is not limited to federal systems of government. It may also result within unitary systems of government, which make up the remaining 160-plus governments on the globe. Importantly, however—and this is the fundamental premise underlying the book—in unitary systems rationality would manifest as a *political* matter rather than as a legal/constitutional matter. In a unitary system, the central government may politically choose not to exercise its legal authority to intervene in destructive subnational appropriation of natural capital, whether because of political pressure from subnational units of government or otherwise. This book, on the other hand, is focused on circumstances where a central authority in a federal system politically *wishes* to legally intervene, but is constrained in doing so by constitutional structure.

Fifth, this book is also not aimed at making normative claims about which type of "fail-safes," as discussed in Chapter 9, would be optimal to forge a remedy for natural capital management problems created by federal structure, or to argue that any one in particular should be used in isolation. Rather the book is aimed at alerting policy-makers and others concerned with the protection of natural capital of the potential legally protected tragedies that may result from federal constitutional structure, and making a normative claim that some natural capital problems, such as those associated with urban development and forest management, require *some* form of legal and policy response to adjust federal structure to adequately address the problem.

Finally, this book is not a microeconomic critique or an economic empirical work. Rather, the book focuses on institutional realities and their commons characteristics as evidenced by legal case-law, the existence or absence of a variety of natural capital policies, and data on the continually dire state of natural capital itself. While Ostrom makes clear that reliance on metaphors may often give rise to bad policy, her work itself incorporates important elements of metaphor, which provide valuable insights into real world problems. This is especially so when the projected ramifications of current policy trends are supported by legal interpretations and text, evidence of growing displacement of natural capital, and the inertia of economic systems grounded in the replacement of that natural capital with human-made capital.

Notes

1 This book arose out of a collection of articles written on the subjects presented. The material constituting significant portions of each chapter originated in the following articles: Blake Hudson and Jonathan Rosenbloom, Uncommon Approaches to Commons Problems: Nested Governance Commons and Climate Change, 64 *Hastings L.J.* 1273 (2013); Blake Hudson, Federal Constitutions, Global Governance, and the Role of Forests in Regulating Climate Change, 87 *Ind. L.J.* 1455 (2012); Blake Hudson, Federal Constitutions: The Keystone of Nested Commons Governance, 63 *Ala. L. Rev.* 1007 (2012); Blake Hudson, Fail-safe Federalism and Climate Change: The Case of U.S. and Canadian Forest Policy, 44 *Conn. L. Rev.* 925 (2012); Blake Hudson, Coastal Land Loss and the Mitigation-Adaptation Dilemma: Between Scylla and Charybdis, 73 *La. L. Rev.* 31

(2012); Blake Hudson, Climate Change, Forests and Federalism: Seeing the Treaty for the Trees, 82 *U. Col. L. Rev.* 363 (2011); Blake Hudson, Reconstituting Land Use Federalism to Address Transitory and Perpetual Disasters: The Bimodal Federalism Framework, 2011 *BYU L. Rev.* 1991 (2011); Blake Hudson, Commerce in the Commons: A Unified Theory of Natural Capital Regulation Under the Commerce Clause, 35 *Harv. Env. L. Rev.* 375 (2011).

2 Garret Hardin, Tragedy of the Commons, 162 *Science* 1243 (1968).

3 Karlson "Charlie" Hargroves and Michael H. Smith, *The Natural Advantage of Nations: Business Opportunities, Innovation and Governance in the 21st Century*. London; Sterling, VA : Earthscan 178 (2005).

4 Brigham Daniels, Governing the Presidential Nomination Commons, 84 *Tul. L. Rev.* 899 (2010).

5 I say "currently" because even though there may be jurisprudential arguments justifying the constitutionality of certain forms of prescriptive federal land-use regulation, the federal government has yet to claim such authority and courts have not had an opportunity to assess it. Furthermore, the federal government maintains very limited *indirect* inputs into land-use planning.

6 Steffen W. Schmidt et al., *American Government and Politics Today* 89 (14th ed. 2009).

7 Edella Schlager and William Blomquist, Water Resources: The Southwestern United States, in *Protecting the Commons* 133, 157 (Joanna Burger et al. eds, 2001) ("[f]ederal, state, and local rules and organizations on the public-sector side are intensely articulated with land-use development … decisions driven largely by private-sector concerns.").

8 Joanna Burger et al., Common-Pool Resources and Commons Institutions, in *Protecting the Commons* 1, 6 (Joanna Burger et al. eds., 2001).

9 Gerald A. Rose et al., Forest Resources Decision-Making in the U.S., in *The Politics of Decentralization: Forests, People and Power* 238, 239 (Carol J. Pierce Colfer and Doris Capistrano eds, 2005).

10 See Canadian Counsel of Forest Ministers, *Sustainable Forest Management in Canada* 4 (2010).

11 Jacek P. Siry, Frederick W. Cubbage, and David H. Newman, *Global Forest Ownership: Implications for Forest Production, Management, and Protection* 3, XIII World Forestry Congress Paper (2009), available at http://www.pefc.org/images/stories/documents/external/global_forest_ownership_FD.pdf. This is not to say, of course, that developing countries with greater standards on paper manage forests better in fact, as enforcement capacity and overall efficacy of the rule of law impact the translation of law into results on the ground.

2 Natural Capital Commons and Keystone Constitutions

The Theoretical Context[1]

Keystone:

1: the wedge-shaped piece at the summit of an arch, regarded as holding the other pieces in place.

2: something that is necessary to connect or support a number of other related things.[2]

Introduction to the Commons

Hardin's *Tragedy of the Commons* describes a pasture open to any and all herders of cattle, each of whom maintains the right to graze in the pasture. This open allocation of rights renders the pasture a "commons," and the grass present upon it a "commons resource." Upon entering the pasture, each herder makes a rational choice to maximize personal economic gain by continually adding cattle to the herder's respective herd. Each herder gains the full benefit of each additional cow, but the negative cost of incremental over-grazing of the grass resource is spread among all herders on the commons. As a result, each herder undertakes a simple, short-term cost–benefit analysis and determines that it is *always* in the herder's best interest to add more cattle, as individual returns invariably outweigh individual costs. As Hardin describes for each herder,

> the only sensible course for him to pursue is to add another animal to his herd. And another; and another ... But this is the conclusion reached by each and every rational herdsman sharing the commons. Therein is the tragedy. Each man is locked into a system that compels him to increase his herd without limit—in a world that is limited ... Freedom in a commons brings ruin to all.[3]

Freedom in a commons brings ruin to all because in a finite world of finite resources, unchecked consumption can ultimately lead to dire consequences for the society reliant on those resources. Hardin provides many modern examples of commons in which this tragedy has the potential to occur, such

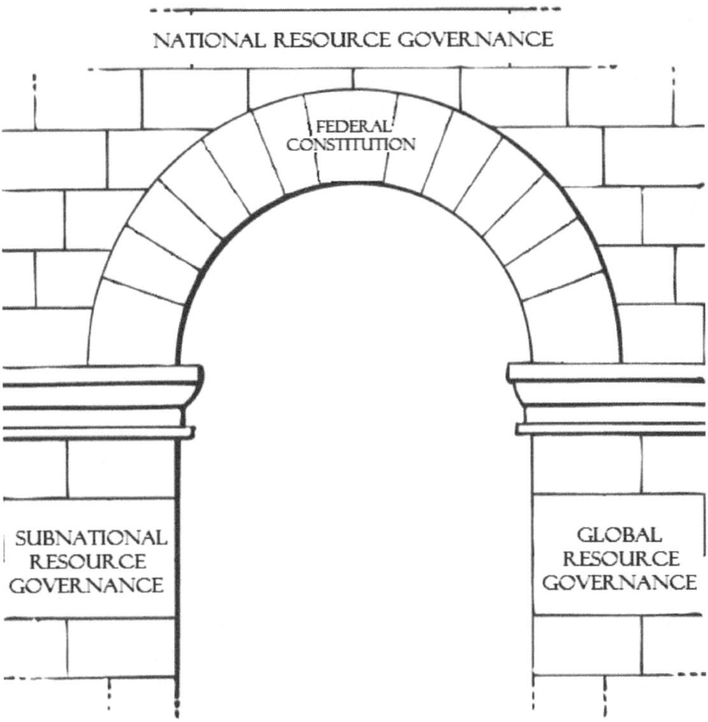

Figure 2.1 The arch of resource governance in federal systems

as national parks, grazing lands, fish stocks, pollution in the atmosphere, and even parking meters. Since the time of Hardin's initial essay, commons scholars have recognized a wide and ever-expanding variety of resources that may be deemed commons in nature and which may be subject to tragedies of overuse and degradation. Commons analysis has been applied not only to "traditional" natural resources, such as fisheries, forests, groundwater aquifers, and the atmosphere, but also to a variety of "new commons" in the form of medical care, parking spaces, sidewalk vending, knowledge, government budgets, silence, email inboxes, and even presidential primaries.[4]

Though the categories of resources to which commons analysis may be applied continue to expand, commons scholars have settled on two key elements that define commons resources: depletability (or rivalry) and non-excludability. Noted commons scholars Keohane and Ostrom have characterized commons resources as "depletable natural or human-made resources from which potential beneficiaries are difficult to exclude,"[5] while Oran Young similarly describes them as resources "used by a group of appropriators that is both non-excludable and depletable."[6] Duncan Snidal asserts that commons analysis

> focuses on the provision and appropriation of goods that are not joint in consumption (like private goods) but where exclusion is difficult (like public goods). Standard cases are natural resources, like forests or water, where the quantity available is less than the desired consumption of potential appropriators.[7]

Stated slightly differently, commons resources are "natural or human-made resources in which (a) exclusion is non-trivial (but not necessarily impossible) and (b) yield is subtractable."[8] To put these terms in context, the grass resource consumed by one herder is no longer available to other, rival herders (depletable), and it is very difficult to exclude any one herder from consuming the resource (non-excludable).

A variety of other terms and concepts are critical to commons analysis. The corpus of resources that make up the commons is known as a "resource system." A resource system is comprised of "resource units," defined as "what individuals appropriate or use from resource systems."[9] The process of withdrawing resource units from a resource system is called "appropriation," and those who withdraw resource units from the system are called "appropriators." When more than one appropriator extracts commons resource units from a resource system—as do the herders in Hardin's example—they are called "co-appropriators." Co-appropriators are "tied together in a lattice of interdependence" so long as they continue to share the commons.[10] Finally, "providers" arrange for the provision of a commons resource, and "producers" are any entities that maintain and ensure the long-term viability of the resource system.

Of particular importance for the concepts of scale presented in this book, resource units "*are not subject to joint use or appropriation*,"[11] meaning that appropriators *can* exclude other appropriators from the resource unit itself. Rather, the non-excludability requirement for a commons resource is met because it is exceedingly difficult to exclude other appropriators from the *resource system*. So whether a resource is in fact part of a commons is largely a matter of scale, and depends upon how one defines both the resource unit and the resource system. As detailed in Chapters 3 and 4, for example, an individual resource *unit* may be defined by private property, state, or national geopolitical boundaries, and the resource *system* is the higher level geopolitical jurisdiction that contains those respective resource units, such as local government commons (with private property herders), state government commons (with local government herders), national government commons (with state or provincial government herders), and global governance regime commons (with national government herders).

Hardin's pastoral commons illustrates commons terminology in a fairly straightforward manner. Hardin's pasture is a resource system and the immediately consumable portion of grass appropriated by each herder is a resource unit. Herders who graze their cattle are appropriators, and the process of grazing is an appropriation of grass resource units—in this way multiple grazing herders may be called co-appropriators. In turn, co-appropriating herders are the providers of a specific pastoral resource system, as they facilitate provision of the commons resource. Even so, the herders may also allow "non-providing" appropriators from surrounding areas to come to their pasture and extract resources for a time. If the co-appropriating herders establish a set of rules to ensure the long-term sustainability of the pasture, then they are also the producers of the resource system. If an external authority (a government, e.g.) mandates rules for long-term viability of the herder's pastoral resource system, then the external authority may be considered the producer.

These terms guide application of commons analysis to any set of resources. Their application assists in determining whether a resource is part of a commons, whether solutions to commons problems are effective, and how those solutions might be adjusted to provide better management of commons resources.

Commons Solutions: No Silver Bullet

Solutions aimed at preventing tragic over-appropriation of both traditional and new commons resources may take a variety of forms, ranging from government regulation on one end of the spectrum to privatization on the other. For example, an external authority may mandate rules for dividing appropriation of the resource among the herders and regulating "what, where, when, and how" appropriation occurs. In the alternative, an external authority might establish rules for fencing the commons and allocating property rights so that each herder has a privatized interest in preserving the grass resource on the herder's portion of property. Of course, a wide range of combined government regulation and private property rights approaches exists between the two ends of the spectrum, and in federal systems an inherent and constant tension is present between property rights and government regulation as mechanisms for managing resources and the environment.

Some scholars, such as Nobel laureate Elinor Ostrom, have established that neither regulation nor privatization is a *necessary* component of responsible commons management. Ostrom posits a third option that does not arise from an external source like the government or the market, but rather internally from among the herders themselves. Ostrom argues:

> One set of advocates presumes that a central authority must assume continuing responsibility to make unitary decisions for a particular resource. The other presumes that a central authority should parcel out ownership rights to the resource and then allow individuals to pursue their own self-interests within a set of well-defined property rights. Both centralization advocates and privatization advocates accept as a central tenet that institutional change must come from the outside and be imposed on the individuals affected. Despite sharing a faith in the necessity and efficacy of 'the state' to change institutions so as to increase efficiency, the institutional changes they recommend could hardly be further apart.[12]

Ostrom posits that both of these extremes are "too sweeping in their claims," arguing that "the capacity of individuals to extricate themselves from various types of dilemma situations *varies* from situation to situation."[13] Stated in more stark terms, Ostrom argues that "[i]nstead of presuming that some individuals are incompetent, evil, or irrational, and others are omniscient, I presume that individuals have very similar limited capabilities to reason and figure out the structure of complex environments," and that more focused study should be undertaken to ascertain the resource management problems individuals face and which circumstances hinder or help them.[14] Indeed, the lynchpin of Ostrom's research leading to her 2009 Nobel Prize in Economic Sciences is her robust insight into the circumstances under which groups of individuals have engaged in successful collective action to sustainably manage resources in the absence of private property rights or governmental regulatory intervention.[15]

Regardless of whether purported commons solutions arise from external governments or markets, or rather from internal arrangements among individuals, commons resources remain subject to potential tragedy due to the imperfect and individually deficient nature of the various solutions. In practical reality, "neither the state nor the market is uniformly successful in enabling individuals to sustain long-term, productive use of natural resource systems."[16] Both market-driven privatization and government-driven regulation, due to their nature as *external* forces on appropriators, result in a variety of negative externalities[17] that remain even in the presence of the purported solution. Furthermore, Ostrom's successful collective action model has its own imperfection, though it is unrelated to the model itself. Rather, this imperfection might best be described as an imperfection of scale—in practice Ostrom's model simply occurs too infrequently on large resource management scales to capture the vast majority of the world's natural capital.

Government Regulation

Invoking Thomas Hobbes' *Leviathan*,[18] Ostrom challenges government regulation ("Leviathan") as the "only way" to resolve commons tragedies, as numerous scholars have argued.[19] The presumption that an "external Leviathan" is necessary to address commons problems has led scholars to recommend that central governments control most natural resource management within nations, or "[t]he central authority will decide who can use the meadow, when they can use it, and how many animals can be grazed."[20] But this approach often fails because central authorities do not maintain sufficient information to estimate the carrying capacity of commons resources or to design the appropriate penalties to induce behavioral change. Crafting resource management policies based on inadequate information results in ineffective policies and continued resource degradation, especially because central governments are often incapable of providing sufficient monitoring and enforcement. Indeed, central government deficiencies are the primary drivers for decentralized resource governance in federal systems, to harness the ability of those closer to the resources to act upon better information regarding resource appropriation and management.

Privatization

Other scholars have argued that stringent imposition of private property rights is the "only way" to prevent commons tragedies—a proposition that Ostrom also challenges. This approach "would divide the meadow in half and assign half the meadow to one herder and the other half to the second herder."[21] As Ostrom notes, however, "each player will be playing a *game against nature* in a smaller terrain, rather than a game against another player in larger terrain."[22] Accordingly, as further analyzed in Chapter 3, individuals perpetually pit themselves against natural capital on private properties, appropriating it and replacing it with human-made capital,[23] even if they are now able to exclude other appropriators from the resource unit of property. In other words, private property may still operate as a commons with regard to the natural capital present upon it. In addition, various market failures, such as imperfect information, "free-riders," transaction costs, collective action problems, and other failures to internalize externalities lead to continued environmental destruction even in the presence of a private property rights system.[24]

Successful Collective Action

What of internal arrangements among herders outside the context of governmental regulation or private property rights? Ostrom is correct that herders are not inevitably locked into a tragic fate and that a variety of small-scale case studies demonstrates successful collective action to protect resources in the absence of private property rights or government regulation. Certainly the great value of Ostrom's work is that it provides a firm foundation for exploring how her models may be scaled up to achieve successful resource management on much larger scales. Nonetheless, her examples *currently* remain a distinct minority of cases.[25]

Until Ostrom's analysis can be infused more broadly into current systems of resource governance and management, an imperfect system for managing natural capital commons remains. This system balances governmental regulation with private property rights and markets, but because that balance has not yet been sufficiently struck, much of the world's natural capital remains in an increasingly tragic plight. The continued over-exploitation of natural capital commons resources demonstrates as much—whether it is world fisheries, an atmosphere increasingly filled with greenhouse gases, Amazonian rainforests, or other landed natural capital increasingly extracted or replaced by human-made capital due to economic development pressures.

Natural Capital Commons

> We must learn to recognize the true value of nature—both in an economic sense and in the richness it provides to our lives in ways much more difficult to put numbers on. Above all, protection of these assets can no longer be seen as an optional extra, to be considered once more pressing concerns such as wealth creation or national security have been dealt with ... healthy ecosystems are central to the aspirations of humankind.[26]

Though "[s]ocieties invest a great deal of effort in monitoring and cultivating their physical, financial, and human-capital ... they typically pay scant attention to their natural capital."[27] The term "natural capital" includes everything from extractable resources like water, minerals, oil, trees, fish, soil, air, and other natural resources, to holistic ecological systems like grasslands, savannas, wetlands, estuaries, oceans, coral reefs, riparian corridors, tundras, and rainforests.[28] Natural capital has two primary components: stocks of non-renewable natural resources, such as fossil fuels and minerals, and renewable natural resources in the form of ecosystems and the services they provide.[29]

Costanza and Daly assert that natural capital is based upon "a more functional definition of capital," as

> 'a stock that yields a flow of valuable goods or services into the future.' ... a stock or population of trees or fish provides a flow or annual yield of new trees or fish, a flow that can be sustainable year after year. The sustainable flow is 'natural income'; the stock that yields the sustainable flow is "natural capital." Natural capital may also provide services such as recycling waste materials, or water catchment and erosion control, which are also counted as natural income. Since the flow of services from ecosystems requires that they function as whole systems, the structure and diversity of the system is an important component in natural capital.[30]

Scholars have increasingly recognized the value of the services provided by natural capital, as evidenced by the growing body of scholarship on ecosystem services. These scholars seek to bring into focus the needed internalization of economic externalities long excluded from market-based decision-making regarding the management and use of natural resources.[31] By some estimates natural capital stock and ecosystem service values worldwide are, at a minimum, an average of $33 *trillion per year.*[32] This value is nearly *twice* the value of the combined gross national product of countries across the globe, which equals $18 trillion per year. Unfortunately, and regardless of the precise worth, the tremendous value of natural capital and ecosystem services is almost entirely excluded from the market and from the metrics by which we gauge the health of our economic systems. This exclusion is one of the most significant disconnects between the economic and environmental systems upon which we depend. As scholars note,

> [j]ust because these services have no market price, however, does not mean that they are without value. Quite the opposite. One cannot begin to understand flood control, for example, without realizing the impact of widespread wetland destruction on the ecosystem service of water retention; nor can one understand water quality without recognizing how development in forested watersheds degrades the service of water purification. The costs from degradation of these services are high, and suffered in rich and poor countries alike.[33]

Despite increased recognition of human dependence on the services provided by natural capital, nearly two-thirds of valuable ecosystem services worldwide are in decline, and "the benefits reaped from our engineering of the planet have been achieved by running down natural capital assets."[34] A root cause of this decline is that

> with rare exception, local, state, and national governments simply do not consider ecosystems as valuable providers of services. Without explicit comparisons between natural and built provision of services, we will continue to miss opportunities where reliance on natural capital provides the lowest cost services for human welfare.[35]

Unfortunately, the metrics of economic growth embedded within our modern society demonstrate that society all too often values the provision and maintenance of human-made capital *at the expense of* natural capital. As a result, we must not only compare the relative services that human or natural capital can provide, but must also analyze the institutional flaws responsible for the current balance of human-made and natural capital management and how those flaws can be rectified. Commons analysis provides a mechanism for exploring those flaws and remedies and specifically establishes a framework for assessing how the federal form of governance exacerbates natural capital commons tragedies.

Applying commons analysis to natural capital resources is nothing particularly new, as those resources have long been considered part of traditional commons—any forest, fishery, or groundwater aquifer that is not privatized or regulated by a government authority, but that is open to appropriation by non-excludable appropriators may be subject to tragic overconsumption. However, current commons and environmental scholarship related to natural capital is incomplete. For example, scholars and policymakers seem to presume that both the commons and the tragedy of overconsumption disappear once a forest is privatized or regulated. Yet natural capital subject to both privatization and regulation remains a commons and can therefore be considered a "new commons" to which commons analysis can and should be applied.

As described later in Chapter 4, natural capital on private lands constitutes a "new commons" resource in the form of "privatized commons resources."[36] Natural capital on private lands is depletable, and in the absence of government regulation it is extremely difficult, if not impossible, to exclude any private property owner from appropriating natural capital and replacing it with human-made capital or from transferring property to another appropriator who would do the same. Thus, natural capital on private lands meets the definition of a commons resource.

The same may be said about the other end of the spectrum—government regulation. And more specifically government regulation in a federal system of government. This is especially the case when a government's institutional structure is designed in a way that facilitates the ability of subnational governments to appropriate natural capital resources with unchecked rationality. When a federal system of government constitutionally grants exclusive control over natural capital appropriation to the numerous subnational governments within its borders, for example, that system provides a framework for a legally entrenched commons—the nation's natural capital is depletable and it becomes extremely difficult, if not legally impossible, to exclude individual subnational governments from appropriating that natural capital (or *allowing* that appropriation) through their individual bodies of land use law. Difficulty of exclusion is exacerbated when governments establish economic policies that align incentives with, and proactively encourage, the replacement of natural capital with built, human-made capital.

Not only do governments affirmatively encourage the replacement of natural capital with human-made capital for the sake of economic development activities, but even when governments act to protect the environment their approaches passively devalue natural capital. As noted by scholars, "[s]pecialized governmental institutions do, of course, pay attention to some [ecosystem] services, but their focus is primarily on the provision of services through modification of the landscape or construction of specialized facilities—that is, through 'built structures.'"[37] Examples would be building dams and levees to control flooding, rather than restoring or conserving wetlands, or building water purification plants rather than protecting and restoring forested watersheds that provide the same water purification benefits.[38]

When governmental policies promote the replacement of natural capital with human-made capital in the name of economic development and the harnessing of human-made capital to provide environmental benefits that could otherwise be naturally provided, the government fails to act as a commons solution or to fundamentally change the commons character of the resources. It is very much like a government requiring herders to pay taxes for their use of the pasture, or providing herders with a subsidized alternative food source in the form of canned and processed cattle food, or mandating that the herders use a particular type of corralling method to prevent herder trampling deaths, but then allowing the herders to appropriate natural capital however they see fit. This attribute may be no different in any system of government due to politics, but a federal system of government not only may politically fail to act as a solution for natural capital commons, but may legally entrench and protect a commons by providing numerous subnational governments exclusive regulatory authority to set rules for natural resource appropriation.

Federal Systems May Legally Entrench a Nested Natural Capital Commons

> [T]he structure of the situations that [commons] actors face, whether at a local or international level, creates strong similarities among problems, even at very different scales. That is, the similarities between local [commons] problems and [commons] problems involving international regimes are sufficiently great that we can learn a good deal from treating them within a comparable framework.[39]

Federal Governments and the Commons Metaphor

As a descriptive matter, federal systems of government resemble Hardin's pasture of rational herders more than perhaps any other form of governance. Hardin's pasture is divided among numerous rational herders making individualized choices about how to appropriate the natural capital over which they have control. Similarly, federal systems are divided among perhaps thousands of subnational governments who make rational, individualized choices regarding the appropriation of natural capital. Through their disparate management rules and regulatory mechanisms these subnational governments dictate appropriation of the natural capital that constitutes the "environment" contained within national boundaries—natural capital distributed with absolute disregard for the numerous subnational geopolitical boundaries segmenting the nation.[40] While the United States's nearly 88,000 separate governmental units facilitates a degree of decentralized governance that certainly provides widely recognized benefits, as discussed further in Chapter 5, it also has the potential to entrench a great deal of individually rational, yet collectively tragic, decision-making on the part of subnational governments.

Ultimately, the primary characteristic shared by Hardin's pasture and a federal system of government is an entrenchment of segmented decision-making by individual entities regarding the appropriation of resources within a defined boundary—whether it be a pasture, a private property, a state, or a nation. In the case of the herders, this shared trait may have no tragic consequences if they can successfully establish and implement management rules from within the group, or if an external actor can do so from without. Similarly, resource management in federal systems may suffer no tragic consequences if higher levels of government maintain the constitutional authority to establish, or to participate in establishing, rules for managing natural capital, or in the alternative if subnational governments themselves establish rules for sustainably managing natural capital within their governmental jurisdictions and are not preempted by higher level governments from doing so. But what if higher level governments do not maintain such power? What if lower level governments maintain *exclusive* constitutional regulatory authority over the appropriation of certain categories of natural capital and fail to act? If so, then subnational governments may in fact operate as rational commons herders on the national commons as they attempt to maximize local benefit to the detriment of the environment more broadly defined by national boundaries. Or what if higher level governments legally preempt lower level government action that would resolve a commons dilemma? In that case lower level governments would be coerced into rationality.

Contrast the status of natural capital within federal nations with its status in unitary systems of government. Unitary systems have subnational governmental units, but those units do not maintain exclusive regulatory authority over resource appropriation.[41] Thus, unitary systems maintain authority to establish uniform rules across a national resource system segmented by subnational governmental boundaries. The national government may therefore act unconstrained by subnational governments in designing rules for appropriating the nation's natural capital. For example, in England the national government maintains the ultimate authority to establish land use planning standards, including urban growth boundaries around municipalities, in order to prevent urban sprawl and preserve the nation's natural capital.[42]

In contrast, the United States national government does not maintain *recognized* constitutional authority to establish urban growth boundaries because this type of direct land use regulation has historically been reserved in jurisprudence exclusively to state and local governments. Even though growth boundaries "reduc[e] the need to extend infrastructure beyond existing service areas and preserv[e] rural lands and open space,"[43] subnational governments in the U.S. are not coordinating natural capital appropriation in a manner that protects the resources both within and without these geopolitical boundaries. There is a striking disparity in the U.S. between the number of subnational governments and the number of urban growth boundaries. Although there are nearly 88,000 subnational governmental units, only "[o]ver a hundred such urban constraint programs are now in place around the United States."[44] To make matters worse, without coordinated action among groups of subnational governments on larger scales—potentially achieved with input by a national government—even these limited efforts may be ineffective. Urban growth boundaries "appear to reduce sprawl and create often vibrant urban communities," yet "[b]uoyed by market pressure and citizen preferences for low-density development, however, new development still often leaks out of the growth boundaries into the countryside"[45]—largely because neighboring governments refuse to participate in any type of coordinated effort.

In the absence of coordinated action to curb continued destruction of natural capital, the 50 state governments in the U.S., as the primary arbiters of land use regulation at the state and local levels, remain free to appropriate natural capital from the national commons in an individually rational way. This gives rise to the potential that one state may maintain more lax land use standards than another in an effort to attract economic development. States with more strict environmental and land use standards may lose out to neighboring states on economic development opportunities, even though their standards may better protect the nation's natural capital in the aggregate. Thus each of the 50 states has a rational incentive to maximize individual economic gain through the maintenance of lax land use standards to the detriment of the nation's natural capital—50 rational herders on the national commons.

The attributes that federal systems of government share with a commons have profound implications for global resource governance. There are over 160 unitary systems of government,[46] while there are only 25 federal systems of government.[47] Though there are far fewer federal systems of government than unitary systems, approximately 46 percent of the world's land base is contained within federal nations' boundaries.[48] With certain other resources, such as global forests, the numbers are even starker. Scholars are increasingly recognizing the importance of the world's forests in combating climate change.[49] Even though federal systems of government only comprise approximately 13 percent of the world's governments, they maintain control over 70 to 80 percent of the world's forests.[50] Thus, the vast majority of the world's forests are contained within systems of government with the greatest potential to constitute a commons. This is both the great irony and the great challenge of our time—the placement of perhaps the most critical resource to combating climate change largely within systems of government that present potentially tragic complications for holistic resource management.

Before moving to the next section, it is important to make a final note on the metaphorical comparison between federal systems of government and Hardin's commons. We might typically imagine that the herders roam around on Hardin's commons as they graze their cattle. It is true that a parcel of private property, a state, and a nation cannot move around their respective commons. Yet, though some traditional commons appropriators take on this characteristic of mobility, such as fishing boats on the high seas or loggers roaming about an open forest, other commons appropriators are quite stationary. Groundwater aquifers, for example, are widely considered the prototypical commons resource. The parties withdrawing water from the aquifer, however, are most often anchored to the surface and contained within defined property boundaries, as is the case with private farms or housing developments. Even though the appropriators are not mobile, their unchecked consumption of the resource leads to its degradation and destruction. Thus it is not the mobility of the appropriator that makes a commons, but rather the intensity of co-appropriators' unchecked use of the resources anchored to the commons.

Likewise, each of Hardin's herders could stand immobile in one spot of the pasture, but may nevertheless continue adding cattle until eventually one herder's cows start merging with the cows of another herder standing far away—it is the increased intensity of use by the addition of more cattle that drives the tragic outcome. This is the same mechanism by which private property owners, states, and nations remain stationary while still appropriating natural capital with increasing intensity in an unchecked fashion.

Furthermore, these entities may do so with constitutional sanction in federal systems of government, rendering federal constitutions the keystone that connects and supports these nested commons and determines whether or not they may be governed in a sustainable manner.

Federal Governments and Nested Governance Commons Theory

Whether it be forests, terrestrial or coastal wetlands, or agricultural resources, a wide range of management approaches may be implemented—or perhaps more frequently *not* implemented—both horizontally within levels of government (global, national, state, or local) or among private property owners, and vertically across levels of government and private properties, that have potentially tragic consequences for global natural capital. Assume, for example, that state governments in the United States are actors appropriating natural capital on one scale of governance—the "national scale."[51] As will be a subject of discussion throughout this book, the U.S. federal government currently maintains no direct inputs into the management of 65 percent of U.S. forests, which are privately or state-owned and subject almost exclusively to state regulatory authority. This represents the *vertical component* in which a higher level of government, the federal government, might attempt to manage, but fails to manage, natural capital by regulating resource appropriation within state jurisdictions situated one scale down.

Simultaneously, U.S. state governments' forest management policies are all over the board on their level of regulatory stringency. While some states maintain fairly stringent forest management standards, others, particularly in the southeastern U.S., maintain none at all. This represents the *horizontal component* in which actors appropriating natural capital on the same scale manage (or fail to manage) natural capital through collective action. This description presents a classic tragedy of the commons problem, whereby a number of actors (here, the 50 state governments) may act as rational herders and appropriate resources from a single resource system (forests within the United States), with many states doing so without instituting appropriate mechanisms of resource management. It is perhaps no surprise, then, that the U.S. Forest Service projects that urbanization and other factors will remove 13 percent of all southeastern forests over the next 50 years, not only creating a significant source of carbon but also removing a crucial carbon sink.[52]

While this example analyzing one scale of governance helps illustrate the classic tragedy of the commons scenario, natural capital resources like U.S. forests, and those in certain other federal systems, are subject to a far more complex commons phenomenon than the classic case—a complexity that arises out of a *three-dimensional* vertically and horizontally integrated resource management arrangement that is exemplified by a federal governance structure. Indeed, descriptions of commons resources and solutions for their management are often oversimplified. In many federal systems, given that there is very little natural capital subject to a pure common-pool arrangement, the resource management challenge is often framed, somewhat two-dimensionally, as merely about striking the appropriate balance between the two extremes of private property and government regulation, or about preserving the values of private property ownership in balance with the values that natural capital provides to the public at large.

One problem with this limited inquiry is that it presumes that once private property rights, government regulation, or both, are in place for managing natural capital, the commons dilemma has disappeared. This presumption is based on the belief that while there were once resources open to all and subject to tragic overconsumption, now those resources are either privatized or regulated, thereby eliminating the commons or associated tragedy. In reality, the commons dilemma has not disappeared. Rather, both the entities labeled commons herders and the scale of the resource system to which they maintain access have simply shifted.

To see this more clearly, consider an illustration based upon the commons terminology presented earlier in this chapter, regarding resource "appropriators" appropriating "resource units" of natural capital from a "resource system." The "scales" referred to in this book contain "resource systems" that are geographically bounded by national, state, or local jurisdictional boundaries. In a federal system of government, there are several scales to which commons analysis may be applied. There is the national scale in which the national resource system is embedded, the state scale in which 50 distinct state/provincial resource systems are embedded, and the local scale in which thousands of local government resource systems and private property resource systems are embedded. Furthermore, each of these resource systems is embedded within the ultimate scale, the global resource system. As we adjust our focus from one type of resource system on one scale to another resource system on another scale, it is necessary to adopt a new perspective on both the entities considered herders on the commons and the common pool of natural capital to which these herders maintain access.

For example, on the national scale, states are the herders who may (or may not) horizontally coordinate their appropriation of resource units of natural capital from the national resource system, or whose appropriation may (or may not) be subject to vertical coordination by the federal government. Yet in shifting to the state scale we see that local governments are the herders who may (or may not) horizontally coordinate their appropriation of resource units of natural capital from the state resource system, or whose appropriation may (or may not) be subject to vertical coordination by the state government (who is now the vertical actor rather than the horizontal actor, as on the national scale). Shifting scales allows us to see that in the absence of horizontal self-coordination (HSC) or vertical regulatory coordination (VRC) by a higher level of government, private property owners may act as herders on local commons, local governments as herders on the state commons, state governments as herders on the national commons, and national governments as herders on the global commons.

Another problem presented by the limited inquiry is that it seemingly assumes that the interplay between appropriators, the commons, and associated resources is relatively identical regardless of, first, the scale on which the vertical or horizontal management approaches are implemented and, second, geopolitical and jurisdictional differences found among resource systems located on the same scale. The limited inquiry is again two-dimensional, oversimplifying both the vertical and the horizontal approaches to commons resource management. This oversimplification fails to fully account for legal differences in the various scales that affect the viability of vertical or horizontal management approaches within specific scales and also fails to take into account geopolitical differences that may arise among similarly situated horizontal actors that can affect their choice of horizontal versus vertical approaches.

Stated differently, there are two important components that together constitute a third dimension of federal governance commons analysis. The first component may be termed "geolegal" differences across scales of governance. These come in the form of legal constraints placed on either higher level governmental entities that prevent vertical regulation or on higher or lower level entities that prevent them from taking successful horizontal collective action for resource management. These constraints may arise out of either constitutional or legislative restrictions. Geolegal differences simply represent that vertical regulation and horizontal collective action do not take place in the same way within different scales due to different legal environments. For example, the federal government may be restrained from regulating some activities at the state and local levels because those powers are reserved to states or provinces. This is a geolegal difference from vertical regulation at the state or provincial level, where the same federal constitutional provision does allow the state/province to vertically regulate lower level scales regarding that subject matter. "Geolegal" also encapsulates different legal circumstances across horizontal jurisdictions. For example, there are good arguments that the U.S. federal government may vertically regulate certain aspects of subnational forest management under the Commerce Clause whereas the Canadian federal government clearly may not under the Canadian Constitution. The second component comes in the form of geopolitical differences horizontally across jurisdictions, whereby vertical or horizontal approaches to commons management may be more or less viable depending on political circumstances in similarly situated horizontal regions.

The limited analysis would conclude that the government within *a single scale* vertically regulates to avoid the commons dilemma (the first dimension) or that actors horizontally coordinate in a way that avoids the commons dilemma (the second dimension), and that both horizontal and vertical action are equally viable as applied to, and take place in a uniform manner across, that single scale, thus ignoring geolegal constraints and geopolitical differences across and within scales (the third dimension). In fact, a federal system of government contains multiple two-dimensional (vertical–horizontal) scales stacked one on top of another, or "nested" one within another. Commons scholars have previously noted that "[p]roperty rights systems, and governance systems more generally, tend to be nested in space ranging from the shared properties of individual families, to the shared resources of communities of families or local governments, to much larger regional and national governmental jurisdictions."[53]

So private property owners may horizontally coordinate with each other or be subject to higher levels of governmental authority, as may local governments, state governments, and even national governments. Furthermore, the multiple, two-dimensional scales of government are embedded in a three-dimensional structure created by distinct geolegal constraints vertically and horizontally across scales and geopolitical circumstances horizontally across jurisdictions. The geolegal and geopolitical environments being different across scales may influence how the herders view and interact with their respective commons and with each other.

By way of illustration and looking at the state scale in isolation, the limited analysis would simply consider whether the U.S. State of Alabama vertically regulates private forest management (the first dimension) or private foresters in Alabama horizontally coordinate their forest management activities (the second dimension), or some combination of the two, to avoid the commons dilemma. This two-dimensional analysis, however, ignores the fact that different scales might also maintain regulatory inputs into Alabama's forest management, such as the U.S. federal government or Alabama's many local governments (the geolegal component). Yet the viability of these regulatory inputs may be quite variable. The federal government, for example, may be subject to constitutional constraints on its authority to regulate private forests in Alabama under Commerce Clause analysis. Similarly, some states may legislatively preempt local governments from setting their own forest management standards in lieu of or supplemental to state mandates, while Alabama or other states may encourage such supplemental regulation. Furthermore, the two-dimensional analysis overlooks the fact that a different balance of vertical regulation or horizontal collective action may manifest within the state scale in different regions of the United States. A vertical private forest management approach may be more likely, for example, in the State of Oregon than in Alabama. In the same way, a vertical regulatory approach to regulating land use planning related to urban growth boundaries might be more appropriate in the U.S. Pacific Northwest, since geopolitics makes such an approach more viable, whereas geopolitical considerations make a vertical regulatory approach far *less* viable in the southeastern United States.

Rather than grappling with this three-dimensional complexity, solutions to the primary problems associated with resource management are often framed as limitations on a readily identifiable number and type of externalities that may spill over jurisdictional boundaries with uniform geopolitical characteristics to create isolated environmental harms. Yet avoiding commons tragedies in the federal governance structure in which private property rights and government regulation are embedded will often require an adjustment of horizontal and vertical relationships among relevant actors within a single scale—the first and second dimensions—and consideration of the geolegal impacts stemming from multiple scales nested one within another and the geopolitical differences across horizontal scales—the third dimension. When scholars focus too acutely on the variety of externalities that exist even in the presence of private property rights or government regulation, the magnitude of the tragedy of the commons attributes of the problem is diminished.

Ultimately, the limited, two-dimensional vertical/horizontal analysis prevalent in current law and policy debates both overlooks the commons attributes of federal systems and ignores the fact that the federal system of government results in *multiple* two-dimensional vertical and horizontal relationships nested one within another that may influence the commons dynamic. It fails to holistically account for the many government scales vertically that may establish rules of resource management for private properties or lower levels of government. Similarly, such analysis fails to account for the ways in which multiple actors on different scales (private property owners or various levels of government) may work simultaneously with other actors on the same plane to tackle commons challenges at each scale, and how their efforts may interact with vertically scaled governments. Once these considerations are fully integrated into commons analysis, we see that, depending upon the relationship between private property rights and government regulation on any one scale, commons tragedies may yet occur for natural capital absent an adjustment in the relationship between the *multiple*, two-dimensional scales where horizontal coordination or vertical regulation may occur—again, nested one within another as depicted in Figure 2.2. The resource management challenge is anything but a two-dimensional balance within single scales of governance.

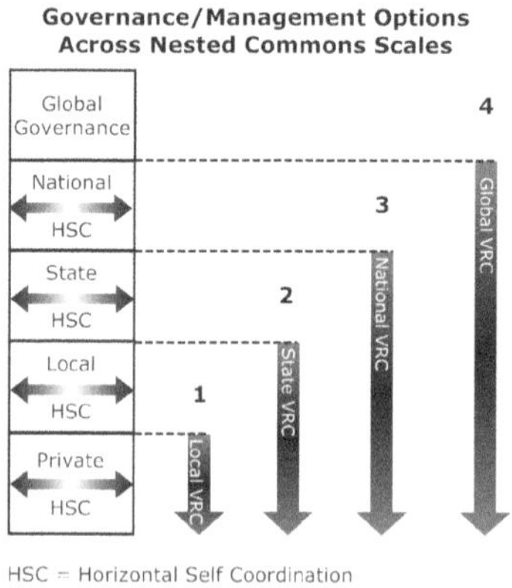

Figure 2.2 Governance/management options across nested governance commons scales

Importantly, the three-dimensional horizontal and vertical interactions themselves, particularly in a federal system of government, can act as what may be termed a "nested governance commons" within which natural resource commons are embedded. Within each horizontal scale, the rules of resource management allowed by the governance framework (what I refer to here as "legal authority"), and the resource management actions actually undertaken at that level (what I refer to here as "political action") interplay with the natural environment to provide a complete picture of the complexity of the commons, as herders may appropriate natural capital from each commons scale and across scales with tragic consequences. So, as alluded to earlier, in the absence of a higher level of government maintaining legal authority or exercising political action to regulate, or in the absence of legal authority or political action to horizontally coordinate with each other, private property owners may act as herders within local government commons, local governments may act as herders within state commons, states may act as herders within national commons, and nations may act as herders within the global commons. The overlay of segmented vertical jurisdictions and vertical regulatory authority over a myriad of individual horizontal jurisdictions creates a nested commons that is especially salient within federal systems of government where regulatory governance jurisdictions are legally divided both horizontally and vertically.

One of the roles that federal systems of government have increasingly assumed, of course, is the management of natural resource commons. Yet, in federal systems we see both rivalry (depletability) and non-excludability, the presence of each being necessary to label something a commons. There is rivalry because, for example, more natural capital governance authority maintained by the federal government may mean less for subnational governments, and vice versa. If subnational governments, such as the 50 states in the U.S., maintain more or nearly exclusive authority, then by virtue of the governance structure those entities are non-excludable in that they are allowed to "roam" on the commons freely, appropriating natural capital without federal coordination and perhaps without coordinating with each other to ensure non-tragic resource management. We see this in the context of land use planning at the subnational level and the resultant urban sprawl that is threatening natural capital globally. In this way, natural resource commons are embedded within the governance framework that sets the rules for appropriation and management of those resources—a framework that itself may be segmented in a way that tracks a commons. Though private property rights and government regulation are the tools used to manage natural resources in the United States (or, traditional commons resources), the federal governance structure within which they are embedded and implemented may also be considered a new commons.

Natural resource commons are often described as multi-scalar, in that resources are contained in vertically and horizontally structured governance scales that include a complex web of appropriators within each scale and across scales. For example, forests are horizontally scaled across the geopolitical boundary between the United States and Canada and vertically scaled within each of those federal nations across national and subnational government jurisdictions and private properties—with numerous entities playing a role in appropriating those resources. But it is important to ask: *precisely* what is it that makes natural resources multi-scalar? It is not the natural environment itself, at least in the primary sense used by governance scholars, since the biota, absent artificial human divisions and consumptive influence, is interconnected in a way that creates a highly functional, integrated, unified, and natural scale globally. What makes natural resources multi-scalar are the artificial geopolitical boundaries and corresponding allocations of governance authority creating the governance systems within which natural resources are embedded. This is what commons scholars mean when they refer to the potential to scale up analysis of local commons to the national and international scales.[54]

There are very few open pastures remaining, with governments and private property owners controlling most natural resources worldwide. And, aside from some ocean resources, the open-access properties that remain are embedded within some country with ultimate governmental authority over them if they choose to exercise it. In this way we can see that it is the *intersection* between natural resource commons and the nested governance commons where modern resource commons problems arise. Ultimately, even though scholars have spent a great deal of time discussing mechanisms for addressing problems associated with commons present within these nested constructs, they have failed to adequately assess situations where the governmental solution itself *becomes* the commons.

To understand the complexity and dynamism of the federal nested governance commons, it is important to first break it down into its constituent parts. This necessitates analyzing each "nest" as a horizontal construct within the vertically nested governance commons, as well as analyzing the relationship of each nest with the successive nest up or down the vertical scale. Within each nest there are two primary components that intersect to determine whether and how natural resources are managed on private or government-owned lands: (1) legal authority of horizontal or vertical governments to enact regulatory policies; and (2) political action on the part of those governments to actually do so. These components intersect in a variety of scenarios, the most notable of which are described below (by no means an exhaustive list, however).

To begin, let us consider scenarios that avoid natural capital tragedies because, first, there are no legal, *institutional* barriers to natural capital management. Second, natural capital tragedies are avoided under these scenarios because horizontal or vertical entities or both have politically exercised their legal authority to sustainably manage natural capital. Management of natural capital resources within each nest may not result in tragedy if at least one of five scenarios manifests (depicted as "NT" [non-tragic] in Figure 2.3 below):

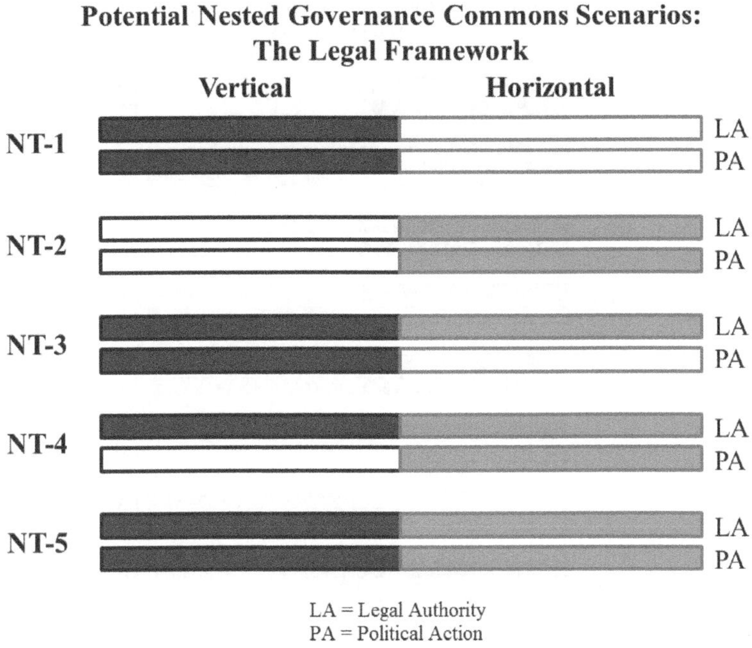

Figure 2.3 Non-tragic nested governance commons scenarios

NT-1 Higher levels of government *have the legal authority* to vertically regulate the resource and exercise that authority through political action, while entities at the lower level *lack the legal authority* to horizontally coordinate.[55]

NT-2 Higher levels of government *lack the legal authority* to vertically regulate the resource, but entities at the lower level *have the legal authority* to horizontally coordinate and undertake HSC through political action.

NT-3 Higher levels of government *have the legal authority* to vertically regulate the resource and exercise that authority through political action, and entities at the lower level *have the legal authority* to horizontally coordinate, but they do not exercise that authority through political action.[56]

NT-4 Higher levels of government *have the legal authority* to vertically regulate the resource, but fail to exercise that authority through political action, and entities at the lower level *have the legal authority* to horizontally coordinate and undertake HSC through political action.

NT-5 Higher levels of government *have the legal authority* to vertically regulate the resource and exercise that authority through political action, and entities at the lower level *have the legal authority* to horizontally coordinate and also undertake HSC through political action.

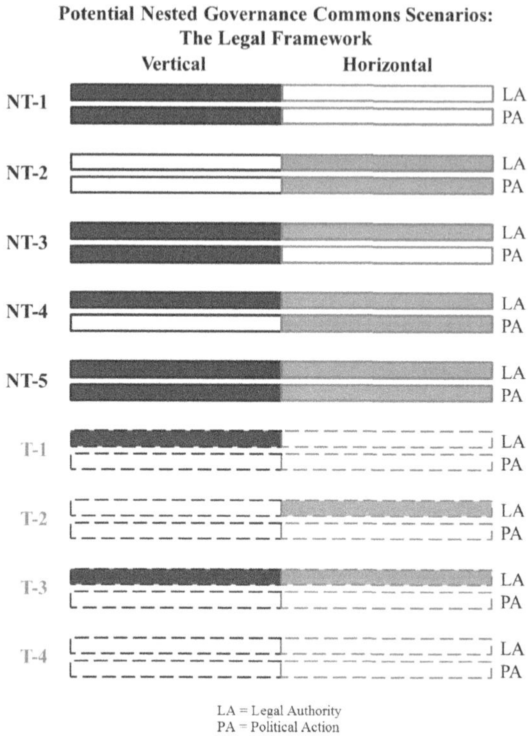

Figure 2.4 Tragic and non-tragic nested governance commons scenarios

Correspondingly, natural capital commons tragedies can result when at least one of four scenarios manifests (depicted as "T" [tragic] in Figure 2.4 above):

T-1 Higher levels of government *have the legal authority* to vertically regulate the resource, but fail to exercise that authority through political action, and entities at the lower level *lack the legal authority* to horizontally coordinate.[57]

T-2 Higher levels of government *lack the legal authority* to vertically regulate the resource, and entities at the lower level *have the legal authority* to horizontally coordinate, but it is not exercised through political action.

T-4 Higher levels of government *have the legal authority* to vertically regulate the resource, but fail to exercise that authority through political action, and entities at the lower level *have the legal authority* to horizontally coordinate, but also fail to exercise that authority through political action.

T-4 Higher levels of government *lack the legal authority* to vertically regulate the resource, *and* entities at the lower level *lack the legal authority* to horizontally coordinate, failing to produce either VRC or HSC. This scenario requires more thorough explication, as it can play out in more complex ways. A useful illustration comes from the United States, where the Tenth Amendment to the Constitution makes it clear that legal authority must reside with the federal government or state governments—if the federal government does not have explicit legal authority to act granted by the text of the constitution, then the states must have it, and vice versa. As a result, there will not be a scenario where both the federal and state governments in the United States do *not* maintain legal authority to act. The T-4 scenario, however, could play out quite frequently at state or local scales, as well as on the global scale. If the federal government, for example, preempts state authority to act, then neither the state nor the local government maintains the legal authority to act, resulting in a T-4 scenario at the state scale. Similarly, if the state government preempts local authority to act, then a T-4 scenario could play out on the local scale, where the local government actors and private property owners do not have the legal authority to act. A T-4 scenario could also occur on the global scale when the state government has the legal authority to act and the federal government does not. In this circumstance, restrictions on nested governance would be operating in reverse, with the federal government not legally permitted to horizontally coordinate with other nations in a way that binds the states, which in turn prevents it from authorizing a global body to vertically regulate via treaty.[58]

Before moving to Chapter 3's review of commons decentralization across global, national, state, and local scales and how these scenarios play out within each scale, I should pause a moment to provide three clarifications of this legal authority/political action framework. First, though unlikely from a practical perspective, theoretically a tragedy could be avoided within a given nest even in the absence of either vertical or horizontal legal authority or political action. In this situation, a critical mass of entities within each nest could *altruistically, but individually,* act against perceived self-interest by limiting their own use of the resource—but they would not do so in coordination with others, nor would they be directed by higher level governments. This book is not concerned, however, with the coincidental de facto coordination of separate actors, but rather with the institutional and legal mechanisms that are needed horizontally or vertically to avoid commons resource tragedies.

Second, this book is concerned, somewhat quantitatively, with whether commons management institutions are or are not in place and whether or not there are legal barriers to such institutions, rather than with a qualitative analysis of policy. As a result, the scenarios presented in this book are focused primarily on the issue of legal authority, though political action is certainly a necessary component of proper commons resource management both vertically and horizontally. Indeed, I do not suggest that simply maintaining adequate legal authority will result in sustainable decision-making and the proper government exercise of that authority, whether vertically or horizontally. For example, there could be authority at the higher level of government that is acted upon through vertical regulatory action, but in a way that does not address the resource management issues and that may even exacerbate the commons conditions—i.e. bad policy. Nonetheless, a necessary precursor to efficacious political action is whether proper institutions are in place to legally facilitate that political will in the first instance. This is why I necessarily presume for the purposes of conveying the theoretical framework that if legal authority exists and political action is taken in the NT scenarios above, then the resulting policy resolves the commons dilemma.

In the real world, of course, policy actions may be taken but not efficacious. For this reason, in the T scenarios dealing with preemption, for example, I do make some qualitative observations—only in furtherance of the framework—noting that legal authority may exist at a higher level of government and may be acted upon, but in a way that does not resolve the commons dilemma. I make this observation in the preemption context merely because in the absence of preemption, the lower level government might be able to resolve said dilemma more effectively than the higher level government. So, to provide a clearer conception of the framework, I am using the efficacy of political action very much like 1s and 0s in binary code—either political action at that level of government resolves the commons dilemma or it does not. Given the complexities of assessing the relative success of policy, this model is purposefully lacking in analysis of policy sufficiency.

Third and finally, as indicated earlier, this book purposefully and over-simplistically discusses scales in relative isolation, leaving the full complexity of cross-cutting scalar interactions to future research. One of the reasons scalar analysis is so complex is because a degree of "scale jumping" may occur, as represented by the T-4 scenario above. For example, this book characterizes private property owners as herders on local commons, but they also may be characterized as the appropriators on the state, national, or global commons. The same might be said of the states on both the national and global commons. In part, constitutions in federal systems dictate how these scale jumping interactions occur, and as described in the next part of this chapter act as a "keystone" by identifying what natural capital resources will become the subject of a legal authority dispute on the global, national, state, or local governance commons. For example, if the U.S. Constitution grants the federal government authority to regulate certain resources all the way down to private individuals, then the federal government may exercise that authority, leading to an NT scenario; or it may preempt state, local, or private action, creating either an NT or T scenario, depending on whether Congress crafts policy addressing the commons dilemma or not; or the federal government may operate concurrently with entities across those lower scales, leading to an

NT or T scenario, depending on whether Congress, states, local governments, or private actors craft policies addressing the commons dilemma.

On the other hand, if the U.S. Constitution does not grant Congress the legal authority to regulate at the state scale and further down, then state constitutional law and legislation become determinative of the ultimate outcome of a variety of T or NT commons management scenarios at those scales. In the same way, lack of national authority in the U.S. Constitution can affect T or NT scenarios at the global level, since entities at the state or local scales may impede the ability of the national government to participate in global scale governance arrangements to address commons problems. Furthermore, the coordinated actions of every private property owner on the earth, theoretically and however unlikely, could resolve the commons dilemma across every higher scale—jumping from the lowest scale to the highest in resolving the problem. Similarly, a global arrangement successfully negotiated and successfully implemented in every country on the globe could potentially, and however unlikely, compel actors at all lower scales to address the commons dilemma—thus jumping from the highest scale to the lowest. And there are a variety of permutations of scale jumping in between. The reality is that these types of cross-cutting interactions do not occur within only these two dimensions of vertical and horizontal. Rather, they occur in different ways within and across different horizontal jurisdictional and geographic lines. It is this aspect of nested governance commons that should be analyzed in future research.

We have now established the basic operation of each nest within a governance commons, and how each nest may or may not result in tragedy depending on the presence or absence of legal authority and political action both vertically and horizontally. As we know, however, there are multiple nests scaled vertically and horizontally in federal systems within which natural capital commons are embedded. So, to gain a clearer and more precise conception of the nested commons in federal systems, we can describe each nest as one of four, scaled from units as small as private properties to the largest unit we can assess, the globe. As described above and further detailed in Chapter 3, the legal entrenchment of commons at each scale can arise out of very different legal authority/political action scenarios, which are in turn determined by matters of simple geopolitics (as in the case of the global commons), constitutional law (as in the case of the national and state scale commons), or legislative preemption (as in the case of some national, state, and local scale commons). On any individual scale, as depicted in Figure 2.2 above, a natural capital commons may occur (notwithstanding the overarching governance commons), and each level may look like the following:

1 In the absence of vertical inputs by a global governance arrangement or HSC among groups of nations, national governments may act as individual herders on the natural capital "pasture" that is the globe. The resource unit is natural capital within a single nation, while the resource system is global natural capital.

2 In the absence of vertical inputs by the federal government or HSC with each other, state governments may act as individual herders on the natural capital "pasture" defined by national jurisdictional boundaries. The resource unit is natural capital within a single state, while the resource system is natural capital within the collection of local governments that make up the state.
3 In the absence of vertical inputs from state governments or HSC with each other, local governments may act as individual herders appropriating natural capital from the "pasture" defined by state jurisdictional boundaries. The resource unit is natural capital within a single local government, while the resource system is natural capital within the collection of local governments that make up the state.
4 In the absence of vertical inputs from local governments or HSC with each other, private property owners act as individual herders appropriating natural capital from the "pasture" defined by local government jurisdictional boundaries. The resource unit is natural capital on private property, while the resource system is natural capital within the collection of private properties that exist within local government boundaries.[59]

While each level in isolation may constitute a typical natural resource commons, whereby individual appropriators appropriate resource units from the resource system, it is the integration of each scale within a federal system of government that creates multi-scalar natural resource management issues. It is the synergy between the natural environment and the system of governance designing rules for its management that presents the complete picture of the commons. In this way, federal systems of government can operate as a nested governance commons that overlays the natural environment—thus adding another layer of complexity to the management approaches needed to address the most pressing natural capital management issues of our time. Chapter 3 looks more closely at this level of decentralization in federal systems and how the commons dynamic plays out within each scale.

The Role of Keystone Constitutions

A key question in commons analysis is "whether there is congruence between the spatial scale of the resource system itself and the spatial scale of the jurisdictions able to take governance and make management decisions related to that resource."[60] This is an important question because "the boundaries of governmental units are usually arbitrarily drawn when viewed from the perspective of most natural resources," and "very often the spatial boundaries of a particular resource are not congruent with any one particular governance unit."[61] In federal systems of government, perhaps more than in any other governmental system, there is likely to be incongruity between the spatial scale of the resource system, stretching from one side of the nation to another, and the spatial scale of the jurisdictions with authority over resource management—which in the U.S. are the 50 states and the thousands of other subnational governments in between. This likelihood increases when federal constitutions grant the myriad subnational governments within national borders exclusive regulatory authority over natural capital appropriation or when federal legislatures and state legislatures and constitutions legally preempt lower level governance authority.

All federal systems of government maintain written constitutions that are the ultimate source from which legal governance flows.[62] The same is true of the many state constitutions that exist on the next scale below the federal scale. Constitutions are a relatively recent governance phenomenon, with the U.S. Constitution being the first written constitution, established in 1787. The use of written constitutions has since become widespread, though the efficacy of constitutions depends upon a wide range of factors, including rule of law considerations and the development of sufficient institutions to facilitate the dictates set out in the constitution. Nonetheless, a constitution provides the framework through which societal order and stability is facilitated.

These constitutions lie at the very center of the nested commons of federal natural capital governance. If a federal constitution grants subnational governments exclusive regulatory authority over natural capital appropriation, then those governments may rationally refuse to exercise that authority. As previously discussed, their failure to act allows rational individuals to appropriate subnational natural capital unchecked and also allows rational subnational governments to appropriate national natural capital unchecked. In turn, the constitutional structure of those national governments likewise constrains global natural capital governance. A federal government that cannot bind subnational governments cannot fully and effectively participate in global treaty-making.

Similarly, a federal constitution may give the national legislature the authority to preempt state or local regulatory authority, thus preventing potential commons solutions at lower scales, and state constitutions may directly preempt, or allow state legislatures to preempt, local government or private party decision-making that might otherwise constitute a solution to the commons dilemma.

Constitutions in federal systems therefore act as a keystone of nested natural capital commons governance, as illustrated in Figure 2.1 in the introduction to this chapter. Constitutions in federal systems either maintain a strong arch of resource governance, the integrity of which adequately addresses commons concerns across resource management scales, or contributes to a weak and vulnerable arch of resource governance, likely to crumble due to a legal entrenchment of a commons not only within national boundaries but also on global scales. In other words, constitutions establish the institutional framework that must facilitate policy formulation if national-level governance is to have legal authority to rectify natural capital commons dilemmas on subnational, national, and international scales, as well as if lower level governance is not to be legally preempted in rectifying such dilemmas.

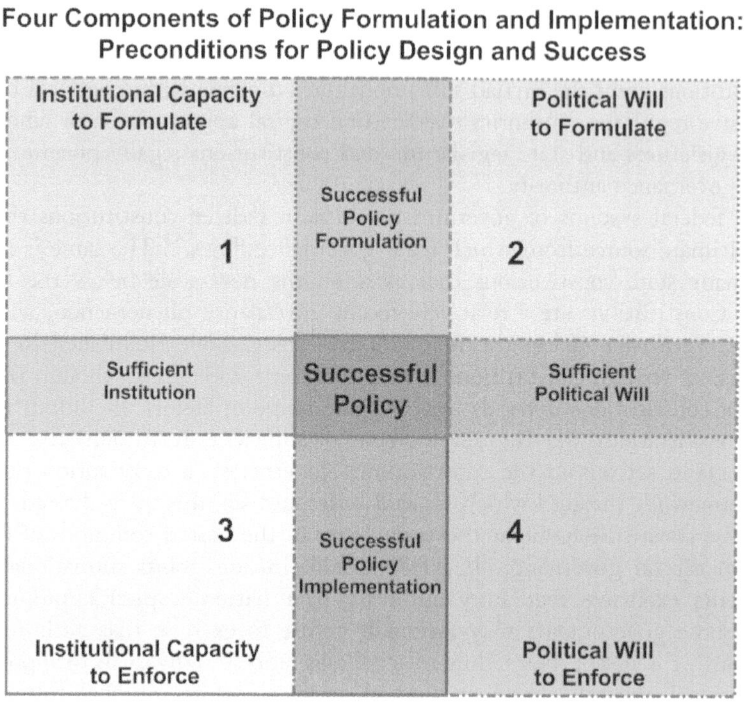

Figure 2.5 Components of policy formulation and implementation

On a very rudimentary level, successful policy formulation and implementation requires four basic components: (1) institutional capacity of the government to formulate policy; (2) political will of the government to formulate policy; (3) institutional capacity of the government to enforce policy; (4) political will of the government to enforce policy. These components intersect as shown in Figure 2.5. While governmental systems can contain any combination of these elements, the presence of all four components can be said to result in a successful policy. The study of federal and state constitutions undertaken in this book falls into quadrant 1 of Figure 2.5, because the constitutional order of a nation is the institution that provides the legal mechanism of policy formulation. Without a government first maintaining such an institution, institutional capacity to enforce and political will to formulate and implement policy are irrelevant.

For example, in the U.S. if the constitution provides federal regulatory authority over some subject matter (component 1) and Congress maintains the political will to pass legislation pursuant to that authority (component 2), then policy formulation can be successful. Such is the case with the Clean Air Act (CAA),[63] for instance, whereby the Commerce Clause provides federal regulatory authority over regulation of industrial pollutants, and Congress acted on its political will to regulate those pollutants through the passage of the CAA. The question that naturally follows is whether a government can achieve successful policy implementation. The Environmental Protection Agency and other administrative tools available to the federal government, as well as the enlisting of state government support in implementing the CAA, provide sufficient institutional capacity to enforce the CAA (component 3). Furthermore, though there are certainly improvements to be made in enforcement, as evidenced by areas of CAA noncompliance around the country, there also exists sufficient political will to enforce the CAA (component 4), as evidenced by the continued monitoring and enforcement actions performed by the institutions responsible for administration of the act. The presence of these four components has resulted in a successful policy, and air quality in the U.S. has improved greatly since CAA passage. While the strength of the success of any policy may always be debated, discernable metrics exist that can be assessed to help observers determine as a general matter whether the policy problem the government sought to remedy has in fact been addressed. In this way, the CAA provides a good example of a successful policy.

Other federal systems of government maintain a different combination of policy formulation/implementation components, leading to a very different outcome regarding the efficacy of governance via national government policymaking. For example, as discussed in Chapter 7, Brazil maintains some of the most stringent, explicit forest-protection mandates in any federal constitution, and the national government is constitutionally empowered to guide policy for subnational forest management. In this way the Brazilian national government has been able to successfully *formulate* forest policy (components 1 and 2)—the Brazilian federal government has had the political will to both include explicit forest provisions in the Brazilian Constitution as well as pass legislation pursuant to that power (component 2), and the constitution, in turn, is the institution that legally empowers the federal government to engage in forest policy formulation (component 1). Nonetheless, as further discussed in Chapter 7, Brazil is missing crucial components of policy implementation, as the national government is unable to enforce legislation under its broad powers.

The U.S. CAA and the case of Brazilian forest policy provide just two examples of how the four components of policy formulation/implementation can exist in a variety of combinations. More study should certainly be undertaken to understand which combination of factors different systems of government maintain regarding a range of policies. Such study will yield valuable insights into the specific drivers of policy failure. The scenario with which this book is concerned, however, is whether institutional capacity to formulate policy exists in the first instance (component 1)—an institutional aspect of policymaking that is far too often overlooked in scholarship. For example, a national government in a federal system may have the political will to formulate a national land use policy (component 2), and may maintain both the institutional capacity (component 3) and political will (component 4) to enforce such a policy. If the constitution does not grant the national government legal authority to act in this manner (component 1), however, then the policy will either never be formulated in the first instance or, even if it is formulated and successful on the ground, it may be challenged and held unconstitutional by the courts. The result, of course, is that the policy's success on the ground will not save it from being struck down as beyond the scope of national government authority. Such is the case in the U.S., where the keystone constitution is very weak regarding natural capital appropriation connected to land use-related development and resource extraction activities, the direct regulation of which has long been considered the exclusive constitutional purview of subnational governments.

The result is a nested natural capital commons, legally entrenched by the very constitutions that provide both the private property rights and governmental system that have supposedly replaced the commons. Chapter 3, next, will analyze the nested commons scales that arise directly out of our efforts to legally decentralize national forms of governance, providing a more thorough description of their composition and function in order to explain how federal constitutional structure is key to solving natural capital commons tragedies within both federal systems of government and the international community.

Notes

1 The material constituting significant portions of this chapter originated in Blake Hudson and Jonathan Rosenbloom, Uncommon Approaches to Commons Problems: Nested Governance Commons and Climate Change, 64 *Hastings L.J.* 1273 (2013) and Blake Hudson, Federal Constitutions: The Keystone of Nested Commons Governance, 63 *Ala. L. Rev.* 1007 (2012).

2 *Keystone Definition*, dictionary.com, http://dictionary.reference.com/browse/keystone.

3 Garret Hardin, The Tragedy of the Commons, 162 *Science* 1243 (1968).

4 Michael Gochfeld, Joanna Burger, and Bernard D. Goldstein, Medical Care as a Commons, in *Protecting the Commons* 253 (Joanna Burger et al. eds, 2001); Brigham Daniels, Governing the Presidential Nomination Commons, 84 *Tul. L. Rev.* 899, 907 (2010). This book argues that the very system of government meant to address commons concerns may itself, when federal in kind, constitute another "new commons." Professor Daniels has noted that:

> New commons resources are *new* in one of two respects. First, they might be considered new in that, like an e-mail inbox, they are a fairly recent invention. Second, they might be familiar but only recently categorized as a commons resource, as in the case of silence or knowledge.

Id.

5 Robert O. Keohane and Elinor Ostrom, Introduction, in *Local Commons and Global Interdependence* 1, 13 (Robert O. Keohane and Elinor Ostrom eds, 1995).

6 Oran R. Young, Problem of Scale in Human/Environment Relationships, in *Local Commons and Global Interdependence* 27, 29 (Robert O. Keohane and Elinor Ostrom eds, 1995).

7 Duncan Snidal, The Politics of Scope: Endogenous Actors, Heterogeneity and Institutions, in *Local Commons and Global Interdependence* 47, 50 (Robert O. Keohane and Elinor Ostrom eds, 1995).

8 Steven Hackett, Dean Dudley, and James Walker, Heterogeneities, Information and Conflict Resolution: Experimental Evidence on Sharing Contracts, in *Local Commons and Global Interdependence* 93, 95 (Robert O. Keohane and Elinor Ostrom eds, 1995).

9 Elinor Ostrom, *Governing the Commons: The Evolution of Institutions for Collective Action* 30 (1990). Ostrom cites fishing grounds, groundwater basins, grazing areas, irrigation canals, bridges, parking garages, mainframe computers, streams, lakes, oceans, and other bodies of water as examples of "resource systems."

10 Id. at 38. Ostrom gives numerous examples of appropriators, such as herders, fishers, irrigators, commuters, and "anyone else who appropriates resource units from some type of resource system." Id. at 31.

11 Id.

12 Ostrom, supra note 9, at 14.

13 Id.

14 Id. at 25.

15 Id. at 90. Such groups include communities managing meadows and forests in Torbel, Switzerland and Hirano, Nagaike, and Yamanoka villages in Japan, as well as communities managing irrigation systems in Valencia, Murica and Orihuela, and Alicante, Spain and in the Philippines. See id. Importantly, many of Ostrom's design principles "appear relevant to the design of institutions to resolve problems of international cooperation as well as those at a strictly local level." Keohane, supra note 5, at 2.

16 Ostrom, supra note 9, at 1.

17 Hal R. Varian, *Microeconomic Analysis* 432–39 (3rd ed. 1992).

18 Thomas Hobbes, *Leviathan* (2009 ed.).

19 Ostrom, supra note 9, at 8.

20 Id. at 9.

21 Id. at 12.

22 Id.

23 Human-made capital includes "factories, buildings, tools, and other physical artifacts usually associated with the term 'capital.'" Robert Costanza and Herman E. Daly, Natural Capital and Sustainable Development, 6 *Conservation Biology* 37, 38 (1992).

24 Amy Sinden, The Tragedy of the Commons and the Myth of a Private Property Solution, 78 *U. Colo. L. Rev.* 533, 538 (2007); Eric T. Freyfogle, *The Land We Share: Private Property and the Common Good* (2003); Robert C. Ellickson, Property in Land, 102 *Yale L.J.* 1315 (1993).

25 See supra note 15. As observed by scholars, "[t]he real world commons problems that Ostrom studies usually involve repeated interactions among a relatively small number of players who are able to develop subtle institutions for monitoring and enforcing a degree of cooperation." Theodore Bergstrom, *The Uncommon Insight of Elinor Ostrom*, 112 *Scandinavian J. of Econ.* 245, 246 (2010).

26 David Hunter, James Salzman, and Durwood Zaelke, *International Environmental Law and Policy* 11 (4th ed. 2010) (citing *Millennium Ecosystem Assessment, Living Beyond Our Means: Natural Assets and Human Well-Being* 5, 16–22 (2005)).

27 Geoffrey Heal et al., Protecting Natural Capital Through Ecosystem Service Districts, 20 *Stan. Envtl. L.J.* 333 (2001).

28 Paul Hawken, Amory Lovins, and L. Hunter Lovins, *Natural Capitalism: Creating the Next Industrial Revolution 2* (1999).

29 Heal, supra note 27, at 334 n.1. Other scholars assert that the natural resources that comprise natural capital are "material that has economic or social value when extracted from its natural state." Susan J. Buck, *The Global Commons: An Introduction* 3 (1998).

30 Costanza and Daly, supra note 23, at 38. In addition, "natural capital" and "natural income" are "aggregates of natural resources in their separate stock and flow dimensions. … " Id.

31 See James Salzman, Integrating Ecosystem Services into Environmental Law, in *Managing Human Dominated Ecosystems* 77 (Victoria Hollowell ed., 2001); James Salzman, Barton H. Thompson, Jr., and Gretchen C. Daily, Protecting Ecosystem Services: Science, Economics,

and Law, 20 *Stan. Envtl. L.J.* 309 (2001); James Salzman, Creating Markets for Ecosystem Services: Notes From the Field, 80 *N.Y.U. L. Rev.* 870 (2005); James Salzman, A Field of Green? The Past and Future of Ecosystem Services, 21 *J. Land Use & Envtl. L.* 133 (2006).

32 Robert Costanza et al., The Value of the World's Ecosystem Services and Natural Capital, 387 *Nature* 253 (1997). The ecosystem services included in the estimate are atmospheric gas regulation, climate regulation, ecosystem disturbance regulation, water regulation, water supply, erosion control and sediment retention, soil formation, nutrient cycling, waste treatment, pollination, biological process regulation, habitat refuge, food production, raw materials, genetic resources, recreation, and cultural values. Id. at 254.

33 Hunter et al., supra note 26, at 11.

34 Id.

35 Heal et al., supra note 27, at 334.

36 See Blake Hudson, Commerce in the Commons: A Unified Theory of Natural Capital Regulation Under the Commerce Clause, 35 *Harv. Envtl. L. Rev.* 375 (2011).

37 Heal et al., supra note 27, at 333.

38 Id. See also, Alice Kenny, *Ecosystem Services in the New York City Watershed, Ecosystem Marketplace* (Feb. 10, 2006), available at http://www.ecosystemmarketplace.com/pages/dynamic/article.page.php?page_id=4130&section=home& eod = 1.

39 Keohane and Ostrom, supra note 5, at 11. Even so, we must remain aware of the "dangers of simplistic reasoning. Macro-scale systems are not merely small-scale systems writ large. Nor are micro-scale systems mere microcosms of large-scale systems. It follows that we cannot simply assume that the mechanisms at work at the two levels are the same." Young, supra note 6, at 42. Even so, "there is considerable scope for cross-fertilization among studies of social phenomena at different scales." Id.

40 See generally, K. Divakaran Prathapan and Priyadarsanan Dharma Rajan, Biological Diversity: A Common Heritage, 46 *Econ. & Pol. Wkly.* 15 (2011).

41 Unitary systems of government "may have subnational levels of governments; but these are not constitutionally empowered to make decisions on major government services and functions; rather, they are subordinate units" (Hans M. Gregersen et al., Forest Governance in Federal Systems: An Overview of Experiences and Implications for Decentralization, in *The Politics of Decentralization: Forests, People and Power* 13, 15 [Carol J. Pierce Colfer and Doris Capistrano eds, 2005]) that are intended to "balance the burden of governance." Ian Ferguson and Cherukat Chandrasekharan, Paths and Pitfalls of Decentralization for Sustainable Forest Management: Experiences of the Asia Pacific Region, in *The Politics of Decentralization: Forests, People and Power* 63, 65 (Carol J. Pierce Colfer and Doris Capistrano eds, 2005).

42 Jack S. Frierson, How Are Local Governments Responding to Student Rental Problems in the United States, Canada, and England? 33 *Ga. J. Int'l & Comp. L.* 497, 507 (2005). This is not to say that all unitary systems of government adequately manage appropriation of natural capital in the national commons, or that no federal systems do. Rather, this exercise is only meant to point out how national governments in federal systems may be *legally* restrained from acting where unitary systems will not be.

43 Paul Goldstein and Barton H. Thompson, Jr., *Property Law: Ownership, Use, and Conservation* 1048 (2006).

44 Id.

45 Id. at 1049.

46 See *Unitary State,* http://en.wikipedia.org/wiki/Unitary_state.

47 *Federalism by Country*, *F. Fed.,* available at http://www.forumfed.org/en/federalism/by_country/index.php.

48 The total surface area of the earth is 148,940,000 km^2. Federal systems of government maintain the following surface areas: Argentina: 2,766,890 km^2; Australia: 7,617,930 km^2; Austria: 83,872 km^2; Belgium: 30,528 km^2; Bosnia and Herzegovina: 51,209 km^2; Brazil: 8,514,877 km^2; Canada: 9,984,670 km^2; Comoros: 2,235 km^2; Ethiopia: 1,104,300 km^2; Germany: 357,021 km^2; India: 3,287,263 km^2; Iraq: 438,317 km^2;

Malaysia: 329,847 km^2; Mexico: 1,972,550 km^2; Micronesia: 702 km^2; Nepal: 147,181 km^2; Nigeria: 923,768 km^2; Pakistan: 796,095 km^2; Russia: 17,075,400 km^2; Saint Kitts and Nevis: 261 km^2; Sudan: 2,505,813 km^2; Switzerland: 41,285 km^2; United Arab Emirates: 83,600 km^2; United States: 9,826,675 km^2; Venezuela: 916,445 km^2. Thus, federal nation total surface area is 68,858,734 km^2, or roughly 46 percent of the world's total surface area.

49 See generally 10(3) *The Int'l Forestry Rev.* 538 (2008).

50 Arnoldo Contreras-Hermosilla, Hans M. Gregersen, and Andy White, *Forest Governance in Countries with Federal Systems of Government: Lessons of Decentralization*, *Center for International Forestry Research Governance Brief* 1, (January 2008, Number 39), available at http://www.cifor.cgiar.org/publications/pdf_files/GovBrief/GovBrief0739E.pdf.

51 Throughout this book, I refer to local, state, and national governments as "appropriating" resources similar to herders on an open pasture. I do not mean that they are necessarily engaged in direct appropriation, though that may be the case. Rather, these governments most often facilitate private appropriation activities through their rules (or lack thereof) for natural capital appropriation.

52 David N. Wear and John G. Greis, *U.S. Forest Serv., The Southern Forest Futures Project: Summary Report* 26–31, 35 (2011), available at http://www.srs.fs.usda.gov/futures/reports/draft/summary_report.pdf.

53 Joanna Burger et al., Common-Pool Resources and Commons Institutions, in *Protecting the Commons* 1, 7 (Joanna Burger et al. eds, 2001).

54 See generally Keohane and Ostrom, supra note 5.

55 Lower levels of government may lack legal authority to horizontally coordinate because higher level governments have preempted them from doing so, have simply not granted them authority to do so, or due to a number of other reasons outside the scope of this chapter.

56 For purposes of this book I refer to the failure to take political action as meaning either the failure to exercise legal authority at all, or rather exercising that authority in a way that does not resolve the commons dilemma.

57 Again, due to preemption by higher level governments, failure of higher level governments to grant legal authority, etc.

58 But see United States v. Pink, 315 U.S. 203, 210–13 (1942) (holding that state laws and presumably local laws, are invalid when conflicting with an international treaty).

59 This book breaks down local governments on the basic line between state level governments and general purpose incorporated subdivisions that are self-governed, including cities, towns, villages, counties (boroughs and parishes), but not special purpose or quasi-public entities (such as housing authorities).

60 Burger et al., supra note 53, at 7.

61 Id.

62 See Martin Edelman, Written Constitutions, Democracy and Judicial Interpretation: The Hobgoblin of Judicial Activism, 68 *Alb. L. Rev.* 585 (2005); see also Ruth Bader Ginsberg, An Overview of Court Review for Constitutionality in the United States, 57 *La. L. Rev.* 1019, 1025 (1997).

63 Clean Air Act, 42 U.S.C. §§ 7401–7671g (2006).

Part II

Decentralization of the Commons

In Part I we established a basis for understanding how natural capital commons have become subject to the parameters of legal institutions, or, "constitutionalized." Even though the purest form of the commons phenomena related to common-pool resources may appear to have been resolved by the institution of private property rights or government regulation, in federal systems of government we can conceive of this natural capital as embedded within a governance system that may legally entrench the commons phenomena and the rationality of governments in their appropriation of resources. Just as Ostrom stated that private property rights do little more than pit an appropriator in a game against nature in a smaller terrain rather than a game against another player in larger terrain, constitutionally decentralized federal systems of government may merely pit private property owner against private property owner in allocating resources, local government against local government, state against state, and nation against nation. Each of these entities might be said to replace Hardin's herders on their respective scales and they may act with legally sanctioned rationality if lower level entities are preempted by higher level authorities from addressing the commons dilemma or if higher level entities are not legally authorized to coordinate lower level entity appropriation activities. What does this legal decentralization look like, and how might it play out in practical reality? This is the question addressed in Chapter 3, next.

3 Federal Systems as a Nested Commons: The Case of United States Decentralization[1,2]

Introduction

The headline read, "Minnesota farmer battles Gulf 'dead zone'"[3]—an intriguing caption to say the least. How could a farmer from the U.S. state of Minnesota directly and positively impact a resource over 1,000 miles away? The article was about the 2010 dead zone in the Gulf of Mexico, one of the largest recorded dead zones in history, scientists say—about the size of the state of New Jersey. The dead zone is caused largely by sedimentation and fertilizer containing nitrogen and phosphorus flowing to the ocean from farms all along the Mississippi River. These chemicals rob the water of oxygen, preventing sea life from respiring. Remarkably, 40 percent of the land in the United States drains into the Gulf of Mexico via the Mississippi River Valley. The dead zone effectively pits farmers against fishermen because fertilizer runoff from farming operations ultimately has an aggregated, substantial effect on commercial fisheries in the Gulf. One of the most dramatic examples of fishery impacts are "suicidal shrimp" that actually leap onto the beach in search of oxygen only to die. Commercial interests, however, are not all that are at stake in the Gulf. Scientists are worried that if yearly dead zones continue to grow, the Gulf's entire ecosystem will reach a "tipping point" from which it may not recover.

The Minnesota farmer in the story said he considered people who live and work near the Gulf of Mexico his "neighbors." The story highlighted the farmer's recognition that "the land, water and air are inextricably tied and that the actions of one farmer can be felt thousands of miles away."[4] The farmer's perspective is unique, of course, as it is exceedingly difficult for most farmers in the Mississippi River Valley to acknowledge, much less establish a plan to rectify, the negative impacts that their activities have on a resource as distant as the Gulf.[5] Noting that he would "much rather eat wild Gulf shrimp than farmed shrimp," however, the Minnesota farmer decided to adjust his farming methods. He stopped tilling his land in order to decrease nitrogen and phosphorus runoff. He planted alfalfa along the edge of his farm—alfalfa is a "greedy" plant that extracts most of the nitrogen and phosphorus before it gets to the waterway. He also, rather cost-effectively, placed a bioreactor in the ground near the stream that removes nitrates from the water. It worked. The farmer's yields actually went up, wildlife he had not seen in years returned, and the water in the area became clearer.

Until more farmers engage in similar conduct, however, Gulf fishermen will not be happy. One commercial fisherman from the state of Louisiana colorfully declared, "you shit in the river, then you shit down here. ... They send us all the garbage; it comes down the river to us," to create what he called "the cesspool of the nation."[6] He continued: "The government ought to have a team of scientists working on that. How bad are they going to let it get before somebody stops it?"[7] Ultimately, the article concluded that more actions like those undertaken by the Minnesota farmer are necessary to prevent further degradation of the Gulf, and that "cleaning up the Gulf from the Midwest will require continental changes."[8]

The story of the Minnesota farmer and the Gulf might as well be a retelling of Hardin's commons metaphor, but on a much greater scale. Here, the herders are the individual states facilitating appropriation of the clean water resource through their citizen's farming activities and creating tragic consequences for the shared inland freshwater and Gulf marine resources. Nonpoint source water pollution from land use-related agricultural activities "is now considered the nation's most persistent and most difficult water quality problem."[9] Over 1.9 million U.S. farms cover nearly half of all the land in the nation. In 1998, agricultural runoff was a primary contributor to the degradation of 59 percent of river miles, 31 percent of impaired lake waters, and 15 percent of impaired estuarine waters. Sedimentation, toxic chemicals such as Polychlorinated Biphenyls (PCBs), mercury, pesticides, hydrocarbons, and, of course, excess fertilizers and animal wastes containing nitrogen and phosphorus plague waters in these watersheds.[10] The inter-jurisdictional impacts are profound.

Nonpoint runoff from agricultural, construction, forestry, and urban development activities sends sediment downstream that results in $1 billion a year in dredging costs for harbors and reservoirs. In addition to the Gulf dead zone, nearly half of all estuaries in the United States contain hypoxic zones due to phosphorus and nitrogen.[11] Nonpoint runoff aggregates at its final point of destination to destroy coral reefs and poison fisheries either directly or through the process of bioaccumulation.[12] There are further biological vector impacts, as runoff has resulted in the outbreak of microorganisms that attack and kill both fish and humans in the Chesapeake Bay, the Neuse River of North Carolina, and the Milwaukee, Wisconsin, watershed.[13]

The problem of Gulf eutrophication is emblematic of the commons complications created by a constitutional division of regulatory authority between the federal and state governments. The federal government does not currently regulate many land use activities related to farming, such as nonpoint source pollution from agricultural sediment and fertilizer runoff, a situation resulting largely from the history of jurisprudence declaring that land use regulation is the "quintessential state and local power" under the Constitution.[14] For example, despite widespread inter-jurisdictional impacts and the nationwide concerns raised by nonpoint water pollution, the federal government does not regulate nonpoint source water pollution under the Clean Water Act (CWA), including from agricultural operations or stormwater runoff not collected in defined stormwater systems. Even sources of pollution that would be considered point sources in other contexts are not regulated by the CWA if they are agricultural. Again, this hesitancy is due in part to conceptions of exclusive state and local authority over land uses, leaving states as the "exclusive regulators of nonpoint source pollution."[15] States, meanwhile, are doing very little to exercise their regulatory authority.[16] As Robin Craig has noted, "[s]o long as Congress operates within constitutional federalism requirements, its statutory judgment calls are subject to revision if new information or awareness indicates that the initial statutory division of power incorrectly reflects the true balance of the national and local interests at stake."[17]

Though the CWA does contain non-prescriptive provisions that might be harnessed to encourage greater state control over nonpoint pollution,[18] neither the CWA nor other programs have "translated into either widespread demonstrable results or clearly defined, coherent regulatory programs," leading to calls for an increased federal presence in the form of minimum federal standards with a great degree of flexibility available to the states in implementation.[19] Such standards might resolve the commons dilemma by addressing the problem of state-level inaction as well as foster more efficient coordination considering the large-scale inter-jurisdictional impacts along watersheds like the Mississippi and the Gulf of Mexico. To the extent that such standards might involve greater federal inputs into state land use planning within potentially affected watersheds, it is necessary to consider how the legal entrenchment of the commons phenomena, through principles of constitutional federalism, might inhibit such inputs.

The Mississippi River Valley can be considered a quintessential commons—in the absence of coordination, either among state and local governments or provided by a higher level authority, such as the federal government, individual subnational governments refuse to address nonpoint source pollution, and their collective inaction damages the shared Mississippi River and Gulf resources. Consider another example from the Mississippi River Valley, regarding the commons mentality of Bay St. Louis Mississippi officials, who recently sought to remove markers along the interstate denoting the high-water flood mark reached during hurricane Katrina.[20] The extent of Katrina's destruction was in no small part due to urban and agricultural development of floodplains that destroyed natural wetland buffer systems. The floodwaters from Katrina in this particular area were so high that they reached the overhead span where Interstate 10 crossed *over* another highway. Even so, a Bay St. Louis council member believed that "the markers are detrimental to attracting businesses that might want to relocate [in the area], especially on undeveloped property around the interstate."[21] In fact, "[s]ome city leaders envision the interstate property as a magnet that will pull in restaurants, motels, and big-box retailers."[22] These commercial establishments may very well be under water during the next Katrina, but local government officials and economic development interests want to keep that information hidden from passersby. In this way communities often want the federal government to bail them out of disaster crises that they themselves are complicit in exacerbating—complicit due to their ability to exercise land use regulatory authority to the legal exclusion of direct regulatory inputs by other levels of government, like the federal government.

Land use planning being a state and local government regulatory role under the U.S. Constitution leads to a number of increasingly concerning commons problems. Sea-level rise associated with climate change shifts the debate about the appropriate role of the federal government in land use planning in coastal areas likely to be inundated. Climate change raises serious questions about whether the federal government should have a greater say in land use decision-making in order to mitigate sea-level rise's devastating effects along the coast, especially given that more than half of the U.S. population lives in the coastal zone. Similarly, wetlands along the coast of Louisiana have long been subject to a certain level of federal regulatory involvement, primarily in the form of the CWA's 404 wetland fill permitting program.[23] Hurricane Katrina, however, exposed more clearly than ever the impacts, socially and economically, of aggregated individual land development projects facilitated by state and local planning that filled in wetlands and destroyed a key hurricane buffer system. This raises questions about how seriously we have taken the role of the federal government in staving off those types of disasters, especially considering the Army Corps of Engineers' high issuance rate of wetland fill permits[24] and state failures to craft more stringent wetland protection regulations. The same can be said for the development of floodplains along the Mississippi River that have greatly exacerbated the destruction caused by flood events.

Finally, as will be discussed in Chapter 5, urban sprawl is projected to dramatically impact forest resources in certain federal nations, a result arising out of land use planning exercised exclusively by subnational governments and the fact that direct forest management has legally been considered a land use regulatory responsibility for state or provincial governments under these countries' constitutions. Ultimately, as this chapter demonstrates, some federal systems are legally over-decentralized, leading to natural capital commons tragedies arising in significant part out of institutional deficiencies.

Benefits and Burdens of Decentralized Governance

To be clear, decentralized governance serves important goals, and scholars have highlighted a number of benefits provided by decentralization. These benefits track the noted benefits of federalism generally: federalism promotes economic growth, reciprocity in the enforcement of the law, safeguards against the potential tyranny of centralized power, encourages local citizen participation in governance and experimentation with new forms of governance (whereby subnational governments become "laboratories for experimentation"), and administrative efficiency as decentralized governments can specifically tailor laws to fit local needs.[25] Scholars have highlighted these benefits for specific forms of natural capital as well, such as forests. Decentralized forest policymaking has been shown to reduce central government bureaucracy, corruption, and political meddling, provide more efficient decision-making and better access to knowledge of local needs and constraints, increased information flow between local and central governments, and greater local cooperation and participation in governance.[26]

On the other hand, decentralized governance can give rise to a number of governance challenges. Federalism makes governance of problems that transcend subnational boundaries more difficult, creates economic inefficiency as overlapping laws conflict, imposes penalties on citizens of neighboring states, creates redundant governance, disenfranchises local minorities at the expense of local majorities, and can cause overall instability.[27] Perhaps most relevant for this book is the potential for federalism to cause a race to the bottom among states or provinces competing for business and growth, which is really just the commons dynamic legally institutionalized at a higher level. These disadvantages track those noted by scholars in the decentralized forest governance context, such as making more difficult the coordination and implementation of national policies, undermining national objectives when local objectives are not consistent, decision-making at local levels that is not socially or environmentally desirable or sustainable, loss of noncommercial objectives of national forest policy, and pressure to extract forest resources for immediate local benefit to the detriment of long-term sustainability, to name a few. Other noted problems are failure to achieve economies of scale, potential increase in arbitrariness and corruption, and the potential for local elites to control decentralized institutions.[28] Each of these challenges compounds the problems that decentralized governance can present for commons resource management.

Over-decentralized Resource Management: Scale by Scale Analysis of the Commons Dilemma

In Chapter 2 we discussed that what makes natural resources multi-scalar are the artificial geopolitical boundaries and corresponding allocations of governance authority creating the governance systems within which natural resources are embedded. We also established how each "nest" in federal systems may result in tragedy depending on the presence or absence of legal authority and political action both vertically and horizontally (the NT-1 through NT-5—non-tragic—or T-1 through T-4—tragic—resource scenarios outlined in that chapter, in Figure 2.4). As also discussed in Chapter 2, there are multiple nests scaled vertically and horizontally within which natural capital commons are embedded (see Figure 2.2), with national governments appropriating resource units of natural capital from the global commons resource system, states doing so from national commons resource systems, local governments from state systems, and private property owners from local systems.

While each level in isolation may see individual appropriators appropriating resource units from a single resource system, it is the integration of each scale within a federal system of government that creates multi-scalar natural resource management issues. Commons scholars have noted how the very systems of government that manage natural capital can take on the characteristics of a commons since "the social structures that bound and define resource commons share the fundamental characteristics of commons themselves."[29] Indeed, "[t]he creation of a new institution itself is indeed a form of collective action" and some resource collapses were due to a tragedy of the commons not just regarding the resource itself, but "in the very legal/political processes that were supposed to counteract such problems. Too many government bodies competed with each other for political resources for any of them to account meaningfully for such diffuse, intangible, or transgenerational values as were really at stake."[30] In the same way, federal systems of government add another layer of complexity to the management approaches needed to address natural capital management across scales, and a legal layer at that.

Global Governance Commons

On the global scale, nations are the individual actors appropriating natural capital resource units from the global commons. In this way, we can look at the legal policies of each nation regarding natural capital protection as a representation of either rational or irrational herder mentality on the global commons. Lack of international input into national policies, either through global governance regimes or cooperative collaborative efforts among distinct groups of nations, renders the depletable natural capital in the global resource system non-excludable because no nation can be excluded from allowing unchecked appropriation of the resource unit of natural capital within each nation's boundaries. Before proceeding, a point of clarification should be made: though not all nations engaging in global governance are federal systems—indeed most are unitary systems—the global governance system itself operates very much like a federal system of government. In international relations, many horizontally situated states with independent sovereignty attempt to resolve governance dilemmas. Importantly, however, the global "federal" system operates like a federal system of government in which the national government has no regulatory authority to coerce state actors, since there is no global government with enforcement authority.[31] As a result, a federation of nation-states with no hegemonic government is the construct within which the international community must operate. It is this construct that takes on the characteristics of a commons. As noted by Snidal, "[l]ocal [commons] and [international relations] have exploitable similarities because both involve collective-action problems, broadly defined, where independent behavior leads to collectively suboptimal outcomes."[32] Additionally, commons scholarship acknowledges that "[s]trong analogies exist between decentralized patterns of cooperation on the local level and patterns of international cooperation, where no external enforcement agency is generally available."[33]

In the climate change context, as one example, individual nations may act alone to curb emissions or establish carbon sinks in forests, wetlands, and agriculture. Yet there are strong disincentives from doing so, not the least of which is that other nations will continue to grow their own greenhouse gas-(GHG) based economies by free-riding on the GHG emissions limitation/sink preservation efforts of others. Indeed, nations face strong economic incentives to rely on the permanent appropriation of natural capital as a metric for the strength of national economies, a fact perhaps best demonstrated by a recent study undertaken by researchers at Brown University. The researchers tracked, via satellite, nighttime changes in the intensity of artificial light over countries around the globe, determining that increases in light parallel increases in that country's household incomes—thus signaling growth in gross domestic product (GDP).[34]

Thus the clearing of evermore land and the subsequent increase in development and generation of electricity facilitates socially desirable outcomes even if at odds with the preservation of crucial global natural capital. This study vividly demonstrates not only local but also global reliance on the replacement of natural capital with human-made capital as a key indicator of strong and growing economies—a result that every rational national government desires. In this way we can see that even in the presence of national boundaries, rational nations are content—even encouraged by economics—to rush toward just the type of tragedy described by Hardin. And yet to address the most pressing environmental issues of our time, like climate change, individual nations must either cooperatively and horizontally coordinate with each other, agreeing to domestically adjust land use, forest, wetland, agricultural, or other resource policies crucial to combating climate change, or they must voluntarily cede sovereignty to an international treaty or other protocol establishing rules of governance that will vertically coordinate those activities through standards set at the international level and implemented by nations.

The global governance commons has the potential to devolve into a tragedy because—absent a legally binding treaty or other arrangement—there is no vertical legal authority at the global level to coordinate the activities of nations engaged in natural capital appropriation, and therefore whether a natural capital commons exists depends entirely on the individual (or incidental collective) political action of nations to harness their authority for natural capital management. At first glance it might appear that horizontal self-coordination among nations and nations coming together to craft a global vertical regulatory structure are one and the same, since the creation of vertical regulatory structure at the global level obviously requires horizontal coordination. Yet nations can go about crafting global resource management regimes in different ways.

For instance, nations might cede all or a degree of sovereignty over domestic resource management to an international body that crafts rules for nations to implement domestically, which results in more direct and robust vertical authority.[35] Or perhaps rules are developed directly by nations engaged in protocol negotiation, and any nation who wishes to be a part of the protocol, at the present or in the future, must abide by those rules and standards. On the other hand, individual nations may not cede rule-making authority to an international body or an international protocol, but may agree to horizontally coordinate with other nations to utilize domestic rule making, with a degree of flexibility, to meet certain resource management targets. The treaty may still be binding, as with a vertical regulatory structure, but in a true horizontal collaboration the individual nations—and not a third party—are responsible for monitoring, sanctioning, and adjudicating disputes regarding other nations' appropriation of the resource.

In addition, horizontal governance at the international level can occur in a variety of additional ways that are not driven by global standards or targets. Horizontal collective action may involve far fewer nations than would a legally binding global governance regime, as a handful of nations may come together to craft rules for localized governance problems that cross only some national jurisdictional boundaries. The United States and Mexico coordinating access to Colorado River resources, or the United States and Canada coordinating management of North American migratory birds would be examples.[36] Even though vertical regulatory coordination and horizontal self-coordination at the global level can be differentiated in some ways, at some point the two begin to merge due to the ceiling that the globe places on governance—unlike at lower levels of government, the vertical and horizontal actors on the global scale are on the same plane.

The presence of a global governance arrangement that establishes binding rules at the international level can result in proper commons resource management at the national scale, even if nations are not individually engaged in domestic rule creation (absent the global push) due to collective action, free-rider, or other commons problems. Referring back to Chapter 2 (especially Figure 2.4) this might be characterized as an NT-3 scenario (non-tragic), at least in part. Yet, since ceding authority to an international body requires some degree of horizontal collective action, it might also be characterized in part as an NT-5 scenario. This is where the merger described above becomes apparent. Similarly, in the absence of rules arising out of an international body and implemented through domestic law, nations may choose to harness their domestic authority to craft their own rules aimed at hitting a resource management target and therefore manage natural capital in a non-tragic way (scenario NT-2).

On the other hand, the lack of a global governance arrangement can devolve into a tragedy if countries do not individually take political action pursuant to their legal authority (scenario T-2). Or, perhaps state or provincial governments have the constitutional authority to act and the federal government does not, which results in the federal government not being legally permitted to horizontally coordinate with other nations and in turn prevents it from authorizing a global body to vertically regulate via treaty (scenario T-4).

Ultimately, the global governance commons exists merely as a matter of geopolitics. There is no global constitution that may be amended to grant global regulatory authority to a global congress or other legislative body. There is also no global enforcement mechanism to ensure compliance, short of military action (though sanctions and other economic mechanisms may be utilized). International law relies solely on the political action of nations to self-regulate natural capital appropriation, voluntarily coordinate with other nations to do so through global agreement on targets, or voluntarily relinquish authority and at least some degree of sovereignty to meet standards set at the international level. As a result, depletable global natural capital is subject to rivalry by non-excludable nations, none of which may be *legally* excluded from appropriating the resource unit of natural capital over which they maintain control from the global resource system.

The goal of this subsection is not to compare the desirability or efficacy of "hard" international law in actually being forged or in fact influencing domestic law, as each depends on a variety of variables from political will to actual enforcement capacity of law on the books. Rather, this part merely describes the operation of the international community as yet a higher level, and potentially legally entrenched, natural capital commons, especially relevant in the context of federal systems of government. This exercise is particularly useful given that certain international environmental agreements have been effective in curbing individual nation rationality in the past (and present), as with the Montreal Protocol on Substances that Deplete the Ozone Layer, hailed as "[p]erhaps the single most successful international agreement to date."[37]

National Governance Commons

At the national scale, the commons dilemma shifts, with the group of rational, self-interested actors changing from national governments to state governments. State governments become herders on the national commons, and avoiding a tragedy of the commons requires self-coordination among the states or vertical coordination arising from federal government regulation.

As highlighted earlier, the federal form of governance in the United States maintains aspects of a commons that currently manifest in the text of the Constitution, primarily with regard to rules of governance related to the allocation and division of governance authority between branches of government or between levels of government.[38] This allocation is in a constant state of rivalry, as demonstrated by two examples in particular: the continued wrangling over the scope of federal authority under the Commerce Clause, described in greater detail in Chapter 4, and the related, subsidiary issue of complete preemption by the federal government of subnational regulatory authority.

Regarding the scope of federal authority under the Commerce Clause, more authority granted to subnational governments means less for the federal government and vice versa (meaning there is rivalry over a depletable governance resource). For example, state governments may wish to maintain exclusive regulatory authority over areas traditionally governed solely by states. So any expansion of federal power that allows either concurrent regulation by the federal government, or perhaps even preemption, results in a depletion of state government authority to exclusively regulate (or authority to see those activities remain unregulated, as they may prefer). In addition, it is very difficult to exclude any commons user (the executive, legislature, judiciary, states, and citizenry) from accessing the institutions that shape the appropriation of that authority over time.

So let us place the national governance commons in the context of our NT and T scenarios from Figure 2.4. The presence of federal legal authority over subnational resource appropriation (via the Commerce Clause) can result in proper commons resource management at the national scale if the national government exercises political action pursuant to that authority to coordinate subnational activities in the absence of subnational action (scenario NT-3), or completely in lieu of subnational action through preemption (scenario NT-1). Similarly, in the absence of federal Commerce Clause authority, subnational entities may choose to harness their authority to manage natural capital in a non-tragic way (scenario NT-2), or they may do so when the federal government maintains legal authority but chooses not to politically act (scenario NT-4). Finally, both the federal and subnational governments may maintain legal authority and both levels exercise that authority through political action to properly manage resources (scenario NT-5). On the other hand, even if the federal government maintains Commerce Clause authority, a tragedy may result if it chooses not to exercise its authority through political action to coordinate subnational activities at the same time that it also preempts the legal authority of subnational governments to manage the resource (scenario T-1). Similarly, the lack of federal Commerce Clause authority can devolve into a tragedy if subnational governments do not act politically on their exclusively held legal authority (scenario T-2). Finally, a tragedy may result if both the national and subnational governments maintain legal authority, but each fails to exercise that authority through political action to manage the resource (scenario T-3).

Ultimately, it is the Constitution's arguable depletion of federal authority over some resource management that legally entrenches a constitutional governance commons scenario. The Constitution grants primary regulatory authority over certain types of natural capital appropriation to a vast quantity of subnational governments. Thus, depletable national natural capital is subject to rivalry by non-excludable subnational governments, none of which may be *legally* excluded from appropriating the resource unit of natural capital over which they maintain control from the national resource system (scenario T-2). Unless subnational actors work together to craft sustainable resource management rules (scenario NT-2), there is no higher level of government with authority to coordinate their activities. It is this vertical overlay of potentially rational governance authority that facilitates the potential rationality of natural capital appropriators along the horizontal plane.

Managers of the governance commons (Congress, the judiciary, the executive, the states, and the citizenry) can always seek to adjust the constitutional structure to redress a legally entrenched commons, further discussed in Chapter 9. Congress could pass a statute claiming authority over natural resources, the regulation of which was previously considered the sole sphere of state governance authority—no legislator is excluded from proposing such a statute and legislators do so in rivalry with those opposing that appropriation or reallocation of governance authority (which would, of course, deplete, at least to an extent, the discretionary governance authority of the states). A president may then veto the statute, or in the alternative sign the legislation to ensure its passage, weighing in either against or in agreement with the new appropriation of governance authority. Any citizen or state that opposes the statute may lodge a challenge against its constitutionality, in rivalry with those citizens or states that would see governance authority appropriated in exactly the manner Congress chose to appropriate it. But unless managers of the governance commons seek to adjust the governance structure in this way, natural resources will remain embedded on a horizontal plane within a vertical governance structure that legally insulates levels of government from inputs by other levels.

Similarly, preemption by the federal government of subnational regulatory authority also may or may not result in commons tragedies. Under this scenario, the federal government forbids subnational governments from exercising what would otherwise be their constitutional authority over natural capital appropriation. It may be that this supplanting of subnational control results in better resource management, as is arguably the case with certain federal preemptive provisions in the CWA and Clean Air Act (CAA) that supplant state or local rules that may conflict with the federal scheme (scenario NT-1). Yet under other scenarios federal preemption may result in a supplanting of state or local authority that prohibits the development of more optimal natural capital appropriation measures (scenario T-1), as is arguably the case in the context of mobile source regulation under the CAA. In the context of climate change, there are a number of examples in which state governments sought to address climate change-related issues but were preempted by federal law, contributing to potentially tragic consequences in the aggregate.[39] This result is represented by T-1 in Figure 2.4, whereby subnational governments do not choose to rush toward commons tragedies, but are actually legally required to act in a rivalrous manner in appropriating depletable resource units of natural capital from the national commons.

So let us take the T-2 scenario—whereby there is no recognized constitutional authority for the federal government to intervene and coordinate state action regarding a particular type of natural capital appropriation, and state governments refrain from utilizing their primary regulatory authority over land uses to intervene in local government or private landowner appropriation of natural capital within state borders. The T-2 scenario is a particular problem in federal systems of government, and is one of the tragic scenarios most prevalent for resource management in federal systems. Each state government maintains a "rational" interest in keeping the land within its borders as open as possible to economic development, an interest driven largely by current economic growth indicators that place far greater value on human-made capital than on natural capital. Thus individual states may maintain lax land use restrictions relative to other states to avoid losing development opportunities and economic growth. This "race-to-the-bottom" among states can stifle innovative land use measures, such as the aforementioned growth boundaries around major metropolitan centers that could assist in preserving natural capital increasingly under development pressures. Professor Stewart aptly described the race-to-the-bottom among states as a form of the tragedy of the commons by noting that:

> States and local communities whose citizens desire environmental quality are also concerned with employment and economic growth. Given the mobility of industry and commerce, any individual state or community may rationally decline unilaterally to adopt high environmental standards that entail substantial costs for industry and obstacles to economic development for fear that the resulting environmental gains will be more than offset by movement of capital to other areas with lower standards. If each locality reasons in the same way, all will adopt lower standards of environmental quality than they would prefer if there were some binding mechanism that enabled them simultaneously to enact higher standards, thus eliminating the threatened loss of industry or development.[40]

Political scientist Neal Woods's empirical study on an environmental race-to-the-bottom concluded that the stringency of state environmental regulatory standards is indeed negatively impacted by the regulatory decisions of regional "competitors" because states "attempt to reduce the cost of doing business in the state in order to maintain current ... production within the state and attract new production."[41] States are especially incentivized to act in this manner on environmental issues because environmental benefits are often diametrically opposed to short-term economic benefits. In other words, the externalities of environmental harm are easy to shift to neighboring jurisdictions, which "allow[s] nations, states, or localities to capture the economic benefits of industrial production within their borders while compelling their neighbors to shoulder the costs"[42] of environmental harm. In addition, "political officials may be motivated to reduce regulatory stringency to gain a competitive advantage over their neighbors, thereby creating an aggregate movement toward the lowest common denominator."[43]

Take, for example, biodiversity as a form of natural capital. Professor Karkkainen has provided a succinct summary of the driver for commons reasoning among state governments in the context of biodiversity protection:

> Despite biodiversity's global benefits, many biodiversity-rich landowners, communities, and states will calculate that they will be better off externalizing the costs of biodiversity by letting local land conversion and development proceed apace, while leaving the costs of conservation to others. Indeed, states and communities with the largest inventories of undisturbed habitat and ecosystems are probably the least inclined to protect them for two reasons. First, from a local perspective, these lands may appear to be an *over*abundant resource. Second, these localities may be reluctant to protect these resources because they would carry a disproportionate share of the localized costs of conservation if they must forego development on a disproportionate percentage of their lands.[44]

Perhaps more importantly, some of the world's top commons scholars have cited federalism as a mechanism for exacerbating commons concerns, since,

> the [United States'] federal structure provides incentives for states to place the priorities of their residents over those of the rest of the nation. Virginia's capacity to meet clean-air standards while its industries contribute considerably to the pollution problems of other states makes it rational for its elected state officials to opt out of pollution agreements to protect the employment and economic growth interests of their constituency. Whereas decentralized governance certainly has a host of virtues, it can also serve as an impediment to meeting the needs of a broader society.[45]

This is not to say that states invariably race-to-the-bottom on all environmental issues. Indeed, under certain circumstances states may race to the top.[46] Yet, in the context of land development and the unchecked appropriation of natural capital in the name of economic development, subnational governments do seem to be sprinting toward the bottom—that is, unless one views widespread urban sprawl as the top.

The land use race-to-the-bottom provides a vivid depiction of the states as rational herders on the national natural capital commons. Not only do states that maintain lax land use standards exacerbate the appropriation of depletable natural capital, but they actually *promote* appropriative non-exclusivity, as their goal is to encourage the replacement of natural capital with human-made capital, new growth, and economic development. As a result, a great deal of natural capital waste and long-term economic inefficiency occurs. This is especially the case when rational developers freely develop greenfields simply because after cost–benefit analysis they determine that redevelopment of brownfields, infill, or other previously used lands would be more expensive.

A dramatic example of land use rationality gone awry is the abandonment of indoor malls in the United States. In the 1980s and 1990s indoor malls were in vogue and were the preferred development of choice for retailers. In the 2000s indoor malls have become far less popular, as developers and retailers have moved to the indoor/outdoor "town center" mall hybrid model.[47] Now, the indoor/outdoor mall is the development of choice for retailers, who abandon their former home for greener pastures, so to speak—rational herders moving from one part of the pastoral commons to another, but only *after* all the natural capital in the former spot is permanently consumed.

Indoor malls are quickly becoming "ghost towns" or "dead malls." Between 2007 and 2009, 400 of the U.S.'s 2,000 largest indoor malls closed.[48] There is even a website, deadmalls.com, dedicated to chronicling the story of hundreds of unused dead malls across the country.[49] The total amount of the nation's natural capital appropriated to create these now-vacant developments is no small amount, as indoor malls are often larger than 2 million square feet—or, in starker terms, 46 acres of permanently-paved land.[50] Not only is the natural capital value lost, but the human-made capital value is significantly decreased because the site of a dead mall "can rapidly turn into a wasteland of overgrown weeds, cracked concrete, and stray animals, with looters picking sites clean of copper tubing, light fixtures, and anything else that can be sold for scrap."[51]

States are complicit in facilitating these duplicative, inefficient, and wasteful uses of developed land, promoting the replacement of natural capital with human-made capital, even though preexisting human-capital could be used for the same economic purpose. Yet the development race between states continues, even in the presence of information regarding the harm caused by wasted developments like dead malls. The actions of states to either encourage new development or to abdicate environmental or land use controls so as not to stifle development is a classic example of rational commons reasoning that,

> [w]hen an individual user of the commons resource unilaterally decides to cut back in the commons resource, the appropriator is only leaving more for others. Particularly in light of how the commons resource allocates benefits and costs, it does not make sense to cut back unilaterally.[52]

It may be argued state races-to-the-bottom are the circumstances under which the federal government is allowed to act under its Commerce Clause authority. Federal involvement in natural resource appropriation can provide a mechanism to coordinate the actions of rational state governments in a way that prevents the destructive effects of states as herders on the national commons. Even so, the federal government's current statutes aimed at natural capital only affect land use activities under fairly limited circumstances—such as in the presence of an endangered species or wetlands considered "navigable waters" of the United States. These statutes only have tangential impacts on powers traditionally reserved to the states under the Constitution, and are not aimed at direct land use regulation such as zoning and other urban planning activities. In short, although race-to-the-bottom has been invoked by the U.S. Supreme Court as justification for federal regulation under the Commerce Clause,[53] the federal government has never been found to have such authority in the land use planning context. This constitutional state of affairs supports the exploration of more creative approaches that facilitate greater coordination of land use decisions at the state and local level.

Ultimately, the national natural capital present across federal nations like the United States takes on the characteristics of a commons when rational state governments fail to utilize their regulatory authority over land use and allow unchecked appropriation of resources of interest to the nation as a whole.[54] In states that decline to intervene in natural capital appropriation, the state boundaries do not act as a sufficient "fence" around each rational state government's resource unit of natural capital in a way that encourages the state to adequately protect the natural resources within its borders. In the absence of federal inputs into natural capital appropriation by subnational entities, either through cooperative federalism arrangements with state governments or pursuant to constitutional regulatory authority based upon the Commerce Clause or some other enumerated power, states may remain rational herders appropriating natural capital from the national commons with potentially tragic consequences. Not only does this state rationality inhibit protection of the national natural capital commons, but it facilitates the legal entrenchment of yet another commons higher up the scale, complicating and potentially inhibiting national participation in managing the global natural capital commons via legally binding international agreements.

State Governance Commons

As the commons dilemma shifts from national to state scale, the group of rational, self-interested actors changes from state governments to local governments. On the state commons, state governments, which constituted the potential herders on the national scale, are transformed into the vertical regulatory authority. Local governments assume the role of potential herders, seeking to appropriate natural capital by growing local economies, generating local revenues, increasing the tax base, and so on, and doing so by competing with other local governments.[55] This competition, a form of "race-to-the-bottom" that can lead to lax land use or forest management standards, for example, results in potentially tragic mismanagement of natural capital in the absence of horizontal self-coordination among local governments or vertical coordination arising from state government regulation.

As Professor Rosenbloom has discussed at length,[56] when the commons dilemma shifts from the national to the state scale, the tussle over legal authority also shifts to a battle between state and local governments. The outcome of this tussle is determined almost entirely by state constitutional and statutory law.[57] Unlike state governments, local governments—the rational, self-interested actors on the state commons—do not exist under the U.S. Constitution.[58] Local governments are a legal concept constructed out of state laws and they do not have inherent regulatory authority under, or protected by, the Constitution.[59] The Constitution is relevant on the state scale, however, because local governments have only that authority granted to them by the states. As a result, exclusive federal government assumption of legal authority to act on the national scale, through preemption or otherwise, leaves state and local governments without the legal authority to act (on either the national or state scale)—avoiding a conflict between state and local governments at the state scale (scenario T-4 in Figure 2.4). Accordingly, avoiding a tragedy at the state scale when the federal government is the sole governmental entity with the legal authority to act on the national scale is dependent upon federal action, as neither state nor local governments on the state scale have the legal authority to act.

Alternatively, if on the national scale state governments maintain the legal authority to act, either exclusively or shared with the federal government, then the potential for a new struggle arises on the state commons—a struggle between state and local governments. One example of this struggle involves, as discussed in the section on the national governance commons, traditional notions of economic pressures described in the *Tragedy of the Commons*, whereby in the absence of state government regulatory restrictions, local governments are engaged in a race-to-the-bottom phenomenon stemming from a traditional, natural capital commons structure. Local governments are believed to appropriate depletable and non-excludable resources in competition with other local governments because of the economic incentives in doing so. An alternative description of the commons dilemma at the state scale is rooted in the legal pressures that actually influence local governments to act rationally. These pressures are frequently overlooked and stem from the fact that state law often compels local governments to manage natural capital resources in a rational, and thus potentially tragic, manner. In particular, local governments are often prohibited from having extraterritorial impacts and are limited to regulating solely within their borders.[60] The combination of multi-jurisdictional natural capital resources and limited local government authority to regulate those resources creates inefficiencies that discourage local governments from seeking innovative solutions to commons challenges.[61]

There are four potential legal scenarios within a state that inform the nested governance commons and influence local government actors' behavior on the state scale. The first stems from an early twentieth-century doctrine—Dillon's Rule.[62] Under this rule a local government may act only if the action is expressly authorized by the state, is incidental to an expressly stated authorization, or is "indispensable" to performing the local government's tasks.[63] Further, any fair, reasonable doubt concerning the existence of the power is resolved by the courts against the local government, and the power is denied.[64] The remaining three state legal scenarios informing the state governance commons are commonly referred to as "home rule" laws. Home rule laws vary in the amount of autonomy granted to local governments and come in three forms: (1) legislative home rule;[65] (2) imperio home rule;[66] (3) hybrid legislative/imperio.[67] Ultimately, all four of these legal scenarios—Dillon's Rule and the three types of home rule laws—limit local government authority to some degree.

State preemption laws determine when a local government has exceeded its legal authority under either Dillon's Rule or the three types of home rule authority, or when the state government has recaptured some of that authority. Incorporated into the home rule and preemption analyses is an inquiry into whether a particular local action has an impermissible extraterritorial impact.[68] While state judicial interpretation of when a local government is acting extraterritorially may differ, many courts "use a finding of extraterritoriality as the basis for the conclusion that [a local government] … has exceeded the [locality's] … powers, or has been preempted by the state legislature."[69]

The combination of Dillon's Rule, home rule laws, and the judicial interpretation of preemption laws coerces local governments to consider only the impacts within their jurisdiction. Local government actors are at a minimum encouraged, and at most legally compelled, not to consider their externalities or to act "rationally," resulting in a legally entrenched commons.[70] Because many natural capital resources are not confined to a local government's borders, any benefit that may stem from one local government's irrational protective action to preserve the resource can be quickly lost. Therefore, the free-riding actions of neighboring jurisdictions discourage "irrational" (responsible) horizontal management of commons resources by those jurisdictions that would otherwise do so. Each locality is therefore faced with both economic and legal pressure to adopt a dominant strategy to benefit its inhabitants—internalizing those benefits—while externalizing the costs to the other state common-pool actors. Each locality is reduced to competing with other localities for the appropriation of natural resources, including those relevant to climate change, such as forests, wetlands, and agricultural resources.

When more authority is assumed by state governments under strict interpretations of Dillon's Rule, home rule, and preemption laws, less authority is granted to local governments and vice versa. In this way, state constitutional and statutory provisions formulate a governance commons that overlays the natural resource commons it was intended to govern at the state level. The presence of Dillon's Rule, home rule, and preemption provisions over local resource appropriation can result in proper commons resource management at the state scale if the state government acts on its legal authority to regulate local activities (scenario NT-1 in Figure 2.4). In the climate change context, state legislation pertaining to GHG reductions enacted in California,[71] Oregon,[72] and Washington[73] represent examples of the NT-1 scenario on the state scale, where state governments have the legal authority to address climate change, take proactive political action to do so, and presumably preempt any local action contrary to the laws. Similarly, if a state constitution grants exclusive legal authority through home rule or specific constitutional protections[74] to local governments to manage a resource, they may choose to harness their collective action and coordinate with each other to manage the resource in a non-tragic way (scenario NT-2).

Because a number of natural capital resources, such as wetlands, forests, and agricultural resources, are simultaneously managed by state and local governments, avoiding a tragedy of the commons could occur when the state vertically regulates local activities pertaining to the resource in the absence of otherwise legitimate horizontal local government political action (scenario NT-3), local governments horizontally coordinate in the absence of otherwise legitimate vertical state political action (scenario NT-4), or the state vertically regulates *and* local governments horizontally coordinate (scenario NT-5). For example, local government collaborations, such as C40 Cities Climate Leadership Group,[75] the U.S. Conference of Mayors,[76] and Union of the Baltic Cities,[77] represent horizontal collaborative attempts to avoid a tragedy relevant to climate change at the state scale. When these attempts are coupled with state legal authority but the state does not take political action, then an NT-4 scenario can arise. Relatedly, when horizontal collaborations similar to these are coupled with state legal authority and political action, an NT-5 scenario can arise and avoid the tragic overconsumption of resources.

Conversely, a tragedy may result if the state has not authorized local governments to act, and the state fails to vertically regulate local activities (scenario T-1 in Figure 2.4). Over the past year, a T-1-like scenario has arisen in several states over zoning and natural gas fracturing (or "fracking"). State laws in Pennsylvania, for example, have attempted to carve out exceptions from local zoning laws for various oil- and gas-related activities.[78] In these circumstances, local governments are powerless to protect the resource, and the state has failed to take action to protect the resource (and some cases, such as fracking in Pennsylvania, have facilitated the consumption of the resource). A tragedy may also occur if local governments that are authorized through home rule or specific enabling laws to manage a resource fail to horizontally coordinate their activities, and the state fails to reclaim the legal authority from local governments (scenario T-2), is prohibited from reclaiming the authority by the state constitution (scenario T-2), or maintains concurrent legal authority and fails to regulate through vertical state political action (scenario T-3).[79]

At the state scale, a legally entrenched nested governance commons results most often from a lack of state political action to vertically regulate local government activities, a lack of local government collective action when authorized by home rule or enabling laws, or a narrow judicial interpretation of home rule provisions and the prohibition on extraterritorial actions preventing local governments from taking actions they otherwise might take. This structure subjects the depletable state natural capital to rivalry by non-excludable local governments that may either choose to appropriate the resource unit of natural capital over which they maintain control from the state if the state does not intervene, or may even be compelled to do so by state law.

Let us look more closely at the operation of the state governance commons, and use the example of private land use regulatory authority in the U.S. The Tenth Amendment of the U.S. Constitution reserves for the states all powers not delegated to the federal government and may act as a limit on Congress's regulatory authority, "particularly in traditional areas of state and local authority, such as land use."[80] State and local governments regulate private property pursuant to their "police power" authority to protect the "general welfare."[81] Numerous scholars have observed that "[t]he weight of legal and political opinion holds that this allocation of power in [the U.S.] leaves the states in charge of regulating how private land is used,"[82] and that "[l]and use law has always been a creature of state and local law."[83] The U.S. Supreme Court case that established the foundation for the land use regulatory patterns we see today, *Euclid v. Ambler Realty*,[84] has been described as a "sweeping paean to the supremacy of state regulation over private property."[85] Furthermore, the U.S. Supreme Court has recognized "the States' traditional and primary power over land ... use,"[86] and that "regulation of land use ... is a *quintessential* state and local power."[87]

States and localities may utilize this paramount authority to set zoning standards for municipalities, to encourage planned land development for economic growth, to set agricultural standards related to land use, and to establish private forest management standards, among a variety of other land use directives that might further the "general welfare." As discussed in greater detail in Chapter 6, though current constitutional interpretations of the Commerce Clause grant the federal government limited, indirect authority to impact land use activities related to, for example, endangered species and wetlands,[88] subnational governments maintain primary responsibility for regulating "if, when, and how" private property owners appropriate natural capital on their private lands.

To be sure, various state governments maintain environmental laws meant to protect natural capital, such as state biodiversity laws.[89] In addition, local governments are quite active in dictating regulations guiding the development of human-made capital on private lands, including the location of residential versus commercial developments relative to each other in a municipality, how tall buildings should be, how far from the road homes should be constructed, minimum or maximum lot size for homes, to name just a few examples. Local governments may even establish "smart growth" plans conditioning the development of new human-made capital upon a showing that the requisite services will be available to new commercial tenants or residents. Even though state and local governments participate quite vigorously in dictating the planning and establishment of human-made capital, these plans are largely development-centric and are focused on the *expansion* of human-made capital—often at the expense of natural capital formerly maintained on the land.

State governments not only passively leave local governments and private property owners to their rationality when they refuse to devise inputs into natural capital appropriation, but they actually encourage the replacement of natural capital with human-made capital. The predisposition of both subnational governments and private property owners to move "rationally" toward a natural capital tragedy does not inevitably flow out of incapacity to choose otherwise—though information problems can explain that potential causal relationship. Rather, this rationality follows quite naturally, again, from the institutional incentives provided by our economic system. Many of the consumer reports and indices that society relies upon to gauge the strength of the economy are explicitly linked to land development activities that *permanently* appropriate natural capital and replace it with human-made capital—"new home starts" are just one example.[90] For instance, in the midst of one of the most serious economic downturns in U.S. history, an April 2011 report on growth in new housing construction raised some analysts' hopes that our nation was on a path toward economic recovery. Commerce Secretary Gary Locke issued a statement, commenting that "[d]espite continued volatility, today's numbers show welcome growth within the housing market," and that "[t]here are positive signs for widespread growth throughout the economy and a stronger housing market in the coming year."[91] These statements appear quite frequently in the news, representing our societal preference for human-made capital over natural capital. Not only do we value "new home starts" because that metric makes us feel good about the state of the economy, but increasing population pressures make the development of new homes a practical reality. Experts estimate that increasing populations in the United States will result in the development of 70 million additional housing units by 2040, 40 million of those being built on *new* residential lots.[92]

Ultimately, natural capital in the form of biodiversity, wetlands, pasturelands, forests, and other resources is subject to overuse and degradation in the absence of state government exercise of constitutional authority to effectively direct land use planning at the local level. In this way, local governments and private parties roam around the state commons appropriating natural capital at will and with potentially tragic consequences.

Local Governance Commons

At the lowest scale on the governance commons, private sector actors compete for vital natural resources most immediately within the bounds of the local government in which their property is situated. Land use activities undertaken by private property owners who fail to self-coordinate or who are not governed by local rules for appropriating natural capital can remove or mismanage vast amounts of natural capital that could, for example, be used to sequester carbon, with tragic climate change impacts. Urban sprawl, subnational forest management, and wetland disturbance/disappearance are valuable case studies of this phenomenon, whereby private property owners are potential herders on the local commons (and every commons at higher scales) in the absence of horizontal self-coordination among property owners or vertical regulatory coordination arising from local government (or state or national) regulation.

In order to avoid a natural capital commons dilemma at the local scale, the local government must have the legal authority to vertically regulate, or private sector actors must have the legal authority to horizontally coordinate. If neither local government nor private sector actors have legal authority to vertically regulate or horizontally coordinate due to federal or state preemption of their ability to do so, then the local governance commons devolves into a T-4 scenario on the local scale, where the vertical and horizontal legal authorities are absent, and avoiding a tragedy of the commons can only occur by higher level action. Higher level action would require a jumping of scales, so to speak, in the form of federal or state vertical regulatory or horizontally coordinated activities.

Alternatively, if states maintain legal authority to act on the national scale, and an individual state allocates some or all of that legal authority to local governments to act on the state scale (through Dillon's Rule or home rule provisions, and without preemption), a tragedy may be avoided at the local scale through vertical regulatory action on the part of the local government. If private parties are left a degree of legal authority to devise their own commons management solutions notwithstanding local government regulation, then it may constitute an NT-3 or an NT-5 scenario (depending on whether private property owners actually do take action, NT-5, or do not take action, NT-3). For example, landowners might come together to create a trust or execute formal private land use controls, such as private covenants, to protect forests or wetlands.[93] They might also enter into forest, wetland, or agricultural cooperatives to achieve sustainable resource management.[94] If local government regulation completely preempts private property owner authority, then it is an NT-1 scenario. For example, Washington County Maryland's Forest Conservation Ordinance, which requires that developers of projects removing 40,000 square feet of forest submit a mitigation plan for approval, arguably represents an NT-1 scenario at the local scale.[95]

It is also possible that the federal or state governments may maintain authority to vertically regulate—and that they will do so in a way that prevents local governments from also acting—but that allows for concurrent, private property owner horizontal action. This is the NT-2 scenario at the local scale, where the local government does not maintain legal authority but private property owners can self-coordinate. Finally, private property owners may horizontally coordinate for proper commons resource management in the absence of otherwise authorized local government regulation (scenario NT-4).

Conversely, scenario T-1 results when a local government maintains legal authority to vertically regulate, but fails to do so *and* prevents private property owners from acting. T-2 results when the state or federal governments withhold legal authority from local governments to vertically regulate a resource but allow concurrent private property owner action that does not then come to fruition. The fracking example mentioned in the previous section represents a T-2 scenario at the local scale, as local governments have been preempted by state authority. Presumably, private landowners still have the authority to refuse to allow fracking on their property, but many have not done so.[96] T-3 results when local governments have the legal authority to act—granted by the state and not preempted by state or federal authority—but fail to take necessary political action at the same time that private property owners fail to exercise concurrent management authority.

To be clear, the system of private property rights as conceived in the modern U.S. can provide numerous environmental benefits, *if* those in control of the property act in an environmentally responsible manner or otherwise do not take on the characteristics of "rational private property owners." In the absence of state or local regulation, private property owners may voluntarily undertake conservation activities regarding natural capital on their property, thus harnessing the power that private property rights can provide for environmental protection. Environmental non-governmental organizations (NGOs) and private individuals have used the vehicle of private property rights to purchase or receive donations of property for the sole purpose of conserving environmental amenities.[97] Others have captured the power of ecosystem services within markets, striking a balance between protecting the environment and facilitating economic revenues and progress, and have therefore gained economic return simply from protecting natural capital.[98] Thus privatization of landed natural capital can serve important societal and environmental interests. Ultimately, a judicially protected private property rights system may be necessary simply because the very same legal system that may protect one person's right to pave an asphalt parking lot over 100 acres of pristine forestland preserves another person's right to conserve the same 100 acres in perpetuity. Without a somewhat shielded private property rights system, and with property rights existing only at the discretion of the government, serious environmental problems can arise. The foremost of these is that a democratically elected majority, unsympathetic to conservation interests and wishing to rejuvenate a suffering economy by investing in sprawling development, might vote to transfer 100 acres of pristine forest from the person wishing to conserve the forest to the person wishing to develop a "big box" retail store, or may vote to condemn property for a downtown redevelopment centered around a private pharmaceutical company, as in the U.S. Supreme Court case of *Kelo v. City of New London*.[99]

Though Ostrom provided key insights into how neither government regulation nor private property rights are prerequisites for effective resource management, property rights is one of the initial mechanisms identified to address commons dilemmas. The purpose as initially conceived is to turn rational individual decisions that lead to collective harms into positive collective outcomes—to turn a prisoner's dilemma, whereby parties with access to a commons resource believe they are making a decision that is in their own "best" interest but that in fact results in a worse outcome for every party involved, into a Pareto-optimal outcome, whereby it would be impossible for a party to make him or herself better off without necessarily making another party worse off.[100] Thus, in the herder's case, fencing off the pasture and dividing it into private property will theoretically cause each herder to prohibit the flock from consuming more grass than can sustain the herd and to add no more sheep than the pasture can sustain. Yet due to various failures in the market, such as imperfect information, "free-riders," transaction costs, collective action problems, and other failures to internalize externalities, environmental destruction remains, even in the presence of our private property rights system.[101]

Private property rights alone ultimately do not succeed in curbing the rationality of property owners regarding the appropriation of natural capital because natural capital on private lands is itself a commons—being depletable, such that appropriation of natural capital by one private property owner renders it unavailable to others for use or appropriation, and it is extremely difficult, if not impossible, to exclude a private property owner from appropriating the natural capital available on his or her property.

What is often overlooked in the private property context is the difference between the legal right to own land and the legal right to *use* land. Private land is not in and of itself a commons, of course. Though the land base is certainly depletable, meeting the first element of a commons resource, property owners are legally entitled to exclude others from the land itself. It is very difficult, however, to exclude any landowner from a use that appropriates a depletable resource unit of natural capital present on private property. Indeed, the very nature of private property, providing stringent protections for both use of property and the right to alienate property, allows natural capital to remain a commons—even though the private land itself is no longer so.

In the context of Hardin's example, we can see this by asking: how did Hardin's rational herder come to have pasturelands in the first place? Perhaps a private property rights system was already in place and the rational herder simply bought the property from a rational forester, who had managed the land for forest products until a shift in the market simultaneously caused the forest products industry to move overseas and agricultural products like grass and sheep to become more valuable. Thus the rational herder came to own the property by paying the rational forester a nice sum—enough for the forester to rationally retire—and then converted the property from forest land to agricultural land with a plentitude of grass resources. Though grass resources remained, the trees were gone, and gone too were the services they provided and other resources present in the forest.[102]

Though an individual herder or forester can legally exclude others from accessing his or her property, no individual herder, forester, or other property owner can, in the absence of government regulation or Ostrom's model, be excluded from either appropriating the natural capital on one's property or from selling it to another who will. So even though the forester's trees were fenced in and privatized, as was the subsequent herder's pasture, a "tragedy" is likely to occur at each step in the chain of ownership regarding various important natural resources—even in the presence of a private property rights system. This is because commons resources "are subtractable resources managed under a property regime in which a legally defined user pool cannot be efficiently excluded *from the resource domain*."[103] Natural capital on private lands meets this definition. Furthermore, scholars have noted the potential of commons resources to be present in privatized space in other property contexts, such as the commons nature of pollutable atmosphere present in airspace while the airspace itself is private property that is "separately owned or controlled."[104]

In the modern context, consider a hypothetical from a later step in the chain of private ownership. Assume that a herder with privatized pasture lands is approached by a rational grocer, who wants to develop a market to sell various agricultural products for human consumption. Because market demand for grocery products is high, the grocer is able to offer the herder an attractive sum of money for the land—an amount substantial enough for the herder to rationally retire. Furthermore, the country where the herder and grocer reside, the "Rational States of America," has established "new grocery starts" as one of its primary metrics of economic growth—the more new grocery starts, the stronger the economy. In order to utilize this development to invigorate the economy the government crafts various policies aimed at promoting new grocery starts.

As a result, incentives are aligned for an increasing number of herders to sell their pasture lands to an increasing number of grocers. Once the grocers obtain a private property interest in the pasture lands it is difficult to exclude their appropriation of depletable natural capital in the absence of government intervention or internal arrangements among grocers. What becomes of the grass? In establishing their places of business, the grocers rid the land of the grass, construct their markets, and pave the property to allow customer parking. Not only is the grass gone, but ambient temperatures in the region rise due to the urban heat island effect,[105] impervious surfaces on the property lead to pollution and greater risk of flooding downstream, the population's water supply is potentially reduced as groundwater aquifer recharge is slowed, and carbon sequestration capabilities are eliminated, to name a few environmental harms. In other words, the grocers' complete replacement of natural capital with human-made capital in an effort to rationally maximize their economic interests provides them with a 100 percent return for their use of the property, but they only suffer a fraction of the negative cost imposed by impervious surfaces, the heat island effect, increased flooding, and loss of carbon sequestration capabilities. Those costs are spread across the collection of private properties in the region.

Thus, upon adjusting our scale of analysis we can see that each individual herder can be replaced by each individual private landowner who owns a segment of private property, and the pastoral commons can be replaced by the network of individually owned private properties which constitutes "the environment." In these circumstances it is in a private property owner's best interest to maximize economic benefit received from property by replacing the natural capital on his or her private land with human-made capital—after all, this act of appropriation puts money in the landowner's pocket and signals a strong economy in the locale and perhaps the nation as a whole. Because the negative cost of the lost natural capital is fractionally spread across the collection of private properties in an area—which we might call the "collective privatized environment"[106]—the true harm occurring in the aggregate is cloaked. In addition, the harm is also fractionally spread across time, as the impacts of losing aggregated natural capital in an area may not be known for many years to come.[107]

Ostrom herself argued that "even when particular rights are unitized, quantified, and salable, the resource *system* is still likely to be owned in common rather than individually."[108] Similarly, Professor Rose has stated:

> [A] private property regime itself—whether governmental or customary—may be understood as a managed 'commons'—a meta-property held in common by those who understand and follow its precepts. In a sense, a movement toward private property is a movement from a 'commons' in a physical resource to a 'commons' in the social structure of individualized resource management.[109]

The collective privatized environment is just the type of resource system envisioned by Ostrom and the managed commons alluded to by Rose, comprised of the aggregated resource units of natural capital contained on "unitized, quantified and salable" private properties within national, state, and local government boundaries.

As discussed in Chapter 2, the critical concept to viewing the natural capital on any one individual's private land as a "resource unit" within a commons is the fact that an individual herder *can* exclude others from "resource units," just as a private property owner can exclude others from coming onto his or her property. Despite the fact that both the herder and the private property owner can exclude others from appropriating the *resource unit* itself, the pasture and the natural capital on private land remains a constituent part of a commons resource *system*. Ostrom explains that though a *resource system* can be jointly held and multiple appropriators can appropriate resource units from the system, the resource units themselves "*are not subject to joint use or appropriation*."[110]

Take, for example, landowners X and Y, whose private properties are adjacent to each other. Each maintains a resource unit of natural capital defined by his or her respective property boundaries. That natural capital is obviously depletable—rendering the first element of a commons resource met. The second element exists as well, as the natural capital within the resource system—that is, across the collection of private properties—is non-excludable. The question of non-excludability does not mean that X cannot exclude Y from X's property, for that is considered one of the most important aspects of property rights, at least in the U.S. Rather, the question is the difficulty, if not impossibility, of excluding any individual property owner from *using* his or her property in a way that appropriates one resource unit of natural capital absent some external vertical regulatory coordination or horizontal self-coordination.

Just as two herders cannot occupy the same spot in the pasture, nor can their cattle graze the exact same blades of grass, no two private property owners' parcels of land can occupy the same spot, nor can their bulldozers remove the same natural capital. Herders may move around in the pasture, just as X and Y may legally swap properties an infinite number of times. Or herders may remain stationary and increase their herd until their herds merge, just as private property owners may remain stationary until a Walmart parking lot abuts a Best Buy parking lot. In each case, however, the pasture and private lands from which the resource units of natural capital are appropriated remain a part of a system that is a natural capital commons. It is equally impossible to exclude herders or private property owners from appropriating the natural capital resource units available to them in their current position in both space and time. In reality, as noted by Ostrom, all our private property rights system does with regards to natural capital is pit each property owner "*against nature* in a smaller terrain, rather than ... against another player in larger terrain."[111]

Indeed, the destruction of privatized natural capital is occurring on wide scales. Developers are appropriating resource units in land at an alarming rate, which threatens irreparable damage to natural capital resource systems. "Rational farmers," for example, are selling formerly valuable farmland to sprawling development interests because "selling all or a portion of a farm for development [is] the only economically sensible option. ... "[112] As a result, "the U.S. is losing nearly twice as much farmland each year as it did in the early nineties ... [and fifty] acres of farmland are converted to development every hour."[113] In addition, almost 1 million acres of forestland were lost to development annually from 1992 to 1997, a rate of nearly 115 acres an hour.[114] As discussed in Chapter 5, the U.S. Forest Service report detailing that population growth and urbanization will reduce forests in the southeastern United States alone by as much as 23 million acres, or 13 percent, over the next 50 years, is emblematic of this phenomenon.[115] In short, developers are rushing to purchase, develop, and permanently remove valuable natural capital from land as quickly as possible. Paraphrasing Ostrom's analysis regarding groundwater basin commons, what a developer does not purchase today in a developing area will be either developed or purchased by rival developers tomorrow. The fear that developers cannot purchase tomorrow what they do not purchase today undermines any countervailing motive to forego current appropriation of natural capital for its future availability. Thus, "[t]he two incentives reinforce one another to aggravate the intensity of the [development] race. Without a change of institutions, [developers] in such a situation acting independently will severely overexploit the resource. Over-exploitation can lead to destruction of the resource itself."[116] Indeed, appropriators like developers "tend to be in competitive relationships with each other; although often fiercely independent, they are also interdependent because they are appropriating from the same [commons] resource or related resources within an ecosystem."[117]

Implications of Over-decentralized Resource Governance in Federal Systems: Tragedy not Inevitable, but Legally Defensible

As noted by commons scholars, "[i]t is popularly believed that the actors involved in [commons] problems, whether individuals or governments, are trapped in an inexorable 'tragedy of the commons' from which they cannot extract themselves."[118] Ostrom herself criticizes much of the body of commons scholarship as regretfully presuming a "remorseless tragedy."[119] Ostrom and other scholars have more recently proven this theory incorrect, as evidenced by Ostrom's successful collective action model.

Indeed, private property owners sometimes harness the power of private property to protect the environment. Due largely to the difficulties nations have experienced in forging a legally binding international climate agreement, local communities and NGOs are even devising their own methods for addressing climate change.[120] Even in the absence of a higher mandate, these individuals and groups are overcoming individual rationality and seeking to escape natural capital tragedies, demonstrating that external rules are not a *necessary* component to spur certain individuals to action.

Nor do state governments necessarily rush toward tragedy. States such as California have led the charge on ratcheting up certain mechanisms of environmental protection, even maintaining more stringent environmental regulations than the national government—a phenomenon of race-to-the-top known as the "California Effect."[121] In this way state governments in the U.S. may often serve as valuable laboratories for governmental experimentation, rather than racing to the bottom.

Even though there are examples of parties extracting themselves from commons tragedies at each level within nested natural capital commons, there is an important difference between inexorability, probability, and reality. Though not inevitably trapped, in reality most private property owners and states remain guided by economic incentives diametrically opposed to sustainable natural capital management—policies that exacerbate urban sprawl and other environmental ills within nations. Likewise, nations are facilitating the destruction of global resources, like tropical forests, world fisheries, and a global atmosphere free of dangerous levels of GHGs, to name only a few examples. Certain federal constitutional structures make these realities more probable, rather than inexorable. At the very least, the above examples of actors overcoming commons tragedies demonstrate that while a few are successful, many more are unsuccessful, indicating that some legal inputs either at a higher level to resolve the dilemma (and not preempting lower level efforts to do so) or horizontally among actors are necessary to coordinate successful action. In the absence of such authority, a natural capital tragedy remains legally defensible.

Federal structure simply adds a layer of *legal* complication on top of already *politically* complicated resource management. While it is not impossible for the varied actors within federal systems to extract themselves from tragic natural capital appropriation, it is far more difficult to coordinate and ensure efforts to do so. Certainly attempts at cooperative or voluntary inputs may be made by governments in these systems, but in the event of successful constitutional challenge there is no legal mechanism—no "Fail-Safe Federalism"—for preventing natural capital tragedies. In federal systems like the U.S., for example, even if the national government politically chose to act, it only takes one private property owner or one subnational government combined with the right mix of U.S. Supreme Court justices to have national action thwarted by constitutional challenge.

This book is not calling for a dramatic tip in the balance toward top-down, prescriptive nationalization of land use or private forest management or other natural capital management, especially since "[g]overnment policies that have ignored the local knowledge of participants or underestimated their ability to solve collective action problems have done great damage."[122] But government policies and governance structures that have relied too heavily on local knowledge of participants or overestimated their ability to solve collective action problems have also done great damage. The latter is the case in federal systems that provide no constitutional mechanism for allowing the appropriate governmental inputs into rules for natural capital appropriation. Leaving this keystone out of the arch of federal nation natural capital governance can lead to damaging "over-decentralization" in federal systems, and can cause the arch of natural capital management, stretching across local, national, and global scales, to crumble.

Notes

1 The material constituting significant portions of this chapter originated in Blake Hudson and Jonathan Rosenbloom, Uncommon Approaches to Commons Problems: Nested Governance Commons and Climate Change, 64 *Hastings L.J.* 1273 (2013); Blake Hudson, Federal Constitutions: The Keystone of Nested Commons Governance, 63 *Ala. L. Rev.* 1007 (2012); Blake Hudson, Coastal Land Loss and the Mitigation-Adaptation Dilemma: Between Scylla and Charybdis, 73 *La. L. Rev.* 31 (2012); Blake Hudson, Commerce in the Commons: A Unified Theory of Natural Capital Regulation Under the Commerce Clause, 35 *Harv. Env. L. Rev.* 375 (2011).

2 Scholars have noted that:

> federations use the principle of *constitutional non-centralization* rather than decentralization. … In other words, when independent states decide to create a federation and a federal system of government, they confer, generally through a constitution, certain specific responsibilities and authorities to the federal government in the interest of all states. … [F]or these reasons, use of the term *decentralized* is somewhat awkward in the case of federal governments.

Hans M. Gregersen et al., Forest Governance in Federal Systems: An Overview of Experiences and Implications for Decentralization, in *The Politics of Decentralization: Forests, Power and People* 13, 14–15 (Carol J. Pierce Colfer and Doris Capistrano eds, 2005).

3 John D. Sutter, *Minnesota Farmer Battles Gulf 'Dead Zone,'* CNN (Aug. 30, 2010), http://articles.cnn.com/2010-08-30/tech/gulf.dead.zone.minnesota.farm_1_dead-zone-gulf-shrimp?_s=PM:TECH.

4 Id.

5 Douglas R. Williams, When Voluntary, Incentive-Based Controls Fail: Structuring a Regulatory Response to Agricultural Nonpoint Source Water Pollution, 9 *Wash. U. J.L. & Pol'y*. 21, 22 (2002).

6 Sutter, supra note 3.

7 Id.

8 Id.

9 Williams, supra note 5, at 22.

10 Id. at 44–46.

11 Robin Kundis Craig, Local or National? The Increasing Federalization of Nonpoint Source Pollution Regulation, 15 *J. Envtl. L. & Litig*. 179, 213 (2000).

12 See James Rasband et al., *Natural Resources Law and Policy* 456 (2d ed. 2009).

13 Craig, supra note 11, at 214.

14 See Williams, supra note 5, at 27 (stating that "[t]he practices that contribute most to nonpoint source pollution are patterns of land use, the control of which has been guarded jealously by local government authorities, making direct federal control at best a touchy political proposition. Current federal programs to control nonpoint source pollution are the product of judgments that controls of this sort should remain with state and local authorities, as has been the traditional practice" (footnote omitted)).

15 See Craig, supra note 11, at 179. Craig argues that "[c]omprehensive federal regulation of nonpoint source pollution would thus arguably engage the federal government in land use regulation—a type of regulation historically viewed as belonging almost exclusively to more local levels of government" and that "because of federalism restrictions, Congress cannot and has not forced states to assume any regulatory burden with respect to non-point sources of water pollution. Therefore, regulation of nonpoint source polluters is left largely to states' individual regulatory discretion." Id. at 182, 186.

16 Williams, supra note 5, at 23.

17 Craig, supra note 11, at 181.

18 See Williams, supra note 5, at 67–91.

19 Id. at 25–29.

20 The Associated Press, Bay St. Louis Officials Oppose Hurricane Katrina High-Water Markers on Highway, *NOLA.COM* (July 23, 2011), available at http://www.nola.com/katrina/index.ssf/2011/07/bay_st_louis_officials_oppose.html.

21 Id.

22 Id.

23 33 U.S.C. § 1344 (2000).

24 Brandee Ketchum, Note, Like the Swamp Thing: Something Ambiguous Rises From the Hidden Depths of Murky Waters—The Supreme Court's Treatment of Murky Wet Land in Rapanos v. United States, 68 *La. L. Rev*. 983, 1011–12 (2008) (footnotes omitted);

Craig Pittman and Matthew Waite, *Paving Paradise: Florida's Vanishing Wetlands and the Failure of No Net Loss* 167 (2009).

25 Keith S. Rosenn, Federalism in the Americas in Comparative Perspective, 26 *U. Miami Inter-Am. L. Rev.* 1, 6–7 (1994). See also Marcus B. Lane, Decentralization or Privatization of Environmental Governance? Forest Conflict and Bioregional Assessment in Australia, 19 *J. Rural Stud.* 283, 284–85 (2003) (emphasis omitted) (citations omitted).

26 Gregersen et al., supra note 2, at 27–28. Rosenn, supra note 25, at 6–7.

27 See Rosenn, supra note 25, at 7–8.

28 Gregersen et al., supra note 2, at 28.

29 Michel Gelobter, Integrating Scale and Social Justice in the Commons, in *Protecting the Commons* 293, 293 (Joanna Burger et al. eds, 2001).

30 Id. at 294.

31 Robert O. Keohane and Elinor Ostrom, Introduction, in *Local Commons and Global Interdependence* 1, 11 (Robert O. Keohane and Elinor Ostrom eds, 1995) (stating that "[w]ithin states, effective hierarchy would be exercised, while in international relations no common government exists.").

32 Duncan Snidal, The Politics of Scope: Endogenous Actors, Heterogeneity and Institutions, in *Local Commons and Global Interdependence* 47, 49 (Robert O. Keohane and Elinor Ostrom eds, 1995).

33 Lisa L. Martin, Heterogeneity, Linkage and Commons Problems, in *Local Commons and Global Interdependence* 72, 88 (Robert O. Keohane and Elinor Ostrom eds, 1995).

34 Measuring Growth from Outer Space, *The Economist,* Aug. 8, 2009, at 63.

35 This mode of vertical regulatory coordination at the international level is termed an "international delegation," defined as "a grant of authority by two or more states to an international body to make decisions or take actions."; Curtis A. Bradley and Judith G. Kelley, The Concept of International Delegation, 71 *L. & Contemp. Probs.* 1, 3 (2008). See also Neil Siegel, International Delegations and the Values of Federalism, 71 *L. & Contemp. Probs.* 93, fn 1 (2008) (stating "international delegations take many different forms, leaving nations and subnational units of nations (for example, U.S. states) with varying degrees of regulatory control regarding the subject matter of the delegation.").

36 We also recognize that a vertical regulatory regime could exist among a handful of nations where those nations cede authority to a third party or newly created entity. See, e.g., Council of Great Lakes Governors, The Great Lakes Charter: Principles for the Management of Great Lakes Water Resources, Feb. 11, 1985, at 1; Treaty Between the United States and Great Britain Relating to Boundary Waters Between the United States and Canada, U.S.-Gr. Brit., 36 Stat. 2448 (1909); The Trail Smelter Case (U.S. v. Canada), 3 R.I.A.A. 1905 (1941).

37 *The Montreal Protocol on Substances that Deplete the Ozone Layer*, United Nations Environment Programme, http://ozone.unep.org/pdfs/Montreal-Protocol2000.pdf. Indeed, Salzman et al. note that:

> [t]o many observers, the traditional non-participatory, consensus-based nature of the international law system has been a major hindrance to efforts to formulate an effective international response to our global environmental crisis, where states are held accountable under the rule of law. Increasingly, however, the limitations inherent in international law are being challenged. As non-State actors and new processes emerge in the international system, international lawmaking is slowly and inevitably developing some of the more robust characteristics of national legal systems.

David Hunter, James Salzman, and Durwood Zaelke, *International Environmental Law and Policy* 274 (4th ed. 2010).

38 See generally Brigham Daniels and Blake Hudson, *Our Constitutional Commons* (unpublished manuscript) (on file with authors).

39 See, e.g., Engine Mfrs. Ass'n v. S. Coast Air Quality Mgmt. Dist., 541 U.S. 246 (2004) (holding that the Clean Air Act preempted state standards pertaining to new motor vehicles and new motor vehicle engine emissions); Cent. Valley Chrysler-Jeep v. Witherspoon, No. CV F 04–6663 AWILJO, 2007 WL 135688 (E.D. Cal. Jan. 16, 2007) (holding that the Clean Air Act preempted state efforts to reduce global warming pollution). But see Green Mountain Chrysler Plymouth Dodge Jeep v. Crombie, 508 F. Supp. 2d 295 (D. Vt. 2007) (holding that Vermont's GHG regulations were not preempted).

40 Richard B. Stewart, Pyramids of Sacrifice? Problems of Federalism in Mandating State Implementation of National Environmental Policy, 86 *Yale L.J.* 1196, 1211–12 (1977).

41 Neal D. Woods, Interstate Competition and Environmental Regulation: A Test of the Race-to-the-Bottom Thesis, 87 *Soc. Sci. Q.* 174, 175 (2006).

42 Id. at 174.

43 Id. Whether heightened restrictions *actually* cause businesses to move elsewhere is a separate question. Woods notes that,

> [s]ocial science research on interstate environmental policy competition thus presents something of a paradox. On one hand, there is little evidence that firms relocate on the basis of regulatory cost differentials. On the other, survey evidence suggests that regulators believe that they do, and this belief appears to affect state environmental policy. [There are] two possible explanations for this paradox: that states are unaware of the actual decision calculus facing firms in deciding where to locate, and that regulators face significant political pressures to reduce the regulatory burden facing industry, regardless of this calculus … both forces may, in fact, be at work.

Id. at 177.

44 Bradley C. Karkkainen, Biodiversity and Land, 83 *Cornell L. Rev.* 1, 74–75 (1997) (citations omitted).

45 Nives Dolsak et al., Adaptation to Challenges, in *The Commons in the New Millennium* 337, 345 (Nives Dolsak and Elinor Ostrom eds, 2003).

46 Richard L. Revesz, Rehabilitating Interstate Competition: Rethinking the "Race-to-the-Bottom" Rationale for Federal Environmental Regulation, 67 *N.Y.U. L. Rev.* 1210 (1992); Henry N. Butler and Jonathan R. Macey, *Using Federalism to Improve Environmental Policy* (1996); David Vogel, *Trading Up: Consumer and Environmental Regulation in a Global Economy* (1995); Matthew Potoski, Clean Air Federalism: Do States Race to the Bottom? 61 *Pub. Admin. Rev.* 335 (2001).

47 Kris Hudson and Vanessa O'Connell, Recession Turns Malls Into Ghost Towns, *The Wall St. J.*, May 22, 2009, at A1; Tony Dokoupil, Is the Mall Dead? *Newsweek*, November 12, 2008, available at http://www.newsweek.com/2008/11/11/is-the-mall-dead.html.

48 The Vanishing Shopping Mall, *The Week*, March 26, 2009, available at http://theweek.com/article/index/94691/The_vanishing_shopping_mall.

49 Deadmalls.com, available at http://deadmalls.com/index.html.

50 *Largest Shopping Malls in the United States*, *Shopping Center Studies at Eastern Connecticut State University*, http://nutmeg.easternct.edu/~pocock/MallsLarge.htm (on file with the Harvard Law School Library).

51 The Vanishing Shopping Mall, supra note 48.

52 Brigham Daniels, Governing the Presidential Nomination Commons, 84 *Tul. L. Rev.* 899, 910 (2010).

53 See Hodel v. Virginia Surface Mining & Reclamation Association, 452 U.S. 264 (1981), and Hodel v. Indiana, 452 U.S. 314 (1981).

54 Scholars have noted that states take on the characteristics of rational herders in other contexts. Brigham Daniels argues that the perpetual moving up of presidential primary dates by states constitutes a classic tragedy of the commons, resulting in damage to the electoral system. See generally Daniels, supra note 52.

55 Several scholars have applied a commons analysis to local governments, including Thomas Gremillion, Setting the Foundation: Climate Change Adaptation at the Local Level, 41 *Envtl. L.* 1221 (2011) (climate change); Sarah B. Schindler, Following Industry's LEED: Municipal Adoption of Private Green Building Standards, 62 *Fla. L. Rev.* 285 (2010) (land use); Hannah Wiseman, Expanding Regional Renewable Governance, 35 *Harv. Envtl. L. Rev.* 477 (2011) (renewables and urban sprawl); Emily C. Powers, Fracking and Federalism: Support for an Adoptive Approach That Avoids the Tragedy of the Regulatory Commons, 19 *J.L. & Pol'y* 913 (2011) (hydro-fracking).

56 See Jonathan Rosenbloom, New Day at the Pool: State Preemption, Common Pool Resources, and Non-Place Based Municipal Collaborations, 36 *Harv. Envtl. L. Rev.* 445 (2012). Significant portions of this section and the next section are a result of the efforts of Professor Rosenbloom, Drake Law School, during the writing and editing of our co-authored *Hastings Law Journal* article on the subject.

57 See Hunter v. City of Pittsburgh, 207 U.S. 161, 174–80 (1907) (holding that local governments are creatures of state law and that the U.S. Constitution does not protect local governments from state government intrusion). But see Avery v. Midland Cnty., 390 U.S. 474, 482–86 (1968) (holding that a state may not create a general purpose local government that apportions voting unequally in violation of the Constitution); Gomillion v. Lightfoot, 364 U.S. 339, 346–48 (1960) (holding that the Constitution protects individuals from state-created local self-government based on race).

58 See Hunter, 207 U.S. at 178.

59 See id.

60 Further discouraging local governments from taking sustainable action on common resources are damage awards stemming from a finding of an impermissible extraterritorial impact. Cf. Owen v. City of Independence, 445 U.S. 622, 651–52 (1980).

61 See Rosenbloom, supra note 56, at 446–62 (discussing state home rule and preemption laws and the impact they have on local governments).

62 John F. Dillon, *Commentaries on the Law of Municipal Corporations* (5th ed. 1911).

63 Rosenbloom, supra note 56, at 448–49. For an example of specific state authorization to act in a Dillon's Rule state, see Va. Code Ann. § 15.2–2280 (1997) (enabling local zoning).

64 Dillon, supra note 62, at 452–53; see Early Estates, Inc. v. Hous. Bd. of Review of Providence, 174 A.2d 117 (R.I. 1961) (applying a narrow view of local authority to act under Dillon's Rule); S. Constructors, Inc. v. Loudon Cnty. Bd. of Educ., 58 S.W. 3d. 706, 711 (Tenn. 2001) (same).

65 See, e.g., Ark. Const. art. X, § 11.

66 See, e.g., Cal. Const. art. III, § 5(a).

67 See, e.g., Iowa Const. art. III, § 38A.

68 See Laurie Reynolds, Home Rule, Extraterritorial Impact, and the Region, 86 *Denv. U. L. Rev.* 1271, 1274 n.19 (2009) (citing Seigles, Inc. v. City of St. Charles, 849 N.E.2d 456, 458) (Ill. App. Ct. 2006) (noting that the court called it "axiomatic" that a local government may not act outside its borders).

69 Id. at 1275.

70 See Rosenbloom, supra note 56, at 453–61.

71 Assemb. B. 32, § 2, 2006 Gen Assemb., Reg. Sess. (Cal. 2006) (Global Warming Solutions Act) (establishing GHG reduction goals and a framework for achieving the goals).

72 H.B. 3543, 74th Leg. Assemb., Reg. Sess. (Or. 2007) (Climate Change Integration Act) (setting specific GHG reduction goals for Oregon, including reducing GHG levels to 10 percent below 1990 levels by 2020 and to 75 percent below 1990 levels by 2050).

73 H.B. 2815, 60th Leg., Reg. Sess. (Wash. 2008) (implementing GHG reduction strategies through trading and vehicle miles traveled).

74 One of the most common specific state constitutional protections includes a state ban on special commissions. See, e.g., S.D. Const. art. III, § 26 (prohibiting the state from delegating enumerated functions over local governments to a special commission). Also

common are state bans on special legislation. See, e.g., Iowa Const. art. III, § 30 (prohibiting the state from passing enumerated special laws).

75 See C40 Cities Climate Leadership Grp., available at http://www.c40cities.org ("Acting both locally and collaboratively, C40 Cities are having a meaningful global impact in reducing both greenhouse gas emissions and climate risks.").

76 The U.S. Conference of Mayors has produced a document in which 1054 mayors representing almost 89 million people have agreed to GHG reductions in a similar fashion to that set forth in the Kyoto Protocol. See *U.S. Conference of Mayors Climate Protection Agreement*, Mayors Climate Prot. Ctr., available at http://www.usmayors.org/climateprotection/agreement.htm.

77 Union of the Baltic Cities, available at http://www.ubc.net ("Union of the Baltic Cities is a voluntary, proactive network mobilizing the shared potential of over 100 member cities for democratic, economic, social, cultural and environmentally sustainable development of the Baltic Sea Region.").

78 58 Pa. Cons. Stat. §§ 2301–3504 (2012) (seeking to preempt local zoning ordinances that regulate oil and gas operations). This law was partially struck down in Robinson Twp. v. Commonwealth, 52 A.3d 463 (Pa. Commw. Ct. 2012). A number of local coastal communities are experiencing similar T-1-like scenarios where states are "transfer[ing] authority over armoring from local to state control."; J. Peter Byrne, The Cathedral Engulfed: Sea-Level Rise, Property Rights, and Time, 73 *La. L. Rev.* 69, 97 n.127 (2012) (citing Maryland's Living Shoreline Protection Act of 2008, MD. Code Ann., Envir. §16–201 (Westlaw 2012); Connecticut's Act Concerning the Coastal Management Act and Shoreline Flood and Erosion Control Structures, S.B. 376, 2012 Reg. Sess. (Conn. 2012)).

79 In theory, a T-2 scenario may also exist where local governments are insulated from state action, and the local governments fail to take action. A more common scenario is T-3, where the state maintains some authority to reassume control or concurrently regulate.

80 James May, Constitutional Law and the Future of Natural Resource Protection, in *The Evolution of Natural Resource Law and Policy* 124–61 (Lawrence J. MacDonnell and Sarah F. Bates eds, Section of Environment, Energy, and Resources, American Bar Association (2009)).

81 See generally Mugler v. Kansas, 123 U.S. 623 (1887).

82 John R. Nolan, Patricia E. Salkin, and Morton Gitelman, *Land Use and Community Development* 17 (Thomson/West 2008).

83 Marci A. Hamilton, Federalism and the Public Good: The True Story Behind the Religious Land Use and Institutionalized Persons Act, 78 *Ind. L.J.* 311, 335 (2003).

84 272 U.S. 365 (1926).

85 Paul Goldstein and Barton H. Thompson, Jr., *Property Law: Ownership, Use, and Conservation* 967 (2006).

86 SWANCC, 531 U.S. at 174 (citing Hess v. Port Authority Trans-Hudson Corporation, 513 U.S. 30, 44 (1944), that "regulation of land use [is] a function traditionally performed by local governments.").

87 Rapanos, 547 U.S. at 738 (2006) (emphasis added) (citing FERC v. Mississippi, 456 U.S. 742, 767, n.30 (1982), that "regulation of land use is perhaps *the quintessential* state activity.").

88 United States v. Riverside Bayview Homes, 474 U.S. 121 (1985); Tenn. Valley Auth. v. Hill, 437 U.S. 153 (1978); Babbitt v. Sweet Home Chapter of Cmtys. for a Great Or., 515 U.S. 687 (1995).

89 See generally Dan Tarlock, Biodiversity Federalism, 54 *U. of Md. L. Rev.* 1315 (1995); Linda Breggin and Susan George, Planning for Biodiversity: Sources of Authority in State Land Use Laws, 22 *Va. Envtl. L.J.* 81 (2003).

90 Ryan Barnes, Investopedia, Economic Indicators: Housing Starts, available at http://www.investopedia.com/university/releases/housingstarts.asp.

91 Ben Rooney, Housing Construction "Encouraging," *CNN.com,* Apr. 19, 2011, http://money.cnn.com/2011/04/19/news/economy/housing_starts_building_permits/index.htm.

92 Arthur C. Nelson and Robert E. Lang, The Next 100 Million, *Planning Magazine*, Jan. 2007, at 4.

93 See, e.g., *Working Conservation Easements*, Pacific Forest Trust, available at https://www.pacificforest.org/working-forest-conservation-easements.html ("Working forest conservation easements provide private landowners the means to permanently conserve their forests for a variety of public benefits while keeping them in private ownership and productive forestry.").

94 See, e.g., Sarah F. Ashton et al., *Forest Management in the Interface: Forest Cooperatives* (2011).

95 Wash. Cnty., Md., Forest Conservation Ordinance (2008).

96 See, e.g., 58 Pa. Cons. Stat. §§ 2301–3504 (2012); Idaho House Bill 464 (requiring "uniformity and consistency in the regulation" of fracking); Ohio Sub. H.B.278 (prohibiting local governments from determining placement or permitting of fracking wells).

97 See Bill Finch, Deal Preserves More Forest Land, *Mobile Press Register*, Mar. 29, 2006, at A1; Greg Fales, IP Donates 2,650 Acres in Mississippi to the Conservation Fund, *Pima's Papermaker*, Apr. 1999, 81(4), at 10. See Press Release, Land Trust Alliance, Private Land Conservation in U.S. Soars (Nov. 30, 2006), available at http://www.landtrustalliance.org/about-us/news/alliance-news/private-land-conservation-in-u.s.-soars.

98 See Alice Kenny, Ecosystem Services in the New York City Watershed, *Ecosystem Marketplace* (Feb. 10, 2006), available at http://ecosystemmarketplace.com/pages/article.news.php?component_id=4130&component_version_id = 6440&language_id = 12; Bradley I. Raffle, Carrots and Sticks: Incentivizing Private Land Conservation, *Ecosystem Marketplace* (May 11, 2006), http://ecosystemmarketplace.com/pages/article.opinion.php?component_id=4349&component_version_id = 6266&language_id = 12.

99 545 U.S. 469 (2005). Scholars have noted this potentiality arising out of *Kelo*; for instance, Professors Somin and Adler argue that the *Kelo* decision "is bad for property owners and environmental protection alike." See Ilya Somin and Jonathan Adler, The Green Costs of Kelo: Economic Development Takings and Environmental Protection, *84 Wash. U. L. Rev.* 623, 623–28 (2006) (citations omitted).

100 Elinor Ostrom, *Governing the Commons: The Evolution of Institutions for Collective Action* 5 (1990).

101 See generally Amy Sinden, The Tragedy of the Commons and the Myth of a Private Property Solution, 78 *U. Colo. L. Rev.* 533, 538 (2007).

102 Such ecosystem services include managed forests' role in watershed protection, flood control, the safeguarding of habitat, biodiversity, genetic resources, and the preservation of cultural and recreational values. See Bastiaan Louman et al., Forest Ecosystem Services: A Cornerstone for Human Well-Being, in *Adaptation of Forests and People to Climate Change—A Global Assessment Report* 14, 17 (Risto Seppälä et al. eds, 2009), available at http://www.iufro.org/science/gfep/embargoed-release/download-by-chapter/ (on file with the Harvard Law School Library).

103 Susan J. Buck, *The Global Commons: An Introduction* 5 (1998).

104 Troy Rule, Airspace in a Green Economy, 59 *UCLA L. Rev.* 270 (2011). Other scholars actually argue that "coastal regions" are a commons "containing many common-pool resources that can be extracted or exploited, are renewable, and can benefit from considerations of the rights and responsibilities of the 'commoners'."; Joanna Burger, Multi-use Coastal Commons: Personal Watercraft, Conflicts, and Resolutions, in *Protecting the Commons* 195, 196 (Joanna Burger et al. eds, 2001). Importantly, Burger includes within these common-pool resources "estuarine land for development."; Id. Burger continues that "[c]oastal commons resources are particularly difficult to manage because there are so many players, including landowners, fishers, other business owners and operators, recreationists, and natural resource managers. Each group contains many diverse subgroups: (1) landowners include public and private owners. ... "; Id. at 200.

105 Daniel Farber, Jim Chen, Robert Verchick, and Lisa Sun, *Disaster Law and Policy 24* (2nd ed. 2009).

106 This phrase is a term of art used to describe the resource system of natural capital on private lands.

107 Ostrom, supra note 100, at 34.

108 Id. at 13 (emphasis added).

109 Carol Rose, The Comedy of the Commons: Custom, Commerce, and Inherently Public Property, 53 *U. Chi. L. Rev.* 711, 746–47 (1986).

110 Ostrom, supra note 100, at 31.

111 Id. at 12.

112 Biodiversity Project, Farmland Loss at a Glance, in *Getting on Message: Making the Biodiversity-Sprawl Connection*, available at http://www.comminit.com/en/node/265588/306.

113 Id. (also noting that "[b]etween 1982 and 1992, 4.2 million acres of farmland were lost to development, [m]ore than 56 percent of our food comes from rapidly developing counties on the edge of urban centers, 32 percent of best quality farmland in highly productive farming regions of the U.S. has already been irretrievably lost to development ... [c]urrently, 70 percent of prime farmland is threatened by sprawl—234,500,000 acres nationwide"). See also Elizabeth Becker, 2 Farm Acres Lost per Minute, Study Says, *N.Y. Times*, Oct. 4, 2002, at A22.

114 Jeffrey Kline, Our National Concern About Forestland Development, *Timber West*, May/June 2005, at 50, available at http://www.fs.fed.us/pnw/pubs/journals/pnw_2005_kline003.pdf.

115 David N. Wear and John G. Greis, U.S. Forest Serv., *The Southern Forest Futures Project: Summary Report* 26–31, 35 (2011), available at http://www.srs.fs.usda.gov/futures/reports/draft/summary_report.pdf.

116 Ostrom, supra note 100, at 109 (citation omitted).

117 Bonnie J. McCay, Community-based and Cooperative Fisheries: Solutions to Fishermen's Problems, in *Protecting the Commons* 175, 175 (Joanna Burger et al. eds, 2001).

118 Keohane and Ostrom, supra note 31, at 1.

119 Ostrom, supra note 100, at 7.

120 Sarah Krakoff, Planetarian Identity Formation and the Relocalization of Environmental Law, 64 *Fla. L. Rev.* 1 (2012).

121 David Vogel, Trading Up and Governing Across: Transnational Governance and Environmental Protection, 4 *J. of Eur. Pub. Pol.* 556 (1997).

122 Keohane and Ostrom, supra note 31, at 21.

Part III

Federalization of the Commons

To this point we have discussed how the "commons," here defined as natural capital subject to both private property rights and governance systems that themselves facilitate the commons dynamic, has been constitutionalized in federal systems of government—with federal and state constitutions and legislative acts made pursuant to constitutional authority establishing rules for the management of natural capital across numerous scales. We then discussed the implications of constitutionalized commons that are legally decentralized, with certain levels of government not maintaining regulatory inputs that might otherwise assist in avoiding commons tragedies within and across scales of governance. This part seeks to address how some of this "over-decentralization" might be corrected through a "federalization" of the commons that re-establishes the legal authority of federal governments to maintain regulatory inputs into natural capital management currently subject to near-exclusive subnational regulatory control. This federalization will be key if a higher level coordinating authority is to be capable of filling the gaps in resource management where subnational actors are acting as rational herders on national commons. This part will focus on examples from one federal nation in particular, the United States, which will be expanded upon in Part IV on Internationalization of the Commons.

4 Commerce in the Commons[1]

> Simply closing the boundaries [of a resource system] is not enough. It is still possible for a limited number of appropriators to increase the quantity of resource units they harvest so that they … totally destroy the resource. Consequently, in addition to closing the boundaries, some rules limiting appropriation and/or mandating provision are needed.[2]

Introduction

While the "tragedy of the commons" is perhaps the primary theoretical driver behind the governance of natural capital, in the United States the Commerce Clause of the U.S. Constitution[3] is the primary tool used by the federal government to enact environmental and natural resource regulation. To paraphrase Ostrom,[4] the Commerce Clause facilitates the creation of appropriation-limiting rules at the federal level that are needed in addition to closing the boundaries of, in our case, the state resource systems. The United States federal government, of course, may only act pursuant to a provision of the Constitution that grants it authority. It is often surprising to the unaquainted to learn that U.S. federal government power over the environment would come from the federal government's authority "to regulate commerce … among the several states." Indeed, the Commerce Clause, likely because of its seemingly odd status as a provision of environmental regulatory authority, has caused a great deal of conflict in both academic scholarship and in practice. Ultimately, in the United States' federal system of government there are some regulatory areas that arguably may not be reached by the federal government under the Commerce Clause. To the extent that some scholars argue there is no such limitation on federal power in the environmental context, that point is somewhat moot because both Congress and states continue to act *politically* as if these legal constraints do exist. So a key question that has yet to be fully explored is how does commons analysis answer questions about the scope of U.S. federal authority under the Commerce Clause? To the extent that there is a legally entrenched commons in the U.S., whereby subnational governments are misappropriating vast quantities of natural capital in the absence of federal minimum standards or other coordination, commons analysis may help assist in making legal arguments that the federal government does maintain authority over far more than is currently recognized. This is not to say that the federal government would exercise this authority properly from an environmental or political perspective, but we may never know how this authority might be exercised if it is not first established that the federal government maintains the legal authority to act.

The United States provides a good case study for applying commons analysis to federal governance authority. Prior to the research upon which this book is founded scholars had yet to apply a commons analysis to Commerce Clause jurisprudence. This is a significant oversight, especially given the persistent questions scholars have raised regarding the "new federalism" introduced in the jurisprudence of *United States v. Lopez*[5] and *United States v. Morrison*,[6] as well as the rejection of federalism limits in *Gonzales v. Raich*[7] and the subsequent raising of more doubts about federal regulatory authority in the recent health-care case of *National Federation of Independent Business v. Sebelius*.[8] It is unclear what this series of cases means for the future of federal environmental legislation in some subject areas—and in particular areas of traditional state authority like land use planning that impacts a wide variety of natural capital, from isolated wetlands to private forests. These concerns justifiably result from the varied and often confused rationales provided by the U.S. Supreme Court in Commerce Clause cases, which have in turn resulted in confusion in the lower courts. This chapter argues, however, that a constant theme has emerged from Commerce Clause jurisprudence: courts have consistently upheld federal authority to regulate depletable natural resources, the appropriation of which is non-excludable—key attributes of a commons. Chapters 2 and 3 discussed how natural capital resources that are privatized may still be subject to the commons dynamic due to the governance framework in which they are embedded—the governance framework itself taking on the attributes of a commons. We might call the depletable natural capital subject to privatization, yet still subject to the commons dynamic, "privatized commons resources." Traditional commons analysis provides a useful method for assessing how the distribution, appropriation, and consumption of these resources affect commercial and economic activity across state lines—i.e., "interstate commerce"—thus facilitating a determination of when federal environmental regulation in the U.S. is constitutional.

Drawing on insights from commons scholars, this chapter provides a new lens through which to view environmental and natural resources jurisprudence in the U.S.: a lens that introduces a clearer, more consistent approach for the treatment of resource regulation under the Commerce Clause. By applying principles arising out of Ostrom's conception of commons resources, we can see that courts have consistently treated appropriation of privatized commons resources as meeting the "substantial effects test" for determining the validity of federal legislation under the Commerce Clause. Use of commons analysis to identify the boundaries of the substantial effects test (1) provides a long overdue, unified justification for U.S. federal environmental regulatory authority; (2) articulates a clearer statement of the jurisprudential approach in federal environmental cases; (3) allows uniform application of judicial standards in lower courts currently divided over how to apply Commerce Clause analysis to federal statutes; (4) introduces more certainty and effectiveness into environmental and natural resources legislation. Commons analysis also assists in answering persistent questions arising in Commerce Clause cases which are crucial to resolving conflicts of federal environmental regulatory authority, including: when the "aggregation principle" may be invoked to find substantial effects on interstate commerce and what the "object of regulation"[9] is in environmental Commerce Clause cases.

For a judicial system based upon establishing stability in the law, adherence to judicial precedent, and steadfast submission to a document written over 200 years ago, jurisprudence and scholarship regarding the scope of federal environmental authority under the Commerce Clause have been anything but stable. This chapter seeks to calm the waters by demonstrating that in the era of the modern regulatory state, courts have consistently upheld federal regulatory protection of privatized commons resources, and have, perhaps unknowingly, defined the scope of the Commerce Clause to include such resources as validly subject to federal regulation because of their substantial effect on interstate commerce.

Commons and the Commerce Clause: Background and Context

Hardin highlighted various solutions that might address the tragedy of the commons, including the creation of a private property rights system, implementation of "polluter pays" principles, and regulation. In the United States, as in most nations, each of Hardin's suggested solutions is used in some capacity to forestall identified "tragedies" of many kinds, particularly regarding the environment. Two of Hardin's solutions, however, have come into sharp conflict with one another, as the modern federal regulatory state has increasingly clashed with both private property rights and state regulatory authority. This clash has effectively pitted the Commerce Clause[10] against the primary and traditional regulators of private property rights and land use—state and local governments. The resulting conflict among private property owners, state governments, and the federal government is one of the most pronounced illustrations of federalism-based legal controversies.

The existence of this controversy is perhaps best evidenced by numerous scholarly works and court opinions debating whether certain applications of environmental statutes—with arguably tenuous ties to interstate commerce—are, or will remain, constitutional under the Supreme Court's modern Commerce Clause jurisprudence. Perhaps the most emblematic of federal environmental statutes in this regard are the Endangered Species Act (ESA) and the Clean Water Act's (CWA) Section 404 wetland fill permitting program, the federal statutes that most directly interfere with state control over private property and land use regulation. Private property owners have argued that wholly intrastate species that have little or no economic value are not properly regulable by the federal government under the Commerce Clause,[11] and in the *Solid Waste Agency of Northern Cook County. (SWANCC)* and *Rapanos* cases the U.S. Supreme Court has raised "constitutional questions" about the federal government's authority to regulate under the 404 program "isolated wetlands" that may lack the requisite degree of connection to interstate commerce.

Even so, analysis of major Commerce Clause cases involving federal resource regulation since the beginning of the modern regulatory state[12] demonstrates that courts have consistently upheld federal authority to regulate a certain class of environmental resources, and specifically a modified form of commons resource, which this chapter describes as privatized commons resources. From wheat,[13] to minerals,[14] to marijuana,[15] to wetlands,[16] to endangered species,[17] courts have consistently validated federal regulatory authority over these depletable natural resources, the appropriation of which is non-excludable—the key characteristics of a commons.[18] These privatized commons resources include two categories of resources: (1) natural resources contained on land (wetlands, endangered species, or other natural capital) that are appropriated by economic development (commercial, retail, housing, industrial, agricultural, etc.); (2) resources appropriated by individuals and tied to an interstate market (wheat, marijuana, or other natural capital commodities).

The cases of *United States v. Lopez* and *United States v. Morrison* had been credited with ushering into the Supreme Court's Commerce Clause jurisprudence a new era of federalism-based protections—the "new federalism"[19]—as they were the first cases since 1937 in which the Supreme Court struck down federal statutes as beyond the scope of the Commerce Clause.[20] This theory was soon put to the test when, in *Gonzales v. Raich*, the Court upheld a federal statute regulating wholly intrastate activities with an arguably tenuous connection to interstate commerce.[21] More recently, however, the U.S. Supreme Court in *National Federation of Independent Business v. Sebelius* gave new life to new federalist arguments by refusing to uphold the Affordable Care Act under the Commerce Clause, instead upholding it under the power to tax. In writing for the majority, Chief Justice Roberts went out of his way to make clear that the Commerce Clause could not sustain the part of the act requiring individuals to purchase health insurance or else face a penalty, because the "Framers [of the U.S. Constitution] knew the difference between doing something and doing nothing. They gave Congress the power to regulate commerce, not to compel it. Ignoring that distinction would undermine the principle that the Federal Government is a government of limited and enumerated powers."[22]

These cases have caused quite a stir among scholars, who have written a flurry of articles questioning their implications for environmental regulation. Scholars have expressed, at the least, criticism for the apparent lack of consistency in the Court's Commerce Clause jurisprudence, and at the most concern about whether *Lopez* and *Morrison* placed environmental statutes in danger of being invalidated on the one hand or whether *Raich* magically erased those concerns in one fell swoop on the other.[23] Other scholars have claimed that in the instant that *Raich* came to the rescue of past and future environmental legislation it also crushed the hopes of federalists for a resurgence in "new federalism" jurisprudence.[24]

The alarmism over both the potential evisceration of federal environmental statutes and the supposed death knell to judicial federalism protections in Commerce Clause cases[25] seems hyperbolic when one views Commerce Clause jurisprudence through the lens of the commons. Upon doing so, we can see that courts have consistently treated privatized commons resources as meeting the substantial effects test for determining the validity of federal legislation under the Commerce Clause. The "new federalism" cases of *Lopez*, *Morrison*, and *Sebelius* did not involve the regulation of zero-sum[26] commons resources, but rather the regulation of non-zero-sum social constructs. The regulated activities in those cases—the carrying of guns near school zones, domestic violence, and health care—are socially constructed problems consisting of individualized decision-making exercised independently of the decisions of other individuals making the same choices. Such decisions do not constitute a commons, as these decisions are infinite within the social construct—thus the Court did not allow their "aggregation" for the purpose of determining substantial effects on interstate commerce. Commons problems, on the other hand, are best characterized as "naturally constructed" problems consisting of individualized decision-making that necessarily affects the consumptive activities of others as well as the total stock of the natural resource base—making aggregation under the substantial effects test quite appropriate. Furthermore, the statutes in *Lopez, Morrison*, and *Sebelius* focused on public safety, security, and health, which may best be characterized as "public goods" rather than a commons, since public safety and health care are non-depletable and non-exclusive (at least in most respects).[27] Therefore, the effects on interstate commerce are arguably more amorphous, and thus federalism protections more appropriate, in the context of the statutes at issue in *Lopez*, *Morrison*, and *Sebelius*. In the context of natural resources and the environment, however, a commons analysis renders the substantial effects test more readily met.

Since individualized decisions regarding the use of commons resources necessarily affect the use decisions of other individuals, as well as the amount and value of resources available to others, regardless of the arbitrary geopolitical boundaries that may or may not divide them, it follows naturally that courts would more easily find that these activities transcend the geopolitical boundary and "commerce" thresholds that form the foundation for application of the Commerce Clause. Though the commons nature of commodities for which a consumptive interstate market is established may be more apparent—such as for wheat, minerals, and, after *Raich*, marijuana—commons principles are equally applicable to other privatized commons resources, such as wetlands and endangered species appropriated by economic development activities. The growing body of scholarship on ecosystem services, which demonstrates the economic internalization of externalities long excluded from market-based decision-making regarding the management and use of natural resources, supports this assertion.[28] When viewed through the lens of the commons, Commerce Clause jurisprudence can be characterized as judicial recognition and internalization of those externalities by acknowledging that the appropriation of privatized commons resources is an economic activity having a "substantial effect" on interstate commerce to the degree required to constitutionally allow federal action under the Commerce Clause.

The Commerce Clause: A Brief Introduction to Relevant Cases

Article I, Section 8 of the U.S. Constitution contains the Commerce Clause, which gives Congress the power to "regulate Commerce ... among the several States."[29] In the area of environmental protection, the commerce power is the most important of all of Congress's powers, as nearly all federal environmental laws are adopted by Congress under Commerce Clause authority.[30]

Judicial interpretation of the scope of the Commerce Clause has gone through numerous shifts over the past 200 years. From the early nineteenth century until the 1890s, a "nationalist perspective" guided the U.S. Supreme Court in Commerce Clause jurisprudence.[31] The Court defined Commerce Clause power broadly and rejected the idea that its exercise violated federalism principles.[32] From the 1890s until 1937, the Court shifted to a "federalist perspective,"[33] narrowly defining the commerce power and accepting the concept that some statutes violated principles of federalism by intruding on areas of state governmental authority.[34] From 1937 until 1995, the Court shifted back to a nationalist perspective, again broadly construing the Commerce Clause.[35] As previously noted, during this period not one federal law was struck down as exceeding Congress's commerce authority.[36] During this era, the Court construed the Commerce Clause broadly to include any intrastate activity that had a substantial relation to interstate commerce when that activity's control was essential or appropriate to protect commerce from burdens or obstructions.[37] The Court also construed "among the states" to mean virtually anything having an aggregate effect on commerce—as long as Congress reasonably believed the effect existed, then the regulation was constitutionally valid.[38] During this period, the Court had an "expansive, and indeed almost unlimited, view of the Commerce Clause."[39]

Perhaps the most important case from this nationalist period, for the purpose of commons analysis, is *Wickard* v. *Filburn*,[40] which the U.S. Supreme Court itself has described as "perhaps the most far reaching example of Commerce Clause authority over intrastate activity."[41] In *Wickard*, the Court upheld Congress's authority under the Agricultural Adjustment Act to regulate farmers growing wheat for home consumption.[42] The Court found that such consumption competed with wheat sold in interstate commerce, and if thousands of farmers were to engage in the same activity, the aggregate impact of such intrastate consumption would have a substantial effect on interstate commerce.[43] Thus, the Court introduced what has come to be known as the "aggregation principle" into Commerce Clause jurisprudence, recognizing the inherent depletable and non-excludable nature of privatized commons resources.[44] For the next 53 years the Court would uphold Congress's Commerce Clause authority in every case in which it was challenged.[45]

In 1995, and then again in 2000, the Court returned to a federalist perspective in the cases of *United States v. Lopez*[46] and *United States v. Morrison*,[47] respectively. At issue in *Lopez* was a high-school student arrested for carrying a concealed and loaded. 38 caliber handgun and was charged with violating the Gun-Free School Zones Act of 1990 (Gun-Free Act).[48] Lopez was convicted and sentenced to six months' imprisonment and two years of supervised release. Lopez appealed, arguing that the statute was unconstitutional and exceeded Congress's Commerce Clause power.[49]

In an opinion written by Chief Justice Rehnquist, the Court detailed that the Constitution created a national government of enumerated powers, emphasizing that Article I limits Congress's legislative powers to those that are express or implied in the Constitution.[50] The Court summarized its Commerce Clause jurisprudence up to that point by noting that Congress can regulate three kinds of activities under the Commerce Clause. First, Congress can regulate the "use of the channels of interstate commerce," such as the regulation of hotels and restaurants during the civil rights movement.[51] Second, Congress may legislate "to regulate and protect the instrumentalities of interstate commerce," such as railroads transporting people and goods in interstate commerce.[52] Lastly, Congress may regulate "those activities having a substantial relation to interstate commerce … *i.e.*, those activities that *substantially affect* interstate commerce."[53]

The Court analyzed the case under the third standard, the substantial effects test, to determine if the Gun-Free Act regulated an activity having a substantial effect on interstate commerce. The government argued that firearms were sold in interstate commerce, and that the carrying of firearms near schools would result in a significant aggregate effect on the economy and interstate commerce. The Court, however, found that the Gun-Free Act was unconstitutional because the mere possession of a firearm near a school zone had no substantial effect on interstate commerce; the activity was primarily non-economic and unsuitable for aggregation, and the regulation of local criminal activities was traditionally a state or local government function. The Court reasoned that upholding such legislation would open the door to federal regulation of anything that could lead to violent crime, or other activities traditionally regulated by the states. Key to the Court's holding was the fact that the activity of carrying a gun near a school zone was itself "non-economic." The Court noted that *Wickard's* aggregation doctrine only allowed Congress to regulate activities that had a substantial *economic* impact on interstate commerce.

The U.S. Supreme Court continued its narrow application of the Commerce Clause in its 2000 *Morrison* decision. The Court used reasoning similar to that in *Lopez* to determine that the civil damages provision of the Violence Against Women Act (VAWA) was unconstitutional because the targeted violence had no substantial effect on interstate commerce.[54] Under the provision, victims of gender-motivated violence could receive a federal civil damages remedy.[55] In passing the act, Congress found that "violent crime against women costs this country at least 3 billion … dollars a year"[56]—a finding that was part of Congress's response to the Supreme Court's criticism in *Lopez* that Congress did not base the Gun-Free Act on sufficient findings of fact.[57] Congress bolstered VAWA with a voluminous record seeking to demonstrate the interstate economic effects of violence against women.[58]

The Court again analyzed the case under the substantial effects test. Despite Congress's finding of billions of dollars of losses due to violence against women, the Court found that the specific, non-economic activity that Congress was attempting to regulate could not be aggregated to find a substantial effect on interstate commerce. The Court noted that "in those cases where we have sustained federal regulation of intrastate activity based upon the activity's substantial effects on interstate commerce, *the activity in question has been some sort of economic endeavor*."[59] The Court then found that "[i]f accepted, petitioners' reasoning would allow Congress to regulate any crime as long as the nationwide, aggregated impact of that crime has substantial effects on employment, production, transit, or consumption."[60] Thus, the Court posited that such an interpretation of the Commerce Clause would create a slippery slope that would allow Congress to regulate all violent crimes in the United States, as well as other non-economic activities that have some aggregated effect on the economy. *Morrison* further clarified the Court's narrower view of the commerce power as expressed in *Lopez*, that "Congress cannot regulate a non-economic activity by finding that, looked at cumulatively, it has a substantial effect on interstate commerce."[61] As a result, in *Morrison* the Court converted the economic activity rationale discussed in *Lopez* into a clear constitutional requirement.[62] The Court in *Lopez* and *Morrison* took this approach on the economic/non-economic distinction "[b]ecause the aggregation of non-economic activities could justify federal usurpation of traditional state functions, [and thus] the Court expressed strong reservations about allowing Congress to aggregate non-economic activities to show a substantial effect on interstate commerce."[63]

In 2005, the Court decided *Gonzales v. Raich*[64]—the first Commerce Clause case since the revival of "new federalism" in *Lopez* that dealt with the constitutionality of federal government regulation of privatized commons resources.[65] Describing the potential implications of *Raich* for the precedential value of *Lopez* and *Morrison*, Professor Claeys posited that in *Raich* "the New Federalism passed from youthful exuberance to middle-aged sobriety."[66] Given the commons nature of the regulated natural capital, however, it is not clear that the new federalism is yet in the midst of a mid-life crisis, as *Raich* is only a natural extension of the Court's longstanding treatment of privatized commons resources under the Commerce Clause.

In *Raich*, the Court considered the validity of the Controlled Substances Act (CSA), which made illegal the possession, distribution, or manufacturing of marijuana.[67] The CSA conflicted with California's Compassionate Use Act, which allowed limited medical use of marijuana.[68] The Ninth Circuit construed *Lopez* and *Morrison* as dispositive in its finding that intrastate, personal medical use of homegrown marijuana was beyond the reach of the federal government, and thus application of the CSA to the plaintiffs was an unconstitutional exercise of Congress's Commerce Clause power.[69]

The U.S. Supreme Court vacated the decision and remanded to the Ninth Circuit, finding that the CSA was within Congress's power under the Commerce Clause.[70] Importantly, the Court noted that the case was both analogous to *Wickard* and consistent with the "new federalism" cases because "[u]nlike [the statutes] at issue in *Lopez* and *Morrison*, the activities regulated by the CSA are quintessentially *economic*."[71] According to some scholars, the Court also established an alternative holding, that Congress has "broad discretion to regulate *non-economic*, intrastate activities as long as it does so in a comprehensive statute."[72] It is not clear, however, that the majority opinion established this test. Though Justice Scalia's concurrence did state that "Congress may regulate even noneconomic local activity if that regulation is a necessary part of a more general regulation of interstate commerce,"[73] the majority never conceded this point, only stating that Congress had the "power to regulate purely *local* activities that are part of an *economic* 'class of activities' that have a substantial effect on interstate commerce."[74] Thus the majority focused on the "local" nature of the activity and the "economic" nature of the class, of which the homegrown marijuana at issue in *Raich* was a part.[75]

Similarly, the *Raich* majority asserted that "*Wickard* thus establishes that Congress can regulate purely intrastate activity that is not itself 'commercial,' *in that it is not produced for sale*, if it concludes that failure to regulate that class of activity would undercut the regulation of the interstate market in that commodity."[76] The activity in *Wickard* was still "economic,"[77] even though not "commercial" in the sense that it would be entering, via sale, an official commercial market.[78] The *Raich* majority's recognition that the wheat production in *Wickard* was not commercial, while leaving undisturbed the *Lopez* Court's previous recognition of the production and consumption as "economic," seems to have been overlooked by scholars.[79] In fact, the Court suggested the activity was economic *for the very reason* that it was not entering the commercial market—being a depletable resource, the appropriative consumption of the resource by non-excludable actors would substantially affect the commercial market when aggregated.[80]

Finally, and as noted earlier, the more recent case of *National Federation of Independent Business v. Sebelius*, saw a majority of the court rule that the Commerce Clause could not sustain the individual mandate portion of the Affordable Care Act, requiring Americans to purchase health insurance by 2014 or else face a penalty. Chief Justice Roberts's opinion distinguished the Commerce Clause analysis from that in the *Raich* case by finding that the statute in *Raich* regulated economic activity, while the individual mandate in *Sebelius* attempted to regulate economic *inactivity*. In this way, Justice Roberts could be viewed as drawing yet another line between the regulation of public goods, like public safety and health care in the *Lopez*, *Morrison*, and *Sebelius* cases and commons resources, like those at issue in *Wickard*, *Raich* and a number of other cases.

To this point we can see that in the major Commerce Clause cases since *Wickard* the U.S. Supreme Court has upheld federal regulatory authority over natural resources that can be characterized as privatized commons resources. The two cases, however, that have perhaps caused the most concern over the scope of environmental Commerce Clause authority are *SWANCC v. United States Army Corps of Engineers*[81] and *Rapanos v. United States*.[82] In *SWANCC* a group sought to purchase an abandoned gravel pit to dispose of nonhazardous wastes.[83] Water within the pit, however, maintained habitat for endangered migratory birds. In denying the group's proposed use, the Army Corps of Engineers (Corps), pursuant to its authority under Section 404(a) of the CWA,[84] applied the Migratory Bird Rule, which asserted that the Corps' jurisdiction extended to intrastate waters "[w]hich are or would be used as habitat by … migratory birds which cross state lines."[85]

The government argued that the rule was appropriate because "protection of migratory birds is a 'national interest of very nearly the first magnitude,' … [and], as the Court of Appeals found, millions of people spend over a billion dollars annually on recreational pursuits relating to migratory birds."[86] The Court proceeded, however, to decide the case upon statutory interpretation grounds in order to avoid constitutional questions about the scope of the Commerce Clause.[87] The Court narrowly construed the CWA as not granting the Corps this authority and held that the act did not apply to intrastate land merely because of the presence of migratory birds. Even though constitutional and federalism questions were raised, however, some have asserted that "*SWANCC* is … noteworthy for its explicit validation of federal regulation of activities that 'substantially affect' interstate commerce and for its continued approval of the 'aggregation doctrine'"—an important fact given the context of federal environmental regulation.[88]

The Court again addressed federal authority to regulate the environment under the CWA in the case of *Rapanos v. United States*.[89] Property owners challenged the Corps' authority to regulate portions of property connected to wetlands by man-made drains. The Court rejected the government's claim that the CWA gave the Corps the power to regulate wetlands regardless of the connection to "navigable waters." The Court, however, as in *SWANCC*, did so based solely upon statutory interpretation grounds, construing the CWA narrowly and refusing to address the constitutional issues raised by the property owners.[90]

Ultimately, the *SWANCC* and *Rapanos* Courts' Commerce Clause discussions express "similar federalism concerns as those expressed in *Lopez* and *Morrison*."[91] Though the types of concerns raised in *SWANCC* and *Rapanos* have caused disquiet among scholars about the future of federal environmental regulation,[92] a commons analysis, as applied to *SWANCC* below, demonstrates that the resources at issue in those cases may be considered privatized commons resources when appropriated by development (as is often the case with wetlands and endangered species) or by individuals as part of a larger, interstate economic market (as with wheat and marijuana). Thus, the appropriation of these resources is in fact intrastate *economic* activity that may be constitutionally regulated under the substantial effects test of the Commerce Clause. Such was the case with the wheat in *Wickard* and the marijuana in *Raich*, and it was decidedly not the case with the public goods at issue in *Lopez, Morrison*, and *Sebelius*—laying the foundation for Commerce Clause jurisprudence that is actually more consistent than has long been perceived, at least in the area of federal environmental regulation.

The Commerce Clause: A Federal Means of Controlling State Herder Rationality?

As discussed in detail in Chapter 3, the natural capital that exists on private lands is depletable and developers are very difficult to exclude from appropriating that natural capital, whether the developer is an individual property owner undertaking development activities or selling the property to another who is in the business of development. Similarly, resources extracted from land by individuals, such as agricultural products (wheat, marijuana), are depletable, and it is very difficult to exclude individuals from consuming and impacting markets related to those resources. Because the regulation of wetlands, endangered species, wheat, marijuana, minerals, and other resources is the focus of the foundational Commerce Clause cases relating to the environment, it is necessary to remind ourselves how these resources may be characterized as privatized commons resources and to explore what the federal government's role is in exercising its Commerce Clause power to control state rationality in exercising its own land use regulatory authority (or perhaps not exercising it).

Chapter 3 laid a foundation for how the rational herder, grocer, farmer, forester, and private property owner can be replaced by the rational state government. Given current indicators of economic growth—i.e. evermore land clearing and electricity generation means strong GDP growth—it is in each rational state government's best interest to keep its land base as open as possible to development interests through the maintenance of lax land use policies in order to avoid losing development interests to neighboring states or local communities. This race-to-the-bottom among states can stifle innovative land use measures that could assist in preserving finite natural capital increasingly under growth and population pressures. In short, in the absence of federal authority to direct or coordinate state land use activities, states are free to act as rational herders on the national commons, rivaling each other to appropriate depletable natural capital in a non-exclusive manner, since no state may be prevented from maintaining lax land use policies. In fact, as highlighted in Chapter 3, lax state land use laws actually *promote* non-exclusivity by preferencing the creation of human-made capital over the preservation of depletable natural capital.[93] So not only do commons tragedies exist, but states are also quite purposeful in promoting tragedies of natural capital commons.

This race-to-the-bottom among states has been a key driver of federal environmental regulation. Indeed, Commerce Clause jurisprudence actually addresses this set of commons problems, and in the context of privatized commons resources. In the related 1981 cases of *Hodel v. Virginia Surface Mining & Reclamation Association*[94] and *Hodel v. Indiana*,[95] the U.S. Supreme Court upheld the Surface Mining Control and Reclamation Act (SMCRA) of 1977 "on the ground that the absence of federal legislation would likely lead to ruinous competition among states lowering state environmental standards in order to retain or attract business from other states."[96] The Court held that provisions of SMCRA protecting disconnected intrastate farmlands were constitutional under the Commerce Clause because of the need to "ensure that production of coal for interstate commerce would not be at the expense of agriculture, the environment, or public health and safety, injury to any of which interests would have deleterious effects on interstate commerce."[97] Perhaps most importantly, the Court noted that "[t]he prevention of this sort of destructive interstate competition is a traditional role for congressional action under the Commerce Clause."[98] Thus states engage in rivalry over businesses appropriating the mineral resource—more for one state means less for another and therefore each fails to appropriately guide responsible extraction and management of the resource. Indeed, each state has an incentive to encourage the greatest amount of extraction possible from the collective privatized environment, just as Hardin's herder ruinously extracts as much grass as possible for the benefit of the herd.

The *Hodel* cases' acknowledgment of the race-to-the-bottom, ultimately grounded in commons reasoning, has jurisprudential implications for other important environmental legislation, such as the ESA. The case of *National Association of Home Builders (NAHB) v. Babbitt*[99] involved a hospital development's "taking" of endangered species habitat. As a basis for upholding the ESA, scholars assert, the *NAHB* court invoked *Hodel v. Virginia Surface Mining*'s finding that Congress has Commerce Clause authority to regulate wholly intrastate activities in order to prevent destructive interstate competition.[100] Judge Sentelle dissented, stating "[a]lthough [Judge Wald] asserts 'striking parallels' between [the *Hodel*] cases and the present one, I see no parallel at all. In [*Hodel*], Congress regulated arguably intrastate *commercial* activities, specifically mining and lumber production for interstate commerce."[101] What is striking is Sentelle's failure to see the parallel—under a commons analysis "intrastate commercial" consumption and appropriation of minerals and lumber for "interstate commerce" is indistinguishable from "intrastate commercial" consumption and appropriation of endangered species, when the development impacting the endangered species would clearly be considered part of interstate commerce. The appropriation of privatized commons resources inextricably links the appropriator (here a developer) and the resource being appropriated (the land containing endangered species), incorporating each into the act of appropriation as one economic transaction.[102] Timber companies appropriate temporally finite lumber resources, mining companies appropriate finite mineral resources, and developers appropriate landed natural capital, including endangered species, water, forests, and other resources present on the land.

In this way, we again see that natural capital present within the United States takes on the characteristics of a commons, with 50 rational state governments maintaining authority over, and vying for, resources of interest to the nation as a whole. The state boundaries are presumably the "fences" around each rational state government's "property." As discussed, however, damage still accrues to the land base when each government acts in its own best economic interest to the detriment of the environment as a whole—such as by maintaining lax land use controls. Enter the Commerce Clause. This is the circumstance under which some scholars argue the framers intended the Commerce Clause to apply—when states are unable to overcome collective action problems to adequately address an economic issue of national concern that could have negative interstate consequences without proper state coordination.[103]

The federal government has made numerous attempts to halt rational actors' destruction of the environment through passage of legislation under the Commerce Clause.[104] Take, for example, the case of a rational state that maintains more lax land use standards than a neighboring state in order to facilitate economic growth, leading to increased eradication of endangered species, wetland, or air quality resources within that state. The ESA, CWA, or CAA, respectively, enter to protect the collective privatized environment and the privatized commons resources present within it. Yet these acts have been met with varying levels of resistance. Congressional authority to regulate clean air, for instance, has met little resistance, as under Commerce Clause analysis air more clearly crosses the "fences" of state boundaries and more apparently affects a neighboring rational state's economic interests (or, the neighboring state's "commerce").

Though water regulation causes slightly more Commerce Clause controversy, particularly in the land use context,[105] water also typically ebbs and flows in discernable patterns across state boundaries, affecting the economy on large scales. In fact, the D.C. Circuit Court of Appeals has explicitly invoked a commons analysis when discussing the race-to-the-bottom among states in the context of water resources, stating:

> [T]he primary purpose of the effluent limitations and guidelines [of the CWA] was to provide uniformity among the federal and state jurisdictions enforcing the [National Pollution Discharge Elimination System] program and prevent the 'Tragedy of the Commons' that might result if jurisdictions can compete for industry and development by providing more liberal limitations than their neighboring states.[106]

Yet, as discussed in Chapters 1–3, land use regulation is a traditional state and local regulatory role under the U.S. Constitution. Thus, the closer the nexus between federal regulation and private land use activities, the more resistance to the federal law. Such is the case with the ESA, which allows the federal government to prevent private landowners from undertaking activities on their property that negatively impact endangered species populations. This restriction may result in Fifth Amendment regulatory "takings" claims by landowners resisting limits on both the use of their property and the economic return that may be gained from their property.[107] State governments may also bring Tenth Amendment claims that the federal government has exceeded its authority under the Constitution by treading on land use regulatory powers reserved to the states.[108] Thus, the regulation of privatized commons resources in the land use context is subject to more resistance than the regulation of other resources, like air and water, that more clearly cross state boundaries. The ESA is perhaps the most emblematic representation of the former.[109] Such resistance would also likely occur if Congress decided in the future to enact "endangered ecosystem" legislation, as some have suggested,[110] or to regulate some other private land use activity that adversely affects privatized commons resources such as isolated wetlands like those at issue in *SWANCC* and *Rapanos*.

Given these circumstances, it is important to understand how a commons analysis informs our understanding of the complex relationship between private property owners, state governments, and the federal government, and how Commerce Clause authority for federal privatized commons resource regulation is an extension of that relationship. Ostrom's commons analysis provides the necessary tools to describe the commons nature of the relationship among individuals, state governments, and the federal government in the context of federal environmental legislation. As detailed in Chapter 2, Ostrom calls those who arrange for the provision of a commons resource "providers," and describes anyone who maintains and ensures the long-term viability of the resource system as a "producer."[111] In this way, we see that individuals engaged in cultivating and appropriating resources subject to an interstate market (such as marijuana or wheat) are *providers* of a privatized commons resource, and the federal government is the *producer* in charge of ensuring the long-term viability of the resource system that supplies those markets. Similarly, in the context of the Commerce Clause, state governments may be characterized as *providers* of natural capital on private lands, as states maintain primary responsibility for regulating land uses related to development. The federal government then acts as the *producer* of the collective privatized environment as it attempts to use federal legislation such as the ESA to maintain and ensure the long-term viability of natural capital on lands primarily regulated by the states.[112] In addition, we can describe the relationship between state governments as the facilitators of land use, and developers, who engage in land use activities, as one between "coappropriators." Co-appropriators, as you recall, are "tied together in a lattice of interdependence" so long as they continue to share the collective privatized environment.[113]

Ultimately, states, private individuals, and developers are co-appropriators of privatized commons resources. When co-appropriators act in an uncoordinated manner, as do Hardin's herders, they have the potential to destroy the resource, as their lack of organization leads to poor management exacerbated by collective action problems. Again, enter the Commerce Clause and federal environmental regulation passed pursuant to it—these constitute, respectively, an organizing constitutional provision and corresponding federal action meant to adequately manage the collective privatized environment in the absence of coordinated state action. Without such federal authority, states may remain rational herders appropriating privatized commons resources from the collective privatized environment with potentially tragic consequences.

In the seminal Commerce Clause case, *Gibbons v. Odgen*,[114] Daniel Webster made the argument, which Justice Marshall accepted,[115] that the purpose of the Commerce Clause is to protect the country from "the embarrassing and destructive consequences, resulting from the legislation of so many different States, and to place it under the protection of a uniform law."[116] This argument extends from that presented to the Constitutional Convention in the Virginia Resolution, which stated that Congress should be able to legislate "in those [cases] to which the States are separately incompetent."[117] This resolution ultimately led to the enumerated federal commerce power and was "accepted without discussion." Scholars have noted that "Marshall's decisional words in *Gibbons* directly connect the concerns of the Virginia Resolution to the scope of the commerce power, and in so doing they state a faithful constitutional understanding of *both* the federal *and* state sides of the commerce power."[118] Justice Marshall's "decisional words" observed that:

> The genius and character of the whole government seem to be, that its action is to be applied to all the external concerns of the nation, and to those internal concerns which affect the States generally; but not to those which are completely within a particular State, which do not affect other States, and with which it is not necessary to interfere, for the purpose of executing some of the general powers of the government. The completely internal commerce of a State, then, may be considered as reserved for the State itself.[119]

Through a commons-based lens it is clear that appropriative consumption of privatized commons resources inherently affects the amount, type, quality, and value of natural capital in other states. This consumption affects entire schemes of intrastate economic regulation, from the various states' chosen form of land use regulation (or lack thereof), to national markets, such as agricultural or illicit drug markets. As such, privatized commons resource appropriation can never be "completely internal" to any one state. As demonstrated in the following section, when viewed through the lens of the commons, both U.S. Supreme Court and lower court Commerce Clause jurisprudence can be interpreted as incorporating Justice Marshall's understanding of the commerce power into decisions involving the scope of federal environmental authority, consistently upholding federal privatized commons resource regulation.

Commerce Clause Jurisprudence Viewed Through the Lens of the Commons: The Economic/Non-economic Controversy and Difficult Questions Arising Under the Commerce Clause

Applying commons analysis to Commerce Clause jurisprudence allows us to see that federal courts, through validation of federal environmental statutes under the Commerce Clause, have effectively recognized the commons nature of privatized commons resources. These courts, through the mechanism of the substantial effects test, have perhaps unintentionally turned the theoretical proposition presented in the three previous sections, on the Commons and the Commerce Clause, into constitutional jurisprudential precedent.

This section establishes how a commons analysis applied to Commerce Clause jurisprudence helps answer two important questions that continually arise in Commerce Clause cases: the "aggregation" and "object of regulation" questions. The first question regards the role of the aggregation principle and whether it should be applied to non-economic activities, or only to those classified as "economic." The second question concerns the controversy over what should be the "object of regulation" focused upon in Commerce Clause cases. For example, under the ESA, should the object of regulation be understood as the endangered species at issue (which may have no recognized economic value in and of itself), or the development impacting the species (which is more clearly linked to interstate commerce)? U.S. Circuit Courts of Appeals decisions are split on this question. The answers to these questions provide a meaningful and unified commons-based rationale to apply in future Commerce Clause cases, providing a long-absent but much-needed clarifying set of principles to the confused mass of Commerce Clause precedent in the area of federal environmental regulation.

Each of these questions is particularly important because each relates to the problems presented by attempts to make an economic/non-economic distinction in Commerce Clause cases. This distinction is useful for Commerce Clause analysis because "when Congress reaches inside a state to regulate or prohibit wholly intrastate activities because of their effect on interstate commerce, requiring that these activities be economic in nature provides some assurance that doing so is a truly necessary means to effectuate the permissible end of regulating interstate commerce."[120] *Lopez* and *Morrison* made "significant changes to the Court's Commerce Clause jurisprudence," since "both decisions emphasized that the Commerce Clause primarily concerns economic regulation and suggested that legislation regulating non-economic activities will receive less deferential review from the Court."[121] Indeed, *Lopez*, *Morrison*, and *Raich* were quite consistent in at least one aspect—they each upheld prior Commerce Clause cases finding that intrastate *economic* activities could be aggregated and regulated as substantially affecting interstate commerce. *Morrison* "explicitly limited Congress's authority to aggregate non-economic, intrastate actions to demonstrate a substantial effect on interstate commerce."[122] However:

> A fundamental problem with both the *Lopez* and *Morrison* decisions is that they failed to provide a workable test for distinguishing between economic and non-economic activities for the purpose of determining which intrastate activities may be aggregated to meet the Commerce Clause's substantial effects test. The two decisions strongly imply that courts should aggregate only economic activities. … Yet, the two cases provide no workable standard for distinguishing between economic and non-economic activities.[123]

The economic/non-economic distinction in the "aggregation" and "object of regulation" questions, however, can be answered with a commons analysis, which provides the "workable standard" currently absent from Commerce Clause jurisprudence. Since privatized commons resources are here defined to be those resources appropriated by economic development of land, or otherwise appropriated by individuals as a component part of a larger interstate market, they will always be economic in nature. In turn, their designation as economic allows aggregation and permits application of the substantial effects test to the "object of regulation" that is the *act* of resource appropriation.

The Aggregation Principle? The Commons is an Inherently Aggregated Economic System

As noted, the Court in *Wickard* introduced the aggregation principle to Commerce Clause jurisprudence, establishing that intrastate consumption of privatized commons resources—even if not directly entering an established commercial market—is economic activity that can be aggregated for the purpose of finding a substantial effect on interstate commerce. Scholars have argued that the *Wickard* Court's formulation of the aggregation doctrine is problematic because it does not clearly establish which intrastate activities are appropriate to aggregate in order to determine the validity of legislation under the Commerce Clause.[124] By using the lens of the commons, however, we can see that the Court's very establishment of an aggregation principle incorporates a commons analysis within Commerce Clause jurisprudence.

Though the question might be different regarding regulation of social constructs, like health care and guns near schools, the aggregation doctrine in the context of privatized commons resources like the wheat in *Wickard* is no more than recognition of the commons nature of the regulated resource. A commons *is itself* a principle of aggregation, because the resources present in the commons are naturally aggregated. The aggregate effects of each herder maximizing economic return and appropriating as much grass as possible from the pasture results in a reduction of resources all across the commons—leading to its potential destruction. The same is true for the rational farmer, forester, developer, or pot-smoker. Thus the appropriation of privatized commons resources by one party, regardless of the nature of the use (e.g., commercial versus home consumption of wheat or marijuana) or the geopolitical or private property boundaries separating appropriators, substantially affects the economic transactions of other appropriators, i.e., "commerce."

An analysis of the rationales presented in *Wickard* and *Raich* supports these assertions. In *Raich*, the majority noted that "[i]n *Wickard*, we had no difficulty concluding that Congress had a rational basis for believing that when viewed in the aggregate, leaving home-consumed wheat outside the regulatory scheme would have a substantial influence on price and market conditions."[125] The *Raich* majority also noted that in both *Wickard* and *Raich* "the regulation is squarely within Congress' commerce power because production of the commodity meant for home consumption, be it wheat or marijuana, has a substantial effect on supply and demand in the national market for that commodity."[126] The substantial influence on price and market conditions demonstrates that the "local" activities in *Wickard* and *Raich* were economic, and also that they took on the characteristics of commons resources because their depletability affects the use, consumption, availability (to rival, non-excludable appropriators), and economic value of resources elsewhere.

In *Raich*, Justice Stevens distinguished *Lopez* and *Morrison* by finding that neither dealt with regulation of activities that were "quintessentially economic." At least one critic has argued that "it is hard to take that argument seriously on a record that establishes only medicinal use, coupled with a total absence of buying, selling, or bartering."[127] But a commons analysis demands serious consideration, as appropriation of these privatized commons resources is by default an economic transaction in a zero-sum world—whether it be characterized in micro-economic parlance as an internalization of externalities or merely as representing the depletion of another rival's consumptive use or preservation elsewhere. In upholding the CSA in *Raich*, the majority noted:

> Like the farmer in *Wickard*, respondents are cultivating, for home consumption, a fungible commodity for which there is an established, albeit illegal, interstate market. Just as the Agricultural Adjustment Act was designed "to control the volume [of wheat] moving in interstate and foreign commerce in order to avoid surpluses … " and consequently control the market price … a primary purpose of the [Substances Act] is to control the supply and demand of controlled substances in both lawful and unlawful drug markets.[128]

In other words, the Court equated the "rational farmer" from *Wickard* with the "rational pot-smoker" in *Raich*. Market price is determined based upon both rivalry over the resource and supply and demand—as parties seek access to a resource in a rivalrous fashion, one party appropriates the resource, which in the aggregate results in less of that resource for other parties. What the Court is describing in *Raich* and *Wickard* as economic activity suitable for aggregation is a commons.

Scholars have argued that *Wickard* and *Raich* were decided incorrectly, since the Commerce Clause does not reach intrastate, *noncommercial* transactions.[129] The commons analysis demonstrates, however, that the activities involved in the cases at issue remain economic in nature, as is the appropriation of any depletable, non-excludable privatized commons resource. The "trade" or "exchange"[130] of such resources, whereby one person's appropriation of the resource reduces its availability to others, may not be explicit, as they may not appropriate the resource directly into an official commercial market.[131] Given the aggregated value of natural capital across the United States, however, an economic effect approximating trade or exchange occurs nonetheless.

A telling illustration of how courts have come to treat regulation of privatized commons resources as meeting the substantial effects test via the aggregation principle is the different outcomes delivered by the Fourth Circuit Court of Appeals in *Gibbs v. Babbitt*[132] and *Brzonkala v. Virginia Polytechnic Institute,*[133] the precursor to *Morrison. Gibbs* was decided by the Fourth Circuit a little more than a year after it decided *Brzonkala*, and less than a month after the U.S. Supreme Court decided *Morrison. Gibbs* has been described as a "doctrinal double-standard" when compared to *Morrison.*[134] *Gibbs* upheld the ESA's prohibition on the taking of endangered red wolves from private property, even though the prohibition conflicted with a North Carolina statute.[135] The Court relied on the *Wickard* aggregation principle in holding that the taking of red wolves would substantially affect interstate commerce,[136] even though the very same Court had rejected the *Wickard* aggregation doctrine in *Brzonkala.*[137] The Court justified its distinction by finding that, unlike the legislation in *Lopez* and *Morrison*, which was aimed at non-economic activity, the legislation in *Gibbs* was aimed at "what is in a meaningful sense economic activity."[138] The Court found that:

> [T]he taking of a red wolf on private land is unlike gender-motivated violence or guns near schools. The protection of commercial and economic assets is a primary reason for taking the wolves. Farmers and ranchers take wolves mainly because they are concerned that the animals pose a risk to commercially valuable livestock and crops. Indeed, appellants' arguments focus quite explicitly on these economic concerns—they want freer rein to protect their property and investments in the land. The relationship between red wolf takings and interstate commerce is quite direct—with no red wolves, there will be no red wolf related tourism, no scientific research, and no commercial trade in pelts.[139]

Some scholars have criticized this distinction as inconsistent,[140] but a commons analysis provides a much more meaningful, consistent distinction. Red wolves are a privatized commons resource being extracted from the collective privatized environment in the name of economic development. As the Court itself describes, without explicitly recognizing it, the *appropriation* of a privatized commons resource, involving both an appropriator (the farmers and ranchers) and the resource being appropriated (the wolves), is the act the federal government is regulating, and the act which in the aggregate substantially affects interstate commerce. In other words, because regulation of privatized commons resources seeks to achieve efficient management of natural capital—allowing *depletable consumption* of resources while *preserving* to the extent possible their continued availability—such regulation can be characterized as an inherently aggregated economic system with substantial effects on interstate commerce.

In summary, "a principle of aggregation was built into the 'substantial economic effects' test."[141] Since the commons is an inherently aggregated system, we see a commons analysis is also built into the test. With the Court in *Raich* "reaffirm[ing] that *Wickard v. Filburn* remains the dominant Commerce Clause case of the last century,"[142] we have perhaps the most important case in Commerce Clause jurisprudence incorporating a commons aggregation principle to find that appropriation of privatized commons resources substantially affects interstate commerce. Thus, the Court has effectively incorporated a commons analysis into its Commerce Clause jurisprudence, at least in the area of natural capital regulation. Viewing the Court's past Commerce Clause jurisprudence through this lens and adopting a commons analysis for future cases provides a unified and simplified rationale for demonstrating an aggregated, "substantial effect on interstate commerce" in the area of privatized commons resources.

The "Object" of Regulation? The Entire Act of "Appropriation"

A related question has arisen in recent Commerce Clause cases at both the Supreme Court and the Court of Appeals levels: what is the "object of regulation" that federal statutes passed pursuant to the Commerce Clause seek to address and that in the aggregate must "substantially affect" interstate commerce? Courts have indicated that this question is important because it informs whether the intrastate activity can appropriately be considered "economic" so as to allow aggregation under the substantial effects test.

In Commerce Clause cases, "a court must determine the central or 'precise' 'object' of a regulatory statute," and "how close the nexus must be between the object and the commercial purposes of the Commerce Clause."[143] *Lopez* and *Morrison* "failed to provide a framework for courts to use in deciding: (1) which, of possibly several subjects regulated by a statute, is the central or precise 'object' for determining whether the statute regulates economic or non-economic activities; (2) whether those activities have substantial impacts on interstate commerce."[144] This is a crucial oversight, as "a court cannot resolve whether an object or activity is 'economic' or 'non-economic' without identifying what that object or activity is."[145] Take an example from Supreme Court jurisprudence: in avoiding the constitutional question in *SWANCC*, the Court stated that to answer the question would require an evaluation of "the precise object or activity that, in the aggregate, substantially affects interstate commerce."[146] The Court was implying that if the "object" that must substantially affect interstate commerce was the simple filling of an isolated gravel pit home to migratory birds, severed from any broader economic activity related to interstate commerce, then the application of the Commerce Clause might be in doubt.[147]

Indeed, the "object of regulation" question has resulted in disagreement regarding whether, under the CWA, wetlands themselves or rather commercial activities impacting those wetlands should be considered the focus of the statute.[148] The divide is perhaps best evidenced, however, by the debate among the Courts of Appeals regarding the appropriate mechanism for upholding application of the ESA. All Courts of Appeals to consider Commerce Clause challenges to the ESA have upheld the statute,[149] but as scholars have noted, the courts have not been able to formulate consistent legal reasoning for doing so. Even so, courts seem determined to uphold the ESA under some rationale, even if they cannot agree on the mechanism of analysis. A commons analysis provides a means by which the varied past rationales of the circuit courts can be reconciled and can be applied in a clearer fashion in the future.

The "object of regulation" question in the context of the ESA takes the form of a split among the Courts of Appeals over whether the ESA regulates the actual taking of protected species or the commercial activities that result in the taking of species. For example, in *Rancho Viejo, LLC v. Norton,* the Court held that the then-Judge Roberts's "hapless toad"[150] was not the object of ESA regulation. Rather, the Court found that the "regulated activity is Rancho Viejo's planned commercial development, not the arroyo toad that it threatens."[151] By contrast, the Fifth Circuit in *GDF Realty Investments v. Norton* (*GDF*) rejected the argument that the economic impact of the development is the appropriate focus of ESA regulation, instead finding that endangered species in and of themselves have substantial effects on interstate commerce when they are aggregated because of their "interdependence."[152] This jurisdictional split is troublesome, because "[t]he [Supreme] Court's failure to define what objects or activities are most important in analyzing whether a statutory scheme may regulate an activity under the Commerce Clause has caused especially difficult problems for courts deciding whether the ESA is constitutional under the [Commerce] Clause."[153] Correlatively, the distinction between the approaches of the Fifth and D.C. Circuits is important because, as noted by Professor Mank:

> If a court focuses on the ESA's means in regulating the economic impact of the activities that harm endangered species, then the government likely can regulate large scale construction projects, but not a lone hiker walking through a forest or perhaps even individual homeowners,

> although in the aggregate both types of activities could cause significant harm to these species. ... By contrast, under the rationale of *GDF*, the government could regulate a lone hiker or landscaping homeowner who harms any endangered species, no matter how insignificant, because the loss of any endangered species threatens the delicate balance of ecosystems, and harm to ecosystems would cause substantial harms to interstate commerce.[154]

The Fifth Circuit based its decision in part upon dicta from the U.S. Supreme Court in *SWANCC*, suggesting that the commercial activities at issue in *SWANCC* were "too far removed from the CWA's 'object' of regulating 'navigable waters.'"[155] Professor Mank argues, however, that "*SWANCC* itself failed to provide a clear answer about how lower courts should decide what is the central 'object' of a statute—either the statute's regulatory 'targets' or its beneficiaries—and how close the relationship must be between the object of the statute and the commercial purposes of the Commerce Clause."[156] Mank argues that the *SWANCC* decision in fact suggested that:

> [N]either the value of the migratory birds nor the commercial activities that motivated the filling in of the wetlands could justify congressional regulation because they were not the precise object of the statute. Instead, the Court implied that the wetlands themselves are the "object" that must substantially affect interstate commerce.[157]

Other scholars have argued that "intrastate water" was the object regulated in *SWANCC*,[158] while yet others have stated that the CWA "is not regulating wetlands use; it is regulating the economic, and often commercial, activity of land use and development."[159]

Commons analysis helps make sense out of this chaos, providing a clear framework within which to analyze the "object" of natural capital regulation. The "interdependence" of species recognized by the Fifth Circuit, and the recognition by the D.C. Circuit that the actor impacting the resource is necessarily tied to the resource itself, are each—though previously considered independent jurisprudential rationales—nothing more than recognition by the appellate courts of the commons nature of the regulated activity, or "object," under the ESA. In fact, scholars have asserted that the ESA provides support for the approach of *either* the Fifth Circuit *or* the D.C. Circuit, because "the statute suggests that both commercial activities that harm species and the species themselves affect interstate commerce."[160] Though these scholars argue that one approach may be more appropriate than the other,[161] this chapter argues that not only is it unnecessary to pick one *or* the other, but to do so is jurisprudentially incorrect. The two approaches cannot be logically separated under the commons appropriation analysis.

Regulation of commons resources cannot be separated into regulation of *either* the appropriator *or* the resource being appropriated. One need only look at the structure of the statutes to determine that wetlands, endangered species, uncontaminated land, air, and other resources are inseparable from the activities impacting them—without this interaction there would be no regulation in the first instance. A developer, for example, is an appropriator of the wetlands resource, or of the endangered species habitat, and the substantial effects on interstate commerce arise out of the *act of appropriation*. Completing the circle, the appropriation substantially affecting interstate commerce is impossible without the constituent sub-elements of an appropriator (the developer) as well as that being appropriated (the wetlands or endangered species). In other words, the "object or activity" of regulations like the ESA and CWA is the *entire act of appropriation* of privatized commons resources, which combines the appropriator (the herder) with the resource being appropriated (the resource on the pastoral commons). It is this act of appropriation that in the aggregate substantially affects interstate commerce.[162]

Regulating *appropriation* of privatized commons resources is the primary purpose of virtually all environmental regulation, to manage how actors within our environment (appropriators) consume, distribute, conserve, and utilize resources (air, endangered species, water, minerals, uncontaminated land). Regulating the act of appropriation is necessary because from a policy perspective dividing the regulation into the constituent sub-elements of appropriation will result in inefficient and ultimately ineffective regulation. Since the "object of regulation" of privatized commons resources is the act of appropriation, which is an economic transaction when implicating land development or external interstate markets, these acts can be aggregated for the purpose of finding a substantial effect on interstate commerce. This renders constitutional privatized commons resource regulation by the federal government under the Commerce Clause.

Conclusion

With every ebb and flow of Commerce Clause jurisprudence, oscillating between federalist and nationalist approaches to the scope of the clause, scholars express concern over federal environmental regulatory authority. Yet environmental regulatory authority has survived, with federal courts content to treat it as fundamentally different from other areas of regulation. Whether it be the different results reached by the U.S. Supreme Court in *Lopez/Morrison/Sebelius* and *Raich*, or the Fourth Circuit coming to strikingly divergent conclusions in *Gibbs* and *Brzonkala*, courts are determined to treat regulation of depletable resources subject to non-excludable appropriation differently than other objects of regulation. We need to understand why.

Viewing Commerce Clause jurisprudence in the context of natural capital regulation through the lens of the commons explains and justifies this distinction. Courts have consistently upheld federal regulation of privatized commons resources since the beginning of the modern regulatory state based upon their aggregated substantial effects on interstate commerce. *Raich* was no outlier—it was merely a continuation of precedent in that regard. Perhaps *Lopez, Morrison*, and *Sebelius* were not outliers either, as they did not involve regulation aimed at commons concerns. It remains to be seen how the U.S. Supreme Court will treat future Commerce Clause challenges to federal environmental and other statutes. In the meantime, commons analysis, with its useful descriptions of appropriators, co-appropriation, producers, providers, and other concepts, provides important and unified answers to much debated questions within Commerce Clause jurisprudence, especially regarding the "aggregation" and "object of regulation" questions. Rather than trying to predict the outcomes of future environmental Commerce Clause challenges based upon single cases, scholarly energy would be better served by recognizing and analyzing the objects of regulation that have received in the past judicial recognition as a valid subject of federal regulatory authority—that is, objects of regulation that constitute commerce in the commons of the United States.

Notes

1 The material constituting significant portions of this chapter originated in Blake Hudson, Commerce in the Commons: A Unified Theory of Natural Capital Regulation Under the Commerce Clause, 35 *Harv. Env. L. Rev.* 375 (2011).
2 Elinor Ostrom, *Governing the Commons: The Evolution of Institutions for Collective Action* 92 (1990) (citation omitted).
3 U.S. Const. art. I, § 8, cl. 3.
4 See text accompanying Ostrom, supra note 2.
5 514 U.S. 549 (1995).
6 529 U.S. 598 (2000).
7 545 U.S. 1 (2005).
8 132 S.Ct. 603 (2011). Justice Roberts, in refusing to uphold the individual mandate portion of the Affordable Care Act as constitutional under the Commerce Clause, stated:

> Construing the Commerce Clause to permit Congress to regulate individuals precisely because they are doing nothing would open a new and potentially vast domain to congressional authority. Congress already possesses expansive power to regulate what people do. Upholding the Affordable Care Act under the Commerce Clause would give Congress the same license to regulate what people do not do. The Framers knew the difference between doing something and doing nothing. They gave Congress the power to regulate commerce, not to compel it. Ignoring that distinction would undermine the principle that the Federal Government is a government of limited and enumerated powers. The individual mandate thus cannot be sustained under Congress's power to 'regulate Commerce.'

See also Tom Scocca, Obama Wins the Battle, Roberts Wins the War, Slate.com, available at http://www.slate.com/articles/news_and_politics/scocca/2012/06/roberts_health_care_opinion_commerce_clause_the_real_reason_the_chief_justice_upheld_obamacare_.html.
9 Bradford C. Mank, After Gonzales v. Raich: Is the Endangered Species Act [ESA] Constitutional Under the Commerce Clause? 78 *U. Colo. L. Rev.* 375, 403 (2007).
10 U.S. Const. art. I, § 8, cl. 3.

11 See, e.g., Rancho Viejo v. Norton, 323 F.3d 1062 (D.C. Cir. 2003); GDF Realty Investments, Ltd. v. Norton, 326 F.3d 622 (5th Cir. 2003); National Ass'n of Home Builders v. Babbitt, 130 F.3d 1041 (D.C. Cir. 1997). Nearly half of all species listed as endangered or threatened under the ESA have habitats limited to one state. Mank, supra note 9 at 428.

12 i.e., since Wickard v. Filburn, 317 U.S. 111 (1942).

13 Wickard, 317 U.S. 111.

14 Hodel v. Va. Surface Mining & Reclamation Ass'n, 452 U.S. 264 (1981); Hodel v. Indiana, 452 U.S. 314 (1981).

15 Gonzales v. Raich, 545 U.S. 1 (2005).

16 United States v. Riverside Bayview Homes, 474 U.S. 121 (1985).

17 Tenn. Valley Auth. v. Hill, 437 U.S. 153 (1978); Babbitt v. Sweet Home Chapter of Cmtys. for a Great Or., 515 U.S. 687 (1995).

18 See, e.g., Brigham Daniels, Emerging Commons and Tragic Institutions, 37 Envtl. L. 515, 523–24 (2007).

19 See Edward T. Swaine, Does Federalism Constrain the Treaty Power? 103 *Colum. L. Rev.* 403, 408 (2003).

20 See, e.g., Randy Barnett, The Original Meaning of the Commerce Clause, 68 *U. Chi. L. Rev.* 101, 101 (2001).

21 545 U.S. 1, at 59 (2005) (Thomas, J., dissenting).

22 132 S.Ct. 603 (2011).

23 See, e.g., Randy Barnett, Foreword: Limiting Raich, 9 *Lewis & Clark L. Rev.* 743 (2005); Eric Brignac, The Commerce Clause Justification of Federal Endangered Species Protection: Gibbs v. Babbitt, 79 *N.C. L. Rev.* 873, 883 (2001); Eric Claeys, Raich and Judicial Conservatism at the Close of the Rehnquist Court, 9 *Lewis & Clark L. Rev.* 791 (2005); Christy H. Dral and Jerry J. Phillips, Commerce by Another Name: The Impact of United States v. Lopez and United States v. Morrison, 68 *Tenn. L. Rev.* 605 (2001); Dan Gildor, Preserving the Priceless: A Constitutional Amendment to Empower Congress to Preserve, Protect, and Promote the Environment, 32 *Ecology L.Q.* 821 (2005); Christine A. Klein, The Environmental Commerce Clause, 27 *Harv. Envtl. L. Rev.* 1, 38 (2003); Mank, supra note 9; Bradford C. Mank, Protecting Intrastate Threatened Species: Does the Endangered Species Act Encroach on Traditional State Authority and Exceed the Outer Limits of the Commerce Clause? 36 *Ga. L. Rev.* 723, 735–36 (2002); Bradford C. Mank, The Murky Future of the Clean Water Act After SWANCC, 30 *Ecology L.Q.* 811, 844–46 (2003); Thomas W. Merrill, Rescuing Federalism After Raich: The Case for Clear Statement Rules, 9 *Lewis & Clark L. Rev.* 823, 844 (2005); John Copeland Nagle, The Commerce Clause Meets the Delhi Sands Flower-Loving Fly, 97 *Mich. L. Rev.* 174 (1998); Sarah D. Van Loh, The Latest and Greatest Commerce Clause Challenges to the Endangered Species Act: Rancho Viejo and GDF Realty, 31 *Ecology L. Q.* 459 (2004); Lori J. Warner, The Potential Impact of United States v. Lopez on Environmental Regulation, 7 *Duke Envtl. L. & Pol'y F.* 321 (1997); Omar N. White, The Endangered Species Act's Precarious Perch: A Constitutional Analysis Under the Commerce Clause and the Treaty Power, 27 *Ecology L.Q.* 215, 235 (2000); Ernest A. Young, Just Blowing Smoke? Politics, Doctrine, and the Federalist Revival After Gonzales v. Raich, 2005 *Sup. Ct. Rev.* 1.

24 See, e.g., Jonathan H. Adler, Is Morrison Dead? Assessing a Supreme Drug (Law) Overdose, 9 *Lewis & Clark L. Rev.* 751, 752–53 (2005); Michael C. Blumm and George A. Kimbrell, Gonzalez v. Raich, the 'Comprehensive Scheme' Principle, and the Constitutionality of the Endangered Species Act, 35 *Envtl. L.* 491, 494–98 (2005).

25 One scholar has stated that "[j]ust as many scholars prematurely heralded *Lopez* as the beginning of a Commerce Clause revolution, others now may be too quick to characterize *Raich* as the end." Robert J. Pushaw, Jr., The Medical Marijuana Case: A Commerce Clause Counter-Revolution? 9 *Lewis & Clark L. Rev.* 879, 884 (2005).

26 "Zero-sum" here is used to mean "of, relating to, or being a situation ... in which a gain for one side entails a corresponding loss for the other side." *Webster's Ninth New Collegiate Dictionary* 1371 (1989).
27 See Ostrom, supra note 2, at 32 (stating that "one's consumption of public security does not reduce the general level of security available in a community" and noting more generally that "propositions derived from a theory of public goods that are based on the nonsubtractive attributes of those goods are *not* applicable to an analysis of *appropriation* and *use* of subtractable resource units"); Mollie Lee, Environmental Economics: A Market Failure Approach to the Commerce Clause, 116 *Yale L.J.* 456, 479, 483, 487–88 (2006).
28 See James Salzman, Integrating Ecosystem Services into Environmental Law, in *Managing Human Dominated Ecosystems* 77 (Victoria Hollowell ed., 2001); James Salzman, Barton H. Thompson, Jr. and Gretchen C. Daily, Protecting Ecosystem Services: Science, Economics, and Law, 20 *Stan. Envtl. L.J.* 309 (2001); James Salzman, Creating Markets for Ecosystem Services: Notes From the Field, 80 *N.Y.U. L. Rev.* 870 (2005); James Salzman, A Field of Green? The Past and Future of Ecosystem Services, 21 *J. Land Use & Envtl. L.* 133 (2006).
29 U.S. Const. art. I, 8, cl. 3.
30 Robert L. Glicksman, From Cooperative to Inoperative Federalism: The Perverse Mutation of Environmental Law and Policy, 41 *Wake Forest L. Rev.* 719, 755 (2006).
31 Erwin Chemerinsky, Lecture on the Scope of the Commerce Clause at Duke University School of Law (Feb. 1, 2005).
32 See Gibbons v. Ogden, 22 U.S. (9 Wheat.) 1, 10–12 (1824) (syllabus).
33 Chemerinsky, supra note 31.
34 See, e.g., Carter v. Carter Coal Co., 298 U.S. 238 (1936); United States v. E. C. Knight Co., 156 U.S. 1, 12–13 (1895).
35 Chemerinsky, supra note 31.
36 Erwin Chemerinsky, *Constitutional Law Principles and Policies* 256 (3rd ed. 2006).
37 Id. at 257 (discussing NRLB (National Labor Relations Board) v. Jones & Laughlin Steel Corp., 301 U.S. 1 (1937)).
38 In other words, the court used a rational basis standard of review for the Commerce Clause. Id. at 262 (discussing Katzenbach v. McClung, 379 U.S. 294 (1964)).
39 Id. at 243.
40 317 U.S. 111 (1942).
41 United States v. Lopez, 514 U.S. 549, 560 (1995).
42 317 U.S. at 127–28.
43 Id.
44 Id. at 130. The court also established the foundation for Gonzales v. Raich, 545 U.S. 1 (2005), discussed below, which was very similar factually and involved the regulation of similar resources. Even though the market for marijuana in *Raich* was an *illegal* market, the appropriation by an individual of that resource, under a commons analysis, would have an impact on that interstate market.
45 Chemerinsky, supra note 36, at 256.
46 514 U.S. 549 (1995).
47 529 U.S. 598 (2000).
48 Lopez, 514 U.S. at 549. The law prohibited the carrying of a gun within a school zone, defined as "in, or on the grounds of, a public, parochial, or private school" or "within a distance of 1,000 feet from the grounds of a public, parochial, or private school." 18 U.S.C. §§ 922(a)(25)(A)–(B) (2006).
49 Lopez, 514 U.S. at 552.
50 Id.
51 Id. at 558 (citing United States v. Darby, 312 U.S. 100 (1941); Heart of Atlanta Motel, Inc. v. United States, 379 U.S. 241 (1964)).
52 Id. (citing the Shreveport Rate Cases, 234 U.S. 342 (1914); S.R.R. Co. v. United States, 222 U.S. 20 (1911)).

53 Id. at 558–59 (citing NLRB v. Jones & Laughlin Steel Corp., 301 U.S. 1 (1937); Maryland v. Wirtz, 392 U.S. 183 (1958)) (emphasis added).
54 United States v. Morrison, 529 U.S. 598, 614–15 (2000).
55 See 42 U.S.C. § 13981 (2006).
56 S. Rep. No. 101–545, at 37 (1990).
57 Louis J. Virelli III and David S. Leibowitz, 'Federalism Whether They Want It or Not': The New Commerce Clause Doctrine and the Future of Federal Civil Rights Legislation After United States v. Morrison, 3 *U. Pa. J. Const. L.* 926, 949 n.142 (2001).
58 Morrison, 529 U.S. at 614.
59 Id. at 611 (emphasis added). Justice Rehnquist wrote:

> Gender-motivated crimes of violence are not, in any sense of the phrase, economic activity. While we need not adopt a categorical rule against aggregating the effects of any noneconomic activity in order to decide these cases, thus far in our Nation's history our cases have upheld Commerce Clause regulation of intrastate activity only where that activity is economic in nature. … [T]he existence of congressional findings is not sufficient, by itself, to sustain the constitutionality of Commerce Clause legislation. As we stated in Lopez, '[S]imply because Congress may conclude that a particular activity substantially affects interstate commerce does not necessarily make it so.'

Id. at 613–14.
60 Id. at 615.
61 Chemerinsky, supra note 36, at 264.
62 Claeys, supra note 23, at 802.
63 Bradford C. Mank, Can Congress Regulate Intrastate Endangered Species Under the Commerce Clause? The Split in the Circuits Over Whether the Regulated Activity Is Private Commercial Development or the Taking of Protected Species, 69 *Brook. L. Rev.* 923, 954 (2004).
64 545 U.S. 1 (2005).
65 *SWANCC* and *Rapanos* dealt with privatized commons resources, but the court did not reach the constitutional issues raised in those cases, deciding the cases on statutory interpretation grounds.
66 Claeys, supra note 23, at 792 (stating also that "[w]hile the New Federalism has not been repudiated, in the future its growth is certain to be far slower and more erratic").
67 See 21 U.S.C. § 841(a)(1) (2006).
68 Cal. Health & Safety Code § 11362.5 (Deering 2011).
69 See Raich v. Ashcroft, 352 F.3d 1222, 1227 (9th Cir. 2003), rev'd sub nom. Gonzales v. Raich, 545 U.S. 1 (2005).
70 See Raich, 545 U.S. at 9.
71 Id. at 25 (emphasis added).
72 Mank, supra note 9, at 410 (emphasis added) (citing Adler, supra note 24, at 764–65; Douglas W. Kmiec, Gonzales v. Raich: Wickard v. Filburn Displaced, 2005 *Cato Sup. Ct. Rev.* 71, 96 (2005)).
73 Raich, 545 U.S. at 37 (Scalia, J., concurring).
74 Id. at 17 (majority opinion) (emphasis added). As noted in Justice Thomas's dissent, the Supreme Court "has never held that Congress can regulate noneconomic activity that substantially affects interstate commerce." Id. at 69 (Thomas, J., dissenting).
75 Id. at 17 (majority opinion).
76 Id. at 18 (emphasis added).
77 Justice Rehnquist stated in Lopez that "*Wickard* … involved *economic* activity in a way that the possession of a gun in a school zone does not." United States v. Lopez, 514 U.S. 549, 560 (1995) (emphasis added).
78 The *Wickard* Court stated that the Agricultural Adjustment Act "extend[ed] federal regulation to production not intended in any part for commerce but wholly for consumption

on the farm." Wickard v. Filburn, 317 U.S. 111, 118 (1942). Scholars seem to interpret this statement as evidence that the *Raich* Court relied on *Wickard* to prove that intrastate, non-economic activities that are part of a broader comprehensive scheme can be reached by federal regulation. See Mank, supra note 9. As noted, however, Justice Rehnquist stated in *Lopez* that *Wickard* involved economic activity. *Lopez,* 514 U.S. at 560. It is completely consistent to say that use of a resource that will not be entering an official commercial market is an economic activity, as is the appropriation, this book argues, of any privatized commons resources.

79 See, e.g., Mank, supra note 9, at 456 (arguing that the *Raich* majority and Justice Scalia's *Raich* concurrence "explain ... that Congress may regulate non-economic, purely intrastate activities as long as they are an appropriate part of a valid comprehensive scheme").

80 Nonetheless, even if the claim that non-economic activity may be reached under the "comprehensive scheme" analysis has merit, this chapter argues that *Raich* did involve an economic activity under a commons analysis, and thus the Supreme Court has yet to declare that non-economic intrastate activities can be reached under a comprehensive scheme analysis. This chapter further argues that failure to recognize the economic/non-economic distinction under the comprehensive scheme analysis would leave little to no judicial federalism protection in place.

81 531 U.S. 159 (2001).

82 547 U.S. 715 (2006).

83 SWANCC, 531 U.S. at 163.

84 33 U.S.C. § 1344(a) (2006).

85 Final Rule for Regulatory Programs of the Corps of Engineers, 51 Fed.Reg. 41,206, 41,217 (Nov. 13, 1986).

86 *SWANCC*, 531 U.S. at 173.

87 Id. at 174. In so finding, Chief Justice Rehnquist stated:

> These are significant constitutional questions raised by respondents' application of their regulations, and yet we find nothing approaching a clear statement from Congress that it intended § 404(a) to reach an abandoned sand and gravel pit such as we have here. Permitting respondents to claim federal jurisdiction over ponds and mudflats falling within the "Migratory Bird Rule" would result in a significant impingement of the States' traditional and primary power over land and water use ... We thus read the statute as written to avoid the significant constitutional and federalism questions raised by respondents' interpretation.

Id.

88 Klein, supra note 23, at 37.

89 Rapanos v. United States, 547 U.S. 715 (2006).

90 See Ilya Somin, A False Dawn for Federalism: Clear Statement Rules After Gonzales v. Raich, 2006 *Cato Sup. Ct. Rev.* 113, 127 (2006). Somin argues that "*Rapanos* probably does not impose significant limits on the scope of federal authority under the CWA." Id. at 130.

91 Mank, supra note 63, at 959.

92 See supra note 23 for a list of examples.

93 See Richard B. Stewart, Pyramids of Sacrifice? Problems of Federalism in Mandating State Implementation of National Environmental Policy, 86 *Yale L.J.* 1196, 1211–12 (1977).

94 452 U.S. 264 (1981).

95 452 U.S. 314 (1981).

96 Mank, supra note 9, at 390–91.

97 Hodel v. Indiana, 452 U.S. at 327–29.

98 Hodel v. Va. Surface Mining, 452 U.S. at 282.

99 130 F.3d 1041 (D.C. Cir. 1997).

100 See Mank, supra note 9, at 441–42. Mank has argued that "[u]nder *Hodel*'s rationale, one could reasonably justify regulation of purely intrastate endangered species on the ground that states might fail to protect them because of economic competition." Mank, supra note 63, at 948.

101 NAHB, 130 F.3d at 1066 (Sentelle, J., dissenting).

102 Ostrom has stated that the goal in addressing commons problems and the destruction of natural resources is to determine "how best to limit the use of natural resources so as to ensure their long-term *economic* viability." Ostrom, supra note 2, at 1 (emphasis added). She also noted that "[s]tandard analyses in modern resource economics conclude that where a number of users have access to a common-pool resource, the total of resource units withdrawn from the resource will be greater than the optimal *economic* level of withdrawal." Id. at 3 (emphasis added). Though appropriation from every commons may not be characterized as economic, this chapter argues that appropriation of privatized commons resources is economic when appropriation occurs due to economic development of land, or in a way that has aggregated impacts on a national market for that resource (whether that market is legal or illegal, such as is the case with marijuana use).

103 Professor Mank has asserted that "Congress may enact legislation under the Commerce Clause to prevent states from engaging in a 'race-to-the-bottom' to attract businesses because such competition would probably result in inappropriate intrastate environmental standards." Mank, supra note 9, at 391. Mank, referencing Professor Engel, has also suggested that "the framers of the Constitution would have approved of congressional legislation—based on the Commerce Clause—designed to prevent harmful national competition that states are unable to regulate effectively." Id. at 441 (referencing Kirsten H. Engel, State Environmental Standard-Setting: Is There a 'Race' and Is It 'To the Bottom'? 48 *Hastings L.J.* 271, 281–82 (1997)). Mank also argues that "there is a significant risk that at least some states would race to the bottom to exploit timber or develop land and would destroy critical habitat currently protected by the ESA." Id. at 443.

104 See, e.g., Clean Air Act, 42 U.S.C. §§ 7401–7671g (2006); Clean Water Act, 33 U.S.C. §§ 1251–1387 (2006); Resource Conservation and Recovery Act, 42 U.S.C. §§ 6901–92k (2006); Comprehensive Environmental Response, Compensation, and Liability Act, 42 U.S.C. §§ 9601–75 (2006); Endangered Species Act, 16 U.S.C. §§ 1531–44 (2006).

105 See Solid Waste Agency of Northern Cook Cnty. [SWANCC] v. U.S. Army Corps of Eng'rs, 531 U.S. 159 (2001); Rapanos v. United States, 547 U.S. 715 (2006).

106 Natural Res. Def. Council, Inc. v. Costle, 568 F.2d 1369, 1378 (D.C. Cir. 1977) (footnote omitted).

107 See Penn. Coal Co. v. Mahon, 260 U.S. 393, 415 (1922).

108 See Missouri v. Holland, 252 U.S. 416 (1919).

109 Yet the ESA itself is a statute intended to prevent the 50 rational states as herders from destroying the biodiversity resource. In *Gibbs v. Babbitt,* the Fourth Circuit asserted that the uniform standards of the ESA enhance interstate commerce by avoiding conflicting state standards. 214 F.3d 483, 501–2 (4th Cir. 2000). States have traditionally failed to protect endangered or threatened species, and "[t]he failure of states to provide effective protection for these species and the advantages of uniform national legislation eventually resulted in Congress's enactment of the ESA in 1973." Mank, supra note 9, at 432–33. The Federal Government "needed to provide uniform standards for protecting all threatened and endangered species to prevent a race to the bottom by states that may be tempted to lower their standards to promote economic development." Id. at 439. Indeed, "states are motivated to adopt lower standards of endangered species protection in order to attract development." Id. at 442 n.332.

110 Noss et al. have noted that numerous scientists and conservationists have called for legislation aimed at protecting endangered ecosystems. Reed F. Noss, Edward T. LaRoe III, and J. Michael Scott, *Endangered Ecosystems of the United States: A Preliminary Assessment of Loss and Degradation*, U.S. Dept. of the Interior, National Biological Service (1995) (on file

with the Harvard Law School Library). Others have actually called for "a constitutional amendment to directly preserve, protect, and promote the environment" to avoid these questions altogether. See, e.g., Gildor, supra note 23, at 821.

111 Ostrom, supra note 2, at 31.

112 Id. Ostrom herself uses a relevant example: she describes a national government that establishes an irrigation system as a "provider" of the resource system. If we look at state governments as appropriators of privatized commons resources—in the sense that through their land use laws they facilitate appropriation of landed natural capital by developers—then we see that "appropriators engage in a considerable amount of trial-and-error learning. Many actions are selected without full knowledge of their consequences." Id. at 34. This is the very reason for the passage of statutes like the ESA. The 50 states are laboratories for law, and some run better trials and have fewer errors than others—thus the Federal Government seeks to regulate the environment in areas in desperate need of coordination in order to rectify individual appropriators' (i.e., states') errors in management.

113 Id. at 38–39.

114 22 U.S. (9 Wheat.) 1 (1824).

115 See Kmiec, supra note 72, at 96.

116 Gibbons, 22 U.S. (9 Wheat.) at 11 (syllabus).

117 Records of the Debates in the Federal Convention of 1787 as Reported by James Madison 389 (Charles C. Tansill ed., Legal Classics Library 1989).

118 Kmiec, supra note 72, at 97 (citing Robert L. Stern, That Commerce Which Concerns More States Than One, 47 *Harv. L. Rev.* 1335, 1340 (1934)) (emphasis removed).

119 Gibbons, 22 U.S. (9 Wheat.) at 195.

120 Barnett, supra note 23, at 748.

121 Mank, supra note 9, at 399–400.

122 Id. at 400.

123 Id. at 400–401 (footnotes omitted).

124 Id. at 387; Nagle, supra note 23, at 179–80.

125 Gonzales v. Raich, 545 U.S. 1, 19 (2005).

126 Id. Justice Stevens also stated that "[o]ne need not have a degree in economics to understand why a nationwide exemption for the vast quantity of marijuana … locally cultivated for personal use … may have a substantial impact on the interstate market." Id. at 28.

127 Kmiec, supra note 72, at 88–89.

128 Raich, 545 U.S. at 18–19.

129 See, e.g., Steven K. Balman, Constitutional Irony: Gonzales v. Raich, Federalism and Congressional Regulation of Intrastate Activities Under the Commerce Clause, 41 *Tulsa L. Rev.* 125, 150 (2005).

130 Id. at 151–59 (noting various sources that describe "commerce" as "trade or exchange").

131 Such is the case with biodiversity, the loss of which in the aggregate, and when appropriated by private parties, would have dramatic effects on the nation's economy. Describing the magnitude of economic impact continued consumptive growth might have on our genetic heritage, the 1973 House Committee Report on the ESA stated that species loss put our genetic heritage at risk and "the value of this genetic heritage is, quite literally, incalculable." H.R. Rep. No. 93–412, at 4 (1973).

132 214 F.3d 483 (4th Cir. 2000).

133 169 F.3d 820 (4th Cir. 1999) (en banc).

134 Virelli and Leibowitz, supra note 57, at 968.

135 See 214 F.3d at 506; see also 50 C.F.R. §§ 17.84(c)(4)(i)–(iv) (2010).

136 Gibbs, 214 F.3d at 493.

137 Brzonkala, 169 F.3d at 836 (noting that the statute "cannot be sustained on the authority of cases such as *Wickard*, which have upheld 'regulations of activities that arise out of or are connected with a commercial transaction, which viewed in the aggregate, substantially affects interstate commerce'"). The court also stated that:

> To extend such reasoning beyond the context of statutes regulating economic activities and uphold a statute regulating noneconomic activity merely because that activity, in the aggregate, has an attenuated, though real, effect on the economy, and therefore presumably on interstate commerce, would be effectively to remove all limits on federal authority, and to render unto Congress a police power impermissible under our Constitution.

Id. at 840.

138 *Gibbs*, 214 F.3d at 492.
139 Id. at 492.
140 See, e.g., Virelli and Leibowitz, supra note 57, at 969–70.
141 Kmiec, supra note 72, at 85.
142 Claeys, supra note 23, at 812.
143 Mank, supra note 9, at 403.
144 Id.
145 Id. (quoting David W. Scopp, Commerce Clause Challenges to the Endangered Species Act: The Rehnquist Court's Web of Confusion Traps More Than the Fly, 39 *U.S.F. L. Rev.* 789, 801 (2005)).
146 Solid Waste Agency of N. Cook Cnty. v. U.S. Army Corps of Eng'rs, 531 U.S. 159, 173 (2000).
147 The court stated that the "object" of regulation was "not clear, for although the Corps has claimed jurisdiction over petitioner's land because it contains water areas used as habitat by migratory birds, respondents now, *post litem motam*, focus upon the fact that the regulated activity is petitioner's municipal landfill, which is plainly of a commercial nature." Id.
148 See Klein, supra note 23, at 38; Michael J. Gerhardt, On Revolution and Wetland Regulations, 90 *Geo. L.J.* 2143, 2163 (2002).
149 Indeed, federal courts in general have been reluctant to rely on *Lopez* and *Morrison* to strike down environmental regulations. See Chemerinsky, supra note 36, at 273. For a more recent update on Courts of Appeals treatment of the ESA specifically, see Robert Thornton, 9th Circuit Rejects Commerce Clause Challenge to Delta Smelt Biological Opinion, *Endangered Species Law & Policy* (March 25, 2011), available at http://www.endangeredspecieslawandpolicy.com/2011/03/articles/court-decisions/9th-circuit-rejects-commerce-clause-challenge-to-delta-smelt-biological-opinion/.
150 Rancho Viejo, LLC v. Norton, 334 F.3d 1158, 1160 (D.C. Cir. 2003), *rehearing denied* (Roberts, J. dissenting).
151 Rancho Viejo, LLC v. Norton, 323 F.3d 1062, 1072 (D.C. Cir. 2003).
152 326 F.3d 622, 640 (5th Cir. 2003).
153 Mank, supra note 9, at 405.
154 Mank, supra note 63, at 926–27.
155 Id. at 929.
156 Id.
157 Id. at 960–61 (citations omitted).
158 Robert H. Bork and Daniel E. Troy, Locating the Boundaries: The Scope of Congress's Power to Regulate Commerce, 25 *Harv. J.L. & Pub. Pol'y* 849, 890 (2002).
159 Marianne Moody Jennings and Nim Razook, United States v. Morrison: Where the Commerce Clause Meets Civil Rights and Reasonable Minds Part Ways: A Point and Counterpoint from a Constitutional and Social Perspective, 35 *New Eng. L. Rev.* 23, 54 (2000).
160 Mank supra note 63, at 931. See also Michael C. Blumm and George Kimbrell, Flies, Spiders, Toads, Wolves, and the Constitutionality of the Endangered Species Act's Take Provision, 34 *Envtl. L.* 309, 327 (2004); Nagle, supra note 23, at 210 (stating "either the means or the ends should be able to provide the requisite connection to interstate commerce") (emphasis removed); Robert A. Schapiro and William W. Buzbee, Unidimensional Federalism: Power and Perspective in Commerce Clause Adjudication, 88 *Cornell*

L. Rev. 1199, 1245–47 (2003) (arguing the ESA may apply to both targets of regulation and beneficiaries). The ESA states that "various species of fish, wildlife, and plants in the United States have been rendered extinct as a consequence of economic growth and development untempered by adequate concern and conservation." 16 U.S.C. § 1531(a)(1) (2006).

161 See generally, Mank, supra note 63.

162 The D.C. Circuit in Nat'l Ass'n of Home Builders v. Babbitt, 130 F.3d 1041 (D.C. Cir. 1997) recognized the commons nature of endangered species when it applied the aggregation doctrine to uphold application of the ESA. The court stated that "[i]n the aggregate … we can be certain that the extinction of species and the attendant decline in biodiversity will have a real and predictable effect on interstate commerce," id. at 1053–54, and "we know that in the aggregate the extinction of endangered species will have a substantial effect on interstate commerce." Id. at 1053 n.14. Though future extinction provides an accurate description of the after-effects on interstate commerce, it does not necessarily provide sufficient judicial justification for the effects on interstate commerce at the time the regulation is enacted and implemented. A better way to characterize the point is to recognize that it is the appropriation of endangered species that is being regulated, and appropriation in the aggregate is what substantially affects interstate commerce.

5 Dynamic Commons Resources, Undynamic Federalism[1]

> Given the wide variety of ecological problems that individuals face at diverse scales, an important design principle is getting the boundaries of any one system roughly to fit the ecological boundaries of the problem it is designed to address. Since most ecological problems are nested from very small local ecologies to those of global proportions, following this principle requires a substantial investment in governance systems at multiple levels—each with some autonomy but each exposed to information, sanctioning, and actions from below and above.[2]

Introduction

Though federalization of the commons may be a key mechanism for filling in gaps in subnational resource management, it is only one part of the picture of effective resource management in federal systems of government. As described in Chapters 2 and 3, commons tragedies for resources that are subject to both private property protections and government regulation may occur due to a number of legal or political scenarios present in federal systems. These include not only constitutional limitations on the federal government that legally prevent regulatory inputs into subnational resource management, but also constitutional or legislative preemption of *lower* governmental regulatory inputs by higher governmental authorities—whether it be the federal government preempting state or local action, or states preempting local action. What scholars of federal systems have come to realize is that effective resource management in federal systems is enhanced when regulatory and other management inputs are legally permissible and politically implemented at all vertically situated levels of government. This is a form of federalism that has become known as "dynamic federalism." Though Ostrom was obviously not explicitly referring to the constitutional structure of federal systems, her assessment[3] that solutions to nested ecological problems require a substantial investment in governance systems at multiple levels, with actions taken from below and above, describes the foundational principle of dynamic federalism.

Dynamic federalism, as described in this chapter, is optimal in federal systems of government because the resources being managed are dynamic in and of themselves. Not only is nature dynamic, but human use of resources adds yet another layer of dynamism over already dynamic natural processes—consider human-exacerbated climate change in making even more dynamic naturally occurring sea-level rise and coastal land loss, carbon accumulation in the atmosphere, wildfires, droughts, invasion of non-native species, among a variety of other resource challenges. Some of these challenges may require a different set of management solutions at local, state or provincial, and national levels.

Yet in some federal systems, the dynamism of federalist approaches in some regulatory areas is very much in question. These nations may maintain dynamic federalism in some regulatory areas, whereby all levels of government may legally maintain inputs into certain types of resource management and actually implement such inputs. But for other subject areas it may be unclear from a legal perspective whether regulatory inputs into resource management at all levels is allowed by the nation's constitution or by subnational consitutions or legislation. In these nations, in other words, a system of "dual federalism" may be in place, whereby there are constitutionally entrenched and separate spheres of governance, and one level of government may not impede on a regulatory area considered the purview of other levels of government—even if those other levels of government are failing to effectively govern that regulatory area. Such is the case, for example, in the United States for certain resources, as well as in other federal systems as described in more detail in Chapter 7. In the U.S., and as demonstrated in Chapter 4, the type or mode of federalism maintained has become the subject of great debate. Though this debate has waged for some time, its relevance renews as we see dynamic shifts in the status of resources affected by changing climate, increasing population and development pressures, and changing economic drivers of supply and demand for natural resources.

Some scholars posit that the United States currently maintains and should continue to expand a system of dynamic federalism whereby any level of government maintains constitutional authority to regulate any subject matter, and which does not preempt lower levels of government from effectively addressing issues of concern. In other words, these scholars would argue that there are no separate spheres of governance as between federal, state, and local governments. Other scholars posit that the U.S. currently does and should continue to maintain a system of dual federalism whereby separate spheres do in fact exist and the respective state and federal governments may not regulate in areas constitutionally reserved for the other. These polar propositions drive much of the judicial and academic wrangling discussed in Chapter 4 over whether under the Commerce Clause the federal government can regulate matters of traditional state regulatory authority or whether state and local governments can regulate matters that the federal government claims are preempted by federal authority.

Thus we see an important reality emerge—a reality that contributes to the legal entrenchment of the commons dynamic. The brand of federalism in certain federal systems is neither fully dynamic nor fully dual. Rather, these systems operate under a type of "Bimodal Federalism,"[4] whereby two modes of federalism operate depending upon the subject matter of regulation. While most regulation in these systems may indeed occur in a dynamic manner, as local governments often regulate matters of state or national import, the federal government often regulates matters of almost entirely local concern, and all levels of government share regulatory responsibility over much subject matter, we also see important remnants of dual federalism impacting governance across scales—and in particular in areas of natural resource management. These remnants remain either because jurisprudence has not yet affirmed the validity of dynamic regulatory approaches in those areas or because legislators *perceive*—based upon either genuine constitutional interpretation or rather political and ideological predisposition—that legal constraints exist and therefore politically refuse to act. A result of political inaction, of course, is that courts do not have an opportunity to assess the validity of dynamic regulatory approaches.

One example of this phenomenon from the U.S. is direct land use planning, where there remains a strong dualist notion that state and local governments maintain exclusive constitutional authority to regulate. As discussed in Chapter 4, even though the federal government in the U.S. maintains indirect regulatory mechanisms that can impact land use planning activities, such as the Endangered Species Act (ESA) or Clean Water Act (CWA), state and local governments exercise a suite of powers, primarily related to zoning authority, almost exclusively. These powers are exercised—or perhaps more importantly, often *not* exercised—in the absence of needed minimum standards set at a higher level of government and aimed at the protection of the nation's aggregated natural capital. This has exacerbated problems of urban sprawl and associated forest loss, water degradation, and species habitat fragmentation among other resource management threats, as courts' continued declaration that land use planning is the "quintessential state and local government activity" causes the federal government to perceive (either legitimately or by political calculation) a lack of constitutional authority to set limits on the mode and expanse of local development activities. As a result, an ever-expanding human-built environment rapidly replaces the natural environment and important associated ecosystem services without the regulatory checks that might be administered by federal inputs into land use planning that, for example, could implement growth boundaries around populous municipalities to rein in urban sprawl. Especially given the threat that rising sea levels pose to municipalities and their citizens in coastal areas, and the threat that those municipalities' aggregated poor land use planning decisions pose for needed national climate adaptation policies, the dualistic, undynamic approach to land use planning is increasingly unworkable.

Another regulatory area where remnants of dual federalism remain in the U.S. (and as discussed in Chapters 7, 8, and 9 in other federal nations) is subnational forest management policy (a subject area that will remain the case study example used in Chapters 6–9). In the U.S., the federal government has never before claimed direct regulatory authority over subnational forests, including the 60 percent of U.S. forests in private ownership, despite the fact that subnational forest management policies are grossly inconsistent across the nation. Federal reticence is due in part to longstanding jurisprudence declaring that private forest regulation is a state and local government activity and placing private forest management as a subcategory of direct land use regulation generally. As detailed in a recent U.S. Forest Service report, however, these forests face serious threats over the next 50 years, with southeastern U.S. states projected to lose up to 13 percent of their forests due to urbanization, population growth, invasive species, and climate change by 2060.[5]

While it may be conventional wisdom to consider deforestation as a problem of the Amazon, Indonesia, or other developing countries, this degree of loss of U.S. forests would be a significant blow to both domestic forest resources and the services they provide, as well as utilization of global forests to combat climate change, given the large contribution of forest destruction and degradation to global carbon emissions. The threat that the aggregated poor forest management standards of subnational governments in certain federal systems pose for domestic forest resources and global climate change mitigation policies cause the dualistic, undynamic approach to subnational forest management to be increasingly unworkable.

Federalism scholarship is rife with descriptive and normative assertions about how the Constitution does or should allocate regulatory authority among levels of government. For example, Butler and Macey's "matching principle" argues that the jurisdiction regulating a resource should match the geographic scope of the regulated resource.[6] This type of descriptive analysis is subject to criticisms that it is oversimplistic, as it does not account for the many externalities that spill over jurisdictional boundaries, the increasing scientific recognition of the intricate interconnectedness of resources in the natural environment, and the benefits that multi-level governance can provide. Nonetheless, the matching principle does seem to drive the perpetuation of dualist notions of private forest management and land use planning—that state (provincial) and local governments are best positioned to direct local development activities due to better access to information and the direct assumption of the local benefits and burdens of development. Similarly, the dualistic argument for forest policy seems to be that private forest landowners and state and local governments are best situated to design management standards for regulating forest resources clearly anchored to specific, discernible plots of land. While this may be true, as demonstrated in Chapters 2 and 3 (and in the words of Ostrom) these parties are also those most likely to be incentivized to "play a game against nature in a smaller terrain, rather than a game against another player in larger terrain," and thus engage in tragic commons-driven appropriation of natural capital in the name of economic development.

Though we have seen a transition to more dynamic understandings of constitutional allocation of regulatory authority in the environmental context over the last century, that transition is not yet "complete," whatever that term may come to mean. We need to better understand the implications of living in a bimodal federalism world in certain federal systems whereby failure to recognize dynamic shifts in resources can lead to a failure to establish sound legal arguments providing constitutional justifications for corollary shifts to dynamic federalism regulatory approaches—approaches that may assist in resolving the commons dilemma presented by federal systems. Otherwise, important resources can be locked in a realm of dual federalism where regulatory authority either stops at the border of each and every state or province and those subnational governments, in turn, may refuse to craft regulatory mechanisms that adequately manage those resources, or higher levels of government interfere with subnational governments seeking to implement successful natural capital management policies.

Deconstructing Dynamic and Dual Federalism Within the Bimodal Federalism Framework

Theories of dual federalism posit that "the states and the federal government inhabit[] mutually exclusive spheres of power,"[7] while dynamic federalism "rejects any conception of federalism that separates federal and state authority under the dualist notion that the states need a sphere of authority protected from the influence of the federal government" and posits that "federal and state governments function as alternative centers of power and *any matter* is presumptively within the authority of both the federal and the state governments."[8] Most dynamic/dual federalism scholarship has arisen out of study of U.S. constitutional federalism, yet the theoretical underpinnings assessing the desireability of dual versus dynamic federal governance of natural resources are equally applicable to other federal systems. Ultimately, both dynamic and dual constitutional federalism interpretations are characterized by both normative claims about what should be the proper operation of federalism and descriptive claims about how federalism in fact operates.

Dynamic federalism theory calls into question previously held duel federalism-driven assumptions that "regulatory authority to address environmental ills should be allocated to one or the other level of government with minimal overlap."[9] Professor Engel has argued that:

> a static allocation of authority between the state and federal government is inconsistent with the process of policymaking in our federal system, in which multiple levels of government interact in the regulatory process. Absent constitutional changes that would lock in a specific allocation of authority, broad, overlapping authority between levels of government may be essential to prompting regulatory activity at the preferred level of government.[10]

Dynamic federalism recognizes the importance of multilevel allocations of regulatory authority in federal systems and "conceives the states and the federal government as alternative—not mutually exclusive—sources of regulatory authority."[11] Dynamic regulatory approaches are practically applied by, for example, crafting federal legislation that allows subnational governments flexibility to regulate *within* a "standards framework" provided by the federal government, such that, for example, "where national uniformity is desired, [the federal legislature] might allow for the development of a single standard by the states themselves, as opposed to the imposition of a single standard by the states themselves."[12] So an effective dynamic governance approach does not supplant authority at lower levels of government, but rather creates a system of supplemental governance at all levels whereby the federal government sets a target, limit, or other regulatory goal and allows subnational governments either the ability to take into account local considerations when designing mechanisms to achieve that target or limit, or the flexibility to design their own regulatory standards supplemental to federal regulations.[13] The synergies that a dynamic approach provides "can lead either, or both, parties to adopt policy positions significantly different from the positions they would have adopted had they been regulating in a vacuum,"[14] and "has important benefits in terms of developing quality, responsive regulation, and spreading regulatory innovations."[15] Despite these benefits, and as Professor Schapiro has noted regarding U.S. federalism, "the basic conception of federalism continues to be a system of independent national and state governments that must be protected from each other" and that "[d]ualist conceptions survive" in some regulatory areas.[16]

Whether regulatory subject matter is subject to dynamic or dual regulatory approaches is a complex question, as dynamism and dualism each have legal and political components. As a result, it is necessary to deconstruct exactly what this chapter means by describing "remnants of dual federalism" that impact natural resource governance. The terms dynamic and dual federalism are here used in the strict sense of *constitutional regulatory* dynamism or dualism, meaning that *either* all levels of government maintain recognized legal authority to directly and prescriptively regulate regarding a particular subject matter (dynamism) *or* rather there are separate spheres of constitutional authority between the federal and state governments within which they must directly and exclusively regulate on a particular subject matter (dualism). Constitutional dynamism/dualism is to be distinguished from political dynamism/dualism, the latter of which can exist for any subject matter notwithstanding constitutional questions of dynamism or dualism. In other words, political dynamism simply means that regardless of potential constitutional constraints, the federal and subnational governments are either constitutionally empowered to maintain inputs into resource management and each level politically acts on that authority, or the federal and subnational governments work out a political arrangement for allowing substantial governance inputs at all levels in the absence of constitutional empowerment. Political dualism, on the other hand, means that because of perceived constitutional constraints the federal and state governments choose to operate politically within separate spheres. This chapter does not explore the nuances of political dynamism or dualism, choosing to focus only on constitutional dynamism and dualism.

Consider some U.S. subject matter examples. In the U.S., the ESA, the two primary statutes aimed at hazardous waste regulation (the Comprehensive Environmental Response, Compensation, and Liability Act (CERCLA) and the Resource Conservation and Recovery Act (RCRA)), the CWA, and the Clean Air Act (CAA), just to name a few U.S. federal environmental statutes, demonstrate constitutional dynamism. Federal authority under each of these statutes has been constitutionally validated, allowing the federal government to prescriptively and directly regulate the resource at issue, at least to a substantial extent. Yet, for each of these subject matters, subnational governments are constitutionally empowered to prescriptively regulate with legislation above or in addition to federal minimum standards. For the most part, states can establish their own endangered species, waste, water, or air regulations, though some actions—mobile sources under the CAA, as just one example—may be preempted by the federal government (an indication that constitutional dualism can run both ways, with the federal government sometimes resisting potentially efficacious subnational regulatory inputs). So, for example, some states maintain wetland protection statutes above and beyond the CWA's section 404 wetland program. Ultimately, regulation of endangered species, waste, water, and air regulation is constitutionally dynamic across scales of government in the U.S.

In other regulatory subject matters, however, U.S. subnational governments are left nearly exclusive constitutional authority. Such is the case with subnational forests and direct land use planning. While there are federal statutes aimed at these areas, these statutes do not even seek to establish constitutional dynamism because they are non-prescriptive and exceedingly limited in scope. Examples include the Coastal Zone Management Act (CZMA) and the Forest Legacy Program (FLP). These statutes seek to merely incentivize certain prescriptive inputs or management actions of subnational governments regarding coastal land use and forest resources. This is not to say that the statutes provide no benefit, or that prescriptive regulation is the only means of achieving resource management gains. By no means is that the case, as a variety of incentive-based, voluntary programs can have significant positive resource management effects. But, as is the common refrain in this book, these statutes provide no means of federal authority in the event that subnational government rationality remains unchecked. The voluntary, incentive-based nature of these statutes seems to be a direct result of remnant notions of constitutional dualism. The federal government, perceiving constitutional federalism constraints for any type of prescriptive regulatory inputs, created programs that the states or private property owners can opt into on a voluntary basis, thus skirting any constitutional federalism constraints. These remnants remain either because jurisprudence has not yet affirmed the validity of dynamic regulatory approaches in those areas or because Congress perceives, based upon either genuine constitutional interpretation or rather political and ideological predisposition, that legal constraints exist and therefore it politically refuses to act. A result of political inaction, of course, is that courts do not have an opportunity to assess the validity of dynamic regulatory approaches.

Though we are talking about constitutional dualism here, an important political element remains. Direct land use planning and subnational forest management (considered, as you recall, a subset of direct land use planning generally in the U.S.) fall into the constitutionally dual category because it is difficult to determine whether the constitutional status of those subject areas is solidly dual based on the jurisprudence and constitutional interpretation (which in turn informs political decisions to treat them as such) or rather whether policymakers have simply politically chosen to leave those areas within the dualist domain and therefore do not test the constitutional waters to see if that legal perception is correct. So legal perception drives political reality and vice versa in these areas—an intellectual endeavor that can be quite like pondering the grandfather paradox of time travel.

Ultimately, federalism theory may be thought of as increasingly integrating principles of dynamic federalism in combination with as of yet unaddressed principles of dual federalism in some federal nations. This integrated view of federalism constitutes "Bimodal Federalism," which more accurately and holistically describes how federalism may operate in the context of present day constitutional scholarly debates and jurisprudence. The word "bimodal" simply means "having or providing two modes, methods, [or] systems"[17]—on some subject matters federalism is dynamic, and on others it is dual.

Scholars arguing for constitutional dynamic federalism argue that federalism should not be judicially or politically protected.[18] Though these scholars question whether courts have the "ability to police the contours of federalism" under doctrines like the U.S. Commerce Clause,[19] remnants of dual federalism demonstrate that judicial protections remain in place and courts will continue to be in "the business of distinguishing between regulatory matters that are left to the states and those that fall within [a legislature's] jurisdictional reach."[20] Other federal nations, like Canada, need not look to judicial interpretation for dualist protections, as the text of their Constitution explicitly establishes dual federalism over certain resources (discussed in Chapters 7 and 8).

This state of affairs has stark implications for natural capital governance in federal systems where dual remnants remain in place. Notions of dualism effectively facilitate the legally entrenched commons problem addressed by this book. In the context of Hardin's metaphor, dual federalism would be similar to the owner of a pasture having no authority to set rules of resource appropriation by the 50 herders who may enter his pasture and over-exploit the resource with tragic consequences. Or, in the preemption context, perhaps the herders would like to set their own rules for sustainable resource appropriation, but the owner of the pasture prohibits them from doing so and does not simultaneously establish any rules of his or her own for sustainable resource appropriation. This is the metaphorical equivalent to dual federalism in federal systems of government.

To adequately manage dynamic resources in federal systems and avoid commons resource tragedies, there should be as much overlap as possible in jurisdictional regulatory authority; and to the extent one level of government is not adequately addressing these subject areas, other levels of government should be able to fill the void.[21] Yet for levels of government to begin to do so, legal perception must change so that political reality can follow in nations like the U.S. For legal perception to change, strong arguments must be made that certain forms of prescriptive regulation of dynamic resources pass constitutional muster. In nations like Canada, it is not legal perception but rather legal reality that must be adjusted to provide the greatest chance of avoiding commons tragedies for certain resources like subnational forests, given the explicit text of the Canadian Constitution.

If these realities and perceptions can be shifted, legislative mechanisms for managing dynamic resources across levels of governance will move beyond being normatively desirable, and will also be constitutionally permissible in areas where currently dualistic notions remain. Such a foundation can serve as a reference point for legislators seeking to implement effective solutions without constitutional complication and for courts adjudicating conflicts over allocation of regulatory authority. As a result, the *balance* of federal and subnational inputs may be struck in a more dynamic way—a balance that may call for greater federal inputs in circumstances where subnational governments fail to engage in effective natural capital management or for less federal interference in circumstances where subnational governments may provide better solutions than does the federal government. The next section highlights two key subject areas where dynamic resources remain subject to dual federalist management inputs within certain federal systems—a duality that exacerbates some of the most pressing commons dilemmas of our time.

Contributing to Commons Dilemmas: Coastal Land Loss and Subnational Forest Management as Remnants of Dual Federalism

Coastal Land Loss in the United States

In the U.S., over half the population lives within the 17 percent of land that is coastal. While population density nationally is 98 persons per square mile, coastal counties average 300 persons per square mile.[22] The U.S. coastal zone also contains a concentrated amount of the nation's economic wealth and resources, and the level and growth rate of per capita income has a strong positive correlation with coastal proximity.[23]

The very things that make the coastal zone important—high concentrations of human and economic capital—also threaten it. Three primary phenomena have converged in the coastal zone to give rise to coastal land loss—population growth, vanishing wetlands due to economic development, and rising sea levels. These phenomena are so inextricably entwined that it is difficult to discuss them in isolation. Increased populations in the coastal zone have led to commercial, industrial, and residential development that has replaced coastal natural capital that would otherwise act as a buffer against sea-level rise and storm surge from hurricane or other flood events, protect coastal water quality, and provide habitat for coastal species, among other services. These population pressures and accompanying economic growth have, in turn, increased the need to protect human-made capital in the coastal zone. As a result, society has constructed evermore dams, levees, sea walls, and other structures that have starved the coast of sediment, replaced wetlands, and caused subsidence that accelerates sea-level rise.

Each of these factors makes clear that though land use planning has traditionally been the subject of state and local government constitutional regulatory authority, dynamic changes in the coastal zone are shifting the risks of development from individual state and local governments to neighboring states and the nation as a whole. Climate change is perhaps the most dynamic driver of all, as the massive amount of carbon released into the atmosphere over the last two centuries is far out of proportion with the natural, relatively static baseline (over geologic timescales).

Populations in the coastal zone are increasing faster than ever. While absolute population numbers in the coastal zone are disproportionate to total U.S. population, so too is *rate* of population growth. Between 1980 and 2003 coastal population increased by 33 million,[24] accounting for nearly half of the U.S.'s total population growth, but only within 17 percent of its land mass.[25] Coastal population is projected to increase by another 27 million by 2017, accounting for *more than half* of the nation's total population increase.[26] This increased *rate* of population growth in coastal counties compared to the rest of the country creates a dramatic increase in population density along the coast, which, combined with the fast growing coastal economy,[27] increases the rate of development in the coastal zone.[28]

Indeed, the rate of population growth and accumulation of wealth in the coastal zone reinforce a feedback loop whereby development pressures increase at rates that greatly *outpace* already exponential population growth. Coastal counties in the U.S. are losing nearly 2,000 acres of farmland a day to urbanization and other development,[29] and "[s]ome large coastal metropolitan areas are consuming land ten times as fast as they are adding new residents."[30] In 1982, 10 percent of coastal watersheds were developed, rising to 14 percent in 1997, and without a change of course more than 25 percent of the U.S.'s coastal watersheds will be developed by 2025. In 1997 the amount of developed coastal acreage was 14 percent, and without a change of pace more than one-quarter of coastal acreage will be developed by 2025.[31] In fact, "[b]y most measures, human impacts to coastal ecosystems have grown faster than the rate of population growth. So, although population statistics paint an alarming picture for coastal management, they actually understate the magnitude of the challenge."[32] Between 1982 and 1997 developed land in the

U.S. increased by 25 million acres (34 percent), which "means that more than one-fourth of all of the land converted from rural to urban and suburban uses since European settlement occurred in only 15 years."[33] While population growth was 15 percent during this time period, the amount of developed land grew by 34 percent, meaning land consumption occurred at a rate more than twice the rate of population growth. Furthermore, "the mismatch between land development and population growth is widening. Between 1982 and 1992, land was developed at 1.8 times the rate of population growth. During the period between 1992 and 1997, that multiple had grown to 2.5."[34] Ultimately, stacking exponential land consumption on top of already exponential population growth causes coastal lands and the natural systems they provide to be appropriated at astonishing rates. As described by the Pew Oceans Commission,

> [b]etween 2000 and 2025, the U.S. population is projected to grow by 22 percent. If the relationship between land use and population in the last decade continues, there will be 68 million more acres of developed land in the contiguous U.S. than there are today ... This newly developed acreage—equivalent to the land area of Wyoming—will almost match the amount of land developed from the founding of the country until 1983.[35]

In other words, "[i]f developed land were expanding at the same rate as population, coastal zone management would be a formidable task. With development vastly outstripping even the relatively high rate of population growth, the challenge is considerably greater."[36]

The impacts of this development on coastal natural capital has been profound. Over the last century, over half of all wetlands in North America have been developed.[37] The loss of wetland ecosystem services "make urban settlements more prone to disaster, amplifying the risks of climate change."[38] Wetlands not only physically maintain coastal land, but also maintain its functionality. Wetlands provide a buffer system protecting against storm surge caused by hurricanes and other events; dissipate and absorb flood waters and stormwater runoff, thus protecting local communities and saving municipalities flood control expenditures; anchor and preserve coastal lands by dispersing coast-building sediment and forestalling coastal erosion; provide water filtration services that clean coastal waters; act as a carbon sink helping regulate climate; and provide habitat for coastal species, among a variety of other services.

Vanishing wetlands are directly tied to rising sea levels, increased populations, and development in the coastal zone. As described by scholars,

> [i]n many parts of the world, developers have drained wetlands ... removing a buffer against tidal floods. Particularly in delta regions, land compaction, subsidence due to groundwater withdrawal and reductions in the rate of sediment deposition (due to water regulation) can lead, in effect,

to sea-level rise, increasing flood risk (as well as creating various other problems).[39]

Take the U.S. state of Louisiana, for example, which is losing 6,600 acres of coastal wetlands per year.[40] Some of this loss is naturally occurring, but "the real culprits are human-made" and include commercial and residential development, levees, navigational channels, and oil-and-gas infrastructure that have interfered with 7,000 years of sediment deposition from the Mississippi River that counterbalanced sea-level rise in large degree.[41] As a result of land subsidence, Louisiana is facing the highest level of relative sea-level rise in the world.[42] Thus Louisiana engages in a vicious cycle whereby even more man-made flood control devices must be constructed and maintained to protect human and economic capital, requiring ever increasing levee height and pump capacity as "land continues to sink and the sea level rises."[43] As noted by scholars, the "[u]nintended consequences of flood protection measures and individual public work projects have increased risks to natural resources and human settlements resulting in a more dangerous place to live and work."[44]

Ultimately, human development activities in coastal Louisiana, facilitated by poor land use planning of the kind described in the Introduction to Chapter 3, have "accelerate[d] coastal land loss by reducing the natural flow of the [Mississippi] [R]iver's freshwater and sediment to wetland areas, where the lost land would then naturally be replenished."[45] Other states face a similarly staggering amount of coastal wetland loss. For example, in only the last 15 years Florida has lost 5,600 acres a year to urban development, or 84,000 acres total.[46] The Chesapeake Bay has lost nearly half of its coastal marshes while more than 91 percent of California's coastal wetlands have been lost.[47] Just between 1998 and 2004, coastal watersheds of the Atlantic Ocean, Great Lakes, and Gulf of Mexico lost about 59,000 acres per year, or 354,000 acres total.[48]

Despite the increasing rate of destruction of coastal wetlands, governments at all levels have largely failed to formulate robust plans for curbing their destruction, restoring them, or designing policies to encourage a shift in development activities further inland. It is not clear that in the face of sea-level rise restoration of wetlands is a surefire, long-term answer to addressing coastal land loss. What is clear is that a history of poor development planning in the coastal zone has contributed to human and economic costs associated with disasters like Hurricane Katrina in 2005. Ultimately, it will fall upon land use planners to adjust policies to account for dynamic shifts in important resources like coastal wetlands and their nexus with the ocean. Though the costs of taking action will be great, the economic costs of *not* curbing wetland destruction as an initial matter, guiding current and future development away from at-risk coastal lands, or restoring wetlands, will only increase, as hurricanes are expected to become both more frequent and more intense as climate change contributes to warmer oceans and rising sea levels.[49]

Rising sea levels is perhaps the most dynamic change in coastal zone requiring a broader perspective than simply individual state regulatory inputs.

It is also the most obvious threat to coastal lands, ultimately requiring coastal land loss mitigation or adaptation policies.[50] Scholars have described climate change, the source of more rapid sea-level rise in the recent past and in the future, as nothing more than "a slow-moving disaster."[51] Sea level rose 0.17 meters over the past century, a rate of roughly 1.7 mm/year, but satellite imagery demonstrates that the rate accelerated to 3.1 mm/year between 1993 and 2003.[52] This increased rate corresponds with increases in atmospheric concentrations of greenhouse gases (GHG) and temperatures over the same time period, and the future impact of a changing climate on sea levels is highly uncertain. One recent report found that "[p]rojections of sea-level rise for the twenty-first century vary widely, ranging from several centimeters to more than a meter."[53] Even these estimates may be revised upward given the continued rise in global temperatures and the rapid loss of Arctic and Antarctic ice sheets. Ultimately, "warming and sea-level rise will continue for more than a millennium, even if carbon dioxide concentrations are stabilized, due to the long time required to remove this gas from the atmosphere."[54] This dire warning has critical implications for the coastal zone, because "rising sea levels ... will ensure increased damage along increasingly developed shorelines,"[55] as rising seas "inundate low areas and increase flooding, coastal erosion, wetlands loss, and saltwater intrusion into estuaries and freshwater aquifers."[56] Furthermore, as indicated earlier, rising sea levels "interact with tides and storms to create more destructive impacts, as extreme high water levels occur with more frequency."[57]

The most salient question in the coastal zone over the coming decades is whether in the absence of direct federal mandates subnational governments will make the difficult choices necessary to shift development out of areas at high risk of loss and unlikely to be saved even in the face of billions spent on restoration and human engineering projects, or to preserve currently undeveloped green spaces further inland to act as a buffer between future settlements near newly established coastlines and rising seas. Economic incentives are actually aligned in the opposite direction, and the failure of subnational governments to responsibly carry out their land use regulatory role in the coastal zone in the past is the exact reason many areas face such a dire situation today. The societal inertia of our coastal zone culture creates more problems, since sea levels rising at exponential rates (over geologic time scales) will meet head-on with a rush of humans heading at exponential rates right into the face of the disaster—an ironic scenario that demonstrates the circular nature of human psychology related to commons resource dilemmas. Humans exacerbate climate change through carbon emissions, and as a result sea levels rise; then humans move in disproportionate numbers into areas likely to be inundated by rising sea levels; then society expects governmental bodies to alleviate their difficulties *after* disaster strikes, through the creation of even more human-made capital or other assistance.

Despite sea-level rise's methodical nature—and perhaps *because* of it—it will have potentially the most substantial interjurisdictional, nationwide impacts of all the threats to the coastal zone. These impacts will compound other disasters like hurricanes and flood events to place increasing pressure on the human-built coastal environment and exponentially increasing populations that live there—especially in the absence of a turn toward innovative and responsible coastal land use planning.

Ultimately, dynamic changes in the coastal zone increase both the importance of, and difficulty in designing, land use policies. In particular, exponential rates of population growth, economic development, and wealth accumulation complicate climate change adaptation policies, and in particular policies aimed at shifting societal development away from areas likely to be lost by rising sea levels or preserving natural capital to act as a buffer zone between society and increasing disaster threats along the coast. If subnational governments refuse to exercise their constitutional authority to direct climate change-related land use planning adaptation policies, then an important question becomes not only should the federal government do so, but can they? The federal government will, after all, increasingly be on the hook for disaster relief when disaster strikes. In addition, the amount of investment needed to implement land use policies will continue to rise since there are more people to protect or move away from encroaching seas, more wealth and investment in the form of development, jobs, and infrastructure to either protect or forestall to preserve needed natural buffer zones, diminishing functionality of natural capital and associated ecosystem services, and increased economic and social inertia that make it difficult to slow down coastal zone growth in the first instance, much less steer already anchored economic and social systems further inland.

It is true that the federal government has work to do of its own in adjusting policies to forestall these problems, such as making drastic changes to the National Flood Insurance Program, which currently encourages development of floodplains and the coastal zone by subsidizing insurance rates in those high-risk areas. Even so, the federal government needs to be able to act within the bounds of constitutionally validated authority if enough political will is ultimately garnered to implement land use-related climate adaptation policies in the coastal zone. A dual federalism approach does not allow the federal government to intervene and shift development patterns in the coastal zone, or set development density requirements, or preserve wetlands in a robust manner,[58] or set growth boundaries or limit lines around major metropolitan areas, or establish any kind of minimum land use planning standards that subnational governments are free to supplement any way they wish.

Congress's only major contemplation of becoming involved in land use planning was the National Land Use Policy Act (NLUPA), which was proposed in 1970 but was never passed. The failure of Congress to pass the NLUPA during the most active time of federal environmental regulatory expansion in history, and the voluntary, bilateral nature of the only federal statute aimed at influencing direct land use planning, the CZMA, demonstrates the dual federalist remnants that remain in the area of land use planning. Indeed, though the CZMA "recognized a national interest in effective coastal management, Congress also recognized that the type of land use planning and management required was traditionally within the domain of state and local governments."[59] Congress has consistently demonstrated a concern over impeding on state constitutional sovereignty over land use by including important carve-outs within other major federal statutes, like the CWA.[60] Given the increasing importance of aggregated land use policies in the coastal zone, a new approach to federalism is needed so that dynamic coastal resources will no longer outpace a constitutional shift to dynamic regulatory responses. In this way, the resultant changing legal perceptions can bring about a new political reality for land use planning along the coast, changing course from the tragic herder mentality of coastal commoners over the last few decades.

Subnational Forests in the U.S. and Canada

Though forests may have historically been thought of as the quintessential local resource, being anchored to the land of individual property owners, the national and global importance of local forests is becoming ever more apparent in light of climate change. Nearly 20 percent of yearly global carbon emissions over the last few decades has resulted from forest loss and degradation, which is more than that emitted by the global transportation sector each year.[61] As a result, mechanisms to protect forests globally have been placed on the agenda of both future international climate negotiations and negotiations related to establishing a global sustainable forest management regime.[62] Not only does forest destruction constitute a substantial *source* of atmospheric carbon, but another recent U.S. Forest Service report found that one-third of global carbon emissions is absorbed by forests each year, making forests the most significant terrestrial carbon *sink* on the planet.[63] As a result, forest preservation has a multiplied effect on greenhouse gas regulation, and, correspondingly, forest destruction doubly amplifies concentrations of carbon in the atmosphere since it constitutes both a source of carbon and the loss of a significant carbon sink.

In perhaps one of the best examples of dual federalism in action, both U.S. and Canadian regulatory authority over forest management is currently divided between federal and state/provincial governments—epitomizing both constitutional and political dualism. In the U.S. the federal government maintains regulatory authority over the approximately 35 percent of forests it owns. State governments are responsible for regulating the nearly 65 percent of forests owned by private individuals (60 percent) and subnational governments (5 percent),[64] with scholars recognizing that "[u]nder the US Constitution, the federal government has limited authority and responsibility; all other powers are reserved for the states. Forestland management and use was one such reserved power."[65] While U.S. federal government forest policies are quite consistent on the 35 percent of forestland it owns, and Canadian provincial forest policies are equally consistent and stringent, U.S. state forest policies are all over the board. Some U.S. states maintain stringent basic forest management standards, and others maintain none at all. Despite these discrepancies the U.S. federal government has never before attempted direct regulation of subnational forest management, even though it does maintain statutes that sometimes will have tangential effects on forest management activities, like the CWA and ESA. Meanwhile, subnational forest management discrepancies have stark ramifications for not only domestic forest resources, but for the global battle against climate change—especially if the U.S. sought to establish a national policy to harness domestic forests as carbon sinks.

In the first comprehensive study of its kind, Constance L. McDermott et al. provided a framework for assessing and comparing the domestic forest policies of governments around the globe,[66] identifying four "styles" of forest policy regulation. The first is "procedural voluntary," which, as the name suggests, encourages the voluntary development of forest management processes or plans, but does not require such plans to be developed. These are contrasted with "procedural mandatory" rules, which require the development of forest management plans or procedures, much as the National Environmental Policy Act (NEPA) requires environmental assessment reports for agency projects. Third are "substantive voluntary" policies, where specific forest practice guidelines exist, but they are not binding on forest managers. Finally "substantive prescriptive" rules "refer[] to mandatory, on-the-ground requirements or restrictions, such as a rule that no timber harvest may occur within x metres of a river of y width."[67] Substantive prescriptive rules are, of course, enforceable at law.

McDermott et al. assessed domestic forest governance policies to determine which of these "styles" of forest policy regulation different governments maintain regarding five types of environmental protection for forests. For each type of protection, the authors assigned an "indicator" used to classify the policy approach as one of the above "styles" of regulation. The types of protection and associated indicators are as follows:

1 Protection of riparian zones in forested watersheds (*indicator*: riparian streamside buffer zone rules);
2 Protection from environmental damage caused by roads (*indicator*: rules for culvert size at stream crossings and road decommissioning);
3 Protection from clear-cutting damage (*indicator*: clear-cut size limits or other relevant cutting rules);
4 Reforestation (*indicator*: requirements for reforestation, including specified time frames and stocking levels);
5 Limitations on annual allowable cut (*indicator*: cut limits based on sustained yield).[68]

The five forest policy standards assessed by McDermott et al. are the most fundamental of forest management and silvicultural standards. In addition to these standards, a variety of additional standards can build upon this baseline to ensure that forests are managed for the full suite of services they provide. The most holistic forest management standards do not merely seek to maximize timber harvest, but may also include the protection of biodiversity, species habitat, ecosystems, genetic resources, and recreational and cultural values, as well as the provision of water purification, flood prevention, and air quality regulation services.[69] The five metrics used by McDermott et al., however, are fundamental and reflect a baseline upon which good silvicultural practices may build and expand.

Protecting riparian zones in forested watersheds prevents erosion that might otherwise take timberland out of production, prevents siltation of waterways that can lead to eutrophication, provides wildlife corridors, regulates water temperatures, protects aquatic habitat, and provides a variety of other benefits.[70] Road building is "one of the 'main causes [of] the environmental degradation of most forest regions.'"[71] Roads degrade forests because they provide greater access for resource extraction (or over-extraction), cause erosion that damages watersheds, and fragment forested landscapes and habitat. As a result, decommissioning roads or limiting their location or extent is an important sustainable forest management objective. Clear-cutting practices can also be highly damaging to the environment and are "perhaps the most controversial forest harvesting practice[s]"—criticized by ecologists, civil society, and forest market scholars alike.[72] Clear-cutting is effectively a complete removal and replacement of the forest. Though subsequent reforestation normally occurs, the removal of so much stored carbon, as well as the carbon sequestering potential of larger trees, has serious consequences for regulating GHGs—not to mention the complete destruction of a variety of other ecological processes and habitats.[73] Finally, reforestation and annual allowable cut policies are aimed at ensuring that no more of the resource is being harvested than is sustainable.[74]

As can be seen in the McDermott et al. Table 10.7 (Figure 5.1), "Summary of jurisdictional approaches to all five forest practice criteria",[75] there are dramatic differences between the "styles" of riparian buffer zone, road, clear-cut, reforestation, and annual allowable cut forest policies applied by the Canadian provinces and those applied by the U.S. states. The chart reflects the styles of "mandatory substantive"[76] in black, "mandatory procedural" in gray, and where the two types of mandatory are both used in some capacity, the chart depicts "mandatory mixed" in grid form. Both styles of voluntary are represented by horizontal lines, while the "no policy" category is blank (white). Different governments are ranked based on an average of the "style" utilized for each of the five indicators, with mandatory approaches landing governments nearer to "10" on the scale (with mandatory substantive the most stringent) and voluntary or no policy landing governments nearer to "0."

The Canadian provinces of Alberta, British Columbia, and New Brunswick, the U.S. state of California, and the U.S. Forest Service (for federally owned forests) each score a "9" on the scale, maintaining very high forest policy

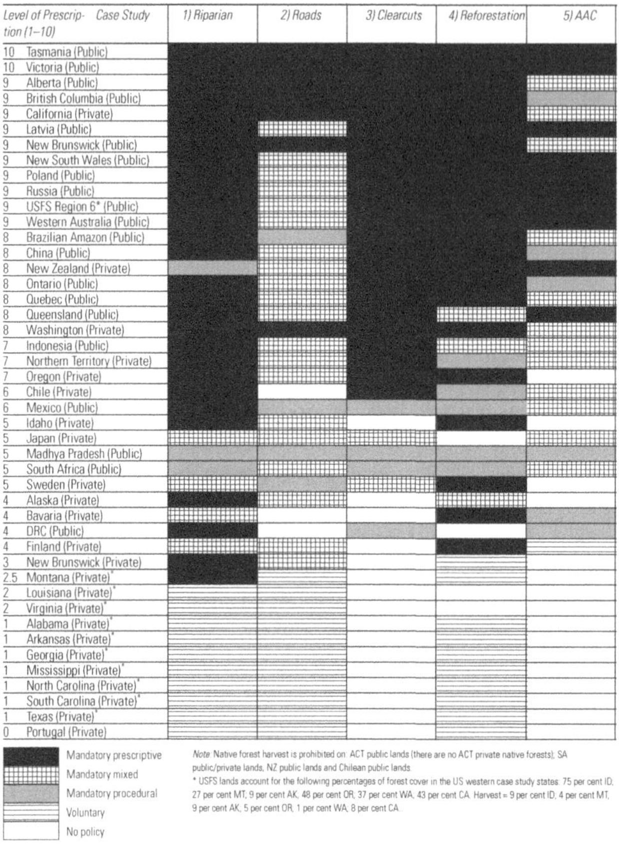

Figure 5.1 McDermott et al. Table 10.7, "Summary of jurisdictional approaches to all five forest practice criteria"

standards.[77] The Canadian provinces of Ontario and Quebec and the U.S. state of Washington score a high "8" on the scale. The U.S. state of Oregon scores a "7" while Idaho scores a "5," and Alaska scores a "4." Lowest on the scale are the states of Montana with a "2.5," Louisiana and Virginia with a "2," and the rest of the southeastern United States—Alabama, Arkansas, Georgia, Mississippi, North Carolina, South Carolina, and Texas with a score of "1." To put the southeastern U.S. states' forest policy stringency in perspective, consider that developing countries average a "6.7" on the scale while nine southeastern U.S. states average a "1.2," maintaining entirely voluntary "guidelines" or no standards at all.[78]

The implications of these lax standards in the southeastern United States for both domestic forest health and global climate change mitigation are profound, providing yet another example about how dynamic changes in our understanding of the nature of a resource (here, a carbon sink needed to combat climate change) demonstrates a need to move beyond dualist notions of federalism in the case of subnational forest regulation.

These profound implications are perhaps best evidenced by the recent U.S. Forest Service's Southern Forests Futures Project Summary Report (Futures Report).[79] The Futures Report highlighted in dramatic fashion the pressure that southeastern U.S. forests will face in the coming decades. The project focused on four factors that would "define the South's future forests,"[80] and include: population growth, climate change, timber markets, and invasive species.[81] Urban development, in particular, is "forecasted to result in forest losses, increased carbon emissions, and stress to other forest resources,"[82] including degradation of a variety of water ecosystem services such as flood control and water filtration—even to the point of threatening public health.[83] Population pressures in the southeast would "result[] in declines in forest cover, increases in demand for ecosystem service[s], and restrictions that complicate the ability to manage forests for the full spectrum of uses."[84] Importantly, both population and economic growth have increased at higher rates in the southeast than anywhere else in the United States, "with the resulting urbanization steadily consuming forests and other rural lands."[85] The Futures Report projected that 30–43 million acres of southern land will succumb to urban development by 2060, while total forest losses could be as high as 23 million acres, or approximately 13 percent of all forestland in the south. This amount of deforestation is roughly equivalent to cutting down all the forests in the states of Georgia or Alabama. The negative repercussions of these projections go beyond the environment, as the important forest industry in the south could also be damaged. The timber production sector in the south contributed more than one million jobs and 51 billion dollars in employee compensation in 2009. In fact, "southern forests are the most intensively managed forests in the U.S."[86] A majority of the United States' lumber is harvested from southern forests, and "since 1986, if the South were compared with any other country, none would produce more timber than this one region of the United States."[87]

Forest losses due to rapid urbanization in the south also profoundly and negatively impact the carbon storage capacity of southern forests. The amount of carbon sequestered in southern forests and their soils is projected to reach a maximum in 2020,[88] and then decline by as much as 5 percent by 2060.[89] Such a decline in carbon storage capacity "would be a challenge for carbon mitigation policies, presenting a dynamic baseline where a first order policy objective would be to *stabilize* rather than expand forest carbon stocks."[90] So even if forest management-driven climate change mitigation policies were enacted by southeastern states, southeastern forests would not only be unable to sequester the additional amounts of carbon needed to fight climate change, but it would be exceedingly difficult to prevent forest carbon stocks from dropping even further and from becoming an even greater source of atmospheric carbon. Furthermore, given the lack of political will to formulate important and fundamental forest management standards in the southeast, it is hard to imagine prescriptive climate mitigation policies even being put into place by southeastern states in the near future. Both the implementation and success of such policies would be undermined because countervailing land use policies promoting and facilitating rapid urbanization are also widespread.

Given the southeastern United States' governance philosophy regarding forests and land use and the high amount of forests privately owned in the southeast, a more dynamic regulatory approach for subnational forest management is needed, whereby the national government maintains constitutional authority to coordinate subnational forest policy with the implementation of basic forest management standards. In the absence of a dramatic shift in governance culture in the southeast, and a voluntary adoption of stronger forest policies by individual states, deforestation of the region will ensue unabated in the absence of a national policy. Alabama's position on voluntary "best management practices" is emblematic of this governance philosophy.[91] The Alabama Forestry Commission declares that it is the "lead agency for forestry in Alabama" but that it is "not an environmental regulatory or enforcement agency" and that it "[avoids] environmental problems through voluntary application of preventative techniques."[92] Yet, as evidenced by recent deforestation and the Forest Report's projected loss of up to 13 percent of the region's forests over the next 50 years, when given the choice between preserving a forest, or managing it for the full range of ecological values, and cutting it down in the name of economic development and urbanization, voluntary choices often do not lead to "preventative techniques" that benefit forests.[93] Even so, most southeastern state administrative agencies operate similarly, as "[t]he implementation of BMPs [best management practices] … generally involves agencies not directly responsible for environmental regulation."[94]

Constitutionally dual federalist forest policy is nothing unique to the United States. Canada's federal government is even more restricted than the U.S. federal government in the area of subnational forest management policy. Canada's provinces actually own 77 percent of the nation's vast forest resources, and also maintain constitutional authority to directly regulate the 7 percent of forests in private ownership.[95] Canada's Constitution actually contains *explicit* provisions relegating forest policy on non-federally owned forests exclusively to the provinces. This has made it virtually impossible for the Canadian federal government to get any foothold whatsoever over subnational forest policy. Even so, the most fundamental of subnational forest policies, as described by McDermott et al., remain fairly robust because of provincial ownership of forests and the fact that the provinces are negotiating with a handful of industry players for the management of forests in what has been described as "quasi-corporatist" negotiations, described in further detail in Chapter 8.

Contrast the situation in Canada with that in the southeastern U.S., where there is not a handful of primary industrial players negotiating with the government regarding the extraction of the government's own resources, but rather forest industries and a vast array of non-industrial private forest owners are managing privately owned forestlands, largely absent of inputs from governments hesitant to place restrictions on private property rights. Eighty-six percent of southern forests are privately owned. While 60 percent of privately owned forests are 100 acres or more, 59 percent of all private forest owners own fewer than nine acres of forestland[96] and family forest holdings in the region average only 29 acres in size.

As a result, a large number of individuals may choose to act "rationally" regarding the appropriation of forest resources, maximizing personal gain to the detriment of the subnational, national, and global resource base—either through poor forest management practices or through replacement of forest resources with human-made capital in the form of urbanization. The high number of private property owners in the southeast correlates strongly with the level of forest policy stringency adopted by the respective subnational governments. In the western U.S., where the proportion of public forests are far greater, forest policy is far more stringent. So, for example, California, Washington, Oregon, Idaho, and Alaska maintain an average 67 percent of forests in public ownership[97] and in turn maintain far more stringent forest policy standards for both public and private forests (a "6.7" average) than do states in the southeastern United States (a "1.2" average) and its 86 percent of privately owned forests.[98] McDermott et al. call this a forest policy spillover effect, where proximity to public forests, which tend to be managed more stringently, influences private forest management policy. It seems that the United States Forest Service's "9" score on the forest policy ranking has spilled over into western forest policy in a way not seen in the southeast. This comes as no real surprise considering that 92 percent of federally owned land is located in the western United States, contrasted with less than 5 percent in the south.[99] Southeastern states simply do not maintain the critical mass of publicly owned forests that would help facilitate a spillover effect, as again, 86 percent of forests are privately owned. Though other factors, such as overall governance culture and the limited administrative capacity of southeastern governments, may also contribute to the region's lax standards, it seems that the lack of a spillover effect further exacerbates continuation of the status quo.

Ultimately, southeastern states' exercise of their discretion on forest policy allows them to avoid the establishment of basic, fundamental forest management standards, much less craft standards meant to curb the loss of 13 percent of southeastern forests over the next 50 years, thus setting the stage for a tragedy of the commons in the forest policy arena, as state governments maximize their own citizens' use of forest resources in their jurisdictions to the detriment of a forest base defined more broadly by national boundaries and that takes into account the value of forests across and beyond subnational boundaries.

Conclusion

In order to adequately address the most pressing commons issues of our time, the bimodal federalism found in certain federal systems will need to be better understood. To be able to keep pace with dynamic shifts in the distribution of and need for certain resources, a more dynamic regulatory response will be needed in federal systems. Once dynamism in federal regulatory responses is achieved, then federal systems of government will be able to most effectively engage in not only domestic commons resource management issues, but also global resource management, the subject of Part IV of this book.

Notes

1 The material constituting significant portions of this chapter originated in Blake Hudson, Coastal Land Loss and the Mitigation-Adaptation Dilemma: Between Scylla and Charybdis, 73 *La. L. Rev.* 31 (2012) and Blake Hudson, Reconstituting Land Use Federalism to Address Transitory and Perpetual Disasters: The Bimodal Federalism Framework, 2011 *BYU L. Rev.* 1991 (2011).
2 Elinor Ostrom, *Understanding Institutional Diversity* 258 (2005).
3 See id.
4 Hudson, supra note 1.
5 David N. Wear and John G. Greis, *U.S. Forest Serv., The Southern Forest Futures Project: Summary Report* 26–31, 35 (2011), available at http://www.srs.fs.usda.gov/futures/reports/draft/summary_report.pdf.
6 Henry N. Butler and Jonathan R. Macey, Externalities and The Matching Principle: The Case For Reallocating Environmental Regulatory Authority, 14 *Yale L. & Pol'y Rev.* 23 (1996).
7 Kirsten H. Engel, Harnessing the Benefits of Dynamic Federalism in Environmental Law, 56 *Emory L.J.* 159, 175 (2006).
8 Id. at 176 (emphasis added).
9 Engel, supra note 7, at 161.
10 Id.
11 Id. at 162.
12 Id. This model echoes Charles Perrow's call for "[f]ederal and state governments [to] establish minimum standards, which states or localities can exceed." Charles Perrow, *The Next Catastrophe: Reducing Our Vulnerabilities to Natural, Industrial, and Terrorist Disasters* 36 (2007). In other words, the goal is to establish floors rather than ceilings of environmental and land-use standards.
13 Indeed, "overlapping jurisdiction may be pivotal to encouraging the more appropriate level of government to respond to a given problem." Engel, supra note 7, at 177.
14 Id. at 171.
15 Id. at 173.
16 Robert A. Schapiro, Toward a Theory of Interactive Federalism, 91 *Iowa L. Rev.* 243, 246 (2005).
17 Definition of "bimodal," *Dictionary.com,* http://dictionary.reference.com/browse/bimodal.
18 Schapiro, supra note 16, at 278–80.
19 Engel, supra note 7, at 174.
20 Id. at 183.
21 As Professor Engel has noted, there is "danger [in] charging any one level of government with environmental protection and closing the door to the policy-making efforts of other levels of government." Id. at 181.
22 Kristen M. Crossett et al., Nat'l Oceanic & Atmospheric Admin., *Population Trends Along The Coastal United States: 1980–2008* 6–7 (2004).
23 Jordon Rappaport and Jeffrey D. Sachs, The United States as a Coastal Nation, 8 *J. of Econ. Growth* 5 (2003).
24 Crossett et al., supra note 22, at 1.

25 See United States Census Bureau, Population Estimates, available at http://www.census.gov/popest/data/historical/index.html.
26 Dana Beach, Pew Oceans Comm'n, *Coastal Sprawl: The Effects Of Urban Design On Aquatic Ecosystems In The United States* ii (2002), available at http://www.pewtrusts.org/uploadedFiles/wwwpewtrustsorg/Reports/Protecting_ocean_life/env_pew_oceans_sprawl.pdf.
27 The median household income of coastal counties is approximately 17 percent higher than noncoastal counties. Crossett, supra note 22, at 12.
28 Id. at 1.
29 Crossett et al., supra note 22, at 16.
30 Beach, supra note 26, at ii.
31 Id. at 5.
32 Id. at 2.
33 Id. at 3.
34 Id. at 4.
35 Id.
36 Id. at 5.
37 David Moreno-Mateos et al., Structural and Functional Loss in Restored Wetland Ecosystems, 10 *PLoS Biology* 1 (2012), available at http://www.plosbiology.org/article/info%3Adoi%2F10.1371%2Fjournal.pbio. 1001247.
38 Gordon McGranahan et al., The Rising Tide: Assessing the Risks of Climate Change and Human Settlements in Low Elevation Coastal Zones, 19 *Env't & Urbanization* 17, 18 (2007), available at http://sedac.ciesin.columbia.edu/gpw/docs/McGranahan2007.pdf. Other resources, such as coastal forests and coral reefs, are similarly imperiled. Roughly one-third of coastal mangrove forests and one-fifth of coral reefs have disappeared. Id. at 19.
39 Id.
40 Robert Verchick, *Facing Catastrophe: Environmental Action for a Post-Katrina World* 19 (2010).
41 Coastal Louisiana Ecosystem Assessment & Restoration (CLEAR), *Reducing Flood Damage in Coastal Louisiana: Communities, Culture and Commerce* 2 (2006), available at http://www.clear.lsu.edu/pdfs/clear_newsletter_20081016112354.pdf.
42 Bob Marshall, New Research: Louisiana Coast Faces Highest Rate of Sea-level Rise Worldwide, *The Lens*, February 21, 2013, available at http://thelensnola.org/2013/02/21/new-research-louisiana-coast-faces-highest-rate-of-sea-level-rise-on-the-planet/.
43 CLEAR, supra note 41, at 2.
44 Id. at 3.
45 Verchick, supra note 40, at 19.
46 Matthew Waite and Craig Pittman, Louisiana Wetlands Serve as Warning, Experts Say, *St. Petersburg Times,* Sept. 6, 2005, at 10.A, available at http://www.sptimes.com/2005/09/05/Worldandnation/Katrina_offers_lesson.shtml.
47 United States Environmental Protection Agency, Coastal Wetlands Outreach, available at http://water.epa.gov/type/wetlands/outreach/upload/coastal_final.pdf.
48 Id.
49 Christophe A.G. Tulou et al., Climate Change and the Marine Environment, in *Ocean and Coastal Law and Policy* 571, 578 (Donald C. Baur, Tim Eichenberg, and Michael Sutton eds., 2008).
50 See Blake Hudson, Coastal Land Loss and the Mitigation-Adaptation Dilemma: Between Scylla and Charybdis, 73 *La. L. Rev.* 31 (2012).
51 Josh Eagle and Meg Caldwell, *Coastal Law* 31 (2011).
52 Tulou et al., supra note 49, at 575.
53 U.S. Climate Change Science Program and the Subcommittee on Global Change Research Report, *Coastal Sensitivity to Sea-Level Rise: A Focus on the Mid-Atlantic Region IX* (2009), available at http://www.climatescience.gov/Library/sap/sap4–1/final-report/default.htm#finalreport.

54 Tulou et al., supra note 49, at 575–76.

55 Id. at 578.

56 U.S. Climate Change Science Program, supra note 53, at IX.

57 Tulou et al., supra note 49, at 578.

58 The CWA's section 404 program is anything but robust, as permits to fill wetlands are approved 99 percent of the time.

59 Kristen M. Fletcher, Managing Coastal Development, in *Ocean and Coastal Law and Policy* 147, 152 (Donald C. Baur et al. eds, 2008).

60 Professor Craig argues that Congress's operation "within constitutional federalism requirements" has seemingly caused it to misjudge the constitutionality of seeking direct regulatory inputs at the federal level into nonpoint pollution under the CWA. Robin Kundis Craig, Local or National? The Increasing Federalization of Nonpoint Source Pollution Regulation, 15 *J. Envtl. L. & Litig.* 179, 179–81 (2000).

61 Erin C. Myers, Policies to Reduce Emissions from Deforestation and Degradation (REDD), *Resources for the Future* 4 (2007), available at http://www.rff.org/documents/RFF-DP-07-50.pdf.

62 Constance L. McDermott et al., *Global Environmental Forest Policies: An International Comparison* 6 (2010).

63 News Release, USDA Forest Service, *US Forest Service Finds Global Forests Absorb One-Third of Carbon Emissions Annually* (July 14, 2011), available at http://www.fs.fed.us/news/2011/releases/07/carbon.shtml.

64 U.N. Env't Programme, *Global Environment Outlook 3: Past, Present and Future Perspectives* 110 (2002), available at http://www.unep.org/geo/GEO3/english/pdf.htm (follow "Forests" hyperlink).

65 Gerald A. Rose et al., Forest Resources Decision-Making in the U.S., in *The Politics of Decentralization*, supra note 4, at 238, 239; see also Jan G. Laitos et al., *Natural Resources Law 849* (2006). Despite maintaining the regulatory authority to do so, most states do not place legally binding forest management standards upon private forest managers. As noted by scholars, "[a]lthough a few states have laws that regulate forest practices on private land, most rely upon *voluntary* best management practices and technical assistance." Rose, supra, at 238 (emphasis added).

66 McDermott et al., supra note 62, at 7–11 (discussing frameworks for comparative forest policy analysis).

67 Id. at 10.

68 Id. at 15–19.

69 See James Rasband et al., *Natural Resources Law and Policy* 1206–9 (2nd ed. 2009); Bastiaan Louman et al., Forest Ecosystem Services: A Cornerstone for Human Well-Being, in 22 *Int'l Union of Forest Res. Orgs. World Series*, *Adaptation of Forests and People to Climate Change—A Global Assessment Report* 15, 16–20 (Risto Seppälä et al. eds, 2009), available at http://www.iufro.org/science/gfep/embargoed-release/download-by-chapter/ (follow "Download chapter 1" hyperlink).

70 McDermott et al., supra note 62, at 15.

71 Id. at 16 (quoting Raffaele Spinelli and Enrico Marchi, *A Literature Review of the Environmental Impacts of Forest Road Construction* (1996), available at http://www.fao.org/docrep/X0622E/x0622e0p.htm).

72 Id. at 18.

73 U.S. Environmental Protection Agency, *Carbon Sequestration in Agriculture and Forestry*, available at http://www.epa.gov/sequestration/.

74 McDermott et al., supra note 62, at 19–20.

75 Id. at 327 tbl.10.7.

76 Id. The chart misidentifies "mandatory substantive" as "mandatory prescriptive" in the key.

77 McDermott et al., supra note 62, at 327 tbl.10.7.

78 To be clear, "it cannot be assumed that regions with higher levels of regulation are actually performing better than those with lesser levels." Id. at 350. A lack of

institutional enforcement capacity and other issues of implementation may render forest standards on paper far less efficacious than voluntary standards in countries with better management practices on the ground. See id. at 10.

79 Wear and Greis, supra note 5, at 4. The report studied 13 states, including: Virginia, North Carolina, South Carolina, Georgia, Florida, Alabama, Tennessee, Kentucky, Mississippi, Arkansas, Louisiana, Oklahoma, and Texas. Id. at 4 fig.1.

80 Id.

81 Id. at 4.

82 Id. Since the 1970s total forest area has been stable, but this stability is a result of agricultural lands being reforested at the same rate that urbanization has reduced forest cover. Id. at 15. While urbanization is expected to increase at even higher rates, conversion of agricultural lands to forests is not expected to continue. Id. at 31.

83 Wear and Greis, supra note 5, at 24.

84 Id. at 26 fig.2. From 1970 to 2010, population in the south grew by 88 percent, and disposable personal income more than doubled. Id. at 6. Further, from 1990 to 2008, population in the south grew at a rate approximately one-third faster than the nation as a whole. Id. at 71. These pressures do not appear to show any sign of letting up. Population in the south is expected to grow yet another 40–60 percent from 2010 to 2060. Id. at 12–13.

85 Id. at 5.

86 Id. at 29.

87 Id. at 17.

88 Id.

89 Robert Hugget et al., Forecasts of Forest Conditions, in *The Southern Forest Futures Project, Technical Report* 17 (2011), available at http://www.srs.fs.usda.gov/futures/reports/draft/Frame.htm (follow "Chapter 5" hyperlink).

90 Wear and Greis, supra note 5, at 34 (emphasis added).

91 McDermott et al., supra note 62, at 82.

92 Id.

93 Wear and Greis, supra note 5, at 35.

94 McDermott et al., supra note 62, at 82.

95 Can. Counsel of Forest Ministers, *Sustainable Forest Management in Canada* 4, (2010).

96 Wear and Greis, supra note 5, at 62.

97 McDermott et al., supra note 62, at 80 tbl.3.3.

98 Wear and Greis, supra note 5, at 58. The 86 percent of forests in the south that are privately owned account for almost the entire amount of timber harvested in the south. Id.

99 Wear and Greis, supra note 5, at 71.

Part IV

Internationalization of the Commons

To this point we have seen how constitutional law in federal systems intersects with natural capital commons (Part I), guides the management of those resources in a legally decentralized system of government (Part II), and how it may (or may not) aggregate a requisite amount of regulatory authority at the federal level to prevent overdecentralization of resource management (Part III). The degree to which authority is or is not maintained by federal governments relative to subnational governments has implications for governance arrangements within the international community, which might actually be considered the ultimate federal system. Nations engaged in global governance negotiations or arrangements are the virtual equivalent of subnational governments in a federal system. Importantly, however, the international community operates like a federal system where regulatory authority over the subject matter in question resides exclusively at the subnational level—making the commons dynamic that is entrenched domestically in federal systems also relevant on international scales. So, if global governance operates by national governments ceding authority or sovereignty to a degree to the global governance regime, what happens when certain nations do not maintain legal authority at the national level over certain types of resource management? What if governments *two levels down* from the global scale (states/provinces) maintain exclusive regulatory authority as a matter of constitutional law, and thus constrain their respective nations in global governance arrangements? How exactly does this version of the T-4 scenario described in Chapter 2 (Figure 2.4) operate? How can it be turned into an NT scenario? This will be the subject of Chapters 6, 7, and 8.

6 Domestic Federalism's Potential Limitation on International Law

A U.S. Forest Case Study[1]

> Nations with federal systems should consider the compatibility of treaties with their constitutional orders before concluding them, because any errors are almost certainly not a basis for extricating themselves afterward. ... International Law obliges nations to explore the limits of their constitutional structure to comply with treaties.[2]

Introduction

A few years ago I visited a parcel of private forestland in the U.S. state of Alabama. I walked downhill to a creek that runs through an impressive stand of oaks, poplars, sycamores, and pines. The creek happens to establish the property line shared with the adjacent landowner. Upon reaching the bottom of the hill I observed that the forest that once stretched across the creek now stopped *at* the creek. The adjacent landowner had recently clear-cut the property and had removed the timber all the way down to the water line on the opposite bank. This Alabama forester's action was clearly contrary to the state of Alabama's Best Management Practices (BMPs) for forests, which *suggest*—but, importantly, do not *require*—that a forested buffer zone like that depicted in Figure 6.1 *should* be left along watersheds to "[p]rotect banks, beds, and floodplains from erosion; control direct deposition of pollutants; provide shade, food, and cover for aquatic ecosystems; [and] filter out pollutants from uplands."[3] Many of the benefits of riparian buffer zones, such as preserving water quality and fisheries, may be considered primarily of local concern. As described in Chapter 5, however, preventing poor forest management decisions destroying such buffer zones not only protects local environmental goods and services, but also provides global goods in the form of carbon sequestration, as governments seek to battle the effects of climate change by including forest carbon in a variety of carbon sequestration programs and policies, market-based or otherwise.[4] Indeed, though as noted in Chapters 1–5, private forest management regulation, and land use regulation generally, have long been the purview of state and local regulatory authority in the United States, federal and international regulatory bodies have taken a growing interest in forest management decisions of the kind made by this Alabama forester.

Figure 6.1 Forest clear-cut with forested buffer zone along watershed[5]

And yet this story presents a curious situation, and one which was the true genesis for this entire scholarly endeavor: if establishment of riparian buffer zones on private forestland is a state and local matter under the U.S. Constitution, then how would that impact the U.S. government's ability to engage in global governance related to forested riparian buffer zones or a variety of other types of forest management standard-setting in the future? In the future, such a regime may be necessary to curb the commons rationality of subnational governments like the state of Alabama. No matter how politically unlikely it may seem today, there may come a time when we look at local and global forests as being as interconnected as local use of chlorofluorocarbons (CFCs) and the global ozone layer, tackled prescriptively and quite stringently by the Montreal Protocol regime.

One way in which the international community has sought to address forest resource commons problems is to seek global standardization of forest management practices—based on both environmental and economic concerns. The global benefits of preventing poor forest management at local scales are enormous, given that a vast majority of the 20–25 percent of annual global carbon emissions resulting from forest and land use activities over recent decades are attributable to forest destruction and degradation.[6] Even so, efforts in recent decades to address national, state, and local forest commons problems and harmonize forest practices within a legally binding international treaty have failed. This failure is due in part to the United States' past unwillingness to support such an agreement, since historically policymakers and scholars have viewed U.S. participation as crucial to the success of global environmental treaties.

A number of international forums have been utilized in an effort to achieve responsible and sustainable global forest management. The United Nations Forum on Forests (UNFF)[7] has been the home for a number of "stand-alone" global forest governance negotiations,[8] which have aimed to promote sustainable forestry, preserve the numerous ecosystem services provided by forests, and address climate change. In addition, due to the importance of forest carbon in regulating climate change, and though coordinated action on climate change via treaty hit a standstill in the first decade of the 2000s, national governments may yet choose to incorporate global forest management into any post-Kyoto climate treaty that may arise.[9] Governments have continued to develop both regulatory and market-based solutions to address climate change, and proposed legislation at both the federal and state levels has explicitly provided a substantial role for forests in mitigating carbon emissions.[10]

Yet if a forest treaty or a climate treaty incorporating forest management were to become the subject of serious negotiation in the future, the relationship between federal and subnational regulatory authority in federal systems may have a negative impact on negotiation and implementation of the arrangement. What if, for example, the federal government is granted authority under the Constitution to negotiate treaties, while subnational governments maintain primary regulatory authority for activities like private forest management?

This chapter seeks to heed Professor Swaine's advice[11] to consider the compatibility of an international treaty that includes forests with the U.S. constitutional order, since "[i]nternational [l]aw obliges nations to explore the limits of their constitutional structure to comply with treaties."[12] The chapter explores the *legal* bases for, and implications of, U.S. federalism's potential limiting effect on the U.S. treaty power in the area of global forest management, to demonstrate how a federal system's constitutional division of power can impact global resource management. The chapter does so by highlighting a vigorous debate among U.S. constitutional law scholars regarding the scope of the treaty-making power established in Article II of the U.S. Constitution. As detailed further below, the view of U.S. federalism known as "new federalism" (introduced in Chapter 4) considers federalism as a restraint on the United States' ability to implement international treaties requiring the passage of federal legislation that would not, standing alone, pass constitutional muster.[13] On the other hand, the "nationalist" perspective of federalism considers that the treaty power is not so limited, and that if a policy is implemented pursuant to an international treaty, the federal government may assert regulatory authority even over subject matters traditionally regulated by state governments and that it would be unable to regulate in the absence of a treaty.[14]

It is unlikely that the debate over whether federalism places limits on the United States' treaty-making power will be resolved anytime soon. Yet, as discussed in greater detail in this chapter, the United States has allowed federalism to inhibit its participation in international treaties in the past. In the event that federal systems like the U.S. are inhibited in participating in certain legally binding global resource governance regimes due to constitutional constraints, then either their constitutional orders will need to be adjusted, as discussed in Chapter 9, or other mechanisms of involvement will need to be explored, such as voluntary, market-based programs that succeed in facilitating private forest owner or subnational government *voluntary* participation in the global regime or federal program. These might take the form of a variety of programs already circulating in the policy arena, such as reduction of emissions from deforestation and degradation (REDD), forest certification, or ecosystem service transaction programs. These mechanisms, unlike prescriptive dictates, allow subnational entities to participate in the federal program on a voluntary basis, and do not require the federal government to directly regulate private land uses. Even so, given the rampant herder rationality demonstrated by national and subnational governments globally regarding forest resources, more direct government standard-setting across scales may be required.

Climate Change: A New Opportunity to Include Forest Management in a Binding Global Treaty

Though global forest management treaty discussions have repeatedly met difficulties over the past two decades, increasing concern over climate change has opened the door for greater coordinated international action on forests. Potential government action on climate change raises many questions for private forest owners in the United States. Would a nationwide climate change scheme enacted pursuant to a global treaty open up carbon offset markets beyond our nation's borders, giving forest owners crucial incentives provided by access to the worldwide carbon market? Could the Alabama forester noted above be persuaded to leave the forest intact under such a scheme if economically valuable carbon credits were made available, or if paid by industrial polluters seeking to offset emissions? If so, these carbon incentives would have the effect not only of preserving carbon values, but also of promoting sustainable forestry and protecting numerous other goods and services provided by forests.

Climate change has also altered the governmental level at which localized private forest management activities are scrutinized. For example, at what scale are sustainable private forest owner activities and incentives most appropriately implemented—at the state, federal, or international level? Which entities are best situated to design forest management directives that will capture the full environmental and economic value of the resource—local communities and state governments, which have on-the-ground access to the best information and are able to more efficiently allocate resources, or national and international governmental, or private bodies, which maintain an increasing stake in how local forest resources are managed?

These considerations and questions exemplify the increasingly complex nature of modern forest management, especially given the role of forests in climate change. A forested watershed in rural Alabama demonstrates how *private individuals*, subject to *state* regulations, could potentially interact in a *federal* regulatory scheme that might arise out of *global* treaty negotiations. Demonstrating how forests may be considered a commons resource as fluid as the fish in the sea, the Alabama forest I visited stretched far beyond the opposite creek bank and actually extended around the world, as forest managers are increasingly considering forests' potential to provide not only local communities, but also the global community, with a wealth of ecosystem and economic resources.

Indeed, international harmonization of forest management practices has occupied an increasingly important place on the world stage during the last 20-plus years. Since the late 1980s, countries promoting formal global action on forest practices have made numerous attempts to forge a legally binding international forest treaty, but repeatedly have met great difficulty. Various international forums have considered the creation of such a treaty: the 1992 UN Conference on the Environment and Development (UNCED) in Rio de Janeiro; four proceedings of the Intergovernmental Panel on Forests (IPF) between 1995 and 1997; four proceedings of the Intergovernmental Forum on Forests (IFF) between 1997 and 2000; and most recently numerous proceedings of the UNFF in the 2000s to the present.[15]

The UNFF remains the primary forum currently facilitating debate on global governance of forests. The UNFF promotes sustainable forestry, solutions to climate change, and preservation of the varied ecosystem services provided by global forests.[16] Yet UNFF negotiations, and negotiations in the number of forums that preceded them, have failed to achieve binding global forest governance for a variety of (primarily) political reasons,[17] and despite some glimmers of hope in recent talks[18] failure to achieve a legally binding stand-alone forest agreement that establishes "one comprehensive set of all rules applicable and desirable for the forest sector" and "reflect[s] each state's responsibility to ensure the sustainable management of its forests … remains a setback."[19] Some scholars have described forest treaty discussions as "a resounding failure."[20] Though scholars have suggested a variety of reasons for these failures,[21] one of the most significant impediments to treaty formation has been the United States' inability to consistently support a legally binding international forest management agreement.[22]

Numerous scholars have argued the United States is the most influential country in the international environmental governance system, and the United States was actually the first country to propose a stand-alone, binding forest convention.[23] Scholars have focused on

> US leadership in the international environmental policy arena, not only because of the US' economic size and influence but also because the US has some of the most stringent environmental regulations in the world. … [T]he US is critical to an effective outcome in global environmental issue areas. … [A] focus on the US as a necessary member of the pro[-forest agreement] coalition is justified by the fact that the US is

likely to bear a far greater proportion—in absolute terms—of the cost of any measures required for manipulating effective agreement than any other single state.[24]

Although the United States was unable to push through a binding agreement in the early 1990s, its official reversal of support for binding international forest management in 1997 made it more difficult for the international community to revisit the issue.[25] Indeed, the United States has forged a "powerful veto coalition in opposition to any further internationally binding instrument" that includes forests.[26] The United States' reversal represented a domestic political shift that embraced the argument put forth by developing countries opposed to a binding treaty—that national sovereignty in the forest sector was more valuable than benefits derived from an international forest treaty.[27]

Despite the international community's failure to achieve a stand-alone forest treaty through the UNFF, global forest governance remains on the agenda of the United Nations Framework Convention on Climate Change (UNFCCC)—though it too has failed to create a binding instrument establishing a significant role for forests in mitigating atmospheric carbon.[28] The current leading UNFCCC treaty on climate change, the Kyoto Protocol, is a multilateral environmental agreement assigning binding carbon reduction targets and timetables to "Annex I," or industrialized nations, as well as general commitments for all member countries.[29] The protocol, however, has largely ignored forest management as a means of achieving carbon sequestration goals, as emissions from deforestation and forest degradation have not been integrated into Kyoto targets.[30] Rather, the protocol's effectiveness has been measured primarily with reference to its direct regulation of industry emitters to achieve a reduction of greenhouse gases (GHG).[31] If a post-Kyoto climate treaty does manifest, the failure to include forests in a meaningful way will need to be remedied, as the UNFF has asserted that "mismanagement [of forests] would have a significant impact on the course of global warming in the twenty-first century," and that "[s]ustainable forest management can contribute towards emissions reductions and to carbon sequestration."[32]

Climate scholars have noted that forest management activities can be augmented to achieve carbon sequestration goals through a variety of strategies, including the increase of forested land through afforestation and reforestation projects, the increase in carbon density of existing forests at both stand and landscape scales, the expanded use of forest products that sustainably replace fossil-fuel driven carbon dioxide emissions, the implementation of programs to reduce deforestation and degradation of forests, and a variety of other methods.[33] Due to the current state of global politics, it seems that the most likely pathways for achieving better forest management globally in the near future are voluntary, market-based programs. Most iterations of proposed domestic carbon cap-and-trade legislation in the United States have provided for industry carbon offsets by investment in, or credit purchases from, approved carbon sequestration projects—in forests or otherwise.[34] It is true that opening up forest markets by increasing and uniformly formalizing the number and types of market-based programs would only increase the viability of U.S. participation in a global climate treaty that includes forests. Furthermore, U.S. backing would capitalize on the aforementioned global inertia toward including managed forest carbon within the post-Kyoto framework and would compensate for Kyoto's failure to adequately utilize the world's forests to fight climate change.

Ultimately, however, although climate change provides a new opportunity to incorporate forest management activities within future UNFCCC and UNFF negotiations, a global treaty including forest management has yet to be achieved, even for voluntary, market-based forest programs. Just as this section demonstrates how including *voluntary* forest management programs in climate negotiations provides the United States incentives to cooperate on a global treaty, the next section explicates how U.S. federalism may disrupt international negotiations on binding forest management if the mechanisms for achieving forest management are *prescriptive* in nature.

U.S. Federalism as a Restriction on Prescriptive Global Forest Management

While climate change provides a new opportunity for the United States to cooperate *politically* with international negotiations on forest management activities, a more important question is whether the United States maintains the *legal* capacity to do so when those negotiations take certain forms. While this question may seem less salient from a political perspective during today's political climate, the question is one that is both important to institutional analysis and that has not yet been addressed in scholarship. Though politics matter a great deal in global environmental governance, without adequate legal institutions to translate politics into policy, global treaties will not be implemented on domestic scales. It is unclear that the United States maintains a sufficient legal institution to implement global forest management objectives domestically, a complication arising directly out of its domestic constitutional structure, because

> the US's own domestic governance structure complicates its role in the creation of any legally binding treaty that involves the potential direct regulation of land use by the federal government. The US's governmental system of federalism, engrained in the US Constitution and receiving protection by the US judiciary, causes domestic implementation of certain international forest governance scenarios to be more viable than others.[35]

While scholars have focused on "decentralized mechanisms" for international forest management, they have largely ignored the effects of domestic institutional structures like federalism on international forest governance.[36] It also appears that U.S. federalism concerns have not entered the calculus in past forest treaty or climate negotiations. As noted, U.S. negotiators' past hesitancy to address forests within a binding treaty appears to have had more to do with defending sovereignty over U.S. resources, concerns over economic impacts of climate legislation, and other political considerations than with anticipating judicial challenges by the states or private citizens to domestic treaty implementation.[37] Going forward, however, the United States should carefully consider potential federalism-based limitations on its ability to implement a treaty aimed at forests.[38] The United States is party to only one-third of existing international environmental agreements, and has failed to sign or ratify many significant international environmental treaties—including most recently the Kyoto Protocol.[39]

Without uncompromised U.S. participation, a future treaty aimed at forest management may not materialize in a way that comprehensively and effectively addresses either the carbon sequestration or many other ecosystem service values of forests.[40] The United States is one of the greatest emitters of carbon in the world and in past climate negotiations the United States sought carbon offsets, such as those potentially provided by forests, to reduce the economic burdens of potential international carbon emissions regulation.[41] And as noted, the United States has included carbon offset mechanisms in various congressional domestic legislative carbon proposals.[42] Ultimately, despite international recognition that U.S. participation is crucial for the success of international environmental agreements, the United States has continued to allow domestic politics to impact its willingness to enter into agreements on both forests and climate.

Importantly, there is a key difference between the domestic *political* issues that hamstrung U.S. negotiators in both previous forest management and climate talks, which were largely ideological, and domestic *legal* issues that could present complications for a future treaty including forest management. There is great uncertainty regarding whether U.S. federalism impedes Congress's ability to implement binding, prescriptive land use regulations even if mandated by international treaty.[43] Indeed, the potential for management conflicts in the area of natural resources law arises directly out of a constitutional structure that is said to have "split the atom of sovereignty,"[44] and thus to have ignited a seemingly unending controversy over the proper division of regulatory authority between the state and federal governments, as seen in Chapter 4, and which manifests especially with regards to the scope of the treaty power.

Suppose that the United States enters into an international treaty that includes prescriptive directives requiring Congress to pass implementing legislation establishing nationwide forest management mandates on publicly *and privately owned* lands—such as the creation of nationwide buffer zones in forested watersheds, stand density requirements, clear-cutting regulations, forest road regulations, and afforestation or reforestation requirements. The nature of the implementing legislation could effectively prohibit U.S.

participation in the treaty because as noted throughout this book, U.S. federalism divides regulatory authority over land use between the federal and state governments. This division of authority presents a unique problem in the United States because even though central governments own roughly 86 percent of the world's forests and wooded areas worldwide,[45] U.S. state and federal governments own no more than 40 percent of U.S. forestland.[46] The remaining 60 percent of U.S. forestland is in private ownership. This public/private divide in the United States is a remarkable break from the global pattern of forest ownership. Furthermore, an estimated 89 percent of the timber harvested in the United States comes from private lands.[47]

In turn, as repeated often in Chapters 1–5, private land use regulation is the primary purview of state governments. To be clear, private land use activities are *affected by* federal regulations passed by Congress under other sources of authority in the Constitution, such as the Commerce Clause or treaty-making power. A number of federal regulations have an *effect* on private landowner activities without violating the Tenth Amendment. Both the Endangered Species Act (ESA) and Clean Water Act (CWA), each passed pursuant to Congress's Commerce Clause power, limit private property owners' land use rights to a degree. Specifically with regard to forests, the ESA prevents certain landowner logging activities that might endanger or threaten species, and the CWA may influence some programs aimed at "nonpoint" sources of water pollution arising out of logging activities.[48] Indeed, courts have rejected state Tenth Amendment challenges to congressional authority to protect endangered species under the ESA,[49] fish under the Magnuson-Stevens Fishery Conservation and Management Act,[50] and air quality under the Clean Air Act (CAA).[51]

The effects of these federal acts on land use activities generally, however, are *tangential* to the primary purposes of the regulations, which are to protect endangered species, water and air quality, and other resources—not to govern directly how private lands are to be managed generally.[52] Rather, states currently maintain direct regulatory authority over private forest management activities and are at present responsible for establishing stand density, reforestation, and riparian buffer zone requirements; governing clear-cutting practices; and implementing a wide variety of other BMPs.[53] In fact, Congress itself has recognized the tangential effects on land use related to its regulation of other resources. For example, the CWA *explicitly* recognizes federalism limitations on Congress's ability to regulate land use, stating that "[i]t is the policy of the Congress to recognize, preserve, and protect *the primary responsibilities and rights of States* to ... plan the development and use (including restoration, preservation, and enhancement) of *land* and water resources."[54] Other scholars have noted that "[a]ll private forests are governed by laws relating to the protection of water quality, wetlands and endangered species; but private forest owners' objectives guide management for other values."[55]

Additionally, federal statutes may *influence* state regulation of forest management, as states may pass or modify state laws to meet federal clean water and endangered species requirements. Even so, a review of U.S. judicial precedent and traditionally accepted forest management practices may distinguish the *permissible*, tangential influencing effects of federal statutes on state regulations from potentially *impermissible* federal interference with primary state authority over forest management. Courts have recognized both the CWA and ESA as valid under the Commerce Clause, despite the limitations they impose on private land use.[56] The validity of private forest management at the federal level, however, has never been judicially tested, as the federal government has never attempted to directly regulate private forest management activities.[57] As noted in Chapter 4, courts have consistently recognized the "quintessential" authority of states to regulate land use, and just as with zoning authority established in *Euclid*,[58] forest management falls squarely within the realm of traditional land use activities regulated by the state.[59] Due to a lack of federal intent to regulate in the area of private forest management, courts have yet to extend application of the Commerce Clause to private forests. As such, it appears that the accepted practice of direct state regulation of private forest activities remains intact.

Also potentially affecting private land use activities are international treaties entered into by the federal government for the protection of certain natural resources—as demonstrated in the 1920 U.S. Supreme Court case of *Missouri v. Holland*,[60] discussed later in this chapter. However, *Holland* may be distinguishable on its facts, as the treaty at issue in that case, like the ESA and CWA, regulates resources tangentially related to the direct land use activities of private property owners. In addition, the federal government has never asserted, by treaty, authority over private forest management practices traditionally regulated by states.[61] In short, even though federal statutes and treaties may affect land use activities of private landowners, the federal government has never before attempted to directly regulate private forest management, and thus courts have never considered the validity of any federal attempts to do so.

Because of U.S. federalism, the types of forest management directives that might arise out of either a post-Kyoto climate framework or a stand-alone forest treaty will impact the viability of the treaty within the United States and, perhaps, even affect treaty formation in the first instance, since the United States' participation in treaty negotiations will be important.[62] This is especially so since the United States has previously invoked federalism as a reason to avoid treaty formation in several other contexts. As noted by Professor Bradley, "in a number of instances in the late nineteenth and early twentieth centuries, U.S. officials declined to enter into negotiations concerning private international law treaties because of a concern that the treaties would infringe on the reserved powers of the states."[63] In addition, in the past,

> U.S. representatives insisted that they could not agree to a treaty regulating certain labor conditions because those matters were within the

> reserved powers of the states. These states' rights concerns continued to inhibit U.S. participation in private international law, labor, and other treaty regimes even after *Holland*.[64]

Other scholars have noted that much more recently perceived federalism limitations have reduced U.S. bargaining power at the negotiating table by encouraging the United States to act in outright opposition to treaty formation, to seek exemptions in treaties that modify the obligations of states, or to provide concessions to the states in domestic implementation.[65] Ultimately, nations with federal systems, like the United States, "may decline altogether to enter into a treaty that poses a serious risk of conflict with their constitutions. At the domestic level, well-grounded constitutional principles may be insurmountable, as may more pedestrian limits imposed by legislation particular to the treaty."[66] Thus, U.S. federalism is predisposed to conflict with principles of international law, not only in the negotiation of treaties, but perhaps more importantly in the implementation of treaties governing areas considered the subject of traditional state authority, like forest management. Because the United States has allowed federalism to limit its ability and willingness to participate in international treaties in the past, it is necessary to gain a complete understanding of the relationship between international law and federalism, and how to avoid conflicts between the two that may arise. Otherwise, we will continue to see yet another example of legal entrenchment of the commons phenomena, and on the highest scale of all those reviewed in this book—the global scale—as herder rationality of some nations involved in global governance becomes not only politically possible, but legally defensible.

International Law on Federalism: A Restraint on Treaty Participation?

Federal government claims of domestic political restraints on treaty implementation are not limited to the United States, but such claims gain particular traction when based on entrenched constitutional grounds, as with the United States. As Professor Swaine has noted,

> [f]ederal states not infrequently seek broader concessions based on the political feasibility of national implementation, but the arguments that have had purchase are based on more genuine constitutional limits. Much the same may be said with respect to … outright refusals to participate based on federalism grounds.[67]

With the United States' federalism principles embedded in the Constitution and with a long history of jurisprudence developing federalism's scope, scholars have rightly questioned what would happen to U.S. treaty obligations if the U.S. Constitution indeed establishes federalism limitations on the treaty power.[68]

International law and U.S. constitutional law have been said to "exhibit a kind of passive hostility toward one another."[69] From the perspective of the U.S. legal system, international law cannot affect the operation of the Constitution, which "operates as an absolute constraint on how U.S. obligations may be observed."[70] From the perspective of international law, however, international law prevails over domestic legislation and constitutions. The rules governing legal agreements among nations, "addressing the formation, application, interpretation, modification, termination, and validity of treaties," are codified in the 1969 Vienna Convention on the Law of Treaties (Vienna Convention).[71] The Vienna Convention has been described as the "treaty on treaties."[72] Article 27 of the Vienna Convention provides that "[a] party may not invoke the provisions of its internal law as justification for its failure to perform a treaty,"[73] and this provision has been described as codification of a "preexisting principle of customary international law that makes no exception for federal states."[74] In addition, Article 26 of the Vienna Convention states that "[e]very treaty in force is binding upon the parties to it and must be performed by them in good faith."[75]

Therefore, international law is supposedly "indifferent" toward federalism.[76] Arguments that a federal domestic governance structure provides an excuse for treaty noncompliance have been described as "heretical"[77] because "a particular country's constitutional difficulties are its own, and a choice in all events that is not to be visited upon the rest of the world."[78] Despite international law's seemingly stern perspective on federalism, however, the U.S.'s internal perspective is quite different—especially considering the rise of the new federalism. Scholars have argued that

> suggestions that international law might actually insinuate itself into the U.S. Constitution, particularly those provisions governing relations among domestic institutions, would surely be resisted. … U.S. courts (usually) try to interpret statutes in conformity with treaty and other international obligations. But *constitutional* law, in the American system, is a different kettle of fish, and in U.S. courts even run-of-the-mill federal statutes—including those protecting state interests—may erase any undesired implications from international law. While Supreme Court justices occasionally preach the need to pay attention to the legal world outside U.S. borders, the Court's case law seemingly limits international law's potential relevance to the new federalism.[79]

The United States' reluctance to allow international obligations to impact domestic governance actually more accurately represents the true state of affairs in international law. In reality, though the position of international law relative to domestic constitutional federalism is stated in fairly stark terms, international law has in fact treated domestic constitutional law with greater deference.[80] As noted, accommodation is frequently made during negotiations for federal states that claim constitutional hurdles to treaty requirements, an occurrence that "reflect[s] a more general understanding that a party's constitutional constraints are less tractable."[81] Even *after* a treaty is formed, international law may concede to the federalist position. For example, the 1999 proceedings regarding two German nationals convicted of murder in Arizona, Karl and Walter LaGrand, were concluded by provisional order that sought to limit the state of Arizona's death penalty procedures as a violation of the Vienna Convention. The United States argued that it could not intervene because its federal system imposed limits that designated such procedures the sole purview of the states and thus not subject to the treaty.[82] The International Court of Justice (ICJ) ultimately issued an order finding that international law "'did not require the United States to exercise powers it did not have, but rather established an obligation 'to take all measures at its disposal' to prevent the German national's execution prior to the Court's final decision."[83] Clearly, the powers that the United States was claiming it did not have in the LaGrand proceedings were powers that instead were reserved for the states under the Tenth Amendment (development of death penalty procedures) and protected by federalism principles.[84]

The ICJ's decision in the LaGrand proceedings actually follows quite naturally from the language of Article 26 of the Vienna Convention, providing that though international treaties are binding, they must be implemented by countries in "good faith."[85] This good faith provision, and the recognition by the ICJ that nation states need not exercise powers they do not have within their domestic regulatory tool belt, is arguably an implicit recognition of the international community that treaties may be constrained by federalism. Furthermore, a "good faith," rather than absolute, performance requirement recognizes the difficulties in overcoming domestic constraints on treaties when there is no enforcement mechanism or when the compliance system of a treaty is non-binding (as is the case with the Kyoto Protocol).[86]

Ultimately, international law sends mixed messages regarding the legitimacy of claimed federalism constraints on domestic implementation of treaties. Though the Vienna Convention asserts that countries may not invoke provisions of internal law as justification for failure to perform treaty obligations, the Convention also requires only that binding treaties be carried out in "good faith," which the ICJ has interpreted as an obligation to take only such measures as are "at the disposal" of the treaty-making branch of the nation's government. Just as with the death penalty procedures at issue in the LaGrand proceedings, direct regulation of private land use activities such as forest management is not a regulatory measure traditionally at the disposal of the U.S. federal government.

In the end, U.S. federalism may act as a domestic constraint on prescriptive "traditional governance" at both the national and international levels, just as do international negotiations noted by scholars.[87] Due to the United States' past tendency of allowing federalism restraints to inhibit it from participating in international treaties, in order for international forest negotiations to result in a legitimate and effective treaty addressing forest management in the future—and one that can be constitutionally implemented in the United States—either measures other than prescriptive, traditional governance regulatory methods will need to be explored, or the U.S. (and similarly situated federal countries) will need to adjust its constitutional structure to allow federal or international inputs.

An Unending Controversy: Does Federalism Limit the Treaty-making Power? The Nationalist Versus New Federalist Debate

During the foregoing analysis, this chapter necessarily presumed that federalism would in fact have a limiting effect on the treaty power. We now turn to the resolution of whether federalism does in fact limit the U.S. federal government's treaty power, or more accurately whether, based upon scholarly interpretations of constitutional law generally, and the U.S. Supreme Court case of *Missouri vs. Holland* specifically, there is likely to be a resolution to this question in the foreseeable future.

U.S. constitutional law scholars are sharply divided regarding whether federalism places limits upon the treaty power. If federalism does not limit the federal government's treaty power, then it matters little, for domestic implementation purposes, what types of forest policy directives are included within a global treaty—whether voluntary, market-based, or prescriptive. The question of the treaty power's scope in light of potential federalism limitations, however, has not been completely resolved.

During one of the most prominent scholarly skirmishes on the scope of the treaty power, Professor Golove provided an accurate and useful summary of the nature of the debate:

> Characteristic of the most enduring constitutional controversies is a clash between fundamental but ultimately irreconcilable principles. Unable to synthesize opposing precepts, we visit and revisit certain issues in an endless cycle. Each generation marches forward heedless, and sometimes only dimly aware, of how many times the battle has already been fought. Even the peace of exhaustion achieves only a temporary respite.
>
> The abiding controversy over the relationship between the treaty power of the national government and the legislative powers of the states is paradigmatic in this respect. … [T]he issue has been among the most passionately disputed questions in our constitutional history. Although temporarily in hibernation, it threatens presently to break out again into full-blown conflict.
>
> Can the federal government enter into treaties on subjects that are otherwise beyond Congress's legislative powers?[88]

Golove's not-so-veiled exasperation with this question was in response to an article by Professor Bradley titled *The Treaty Power and American Federalism*, in which Bradley argued that the treaty power is not unlimited in scope and could be restrained by federalism principles.[89] Bradley's article evaluated the nationalist position on the treaty power, which, based largely on *Missouri v. Holland*, rejects both the idea that the Tenth Amendment placed any restrictions on the treaty power and the notion that there are any subject matter limitations upon the treaty power.[90] Bradley "question[ed] the nationalist view," asserting that the treaty power "is a power to make supreme federal law. If such law can be made on any subject, without regard to the rights of the states, then the treaty power gives the federal government essentially plenary power vis-à-vis the states. Such plenary power, however, is exactly what American federalism denies."[91] Thus Bradley's view supports the notion that, absent some other constitutional provision granting the federal government regulatory authority, American federalism legally entrenches a commons scenario, whereby the 50 states are allowed to act as rationally as they please on certain subject matters, even in the presence of a global governance arrangement that the U.S. federal government fully wishes to implement domestically.

Bradley articulated that if federalism means anything under past or current understandings of constitutional law—i.e. the new federalism—then the treaty power should not be given special immunity from federalism limitations.[92] Other scholars have made similar arguments.[93] Bradley ultimately argued that the treaty power should be subject to the same federalism limitations that apply to Congress's legislative powers, with the result that "the federal government should not be able to use the treaty power … to create domestic law that could not be created by Congress."[94] Professor Swaine agreed, stating that the Supreme Court "might adopt the presumption, for example, that neither treaties nor their domestic implementation were intended to exceed the federal government's legislative authority. … [A] presumption that treaties ought not be construed in excess of otherwise applicable limits on the national government's power … has precedent."[95] Given the new federalism, the interpretation that the federal government's treaty power cannot exceed Congress's authority to legislate pursuant to its other constitutional powers would put federal management of land use activities like forestry in serious doubt.

The new federalism that arose in the 1990s included a number of cases where the Supreme Court, for the first time since 1937, limited the scope of Congress's domestic powers and correlatively protected states' rights and the traditional subjects of state regulatory authority under the Tenth Amendment.[96] As noted in part in Chapter 4, the Supreme Court invoked federalism principles to strike down federal statutes in *New York v. United States*,[97] *United States v. Lopez*,[98] *City of Boerne v. Flores*,[99] *Printz v. United States*,[100] and *United States v. Morrison.*[101] In *New York*, the Court found the statute invalid because it was "inconsistent with the federal structure of our Government established by the Constitution,"[102] while in *Printz* the Court found the statute invalid because it "compromise[d] the structural framework of dual sovereignty."[103] Furthermore, in the Court's subsequent unanimous decision in *Reno v. Condon*, the Court stated that "[i]n *New York* and *Printz*, we held federal statutes invalid, not because Congress lacked legislative authority over the subject matter, but because those statutes violated the principles of federalism contained in the Tenth Amendment."[104]

Though this shift in the Supreme Court's perspective on domestic federal authority might seem a victory for those supporting federalism principles, Bradley warned that the Supreme Court's reassertion of federalism protections "is likely to increase the importance of the scope of the treaty power. If the treaty power is immune from federalism restrictions, as the nationalist view maintains, then it may be a vehicle for the enactment of legislative changes that fall outside of Congress's domestic lawmaking powers."[105] Once again, Swaine agrees, stating that "[t]he new federalism decisions also invite fresh scrutiny of the treaty power by encouraging its creative use to circumvent federalism restrictions."[106] Swaine cited scholars arguing that the statutes struck down in *City of Boerne* and *Morrison* could (and should) effectively be reenacted if legislated pursuant to an international treaty.[107] Both the CWA and the ESA have received similar attention, as scholars have asserted that potential "as applied" constitutional challenges to these acts could be rendered moot if the resources in question were protected pursuant to an international treaty.[108] Nonetheless, "[b]ecause such arguments rely on an apparent inconsistency between *Holland* and the new federalism, they arguably increase its vulnerability to being reinterpreted, narrowed, or overruled."[109]

Professor Kuh framed the balance between the new federalism and the treaty power more directly, and assessed "*how* the treaty power will be recast in a manner consistent with the Supreme Court's revitalized approach to federalism."[110] Kuh stated that the nationalist view of the treaty power as unlimited in scope "ignores both historical uncertainty about the bounds of the treaty power as well as new legal scholarship questioning the continued vitality of strong versions of the treaty power in light of the Supreme Court's recent federalism jurisprudence."[111] Kuh argued that the holding in *Missouri v. Holland,* to the extent that the nationalist camp interpreted it as immunizing the treaty power from the constraints of the Tenth Amendment, may be called into question given recent new federalism jurisprudence in the Court.[112] She ultimately concluded that "as scholars undertake critical examinations of the treaty power, they will generally agree that *some* type of limitation on the treaty power is imminent and/or warranted. … [A]rticulation of a limitation on the nationalist view of the treaty power is both inevitable and advisable."[113]

Golove responded rather forcefully to what he viewed as misguided new federalism reinterpretations of the nationalist perspective on the treaty power.[114] In Golove's view, the question was simply a matter of whether the treaty power was an independently granted "delegated" power to the national government, taking it outside any restrictions generated by the Tenth Amendment and placed on other federal powers, like the Commerce Clause.[115] Golove came to the conclusion that the treaty power was an independently granted delegated power. Furthermore, Golove took issue with

Bradley's interpretation of the constitutional history relied upon by the nationalist camp, asserted that Bradley's view was "entirely unwarranted," and argued that it is actually "the states' rights view that must stretch for historical validation."[116] The tense disconnect between the two camps was apparent as Golove accused Bradley of ignoring contrary precedents and found Bradley's approach "particularly inadequate" and "entirely without support in the Constitution."[117] Golove also found "unpersuasive" Bradley's contention that the treaty power would be virtually unlimited without federalism restraints.[118]

Bradley counterpunched even more forcefully, describing portions of Golove's analysis as "polemical and exaggerated in tone and substance."[119] Bradley claimed that Golove inhibited debate on the scope of the treaty power by "largely fail[ing] to engage" his critique.[120] Also, Bradley stated that Golove's analysis "reflects a false assumption about the views of other foreign affairs scholars" and that it "more importantly, lacks any meaningful content."[121] Bradley asserted that Golove, while purportedly accepting the new federalism, provided analysis that is "inconsistent" with the decisions upon which new federalism is based.[122] Bradley was particularly critical of Golove's historical analysis, finding it to be "methodologically inconsistent and tendentious."[123] Even more pointedly, Bradley asserted that "[a] central complaint about the use of history by legal academics (and judges) is that it is shaped and twisted in order to support a particular conclusion. It is in this sense that, notwithstanding its length, Golove's historical discussion may be considered law office history."[124]

Ultimately, this scholarly skirmish demonstrates—at the very least—that the issue of whether federalism places limits on the treaty power is highly contentious among prominent scholars and is as of yet unresolved. As Bradley stated:

> The scope of the treaty power has been debated numerous times throughout this nation's history. The issue has resurfaced in recent years for a number of reasons, including the Supreme Court's revitalization of federalism restraints in the domestic arena and an expansion in the scope and range of U.S. treatymaking. …
>
> Golove's article fails to appreciate the legitimate reasons why the treaty power question has been a persistent feature of American political and legal discourse, and why, in this age of globalization, the question once again merits our attention.[125]

The constitutional certainty surrounding the scope of the U.S. federal government's treaty power, combined with the similar uncertainties surrounding the scope of the Commerce Clause, as detailed in Chapter 4, lends support to the fact that U.S. federalism may very well legally entrench a governance commons in the context of international law, whereby the national government is limited in engaging in certain forms of global natural capital governance due to constitutional federalism limitations. The next section, however, turns to *Missouri v. Holland*, assesses it in the context of the recent scholarly debates on the scope of the treaty power, and analyzes where land use activities, like forest management, fall along the spectrum of the treaty power's scope. The next section also analyzes an alternative treaty power limitation put forth by Professor Hollis, arising out of the executive branch, which could complicate forest treaty formation even if the judiciary ultimately refuses to revisit *Missouri v. Holland.*

Missouri v. Holland: Death by Judicial Review or Executive Federalism?

Scholars have described *Missouri v. Holland* as the "benchmark" for the Treaty Clause authority of the federal government to regulate certain natural resources[126] and "perhaps the most famous and most discussed case in the constitutional law of foreign affairs."[127] Importantly, scholars have observed that *Holland* "is in deep tension with the fundamental constitutional principle of enumerated legislative powers, and it is therefore of enormous theoretical importance."[128] The following review of *Holland* is not meant to resolve the constitutional questions presented but rather to demonstrate that the debatable nature of the case's precedential value for forest regulation creates even more uncertainty regarding federalism's potential limits on the treaty power.

The events giving rise to *Holland* arose out of a December 8, 1916 treaty between the United States and Great Britain recognizing that "many species of birds [that] in their annual migrations traversed many parts of the United States and of Canada ... were of great value as a source of food and in destroying insects injurious to vegetation, but were in danger of extermination through lack of adequate protection."[129] The two countries agreed to pass domestic conservation legislation to implement the treaty. To that end, the United States passed the Migratory Bird Treaty Act (MBTA) to prohibit the killing, capturing, or selling of any migratory birds covered by the treaty. The state of Missouri challenged a U.S. game warden's authority to enforce the MBTA, arguing the act was unconstitutional as an interference with the rights reserved to the states under the Tenth Amendment. Missouri also asserted the tradition of state control over wildlife to support its claim. In response, the federal government argued the statute was valid under the treaty-making power granted to it by the Constitution.

The Supreme Court began its analysis by noting that Article II of the U.S. Constitution expressly delegates authority to the federal government to create treaties.[130] Furthermore, the Court noted that Article VI declares that treaties are made under the "authority of the United States," and federal laws passed under the Constitution are the supreme law of the land. The Court found that "[i]f the treaty is valid there can be no dispute about the validity of the [MBTA] under Article 1, Section 8, as a necessary and proper means to execute the powers of the Government."[131] The Court found that the MBTA did not contravene any specific portion of the Constitution, and thus was valid—*unless* it was prohibited by the Tenth Amendment under the facts of the case. The Court stated that "[t]he language of the Constitution as to the supremacy of treaties being general, the question before us is narrowed to an inquiry into the ground upon which the present supposed exception is placed,"[132] and that "[n]o doubt the great body of private relations usually fall within the control of the State, but a treaty may override its power. … [I]t only remains to consider the application of established rules to the present case."[133]

Scholars have largely assumed that the Court's analysis stopped at a review of the treaty power.[134] If so, this would lend support for the U.S. federal government's authority to enter into an international agreement imposing domestic restrictions on forest management practices on private lands. However, the Court's subsequent Tenth Amendment analysis, *as applied to the specific facts of Holland*, makes this assertion less clear, especially when the resource in question is private forestlands.[135] For example, the Court noted that "[w]ild birds are not the possession of anyone … [t]he whole foundation of the State's rights is the presence within their jurisdiction of birds that yesterday had not arrived, tomorrow may be in another State and in a week a thousand miles away."[136] Thus, the *migratory nature* of the resource weakened the state's claim of reserved Tenth Amendment regulatory authority over them. In other words, because the MBTA involved a resource that moved across international boundaries, Congress could enter into a treaty to regulate the resource without violating the "general terms of the Tenth Amendment."[137]

The Court also invoked the national interest at stake as support for finding no Tenth Amendment restraint on the federal government's legislative authority:

> Here a national interest of very nearly first magnitude is involved. It can be protected only by national action in concert with that of another power. The subject matter is only transitorily within the State and has no permanent habitat therein. But for the treaty and the statute there soon might be no birds for any powers to deal with. We see nothing in the Constitution that compels the Government to sit by while a food supply is cut off and the protectors of our forests and our crops are destroyed. It is not sufficient to rely upon the States. The reliance is in vain, and were it otherwise, the question is whether the United States is forbidden to act.[138]

It is unclear whether it is "sufficient to rely upon the States" to regulate forest management properly.[139] Though evidence presented in this book indicates that it may very well be insufficient to rely on the states, if all states politically chose they could establish rules for the sustainable management of forests and their many services without coordinating with another country to do so, since forests are a stationary resource. On the other hand, it does seem clear that *climate change* is a "national interest of very nearly the first magnitude," which can be addressed only "by national action in concert with that of another power," indicating that this question relies completely on how one characterizes the forest resource.[140] As a climate change regulating resource, forests are not stationary, but resemble more closely the aquifer discussed in Chapter 2. Nonetheless, the Court in *Holland* primarily relied on the migratory nature of the birds and the lack of "possession" by any party, whereas forest resources are not migratory and can be legally possessed. Furthermore, there is no question that the federal government historically has regulated wildlife, so that *general* invocation of the Tenth Amendment by states in *Holland* could not overcome the federal government's treaty authority to regulate that particular resource.[141] This is a very different scenario from private forest management, which, as discussed above, traditionally has been considered a "land use" regulatory responsibility reserved to states.

Additionally, the history of state control over private forest management (and land use generally) demonstrates that the federal government customarily has not been considered a *necessary* party to private forest management—and forests are not "protected *only* by national action in concert with that of another power"—even if the federal government is a necessary party to climate change negotiations. These facts, coupled with the reassertion of federalism protections by the Court, may argue *against* the domestic validity of an international treaty regulating private forest management and *for* the invocation of a Tenth Amendment power reserved to the states, and they could prohibit a *Holland*-type ruling on challenges to an international forest management treaty.

In fact, Professor Swaine, noting Justice Holmes's reliance in *Holland* on the national interest at stake, the need for international cooperation, and the inability of states to regulate the resource in their own right, asserted that:

> *Holland* … instances an interpretative presumption for the treaty power—we should prefer interpretations permitting U.S. federalism to be reconciled with the national government's ability to negotiate and adhere to treaties—based on the insight that the state-based alternative to the treaty power is inadequate.[142]

In the case of forest management, it is *politically* arguable, but *legally* unclear, that the state-based alternative is inadequate—especially considered in light of the new federalism. The Court reasserted federalism protections in *Lopez* and *Morrison* in part because the Court "perceived that dual federalism required that some matters be left to the states—and, implicitly but unmistakably, that the states were capable of regulating the matters in question."[143] Thus the Court indicated that "traditional exercise of state authority … was worth respecting not only for tradition's sake, but also because it demonstrated that the states could take over precisely where the national government was forced to stop."[144]

Ultimately, a reading of *Holland* that comports with the nationalist view of the treaty power may, as noted by Professor Rosenkranz, "run[] counter to the textual and structural logic of the Constitution," and could result in Congress's legislative power being "expandable virtually without limit."[145] Rosenkranz finds such a scenario "in deep tension with the basic constitutional scheme of enumerated legislative powers, and it stands contradicted by countless canonical statements that the powers of Congress are fixed and defined."[146] Such an expansion of Congress's legislative power is not, Rosenkranz argues, "consistent with the text of the Constitution or with its underlying theory of separation of powers."[147] Rosenkranz is especially critical of the *Holland* Court's failure to cite a particularly germane 1836 Supreme Court decision—*New Orleans v. United States*—recognizing the principle that "the government of the United States ... is one of limited powers. It can exercise authority over no subjects, except those which have been delegated to it. Congress cannot, by legislation, enlarge the federal jurisdiction, nor can it be enlarged under the treaty-making power."[148] As demonstrated in the next section, Treaty Power and Private Property Rights, *New Orleans* is all the more relevant to an analysis of any treaty regulating land uses like forest management, as the treaty at issue in that case sought to impede traditional state control over property rights.

The *Holland* Court's Tenth Amendment analysis may be limited to the specific fact pattern of *Holland*, resting upon the Court's characterization of the birds as being wildlife of a migratory nature and the necessity of countries collaborating for the management of transboundary resources. Scholars have asserted as much, Professor Bradley noting that "although *Holland* has been construed as giving the treaty power complete immunity from federalism limitations, the decision itself can be read much more narrowly,"[149] and Professor Swaine arguing that "there is a substantial risk that subject-matter limitations ... [may be] applied to the exercise of the treaty power. While *Missouri v. Holland* may survive for the foreseeable future, it will likely be read narrowly."[150] Or, as summarized by Kuh:

> [T]he expansive, nationalist view of the treaty power is unlikely to survive sustained analysis intact and will likely be cabined by some type of limiting principle. When presented with arguments that the treaty power justifies congressional power to act in an area outside of the bounds of the Commerce Clause and other enumerated powers, the Supreme Court will be forced to reexamine in a serious way, for the first time in nearly eighty years, an ill-defined, poorly understood constitutional doctrine (the nationalist view), the wholesale adoption of which could easily be argued to undermine the concept of enumerated powers so recently embraced by the Court in its Commerce Clause, Eleventh Amendment, Tenth Amendment, and anti-commandeering decisions. It only seems prudent to anticipate that instead of feeling inexorably bound by relatively moribund precedent, the Court will instead endeavor to assimilate the treaty power into the revived federalism that it has put forward with such frequency.[151]

Rosenkranz is even more direct, stating that "*Missouri v. Holland* may be canonical, but it does not present a strong case for the application of *stare decisis*. It is wrongly decided, and it should be overruled."[152]

Not every scholar who asserts likely federalism limits on the treaty power believes such limits will arise out of the judiciary. Hollis, for instance, does not believe that the Supreme Court will revisit *Missouri v. Holland* anytime soon.[153] Although agreeing that federalism restraints likely will be placed on the treaty power, Hollis asserted these limitations will arise out of the executive branch, rather than the judiciary. Hollis claimed that both nationalists and new federalists are fixated misguidedly on *Missouri v. Holland*—nationalists believing *Holland* rightly held there were no federalism restraints on the treaty power, and new federalists seeking to justify overturning *Holland* or "dramatically restricting its scope."[154] Hollis cited various rationales supporting his conclusion, but his primary rationale was that the executive's protection of federalism principles may prevent the Court from ever having a chance to revisit *Holland.*[155] Hollis noted that:

> The executive, in exercising its Article II power, has consistently held the reins on accepting U.S. treaty obligations ... it is ultimately the executive that negotiates and concludes U.S. treaties and determines the scope of the obligations it wishes to assume. Thus, it is the executive's choice, first and foremost, whether to defer to federalism in treaty-making. Of late, it has done so with increasing frequency. As such, the Court may never have a chance to revisit *Missouri*. The treaties the president concludes today simply do not implicate the legal authority questions [the Court] had to address.[156]

Hollis argued that the executive has adopted at least six distinct approaches to federalism during treaty-making: (1) no accommodation at all (either when federalism is not an issue or on matters involving foreign persons or transnational conduct); (2) rejecting the treaty; (3) modifying the treaty to account for federalism; (4) modifying U.S. consent to the treaty; (5) limiting federal implementation of the treaty; (6) limiting federal enforcement of the treaty.[157]

Hollis observed that the executive increasingly has implemented federalism restraints during U.S. treaty-making, and has "limited treaties from expanding federal law-making beyond Congress's legislative powers or interfering with activities traditionally regulated by the states."[158] Hollis agreed with other scholars that federalism's potential restraining effect on the treaty power may limit the United States' ability to engage successfully in treaty-making, noting that Executive Federalism

> may prevent the United States from joining treaties it might otherwise have an interest in joining. It may restrain the United States from obtaining concessions from other nations with regard to their behavior

> because of the knowledge that the United States would not be able to reciprocate given states' rights concerns.[159]

Importantly, Hollis concluded that "even if the Court somehow reengages the issue, Executive Federalism offers evidence of treaty power limits from the power-holder's perspective—limits to which the Court is likely to defer."[160]

Regardless of whether the judiciary narrows or overrules *Holland,* or the executive places its own federalism restraints on the treaty power, the potential complications for a forest treaty that fails to take into account U.S. federalism are potentially significant. The next section concludes this review of federalism and the treaty power in the U.S. by demonstrating that even the nationalist view, as put forth by Golove, may allow for federalism restraints on the treaty power in the area of land use activities and property rights, such as are at issue in forest management activities—creating yet more uncertainty for any future global treaty that might incorporate prescriptive dictates aimed at forest management.

The Treaty Power and Private Property Rights

> [N]either life nor property of any citizen, nor the particular right of any state, can be affected by a treaty
>
> Edmond Randolph[161]

The treaty power's relationship with private property rights provides yet another example of the uncertainty surrounding the treaty power's scope and federalism's potential limits upon it. Even under the broad, nationalist reading of *Holland*, direct regulation of private property rights and land use activities, like forest management, may be outside the scope of the treaty power. Both Bradley and Golove, though on opposite ends of the debate, have indicated as much, and federalism-based protection of private property rights from an encroaching treaty power has deep historical roots. Bradley cited an 1819 opinion of the Attorney General that suggested a limitation on the treaty power in the area of private property rights.[162] The opinion stated that "the federal government could not alter by treaty state inheritance law concerning real property."[163] Similarly, in *New Orleans v. United States*, the issue was whether, pursuant to a treaty with France, the federal government had acquired trust rights over certain properties in the city of New Orleans, or whether those property rights remained in the local government.[164] The Court ruled in favor of the city, finding, as noted above, that the federal government "is one of limited powers," and its power cannot be "enlarged under the treaty-making power," thus suggesting a federalism limitation on the treaty power in the area of property rights.[165]

Furthermore, it was not only the judicial branch that asserted federalism limitations on the treaty power in the area of property rights. Ralston Hayden, an early twentieth-century scholar who wrote extensively on the treaty power and states' rights, noted that between 1830 and 1860 "the Senate and the executive entertained grave and increasing doubts concerning their authority to make treaties" in the area of real property rights and that "in every particular instance in which conflict arose the treaty in question was amended to bring it more nearly into accord with the states' rights theory."[166]

Though Golove's analysis of property rights as a states' rights limit on the treaty power is rather disjointed, upon closer review it arguably *supports* federalism as a restraint on the treaty power in the area of property rights. Golove consistently cited treaties the United States entered into that limited state authority over property rights as foolproof examples of how the treaty power can trump powers traditionally left to the states.[167] Yet Golove's examples may not prove as much as he would prefer. Every example Golove cited dealt with property owned by *foreign nationals*. For example, Golove asked "[c]an the federal government enter into treaties on subjects that are otherwise beyond Congress's legislative powers? Consider some typical examples from the nation's past: treaty stipulations overriding traditional state laws preventing aliens from owning real property ... "[168]

Golove cited another treaty that allowed citizens of the United States and citizens of France to

> own real and personal property in the territory of the other and dispose of it by testament, donation, or otherwise to whomsoever they chose. This stipulation altered the traditional common law rule of the states, which denied aliens the right to own real property.[169]

Noting the "close relationship between real property and state sovereignty," Golove asserted that "the provision was bound to raise questions about the scope of the treaty power" and that:

> [T]his provision, found in the very first treaty of the new nation and repeated in countless treaties thereafter, raised the single issue over which the states' rights and nationalist views of the treaty power would most recurrently contend for the next century and a half[170]

—that is, the treaty power versus state control over property rights of citizens *of other nations.*

Indeed, Golove spent a remarkable amount of time discussing various treaties that trumped state regulatory authority over property rights—but in each case, the treaty only trumped state property rights authority as it related to *aliens* owning property in the United States. A treaty power scope that subsumes traditional state authority over property only in the narrow circumstances of foreign citizens' ownership rights is hardly surprising, as it is consistent with *Holland*'s focus on treaty subject matters that necessarily implicate the involvement of the federal government—i.e. treaties that necessarily involve the participation of, or interaction with, a foreign power.[171] Given one of the primary justifications for the treaty power—the need to speak with one voice in international affairs[172]—the federal government would necessarily engage with a foreign power over rights of foreign citizens living in the United States and would do so constitutionally.

In fact, the Supreme Court holdings that Golove cited make clear that the Court only upholds treaty stipulations over traditional state authority under circumstances where the treaties are "for the protection of citizens of one country residing in the territory of another"[173] or are "agreement[s] with respect to the rights and privileges of citizens of the United States in foreign countries, and of the nationals of such countries within the United States."[174] It may be a stretch to assert that Golove's nationalist perspective on the treaty power would carry the day over traditional state authority in the area of private forest management, when no foreign power or its citizens were involved. Golove indicated as much, ultimately asserting that:

> [A] treaty cannot ... adopt domestic standards just because the President and Senate believe them to be laudable. A treaty is unconstitutional if it does not serve a foreign policy interest or if it is concluded not to affect the conduct of other nations but to regulate our own.[175]

Perhaps most tellingly, although Golove is one of the most vocal proponents of the nationalist view, his ultimate analysis actually argued against the use of the treaty power to trump traditional state authority over property rights. Golove provided context by stating that:

> [N]ationalist view proponents do not argue that the treaty power, because it is exclusively granted to the federal government, is therefore free from federalism limitations that would apply to concurrent powers. ... [A]s I have also previously pointed out, they do not contend that the treaty power is categorically exempt from either affirmative federalism limitations, such as ... the general Tenth Amendment declaration that exercises of nondelegated authority are unconstitutional.[176]

Golove then made an analogy between separation of powers limitations and federalism limitations on the treaty power, noting that a treaty "purporting to authorize the President rather than Congress hereafter to make laws regulating interstate and foreign commerce would violate the separation of powers. Even though a treaty can regulate particular matters falling within those subjects, it may not change the internal distribution of power between Congress and the President."[177] Strikingly, Golove argued that:

> Likewise, a treaty purporting to grant Congress hereafter legislative authority over, say, *real property in the states, would fall afoul of federalism.* Although a treaty can regulate particular aspects of real property relations

> in the states, it cannot transfer legislative authority over those subjects from the states to Congress. Beyond these cases, treaties are as subject to federalism as they are to the separation of powers.[178]

Although this statement can be read merely to mean that Congress cannot aggregate unto itself a general authority to regulate private property directly, Golove failed to explain how such an aggregation would be fundamentally different than allowing individual treaties to "regulate particular aspects of real property relations." Apparently, based upon Golove's own lengthy summary of examples, he would confine such regulation in the area of property rights to treaties affecting real property owned by foreign nationals.

In the final analysis, regardless of the contentious outcome of the "new federalism" versus "nationalist" debate on the scope of the treaty power—in the legislature, the courts, and the scholarly literature—it appears that it is at the *least* uncertain whether the federal government can claim authority over private property rights, and land use activities like forest management under the treaty power, in light of potential federalism limits upon it. Not only does *Missouri v. Holland* raise such doubts, but so do the scholarly writings of parties on *both sides* of the "new federalism" versus "nationalist" debate. If federalism does so limit the treaty power, then if none of the other enumerated powers under the Constution, such as the Commerce Clause, provide authority to the federal government over direct subnational forest management standard-setting, the federal government would not be able to implement prescriptive, "traditional governance" forest management directives on private lands pursuant to an international treaty. Any attempt to do so would result in Tenth Amendment judicial challenges, likely brought by both private landowners and state governments.

Conclusion

The international community is properly increasing its focus on global forest management in the battle against climate change and is rightly taking an interest in forest management activities on a local scale, such as the activities engaged in by the Alabama forester. This focus is essential to capture the full carbon sequestration value of the world's forests, as well as to preserve the numerous other ecosystem services provided by sustainable forestry. Achieving either a successful binding, stand-alone forest treaty or a climate treaty incorporating forest management, however, may depend in large part on the United States' willingness and ability to enter into and implement such a treaty. U.S. federalism complicates the United States' role in the formation of any treaty aimed at forests, since the federal government is granted authority under the Constitution to negotiate treaties, while state governments maintain primary regulatory authority over land use activities like forest management. We saw this complication in our earlier discussion of the scope of the Commerce Clause at the domestic level. Debates over the scope of the U.S.

treaty power demonstrate how natural capital management approaches one scale up—the international scale—are also complicated by questions of federalism. But it is not only the U.S. that maintains a federal structure that potentially complicates coordination of natural capital appropriation among countries at the global level. As we will see in Chapter 7, around three-quarters of the global forest commons is contained within federal systems that might potentially facilitate legal complications for global forest management. Thus we need to better understand the nature of these institutions, which are the most likely of all governance structures to legally entrench the commons dynamic.

Notes

1 The material constituting significant portions of this chapter originated in Blake Hudson, Climate Change, Forests and Federalism: Seeing the Treaty for the Trees, 82 *U. Col. L. Rev.* 363 (2011).

2 Edward T. Swaine, Does Federalism Constrain the Treaty Power? 103 *Colum. L. Rev.* 403, 456, 492 (2003).

3 Ala. Forestry Comm'n, Alabama's Best Management Practices for Forestry 4 (2007), available at http://www.forestry.state.al.us/Publications/BMPs/2007_BMP_Manual.pdf [hereinafter Alabama's Best Practices].

4 See Erin C. Myers, Policies to Reduce Emissions from Deforestation and Degradation (REDD) in Tropical Forests: An Examination of the Issues Facing the Incorporation of REDD into Market-based Climate Policies 4 (2007), available at http://www.rff.org/documents/RFF-DP-07-50.pdf. See also California's AB-32 climate legislation, Assemb. B. 32, § 2, 2006 Gen Assemb., Reg. Sess. (Cal. 2006) (Global Warming Solutions Act) (establishing GHG reduction goals and a framework for achieving the goals).

5 Alabama's Best Practices, supra note 3.

6 Myers, supra note 4.

7 The UNFF (U.N. Forum on Forests) concluded its tenth session in April 2013. See *UNFF10 Voluntary Reports*, United Nations Forum on Forests, available at http://www.un.org/esa/forests/reports-unff10.html.

8 By "stand-alone" this book refers to negotiations that are outside the context of climate treaty negotiations.

9 At UNFF-8 in April 2009, many called for both forest carbon and non-carbon values to be addressed within any future climate agreement. UNFF8 Discusses Role of Forests in Future Climate Change Regime, Climate-L.org (Apr. 21, 2009), available at http://climate-l.iisd.org/news/unff8-discusses-role-of-forests-in-future-climate-change-regime/ (also see referenced press releases). Also in April 2009, the UN-DESA issued a policy brief asserting that "[t]he global climate change agreement should include actions on deforestation and forest degradation within the wider context of sustainable forest management." U.N. Dep't of Econ. & Soc. Affairs, *UN-DESA Policy Brief No. 15, Finance for Forests and Climate Change* (2009), available at http://www.un.org/esa/policy/policybriefs/policybrief15.pdf.

10 James Rasband, James Salzman, and Mark Squillace, *Natural Resources Law and Policy 1203* (2nd ed. 2009). See also William Boyd, Deforestation and Emerging Greenhouse Gas Compliance Regimes: Toward a Global Environmental Law of Forests, Carbon and Climate Governance, in *Deforestation and Climate Change: Reducing Carbon Emissions From Deforestation and Forest Degradation* 1, 9–13 (Valentina Bosetti and Ruben Lubowski eds, 2010).

11 See Swaine, supra note 2.

12 Id.

13 See United States v. Morrison, 529 U.S. 598 (2000); Printz v. United States, 521 U.S. 898 (1997); City of Boerne v. Flores, 521 U.S. 507 (1997); United States v. Lopez, 514 U.S. 549 (1995); New York v. United States, 505 U.S. 144 (1992); Swaine, supra note 2, at 403; see generally Curtis A. Bradley, The Treaty Power and American Federalism (pts. 1 & 2), 97 *Mich. L. Rev.* 390 (1998) [hereinafter Bradley I], 99 *Mich. L. Rev.* 98 (2000) [hereinafter Bradley II]; Duncan B. Hollis, Executive Federalism: Forging New Federalist Constraints on the Treaty Power, 79 *S. Cal. L. Rev.* 1327 (2006); Katrina L. Fischer, Harnessing the Treaty Power in Support of Environmental Regulation of Activities That Don't "Substantially Affect Interstate Commerce": Recognizing the Realities of the New Federalism, 22 *Va. Envtl. L.J.* 167 (2004); Nicholas Q. Rosenkranz, Executing the Treaty Power, 118 *Harv. L. Rev.* 1867 (2005).

14 David M. Golove, Treaty-Making and the Nation: The Historical Foundations of the Nationalist Conception of the Treaty Power, 98 *Mich. L. Rev.* 1075, 1258 (2000). See also Hollis, supra note 13, at 1330–31. As discussed in Chapter 4, in the context of Commerce Clause scope the jurisprudence supporting these polar positions has shifted numerous times during U.S. history. While we are currently still in a nationalist phase, and despite some cases supporting the new federalist position (*Lopez*, *Morrison*, and *Sebelius*), there is no reason to think that a shift back toward stringent federalism protections could not occur in the future. As a result, scholars should develop a more holistic view of the structure of American federalism over a longer time span than just the present controversies. Otherwise, we view a historically fluid doctrinal subject area through a myopic lens.

15 See United Nations Forum on Forests, available at http://www.un.org/esa/forests/session.html; Radoslav S. Dimitrov et al., International Nonregimes: A Research Agenda, 9 *Int'l Stud. Rev.* 230, 243 (2006); *accord* S. Guéneau and P. Tozzi, Towards the Privatization of Global Forest Governance? 10 *Int'l Forestry Rev.* 550, 552 (2008); Deborah S. Davenport and Peter Wood, Finding the Way Forward for the International Arrangement on Forests: UNFF-5, -6, and -7, 15 *Rev. of Eur. Cmty. & Int'l Envtl. L.* 316 (2006). See Davenport and Wood for a thorough description of the chronology of discussions over a forest treaty since 1992. Id. at 316–17.

16 See Bastiaan Louman et al., 1: Forest Ecosystem Services: A Cornerstone for Human Well-Being, in *Int'l Union of Forest Research Orgs., Adaptation of Forests and People to Climate Change—A Global Assessment Report* 16–20 (Risto Seppälä, Alexander Buck, and Pia Katila eds, 2009), available at http://www.iufro.org/science/gfep/embargoed-release/download-by-chapter/ (follow "Download chapter 1" hyperlink).

17 Radoslav Dimitrov, Knowledge, Power, and Interests in Environmental Regime Formation, 47 *Int'l Stud. Q.* 123, 135–37 (2003).

18 See the 2007 Non-legally Binding Authoritative Statement of Principles for a Global Consensus on the Management, Conservation, and Sustainable Development of All Types of Forests, *G.A. Res.* 62/98, annex, U.N. Doc. A/RES/62/98, at 3–4 (Jan. 31, 2008), available at http://www.fao.org/forestry/14717–03d86aa8c1a7426cf69bf9e2f5023bb12.pdf.

19 Katharina Kunzmann, The Non-legally Binding Instrument on Sustainable Management of All Types of Forests—Towards a Legal Regime for Sustainable Forest Management? 9 *Ger. L.J.* 981, 1005 (2008), available at http://www.germanlawjournal.com/pdfs/Vol09No08/PDF_Vol_09_No_08_981–1006_Articles_Kunzmann.pdf.

20 Dimitrov et al., supra note 15, at 134.

21 Blake Hudson and Erika Weinthal, Seeing the Global Forest for the Trees: How U.S. Federalism can Coexist with Global Governance of Forests, 1 *J. Nat. Resources Pol'y Res.* 353, 353–54 (2009). See also Dimitrov, supra note 15, at 135; Tom Griffiths, Forest Peoples Programme, *Seeing 'RED'? 'Avoided Deforestation' and the Rights of Indigenous Peoples and Local Communities* 1 (2007), available at http://www.forestpeoples.org/documents/ifi_igo/avoided_deforestation_red_jun07_eng.pdf.

22 See Deborah S. Davenport, An Alternative Explanation for the Failure of the UNCED Forest Negotiations, 5 *Global Envtl. Pol.* 105, 105 (2005); see also Radoslav Dimitrov,

Hostage to Norms: States, Institutions and Global Forest Politics, 5 *Global Envtl. Pol.* 1, 9–10 (2005).

23 Davenport, supra note 22, at 105.

24 Id. at 111.

25 Id. at 126–37.

26 See Imme Scholz, A Forest Convention—Yes or No? *Ger. Dev. Inst.* (DIE) Discussion Papers, 9 (2004), available at http://www.isn.ethz.ch/isn/Digital-Library/Publications/Detail/?ots591=0C54E3B3-1E9C-BE1E-2C24-A6A8C7060233&lng=en&id=27768 (follow "English PDF" hyperlink).

27 Id. at 15.

28 For discussion of Kyoto's failure to adequately incorporate forest management, see Kelly Levin, Constance McDermott, and Ben Cashore, The Climate Regime as Global Forest Governance: Can Reduced Emissions from Deforestation and Forest Degradation (REDD) Initiatives Pass a 'Dual Effectiveness' Test? 10 *Int'l Forestry Rev.* 544 (2008). See generally Benjamin Cashore, Constance McDermott, and Kelly Levin, The Shaping and Reshaping of British Columbia Forest Policy in the Global Era: A Review of Governmental and Non-governmental Strategic Initiatives (2006), available at http://www.yale.edu/forest-certification/pdfs/ABCFP.pdf.

29 See Levin et al., supra note 28, at 543–45.

30 Id. at 544.

31 See Levin et al., supra note 28, at 45–48.

32 United Nations Forum on Forests, *Recent Developments in Existing Forest-Related Instruments, Agreements, and Processes* 12 (U.N. Forum on Forests Background Doc. No. 2, Working Draft, 2004), available at http://www.un.org/esa/forests/pdf/aheg/param/background-2.pdf.

33 Josep G. Canadell and Michael R. Raupach, Managing Forests for Climate Change Mitigation, 320 *Sci. Mag.* 1456, 1456 (2008).

34 See Lieberman-Warner Climate Security Act, S. 2191, 110th Cong. (2007); see also American Clean Energy and Security Act (Waxman-Markey Bill), H.R. 2454, 111th Cong. (2009); Dingell-Boucher Cap-and-Trade Bill, Inst. for Energy Research (Oct. 7, 2008), available at http://www.instituteforenergyresearch.org/2008/10/07/dingell-boucher-cap-and-trade-bill.

35 Hudson and Weinthal, supra note 21, at 354 (citation omitted). Though the balance of power between the state and federal governments shifts periodically in U.S. constitutional jurisprudence—thus leading to court "protection" of states' rights to a greater or lesser degree than federal power—the judicial system resolutely protects the principle that is U.S. federalism. As one scholar noted, "[i]n the United States there have been fluctuations in the relative strengths of the national and state governments." Ronald Watts, The American Constitution in Comparative Perspective: A Comparison of Federalism in the United States and Canada, 74 *J. Am. Hist.* 769, 773 (1987). It remains, however, that "the courts and particularly the Supreme Court have come to play a prominent role through their exercise of judicial review to ensure the constitutionality of legislation and executive and administrative action relating to … the distribution of jurisdiction between the national and state governments." Id. at 789.

36 Some scholars argue that to achieve optimal results at the local level, any global forest management scheme should provide the greatest amount of flexibility in managing forests—or, a "bottom-up" approach. See Peter Glück et al., 7: Governance and Policies for Adaptation, in *Int'l Union of Forest Research Orgs.*, supra note 16 at 187, 190, 195–97 (follow "Download chapter 7" hyperlink). These scholars contend that forest governance should retreat from prescriptive approaches—i.e. "traditional governance"—because "traditional governance, focusing on a hierarchical, top-down style of policy formulation and implementation of the nation state and the use of regulatory policy instruments, will be incompatible with this demand for flexibility." Id. at 190. See generally Peter Glück et al., 4: Changes in the Governance of Forest Resources, in Int'l Union of Forest

Research Orgs.; *Forests in the Global Balance—Changing Paradigms* 51, 72 (2005), available at http://www.iufro.org/science/special/wfse/forests-global-balance (follow "Changes in the Governance of Forest Resources" hyperlink). While this may be the case, severe over-decentralization in the forest sector and the legal institutions that facilitate it may require adjustment in the future through more direct, top-down mechanisms. When given global commons problems like climate change, no option should be left off the table nor should a thorough understanding of any option be ignored by scholars and policymakers.

37 See Scholz, supra note 26, at 15.

38 Hudson and Weinthal, supra note 21, at 355.

39 Fischer, supra note 13, at 199. Though the United States signed the Kyoto Protocol, it never ratified it domestically.

40 Hudson and Weinthal, supra note 21, at 356.

41 Id. at 356. See David M. Reiner, Climate Impasse: How The Hague Negotiation Failed, *Environment*, Mar. 2001, at 36, 38.

42 Hudson and Weinthal, supra note 21, at 356.

43 Id.

44 U.S. Term Limits v. Thornton, 514 U.S. 779, 838 (1995) (Kennedy, J., concurring).

45 See Arun Agrawal, Ashwini Chhatre, and Rebecca Hardin, Changing Governance of the World's Forests, 320 *Sci. Mag.* 1460, 1460 (2008).

46 U.N. Env't Programme, *Global Environment Outlook 3: Past, Present, and Future Perspectives* 110 (2002), available at http://www.unep.org/geo/GEO3/english/pdf.htm (follow "Forests" hyperlink).

47 Id.

48 Rasband et al., supra note 10, at 1308.

49 Wyoming v. U.S. Dep't of Interior, 360 F. Supp. 2d 1214, 1238–42 (D. Wyo. 2005).

50 Connecticut v. United States, 369 F. Supp. 2d 237, 248 (D. Conn. 2005).

51 Virginia v. Browner, 80 F.3d 869, 883 (4th Cir. 1996).

52 See Paul Ellefson, Anthony Cheng, and Robert J. Moulton, State Forest Practice Regulatory Programs: An Approach to Implementing Ecosystem Management on Private Forest Lands in the United States, 21 *Envtl. Mgmt.* 421, 421–22 (1997).

53 See Jan G. Laitos et al., Natural Resources Law 849 (2006). It should be noted that logging is only one activity in which forest owners potentially engage. Nonindustrial uses of private forests are even more clearly in the zone of power reserved to the states, as they are subject to state and local zoning and development laws. It seems clear that at the present time the federal government does not maintain the recognized authority to establish zoning schemes for states or municipalities. Some municipalities even use zoning as a means of regulating land use related to forestry. For example, a Pennsylvania municipality's zoning ordinance prohibits clearcutting of forests on tracts which are larger than two acres and on slopes greater than 15 percent. Id. at 871 (citing Williams Township Zoning Ordinance 2001–3).

54 33 U.S.C. § 1251(b) (2006) (emphasis added).

55 Gerald A. Rose et al., Forest Resources Decision-Making in the U.S., in *The Politics of Decentralization: Forests, People and Power* 238 (Carol J. Pierce Colfer and Doris Capistrano eds, 2005).

56 See generally Paul Goldstein and Barton H. Thompson, Jr., Property Law: Ownership, Use, and Conservation 1086–1102 (2006) (ESA); Rasband, supra note 10, at 826–27, 853–65 (CWA).

57 Hudson and Weinthal, supra note 21, at 357.

58 272 U.S. 365 (1926).

59 Ellefson et al., supra note 52, at 429.

60 252 U.S. 416 (1920).

61 Hudson and Weinthal, supra note 21, at 357–58.

62 Id. at 358.

63 Bradley II, supra note 13, at 131–32 (citing Kurt H. Nadelmann, Ignored State Interests: The Federal Government and International Efforts to Unify Rules of Private Law, 102 *U. Pa. L. Rev.* 323 (1954); Harold W. Stoke, *The Foreign Relations of the Federal State* 187–88 (1931)).

64 Id. at 132.

65 Swaine, supra note 2, at 410. Professor Swaine noted that, based upon perceived federalism limits, the United States flatly opposed the Convention on the Rights of the Child, sought treaty exemptions for the states with a variety of human rights treaties and the Agreement on Government Procurement, and provided concessions to the states in domestic implementation of trade matters like the Uruguay Round Agreements Act. Id. at 409–10. Swaine noted that:

> [R]ecent U.S. practices may persuade [the Supreme Court] to look more skeptically at the equivalence of a treaty and its legislative implementation. ... Congress did take specific steps to implement the Uruguay Round Agreements and NAFTA, but in each case pointedly impaired the effectiveness of the agreement for the states' sake; in other matters, like the Agreement on Government Procurement, the United States more forthrightly negotiated internationally and domestically for purely voluntary subscription by American states.

Id. at 420–21.

66 Id. at 461–62.

67 Id. at 445–46.

68 Id. at 449.

69 Id.

70 Id. Professor Hollis has described "the treaty" as

> liv[ing] a double life. By day, it is a creature of international law, which sets forth extensive substantive and procedural rules by which the treaty must operate. ... By night, however, the treaty leads a more domestic life. In its domestic incarnation, the treaty is a creature of national law, deriving its force from the constitutional order of the nation state that concluded it. Within the United States, therefore, the Constitution governs. Just as we look to international law to discern treaty rules on the international plane, so too must we look to the Constitution for substantive or procedural rules by which the treaty functions within the U.S. legal system.

Hollis, supra note 13, at 1327–28.

71 Daniel Bodansky, *The Art and Craft of International Environmental Law* 156 (2010).

72 Id.

73 Vienna Convention on the Law of Treaties art. 27, May 23, 1969, 1155 U.N.T.S. 331.

74 Swaine, supra note 2, at 450.

75 See Vienna Convention, supra note 73, at 339, 340. Swaine has further elaborated that

> international law addresses federalism indirectly through the meta-obligation of *pacta sunt servanda*—the fundamental principle that treaties are to be obeyed—and its corollary duty of good faith (to which I will refer, in the aggregate, as a duty of good faith). ... This principle ... supports, of course, the notion that a state's international responsibilities prevail over any inconsistent domestic law. More particularly, it imposes an affirmative duty to bring internal legislation, at whatever level of government, into line with treaty obligations. Nations are unambiguously responsible for enacting domestic legislation necessary to implement their treaty obligations, and likewise cannot enforce laws that conflict with their international duties.

Swaine, supra note 2, at 453–54.

76 Swaine, supra note 2, at 450.
77 Id. at 452. Swaine stated, however, that it "remains ... manifestly harder for federal governments to ensure compliance, and the abstract availability of remedies for noncompliance hardly makes up the difference." Id.
78 Id. at 451.
79 Id. at 468–70.
80 Id. at 456.
81 Id. at 457.
82 LaGrand Case (Ger. v. U.S.), 2001 I.C.J. 466, 500 (June 27) (noting that U.S. pleadings cited as a "constraining factor ... the character of the United States of America as a federal republic of divided powers").
83 Swaine, supra note 2, at 457 (quoting LaGrand, 2001 I.C.J. at 508).
84 See generally Evan Mandery, Federalism and the Death Penalty, 66 *Alb. L. Rev.* 809 (2003).
85 Vienna Convention, supra note 73, at 339.
86 Bodansky, supra note 71, at 86–87.
87 See Hudson and Weinthal, supra note 21, at 355; see generally Glück et al., supra note 36, at 190, 195–97.
88 Golove, supra note 14, at 1076–77.
89 See generally Bradley I, supra note 13; Bradley II, supra note 13.
90 Bradley I, supra note 13, at 393–94.
91 Id. at 394. Bradley stated that "we must decide whether federalism is worth preserving. If it is, the nationalist view of the treaty power should be reconsidered." Id. at 461.
92 Id. at 394.
93 Swaine, supra note 2, at 474–75 (stating that federalism limits "might leave the United States with a gap between its international treaty obligations and its ability to implement them, and that gap may be relatively more difficult for the government to fill. ... If the national government is indeed supposed to be a creature of limited authority, shouldn't the treaty power enjoy boundaries just like any other?"); see also Fischer, supra note 13; Rosenkranz, supra note 13; Hollis, supra note 13.
94 Bradley I, supra note 13, at 450. See also Id. at 456.
95 Swaine, supra note 2, at 422.
96 Rosenkranz, supra note 13, at 1936.
97 See New York v. United States, 505 U.S. 144 (1992) (invalidating a federal statute that effectively compelled state disposal of radioactive waste).
98 See United States v. Lopez, 514 U.S. 549 (1995) (invalidating a federal statute criminalizing the possession of firearms near school zones).
99 See City of Boerne v. Flores, 521 U.S. 507 (1997) (invalidating a federal statute for exceeding Congress's powers under the 14th Amendment).
100 See Printz v. United States, 521 U.S. 898 (1997) (invalidating a federal statute requiring state law enforcement officials to conduct background checks on handgun purchasers).
101 See United States v. Morrison, 529 U.S. 598 (2000) (invalidating a federal statute providing a civil remedy to victims of gender-based violence, even when no criminal charges were filed).
102 505 U.S. at 177.
103 521 U.S. at 932. Bradley noted that "[i]t was obvious by [Printz] that the Court was treating the Tenth Amendment (broadly defined) as a restraint on delegated powers. Indeed, two concurring justices, including the author of the earlier New York decision, stated this expressly." Bradley II, supra note 13, at 115. See also Thomas Healy, Note, Is Missouri v. Holland Still Good Law? Federalism and the Treaty Power, 98 *Colum. L. Rev.* 1726, 1739–40 (1998).
104 Reno v. Condon, 528 U.S. 141, 149 (2000).
105 Bradley I, supra note 13, at 400.
106 Swaine, supra note 2, at 417.

107 Id. See also Bradley II, supra note 13, at 100.

108 Fischer, supra note 13, at 173–74 ("Although the Supreme Court did not reach the issue, commentators on the SWANCC decision have suggested that the treaty power provides a ground independent of the Commerce Clause for upholding the constitutionality of the CWA's reach to include isolated, intrastate water bodies. Gavin R. Villareal and Omar N. White have evaluated (in separate articles) the possibility of employing the treaty power to support the ESA.") (citing Stephen M. Johnson, Federal Regulation of Isolated Wetlands After SWANCC, [June 2001] 31 *Envtl. L. Rep.* (Envtl. L. Inst.) 10,669; Gavin R. Villareal, Note: One Leg to Stand On: The Treaty Power and Congressional Authority for the Endangered Species Act After United States v. Lopez, 76 *Tex. L. Rev.* 1125 (1998); Omar N. White, The Endangered Species Act's Precarious Perch: A Constitutional Analysis Under the Commerce Clause and the Treaty Power, 27 *Ecology L. Q.* 215 (2000)).

109 Swaine, supra note 2, at 417.

110 Fischer, supra note 13, at 175. Professor Kuh was known as Professor Fischer at the time this article was written.

111 Id. at 177.

112 Id. at 180.

113 Id. at 180–81.

114 Golove, supra note 14, at 1079 ("Given a seven-to-two decision rendered by a Court well known for its sensitivity to federalism concerns—a decision that has been on the books for eighty years, repeatedly reaffirmed and never questioned by the Court, and the object of a highly publicized but failed effort to amend the Constitution—it is difficult to see what justification there could be now for overruling such a venerable decision. Yet, that is precisely what Professor Curtis Bradley forcefully advocated.").

115 Id. at 1087–88 ("Under this view—the nationalist view—the treaty power is the same as any of the other enumerated powers, except that it is granted to the President and Senate in Article II, rather than to Congress in Article I. In contrast, the states' rights view, at least in its most plausible formulation, denies that the treaty power is, in the relevant sense, 'delegated.' Rather, it is just another method for exercising the powers given to the national government in Article I.").

116 Id. at 1278.

117 Id. at 1278–79.

118 Id. at 1287.

119 Bradley II, supra note 13, at 98.

120 Id. at 99.

121 Id.

122 Id.

123 Id. Notably, Bradley argued that Golove "overstates the degree to which Supreme Court precedent resolved the treaty power issue prior to Holland. Most of the decisions Golove cites as 'affirming the nationalist view' simply held that valid treaties preempt inconsistent state law." Id. at 130.

124 Id. at 124.

125 Id. at 132–33.

126 Laitos et al., supra note 53, at 1200–201.

127 Louis Henkin, *Foreign Affairs and the United States Constitution* 190 (2nd ed. 1996).

128 Rosenkranz, supra note 13, at 1869.

129 Missouri v. Holland, 252 U.S. 416, 431 (1920).

130 *Holland*, 252 U.S. at 432.

131 Id.

132 Id. at 432.

133 Id. at 434–35.

134 See Rosenkranz, supra note 13, at 1885–88 ("Justice Holmes contented himself with just a single conclusory sentence: 'If the treaty is valid there can be no dispute about the

validity of the statute under Article I, § 8, as a necessary and proper means to execute the powers of the Government.'").

135 Importantly, the Court stated:

> We do not mean to imply that there are no qualifications to the treaty-making power; but they must be ascertained in a different way. It is obvious that there may be matters of the sharpest exigency for the national well being that an act of Congress could not deal with but that a treaty followed by such an act could.

Holland, 252 U.S. at 433. In addition, it is unclear that the Court today even would consider the facts of *Holland* under the treaty-making power, as "since 1937 the Supreme Court's broad reading of the Commerce Clause as a source of congressional power has led to more reliance upon it to uphold federal regulation of wildlife." George C. Coggins et al., *Federal Public Land and Resources Law* 178 (6th ed. 2007). In fact, the MBTA itself subsequently was justified independently under the Commerce Clause. See e.g., Andrus v. Allard, 444 U.S. 51 (1979).

136 *Holland*, 252 U.S. at 434.

137 Hudson and Weinthal, supra note 21, at 360.

138 *Holland*, 252 U.S. at 435.

139 Indeed, state governments are likely to exercise less stringent environmental controls over forest management activities on state-owned and private forests than those the federal government exercises over federal forests. Scholars have noted that "federal officials consistently exhibit greater levels of ecosystem-level management, rare species identification and protection, ecosystem research and monitoring, and soil and watershed improvement" than do state officials; and "agency officials at higher levels of government are likely to favor goals other than economic development more than are agency officials at lower levels of governance." Tomas M. Koontz, *Federalism in the Forest: National Versus State Natural Resource Policy* 77–78.

140 *Holland*, 252 U.S. at 435. This statement arguably does not apply, however, regarding forest management in isolation from the climate issue. It seems clear that the United States could manage its forests responsibly and sustainably without reliance on the cooperation of any other nation.

141 In Palila v. Hawaii Dep't of Land & Natural Res., 471 F. Supp. 985, 992–93 (D. Haw. 1979), the court characterized the holding in *Holland* as the authority of "the federal government [to] preempt state control over *wildlife* under federal legislation implementing a ... [t]reaty" (emphasis added).

142 Swaine, supra note 2, at 479.

143 Id.

144 Id.

145 Rosenkranz, supra note 13, at 1893.

146 Id. at 1894. Rosenkranz continued:

> Just recently, Chief Justice Rehnquist wrote for the Court that 'Congress' regulatory authority is not without effective bounds.' But it was Chief Justice Marshall, almost two centuries before, who explained why in the clearest terms: 'enumeration presupposes something not enumerated,' or more emphatically, '[t]he powers of the legislature are *defined*, and *limited*; and that those limits may not be mistaken, or forgotten, the constitution is written.'

Id. (alteration in original) (citing Gibbons v. Ogden, 22 U.S. (9 Wheat.) 1, 195 (1824); Marbury v. Madison, 5 U.S. (1 Cranch) 137, 176 (1803)).

147 Id. at 1899.

148 Mayor of New Orleans v. United States, 35 U.S. (10 Pet.) 662, 736 (1836).

149 Bradley I, supra note 13, at 459.
150 Swaine, supra note 2, at 412.
151 Fischer, supra note 13, at 186.
152 Rosenkranz, supra note 13, at 1937.
153 Hollis, supra note 13, at 1360.
154 Id. at 1344–45.
155 Id. at 1353–60.
156 Id.
157 Id. at 1371–86.
158 Id. at 1363.
159 Id. at 1394–95.
160 Id. at 1386.
161 The Debates in *The Convention of the Commonwealth of Virginia*, reprinted in 3 Elliot's Debates 504 (Jonathan Elliot ed., 2nd ed. 1888).
162 1 Op. Atty. Gen. 275 (1819).
163 Bradley I, supra note 13, at 416.
164 35 U.S. (10 Pet.) 662 (1836).
165 Id. at 736.
166 Ralston Hayden, The States' Rights Doctrine and the Treaty-Making Power, 22 *Am. Hist. Rev.* 566, 585 (1917). In turn, Bradley notes, Hayden "explains that, when President Fillmore submitted a proposed treaty between the United States and Switzerland to the Senate in 1850, he asked for and obtained amendments from the Senate to protect the reserved powers of the States." Bradley I, supra note 13, at 421 (citing Hayden, at 575–76).
167 See generally Golove, supra note 14; Hollis, supra note 13.
168 Golove, supra note 14, at 1077.
169 Id. at 1106–7.
170 Id. at 1107.
171 Missouri v. Holland, 252 U.S. 416, 435 (1920).
172 Am. Ins. Ass'n v. Garamendi, 539 U.S. 396, 424 (2003).
173 Asakura v. City of Seattle, 265 U.S. 332, 341 (1924).
174 Santovincenzo v. Egan, 284 U.S. 30, 40 (1931). Golove provided other examples of treaty power trumping traditional state authority, but each instance, again, involved foreign nationals. Golove, supra note 14, at 1270–72 (quoting *Asakura*, 265 U.S. at 341, quoting *Santovincenzo*, 284 U.S. at 40).
175 Golove, supra note 14, at 1287–88.
176 Id. at 1285.
177 Id. at 1286.
178 Id. (emphasis added).

7 Forest Commons, Climate Change, and Federalism Beyond the United States

A Survey of Federal Systems[1]

> Nations concerned about the difficulty of accommodating particular obligations within their constitutional schemes ... may decline altogether to enter into a treaty that poses a serious risk of conflict with their constitutions. At the domestic level, well-grounded constitutional principles may be insurmountable.[2]

> Federalism and a spirited foreign policy go ill together.[3]

Introduction

In 2010, at the United Nations Global Conference on Environmental Governance and Democracy,[4] numerous scholars expressed concern over political disconnects among countries engaged in international negotiations on climate change, perhaps the most complex and challenging environmental issue of our time. Much of the conference discussion focused on strengthening governance at various levels to forge political will for action on climate change, either through the creation of new legislation facilitating climate change mitigation and adaptation or through improved enforcement of existing climate change laws.[5] Political will to create and enforce effective regulatory mechanisms on international and domestic scales is undoubtedly critical to effective global environmental governance, especially in an area as contentious as climate change. As highlighted in Chapter 6, however, another question necessarily precedes an inquiry into political will—that is, does an adequate legal institutional framework exist within participant countries to ensure that in the presence of political will, if and when it occurs, international treaties can be successfully negotiated and implemented domestically? Without adequate legal institutions to effectively translate global politics into domestic policy, the most robust of international treaties will not be effectively implemented on domestic scales.

Indeed, as demonstrated in Chapter 6, domestic governance limitations in the form of constitutional federalism may complicate the implementation of a non-self-executing, legally binding climate change treaty that addresses global forest management via certain regulatory mechanisms, or perhaps even complicate treaty formation altogether. In this way, Professor Swaine's assertion[6] that nations concerned with the interplay between potentially insurmountable domestic constitutional law and international treaty obligations may decline to enter into a treaty may ring true in the forest management context. As Professor Wheare acknowledged 60 years ago,[7] federalism and participation in international governance regimes may very well "go ill together" under some circumstances.

Chapter 6 bears out these potential complications with regard to forest management in the U.S., where regulatory authority over forest management is currently constitutionally divided between the federal and state governments, with state governments responsible for regulating the nearly 65 percent of "local" U.S. forests that are in either state ownership (approximately 5 percent) or private ownership (approximately 60 percent).[8] Yet as discussed in Chapter 6, forests are of both local and global importance, and

> [t]he challenge is to find a governance framework that can balance the various local, national and global interests related to forests. Everyone agrees that local groups should be allowed to come up with solutions that reflect their own needs and circumstances; but regional, national and global concerns must also be addressed.[9]

In other words, in federal systems we need not take away the ability of national, state, and local herders to maintain inputs into forest resource management. Rather, consistent with dynamic federalism as outlined in Chapter 5, we need to remove the commons dynamic by coordinating their activities in a way that takes into account global forest needs.

Federal systems are ostensibly designed to maximize the ability of local groups to meet their own needs and design policies suited to their own circumstances. Yet from a legal perspective there is a sharp contrast in how federal systems and nonfederal nation-states with centralized, unitary forms of government function during international negotiations. As discussed in Chapters 1 and 2, unitary systems may operate without *legal* constraint during international negotiations—the lack of exclusive areas of subnational constitutional authority in these countries allows central governments to more freely obligate their respective nations to the dictates of a legally binding treaty.[10]

As depicted in Figure 7.1, though federal systems of government comprise only approximately 13 percent of the world's governments, they maintain control over 70 to 80 percent of the world's forests.[11] As a result, the domestic constitutional governance structures of federal systems controlling important forest resources need to be analyzed to better understand potential complications that may arise during international climate or other negotiations related to forests. As the threat of climate change becomes more apparent and the resulting law and policy responses adjust over time, it will be crucial that world governments maintain, and are able to effectively utilize, every legal and policy tool at their disposal. A collaborative international

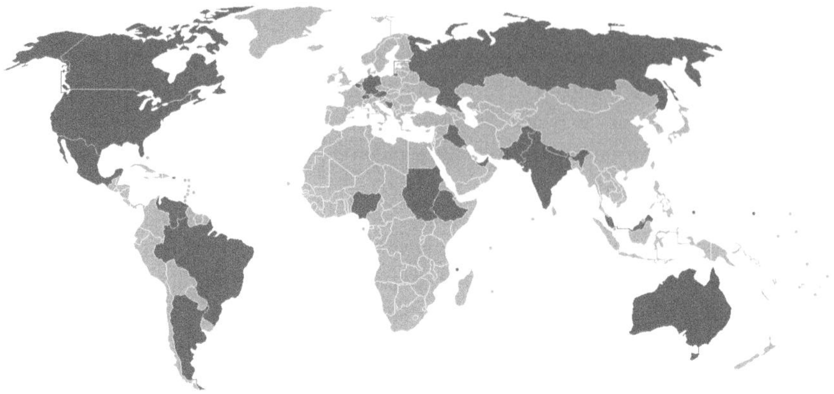

Figure 7.1 Federal nations of the world (shaded)

response to climate change can certainly take many forms, ranging from individualized action by single nations, to transnational forms,[12] to a legally binding global treaty. The utilization of a binding treaty, however, may be diminished if constitutionally decentralized federal systems controlling important forest resources are unable to fully participate. And it is the inability to utilize an international legal regime that would legally entrench the commons dynamic at the global level, absent the incidental "irrational" actions of the many nations controlling crucial forest resources.

In addition to the United States, five federal systems in particular—Australia, Brazil, Canada, India, and Russia—account for 54 percent of the world's total forest cover,[13] and are thus vitally important to international negotiations on forests. Regardless of past and present *political* impacts on climate treaty formation, such as insufficient domestic political will or political disagreements between the developed and developing world, such an assessment is clearly warranted to determine whether a sufficient *legal* institutional framework exists in federal systems to facilitate the full range of market-based *and* regulatory options within international agreements that incorporate forests. If the constitutional framework in a federal system limits the national government's authority to effectively implement a treaty on a subject matter reserved to subnational governments, a more important question will be how to craft constitutional approaches in these systems that best facilitate international agreement, the subject of Chapter 9.

An equally important question is how to balance global climate and forest governance with the benefits that decentralized forest management provides on local scales. The reason that some federal systems may legally entrench the commons dynamic and create innumerable herders on multiple scales engaged in forest or other natural capital appropriation is so that those subnational entities can maintain greater sovereignty over resource management.

In other words, though certain federal systems, like the United States, present challenges for national and international policy on higher scales of forest resource governance, those same systems may more readily facilitate benefits on local scales. Indeed, constitutionally decentralized federal systems provide a variety of governance benefits for local resource managers. Balancing the provision of global forest goods and services (such as climate change mitigation) via the implementation of international agreements with the provision of national and local goods via sustainable decentralized forest policy is a particularly challenging task within federal systems.

This chapter once again uses the lens of climate change and the role of forest management in facilitating climate change solutions to explore the realities of balancing domestic constitutional federalism with both global environmental governance and sustainable national and local forest management. The chapter does so by assessing how the division of regulatory authority over forests between national and subnational governments in the above federal systems may affect global climate negotiations. More specifically, the chapter analyzes whether—and to what degree—the federal countries here reviewed maintain adequate constitutional capacity to enter into a viable climate or other treaty including forest management, to successfully implement such a treaty domestically, and to do so in a way most conducive to capturing the benefits of decentralized forest policy. Included in this assessment is a review of the split in public and private ownership of forests, which is of critical importance because different levels of government in federal systems maintain constitutional regulatory authority over forests depending on whether the forests are publicly or privately owned. The split in national/subnational authority and public/private forest ownership can be represented as two axes of disparity among federal systems in the area of forest management, with different federal systems falling into different quadrants. Figure 7.2 below provides a visualization of the widely divergent positions from which federal nation-states approach international climate negotiations aimed at forests.

Where a federal system falls along these axes affects its legal domestic treaty implementation capabilities, as well as the political will it maintains to negotiate a treaty in the first instance. As explained below, the U.S. and Canadian national governments have extremely limited control over direct forest management activities on both state/provincial forestlands and private forestlands because "constitutional primacy" over decentralized forest policy remains with the subnational states or provinces. While these systems obviously place value on constitutionally decentralized forest governance, their chosen constitutional structure makes it very difficult to bind subnational governments to specific forest management directives via international treaty. By contrast, the Brazilian and Russian national governments maintain far more authority over forest resources relative to subnational governments, thus giving those countries what may be termed "national constitutional primacy" over decentralized forest policy. Furthermore, 75 percent of Brazil's forests,

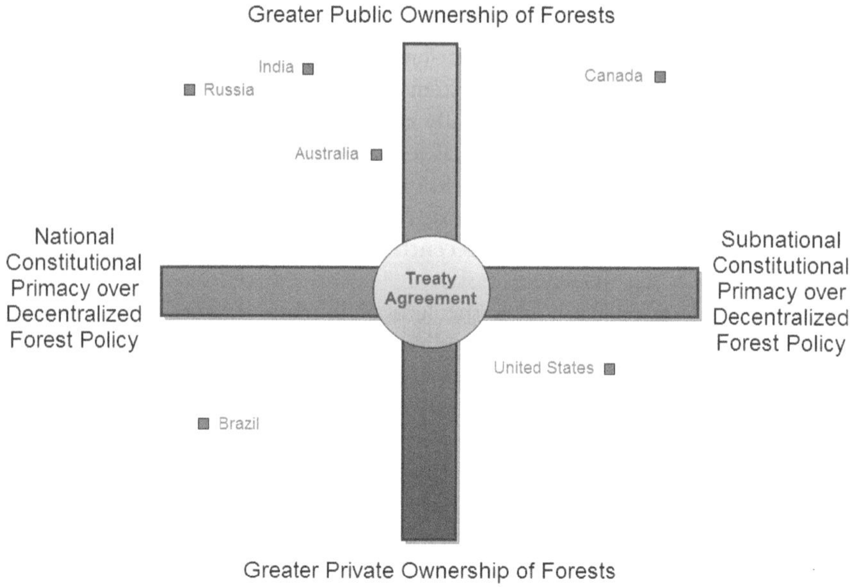

Figure 7.2 The public/private forest ownership and national/subnational regulatory control disparity in federal systems

60 percent of the United States's forests, and 26 percent of Australia's forests are privately owned, whereas 93 percent of forests are publicly owned in Canada, 92 percent in Russia, and 97 percent in India—further complicating global forest governance negotiations among federal systems. Because different levels of government, with different levels of constitutional authority, may directly regulate different categories of forest ownership, federalism and property-rights issues further complicate international negotiations among federal systems. This chapter aims to identify potential federalism-based legal impediments to future climate and forest negotiations by analyzing the constitutional structures of these federal nation-states—a key step toward assessing how to craft constitutional approaches in federal systems that balance the global and local communities' interests in forests while remedying the potential legal entrenchment of the commons dynamic at the global level.

Elements of Federal Constitutional Orders that Best Balance Global Forest Governance and Decentralized Forest Policymaking

The United States is not alone in its status as a federal system potentially constrained in international climate negotiations by subnational units of government. Numerous other federal systems control important forest resources worldwide and present potential difficulties for international negotiations.

As a result, a variety of countries at the negotiating table could each be legally constrained in domestic treaty implementation.

This section introduces and describes the three elements of federal constitutional orders that allow these systems to avoid such difficulties at the global scale while at the same time preserving the benefits of sustainable decentralized forest governance on local scales—a necessary precursor to this chapter's later comparative analysis of the constitutional orders of Australia, Brazil, Canada, India, and Russia in the context of forest management. Analysis of those nations' federal structure permits a determination of which of the three elements each system currently maintains, which in turn allows for both a better understanding of the potential consequences that federal constitutional structure may have for international negotiations on forests, as well as an indication of which federal systems maintain constitutional orders that would require adjustment to strike the difficult balance between global climate governance and decentralized forest management.

Though the potential for subnational governments to place constitutional constraints on national governments may cause federal systems to present more difficulties for international climate negotiations than do unitary systems of government, it is a mistake to assume that federal systems uniformly do so. The five federal systems assessed below maintain constitutions that vary greatly in their allocation of constitutional authority over forest management between the national and subnational governments. In fact, certain federal systems maintain constitutions that allow their involvement in climate change negotiations to approximate the operation of unitary systems of government—at least from a legal perspective—and even to facilitate potentially more effective treaty implementation than unitary systems, as the benefits of decentralized forest *management* may be more readily achieved in federal systems that are already constitutionally decentralized.

To most effectively balance decentralized forest governance in federal systems with successful negotiation and implementation of a treaty aimed at forest management, however, federal systems must maintain three key elements: (1) national constitutional primacy over both national and subnational forest policy; (2) national sharing of constitutional authority over forest policy with subnational governments; (3) forest policy institutional enforcement capacity. The following description of these three elements provides context for this chapter's subsequent survey of which federal systems here reviewed currently maintain all or some of these elements. Likewise, the subsequent survey will make more clear the meaning and implications of each of these elements through the provision of tangible examples.

National Constitutional Primacy Over Forest Policy

> When the present needs are especially urgent, and local costs of exploitation are not immediately incurred, resources are exploited. Achieving positive environmental and

> social outcomes requires standards and means for ensuring that nationally defined environmental and social concerns are taken into account.[14]

"National constitutional primacy" is a term that describes the attribute of a federal system whereby the national government maintains constitutional authority to guide regulatory or management standards for a resource that may be the subject of domestic legislation passed pursuant to an international treaty—here, forest management included within a climate or other treaty. National constitutional primacy over forest policy is a key element for federal system participation in such a treaty for the simple reason that a national government ultimately unconstrained by subnational interference in domestic policy can more freely arrange its international obligations. To be clear, the introduction of this element is not advocating an evisceration of decentralized forest policy.[15] Indeed, as discussed in Chapter 5, the numerous benefits of decentralized forest governance are well documented: reduction of central government bureaucracy resulting in more efficient decision-making; better access to local knowledge leading to increased understanding of local needs and constraints; better information flow between local and central governments, as well as between the government and private sector; greater local cooperation and stakeholder interest in governance participation; and reduction of central government "political meddling" and corruption.[16] Each of these is a crucial component to effective resource governance on local, national, and international scales.

Despite these well-recognized, tangible benefits of decentralized local forest governance, scholars have noted that,

> while there is a trend toward decentralization of forest governance within many countries, there also are developing clear arguments for mechanisms, central or even international (e.g. through global conventions), to ensure that activities and events that affect more than one state and that are involved in the production of national or global public goods associated with the environmental services derived from forests are being adequately considered by those with the mandate to manage them.[17]

Indeed, climate change has been perhaps the foremost driver for "clear arguments" against over-decentralization, as the role of forests in regulating global atmospheric carbon has been increasingly recognized over the last 20 years. Suddenly the aggregated effects of decentralized, local decision-making regarding forest resources have taken on global significance, as sequestration of carbon is perhaps the most important "environmental service" performed by forests in modern times. In short, "[d]ecentralization offers great opportunities for improved forest management, but also great challenges. It is far from being a final solution to the ills of the forest sector because significant possible disadvantages and dangers threaten its potential benefits."[18] National constitutional primacy provides a check on the well-recognized disadvantages of decentralized forest governance, which include making more difficult the coordination and implementation of national policies, undermining national objectives when local objectives are not consistent, decision-making at local levels that is not socially or environmentally desirable or sustainable, loss of noncommercial objectives of national forest policy, and pressure to extract forest resources for immediate local benefit to the detriment of long-term sustainability, to name a few.

National governments in federal systems often maintain regulatory responsibility for forest resource issues that have effects across subnational boundaries or that provide national or international ecosystem services and public goods, and "[o]ften, the federal government influences or controls state activity through federal laws, incentives and checks and balances related to the use of resources."[19] Even so, some federal systems controlling vast forest resources do not maintain a constitutional framework for broad national forest policy formulation that ensures the benefits of decentralized management are maximized in balance with national or global provision of public goods. Pursuing mechanisms for addressing this constitutional gap in these systems is important, as the policy goals of decentralized forest management may best be achieved if federal systems will "[i]dentify which national policies should override the preferences of decentralized bodies and establish clear rules for their enforcement at [the] national level" and "[e]stablish forest management minimum standards for decentralized institutions."[20] In fact, a report issued to the Fourth UNFF (United Nations Forum on Forests) by participants of the Interlaken decentralization workshop stated as one of the guiding principles of effective forest policy decentralization implementation that "[d]ecentralization in the forest sector should not be implemented in isolation from a general national forestry strategy, such as national forest programmes."[21]

Given the importance of a national government's ability to spur effective decentralized forest governance, what this book argues best facilitates federal nation-state agreement on global forest governance is not direct national *control* per se over forest policy at all levels, but rather national constitutional authority to act as a *safety net*—a function discussed in Chapters 8 and 9 that may be termed "Fail-safe Federalism." In other words, "national constitutional primacy" denotes national governments maintaining legal authority to guide forest policy—including the ability to enter into international climate and forest treaties unconstrained—while leaving subnational governments with primary regulatory and management roles.

To be certain, too much national control over forest management can also be detrimental to forest governance. Scholars note that "[c]entral governments … commonly maintain control over forest management through extensive bureaucratic procedures, such as forest management plans, price controls, marketing and permits for cutting, transport and processing. In some cases this represents a loss of local decision-making authority."[22] And, of course, Ostrom and other commons scholars have criticized centralized authorities for exacerbating commons resource management ills. Rather, the type of national constitutional primacy that can most effectively balance global governance with the benefits of subnational decentralized policy is that which establishes a minimum forest management standards framework within which subnational governments may operate with discretion,[23] and which subnational governments can supplement with even higher standards if they so choose. Importantly, as discussed in Chapter 9, national constitutional primacy need not flow out of top-down, prescriptive constitutional mandates at the national level, as it can arise bilaterally out of cooperative federalism arrangements or even horizontally out of regional agreements among subnational governments.

Achieving the appropriate degree of national government oversight is crucial because "[a]lthough too much oversight of local governments can be detrimental, checks and balances on local authority over forests are essential for good governance and to protect resources."[24] Other scholars note that:

> [E]ven where secure decentralization has been implemented, support from central government and others are [sic] needed to ensure that natural resources are not over-exploited. … Some of these efforts include minimum environmental standards. … Central government must play a key role in advancing reforms needed to achieve effective decentralization.[25]

Stated differently, "simply devolving power to communities can produce either no positive change or even negative change, if devolution reduces the power of the national government to stop local resource misuse that might once have been limited by national policy."[26]

Ultimately, scholars who are well aware of the value of decentralized forest policy recognize that a "minimum standards" approach is "an important role of central governments," because,

> minimum environmental standards are a complementary means of codifying … principles [of decentralization] in law, thus establishing greater local autonomy in natural resources management and use. The minimum-standards approach complements decentralization by specifying the boundaries to the domain of local autonomy without restricting discretion within those boundaries. …
>
> A minimum environmental standards approach—a set of restrictions and guidelines for environmental use and management—would replace the centrally directed micromanagement approach currently exercised through elaborate plans and planning processes.[27]

The type of Fail-safe Federalism facilitated by national constitutional primacy strikes a balance between centralized planning and minimum standards at the federal level and decentralized implementation, harnessing of local information and expertise, and other benefits at the subnational level.

Despite the importance of Fail-safe Federalism and minimum national standards, national government involvement in federal system decentralized forest policy cannot be divined from thin air. If a federal constitution does not permit national constitutional primacy over forest policy at all levels (as is arguably the case in the United States where the national government only maintains primacy over 35 percent of forests) then the benefits of decentralized management may not be balanced with the provision of national environmental goods and other goals—at the very least there will be no *legal* mechanism for ensuring that they are. Thus, national constitutional primacy provides a legal mechanism that facilitates the benefits of both decentralized management and responsible centralized forest planning in a way that is realized not only by the individual nation, but by the international community engaged in creating effective solutions to global environmental problems such as climate change.

National Sharing of Constitutional Forest Authority

National sharing of constitutional forest authority can be summarized simply as a national government maintaining constitutional primacy over forest policy at both national and subnational levels, while at the same time voluntarily and cooperatively sharing that authority with subnational governments to achieve the most effective management on localized scales. It is, in effect, the other side of the "national constitutional primacy" coin—a federal system cannot maintain this element unless it first maintains national constitutional primacy over forest management. A federal system may, on the other hand, maintain national constitutional primacy and choose to "over-centralize" national forest policy by refusing to share that authority with subnational governments in a way that is consistent with theories of dynamic federalism, as discussed in Chapter 5. From a treaty negotiation standpoint, having legal authority to implement domestic policy allows a national government to enter into an international agreement unconstrained, while its willingness to share decentralized forest management responsibilities facilitates more effective domestic implementation of the agreement. Even outside the context of an international agreement, this element also aligns the benefits of sustainable decentralized forest policy with the provision of global goods and services, since the national government is more likely to value a wider range of forest goods and services than do individual subnational governments. This sharing of authority is crucial, as a condition of good decentralized forest governance is "[e]ffective and balanced distribution of forest related responsibilities and authority among levels of government" and "[c]ertain forest management decisions are better made at the subnational, or even local levels of government, while others may best be retained at a central level."[28] In other words, this element allows the national government to act as the aforementioned fail-safe via a "minimum standards" approach without giving rise to the myriad of problems caused by a national government that micromanages policy decisions on local scales.

As noted above, suitable responsibilities to be maintained by the national government include providing coherent forest management on issues that may have spillover effects across political and geographic boundaries of subnational units and the provision of national and even international goods and services. There is a need for "strong central government guidance and overall leadership," and "[d]ecentralized forest management does not mean less need for a strong central government."[29] Nonetheless, in order to preserve the resource management gains made during the global shift toward decentralized forest policy, it is important that even in the presence of constitutional authority to do so, national governments in federal systems do not overcentralize in a way that usurps forest policy decisions best left to subnational governments.

National governments that are limited in their ability to implement a treaty effectively on domestic scales will be less inclined to enter into an international agreement—rendering national constitutional primacy of great importance. National sharing of constitutional forest authority, however, achieves the crucial balance of ensuring that international obligations to which the national government can unilaterally agree are domestically carried out in the most effective manner possible and in a way that is most consistent with the federal form of governance chosen by many nations controlling crucial forest resources.

Institutional Enforcement Capacity

Scholars have noted that "forest governance is strongly dependent on the institutional and political conditions of the government in general"[30] and that "[c]losing the gap between law and on-ground outcomes is one of the main challenges in the forest sector … so issues of enforcement and compliance are amongst the most important arenas of policy analysis."[31] Indeed, institutional enforcement capacity[32] is a crucial element for federal-system treaty agreement and implementation for another obvious reason—without the ability to adequately enforce domestic policy, international obligations cannot be met, and, therefore, national governments will be less likely to agree to obligations in the first instance. It is true that "[r]elationships between the central and sub-national governments are never constant in a country and changes are to be expected in a democratic country with a federal system of government."[33] Yet these political shifts in ability or willingness to implement national policies are distinct from having a constitutional, legal capacity to do so.

As seen below, federal systems without adequate institutional enforcement capacity over forest management are hampered by unclear constitutional divisions of power between national and subnational governments, and between branches of the national government, and are further subject to corruption and other institutional maladies—resulting in direct, negative effects on international negotiations. A thorough assessment of institutional environmental enforcement problems is beyond the scope of this book, and is otherwise thoroughly documented in the literature. It is important, however, to introduce this element here since, unfortunately, certain federal systems analyzed below maintain the first two key constitutional elements for facilitating climate treaty agreement and implementation but lack institutional enforcement capacity.

The next section now undertakes a comparative constitutional assessment of different federal systems that control important forest resources to analyze which systems maintain the key elements presented thus far.

Impacts of Select Federal Constitutions on International Forest and Climate Negotiations: Survey of Constitutional Authority and Forest Ownership

As noted in Figure 7.2, federal nations controlling important forest resources enter international climate negotiations from widely divergent positions—both with regard to the division of constitutional authority over forest policy, as well as to the public–private allocation of forest ownership. Some federal constitutions place constitutional regulatory authority over all of a nation's forests in the hands of the national government, which presents fewer difficulties for global climate change governance as national governments can act without constitutional constraints during international negotiations. Other federal constitutions can be interpreted as authorizing virtually exclusive subnational government regulation of a vast majority of the nation's forests, effectively *prohibiting* a prescriptive regulatory role for the national government in setting management standards. While this approach limits the national government's ability to bind the nation to a treaty aimed at forests, it may better facilitate sustainable decentralized forest governance since it provides legal protection from the disadvantages of over-centralization. In addition, private forests make up a majority of the forested land in some federal systems, with private forest management subject to exclusive subnational constitutional control; while in other systems, private and even subnationally owned forests may be subject to national regulatory authority. Various other federal systems fall somewhere in between these extremes of constitutional authority and forest ownership.

The following review describes which federal systems come from which divergent position in order to gain insight into the impacts those systems' domestic constitutional structures have on international climate negotiations. The review suggests that the federal systems here assessed—Australia, Brazil, Canada, India, and Russia, along with the United States via comparative analysis—can effectively be placed into three categories (Table 7.1), based upon their retention of certain key elements discussed above. Nations with all three elements provide models of federal systems that are most capable of engaging in global forest governance balanced with the realities of domestic federalism and the protection of local forest goods and services.

Australia

Constitutional Primacy, National Sharing, and Institutional Enforcement

The Australian Constitution provides no explicit environmental regulatory authority to either the national (or "Commonwealth") government or the

Table 7.1 Elements of federal constitutional structure most conducive for balancing global forest governance with decentralized policymaking

Federal Nations	*1) National Constitutional Primacy*	*2) National Sharing of Constitutional Authority*	*3) Institutional Enforcement Capacity*
Australia	X	X	X
India	X	X	
Brazil	X	X	
Russia	X	X	
Canada			X
United States			X

states and territories.[34] As such—similar to the United States—general authority to protect the environment is vested in the states,[35] and state and territory governments generally maintain constitutional authority to establish the legal and policy framework under which both public and private forests are managed.[36] A governance structure where subnational governments maintain primacy over domestic forest policy might be expected, as in the United States, to result in a domestic legal roadblock to the formation and implementation of an international treaty aimed at forest management activities.

Unlike the United States, however, the Australian High Court has definitively ruled that the Australian national government can gain regulatory authority over *any* subject matter if such regulation is based upon an international treaty, even if in an area of traditional state constitutional authority—a very different outcome than the much narrower result of *Holland*.[37] The Australian High Court, in *Commonwealth v. Tasmania*,[38] "confirmed the Commonwealth's authority to intervene in the management of natural resources in order to meet its international obligations" and "reinforced an earlier High Court decision … which set the Commonwealth's international obligations above state's rights."[39] The constitutional power upon which the *Tasmania* decision was based is Section 51 of the Australian Constitution, the "external affairs" power, which grants the Commonwealth government the authority to pass laws governing "external affairs."[40] As a result, the Australian national government can now "legislate comprehensively in respect of state properties in reliance on an international treaty,"[41] and "Parliament does not lack power to implement treaties to which Australia is or intends to become a party, *whatever the subject matter*."[42] Regarding *Tasmania* and related cases, scholars have argued that,

> [o]ver time, the legal and political implications of these decisions became clear: environmental policy was a jurisdiction shared by both the states and the Commonwealth. In time, this led to increased institutional experimentation at the national level to cope with the 'forestry question'

> [sic]. A variety of new land management arrangements emerged, including new policies and structures of management.[43]

Ultimately, the Australian High Court's jurisprudence firmly establishes that the Australian national government, when acting pursuant to an international treaty, has constitutional primacy over decentralized forest policy (element 1).[44]

As a result, even though subnational governments maintain primary constitutional authority for regulating forests in Australia, the Commonwealth and its agencies have exercised increasing influence over forest governance in the states,[45] and "the politics of federalism" have had "an important impact on forest policy."[46] Indeed, forest conflicts in Australia have been "at the forefront of altering the character of federal relations in Australia."[47] *Commonwealth v. Tasmania* and related cases involving federal intervention in areas of traditional state sovereignty[48] have "had a profound impact on the distribution of power within the Australian federation" and have "substantial implications for Australian federalism,"[49] as they establish "an expansive view of the Commonwealth's power to implement treaties to which Australia is a party by enacting appropriate domestic legislation."[50] Consequently, the Australian government is "constitutionally and legally empowered to act on environmental matters"[51] and is "increasingly politically obliged to involve itself in contentious matters of natural resource policy,"[52] especially since "an expectation was created within the environmental movement that it could now appeal to the Commonwealth against any state decision."[53] In other words,

> the nature of Australian federalism has been fundamentally altered. Whereas it had long been assumed that natural resource policy was a state jurisdiction and that the Australian government had a *co-ordinating* function in which each level of government had distinct jurisdictions, it was now clear that the states shared resource policy with the Commonwealth in a *concurrent* federation.[54]

Take, for example, the Environment Protection and Biodiversity Conservation Act (Conservation Act),[55] passed by the Australian national government in 1999 in order to "allow Australian Government involvement in environmental matters," and particularly management of native forests.[56] Because the Conservation Act invokes powers constitutionally reserved for the states, some of its sections are not applied in the presence of political agreements between the federal and state governments. The Conservation Act, however, is just one component of an increasing trend of federal involvement in forest matters, as "[s]everal national issues, including climate change, environmental heritage, water conservation and the protection of endangered species, have become more important since the implementation of the National Forest Policy Statement of 1992," and "[s]everal stakeholders are interested in having increased Australian Government intervention to coordinate a strategy to address the national issues that are independent" of political agreements between the federal and state governments (that is, cooperative federalism).[57]

Importantly, however, the Conservation Act has implications for both sides of the "national constitutional primacy" coin—though the Australian national government maintains constitutional primacy in the presence of an international treaty, the Conservation Act also demonstrates the Commonwealth government's commitment to sharing constitutional forest policy authority (element 2). In other words, the Australian national government has been quite vigorous in establishing principles of cooperative federalism whereby it retains the authority to intervene in state management of forests under its "external affairs" power, but leaves primary forest governance in the hands of the subnational governments for political and management reasons.

This approach is perhaps best evidenced by Australia's 1992 Inter-Governmental Agreement on the Environment (Inter-Governmental Agreement),[58] which "sought to reduce intergovernmental conflict by committing all governments to an agreement about their respective roles with respect to environmental issues."[59] Under the Inter-Governmental Agreement, the Commonwealth voluntarily limited its role in resource policy to specific circumstances, including "[r]epresenting the national interest"[60] in circumstances "where the regional implications of proposals for the use of a resource transcend State boundaries and affect two or more jurisdictions ... where there are relevant responsibilities under Commonwealth Acts of Parliament such as the *Environment Protection (Impact of Proposals) Act* [of] *1974*," and "where, in the light of scientific evidence, the Commonwealth has obligations under international conventions."[61] The Inter-Governmental Agreement is a political concession rather than a legal obligation, whereby the national government ceded part of its authority to the states by placing self-imposed restrictions on its power to regulate the environment.[62] Though the government may have *politically* ceded this authority, it did not do so *constitutionally*, as the High Court's rulings in *Tasmania* and related cases are dispositive on the question of constitutional authority. In other words, "the Commonwealth has, regardless of its legal and constitutional powers and capabilities, defined for itself a role narrower than its legal responsibilities,"[63] and has "generally approached its relationship with the states in a spirit of cooperative federalism [and] self-imposed restraint in exercising its constitutional powers."[64]

Similar to the Inter-Governmental Agreement, the Commonwealth and the states have entered into agreement on the 1992 National Forest Policy Statement (Forest Statement),[65] which established broad-based goals for Australia's native forests, including to "maintain an extensive and permanent native forest estate in Australia and to manage that estate in an ecologically sustainable manner so as to conserve the suite of values that forests can provide for current and future generations."[66] The Forest Statement was also meant to establish a framework for cooperation between the federal and state governments on forest management and was "devised to give expression to the [Inter-Governmental Agreement] in terms of devolving policy control for resource management issues to the states."[67] The Forest Statement establishes that:

> State and Territory governments have primary responsibility for forest management, in recognition of the constitutional responsibility of the States for land use decisions and their ownership of large areas of forest. The States and Territories have enacted legislation that allocates forest land tenures and specifies the administrative framework and policies within which public and private forests are managed. Local governments have responsibilities for local land use planning and rating systems, which affect public and private forest management and use.[68]

Under the Forest Statement, the national government, while maintaining no explicit constitutional authority over forest policy except that relating to nationally owned forests, is primarily responsible for "coordinating a national approach to both environmental and industry-development issues ... including a national approach to forest issues"[69]—a recognition of the Commonwealth's implicit constitutional authority to order its international obligations under its "external affairs" power.

Other examples of the Commonwealth's sharing of national constitutional primacy are the Regional Forest Agreements (RFAs) negotiated between the national and state governments. RFAs constitute an attempt to navigate the politics of the national government having potentially unfettered regulatory authority over environmental resources and private property rights under its "external affairs" power. RFAs are 20-year plans meant to guide the management of forests, to establish "long-term, durable agreement on the use of forests in order to provide industry with access to forest resources while protecting the environmental and cultural values of forest areas,"[70] and to "mediat[e] the tension between different levels of Government."[71] Because "Commonwealth governments of all political persuasions have felt the electoral and policy impact of conflict with the states on environmental matters ... [t]he RFA process [provides] a means of establishing a long-term resolution to questions of forest allocation and use in a way that reasserts the primacy of the states in forest management."[72]

RFAs effectively constitute a political maneuver on behalf of the national government as a means of navigating "forest politics" in Australia by establishing shared authority with subnational governments in the area of forest management. Indeed, "[t]he political purpose of the RFA process ... was to take forest issues off the political agenda by securing Commonwealth and State cooperation."[73] As a result, RFAs also encapsulate both national constitutional primacy and national sharing of forest authority. With regard to primacy, RFAs allow the Commonwealth to directly participate in forest planning to take into account biodiversity, water production, wood production, and social and economic values. As a result, "the long-standing argument that forestry is a State responsibility under the Constitution has been superseded by these arrangements."[74] Yet RFAs also represent a voluntary ceding of regulatory authority from the national government to the states, given that "RFAs have surrendered much of the [forest regulatory] powers to the states."[75]

In sum, the Australian model of federalism, specifically in the context of climate change and forests, may be summarized as follows:

> One response during the past ten years to the expanded scope of the Commonwealth Parliament's power over external affairs has been to adopt a more cooperative approach to federalism in Australia. Through this process, the states have had a greater policy input into decisions concerning Australia's treaty relations, and an expanded role in the domestic implementation and enforcement of the obligations imposed by those treaties. This approach has generally been a successful one provided there has been a clear division of responsibility between Commonwealth and states over the relevant subject matter and the Commonwealth has been able to gain the cooperation of the states in creating a cooperative legislative scheme.[76]

In the final analysis, Australia maintains all three elements conducive to maximizing flexibility in international negotiations among federal systems of government, while also retaining the benefits of decentralized forest governance. National constitutional primacy allows the Australian national government to enter into an international treaty on climate and forests unconstrained and to act as a fail-safe in the absence of sound subnational forest policy—a legal entitlement to remedy natural capital commons tragedies on state and local scales as well as to participate in attempts to resolve global commons challenges. National sharing of constitutional authority facilitates mechanisms that allow subnational governments to both successfully implement the treaty and perform their functional role within a federal system to achieve the benefits of decentralized forest management. Institutional enforcement capacity in Australia allows the treaty and implementing legislation to be enforced.[77]

Public/Private Forest Ownership

Approximately 74 percent of Australian forests are publicly owned and 26 percent are privately owned.[78] As noted, Australian state and territory governments have primary responsibility for regulating both public and private forests, though both are also subject to federal regulation under the Commonwealth's "external affairs" power in the presence of an international treaty. Since the "external affairs" power received expanded interpretation in *Tasmania*, the national government has taken an even greater role in private forest management. The Forest Statement includes as one of its goals the sustainable management of privately owned forests, which is to be undertaken "through a combination of measures that may include dissemination of information about and technical support for forest management, education programs, conservation incentives, land-clearing controls, harvesting controls, and codes of forest practice."[79]

Due to the high proportion of publicly owned forests, "[f]orest and timber resources on private lands … have largely escaped public scrutiny and regulation" and "[t]he practice and profession of forestry is primarily focused on public lands."[80] Even so, due to both the high proportion of public forest ownership, and the fact that both public and private forests are subject to Commonwealth exercises of its "external affairs" power, the Australian national government maintains the constitutional capacity to prevent its limited private ownership of forests from derailing its involvement in international negotiations on forests—in stark contrast to the United States, where the treaty power may not trump subnational regulatory control over the 60 percent of forests in private ownership. What this ultimately means is that the division of forest ownership between private and public entities does not legally impact the ability of the national government to agree to and implement a climate treaty, because it is not legally constrained by either subnational units of government or private property interests in the exercise of its "external affairs" power.

Brazil

Constitutional Primacy, National Sharing, and Institutional Enforcement

Prior to the 1988 Brazilian Constitution, which aimed to decentralize forest management, Brazilian forest policy at all levels was administered exclusively by the national government.[81] The national government exercised this authority under the first major forest law in Brazil, the Forest Code of 1965,[82] which provided the general framework for forest laws, established protected forest areas and the process for designating them, and put into place "detailed forest practice guidelines for protected areas and reserves on all forestland in the country."[83] The constitutional authority for managing forests, however, was reallocated in 1988 with the establishment of a new Brazilian Constitution.

Unlike the U.S. and Australian constitutions, the Brazilian Constitution contains explicit forestry provisions. Article 225 states that the Brazilian forests are "part of the national patrimony, and they shall be used, as provided by law, under conditions which ensure the preservation of the environment."[84] Article 23 declares that the national, state, and local governments have the power to "preserve the forests," while Article 24 establishes that they may do so with concurrent legislative competence in the area of forest management. Regarding concurrent legislation, Article 24 supposedly limits the national government's role to the "establishment of general principles," and preserves the "supplementary competence of the states" to legislate.[85] Article 24 declares, however, that "[t]he supervenience of a federal law over general rules suspends the effectiveness of a state law to the extent that the two are contrary."[86]

The "supervenience" element of the Brazilian Constitution has proven crucial to defining the true division of forest regulatory authority between the Brazilian national and subnational governments. Scholars interpret the "concurrent legislation" clause in Article 23 to mean that "the federal government has absolute power (plenary power) to establish laws and regulations, and the states and municipalities have only limited power."[87] Indeed, forest policy in Brazil might be characterized as completely "supervened" by the national government. The primary national agency responsible for implementing and enforcing forest laws, the Brazilian Institute of the Environment and Renewable Natural Resources (IBAMA), is said to have adopted the pre-1988 Constitution "centralized administration model" of governance, despite the fact that the 1988 Constitution was designed to facilitate general decentralization of governance.[88] IBAMA had traditionally regulated all public and private lands, and though new laws have sought to transfer some of that authority to subnational governments,[89] IBAMA still retains superseding authority over forest resources.[90] In fact, state and local governments have largely "taken very little or no responsibility for the implementation of forest policy, including enforcement."[91]

Due in part to general principles of constitutional interpretation by the Brazilian judiciary, the 1988 Constitution's legal framework for transitioning to a more decentralized form of forest management has not been very successful. The Brazilian High Court, the *Supremo Tribunal Federal* (Supremo Tribunal), has affirmed Brazil's commitment to a more centralized form of federalism than that present in the United States. Unlike the U.S. Supreme Court, the Supremo Tribunal has never invalidated federal legislation for intruding into traditional "reserved" powers of the states, nor has the Supremo Tribunal debated whether its decisions should be governed by federal or state law.[92] The Supremo Tribunal's more centralized view of federalism results from the fact that "Brazilian Constitutions have granted far greater powers to the federal government than the U.S. Constitution."[93] As a result, Supremo Tribunal justices have never "assumed the role of protecting states' rights from infringement by the federal legislation."[94]

Ultimately, even though there is constitutional concurrence between the national and subnational governments for forest legislation in Brazil—establishing the legal framework for decentralized forest governance—the national government's power to "supervene" subnational authority gives it national constitutional primacy (element 1) over forest management. Recently, however, the Brazilian government has attempted to remedy the problem of subnational governments not capitalizing on their constitutional authority to establish forest policy. New laws aim to transfer the approval and enforcement of forest management plans to state environmental agencies, and both the national and state governments have shown an increased focus on greater subnational involvement in forest regulation.[95] Given explicit constitutional concurrence over forest policy, and an increased focus on decentralized forest governance, Brazil does maintain a national sharing of constitutional forest policy authority (element 2)—though it has proven slow to come to fruition and the national government "retains much of its traditional command and control regulatory powers."[96]

Despite a high concentration of national government *legal* authority over forests and the fact that Brazil has some of the most complex forestry laws in the world, Brazil's forest management constitutional provisions have been largely ineffective.[97] Thus, even though Brazil maintains the first two elements facilitating flexibility in global climate negotiations related to forests, lack of institutional enforcement capacity (element 3) has severely impeded *actual* implementation of environmental constitutional provisions and legislation in Brazil.[98] Scholars argue that "[t]he ineffectiveness of laws alone to protect the environment is nowhere as evident as in the contemporary destruction of the Amazonian … forests,"[99] and that "[a]ttempts to embody environmental protection clauses in national constitutions, such as Brazil's, do not appear to have appreciably influenced the prevailing bureaucratic culture."[100] Article 26 of the Brazilian Constitution actually makes destruction of the Amazonian and Atlantic forests a crime under the penal code,[101] but rarely has this constitutional provision been enforced.[102] The Brazilian government's own reports demonstrate that "the federal government has failed to enforce forestry regulations in relation to forest management, indicating widespread failure to implement forestry laws."[103] In 1996, Brazilian government audits found the compliance rate with forest laws to be just 30 percent, and that "even among the 30% of projects which appeared to fully comply with forest management laws, the management plans were not designed as a tool to produce sustainable timber, but rather as a means to satisfy legal requirements to procure logging permits."[104]

The lack of enforcement results largely from prosecutorial inaction, a conservative judicial system, public apathy, general corruption, deficient legal structures, severe budgetary constraints on local governments,[105] faulty land ownership structures, mistrust of government,[106] and other institutional problems.[107] Thus, in Brazil, even in the presence of explicit forest-protection mandates in the national constitution, the national government is unable to enforce legislation under its broad powers. Without a strong judiciary, financial resources, a culture of enforcement and overall political will, the central government is impeded from guiding forest policy through international mechanisms—though it certainly maintains the constitutional authority to do so. Indeed, "Brazilian environmental agencies, while varying widely in their capacities, have not lived up to the promise of Brazilian environmental law. … The result is a profound disconnect between environmental law 'on the books' and environmental law as it operates in practice."[108] Others assert that "[o]n paper, constitutional rights are better protected in Brazil than in virtually any other country,"[109] but that "[t]he problem is in the disturbing distance that separates the rights inscribed on paper from their effective exercise, and above all in the guaranty of their exercise in practical life."[110]

Though Brazil retains two key elements conducive to balancing global forest governance with federal decentralized domestic forest policy—national constitutional primacy and national sharing of constitutional authority—lack of institutional enforcement capacity prevents Brazil from being fully capable of effective forest policy at either end of the local-global forest governance spectrum. As noted by one scholar, "[t]he case of Brazil ... highlights the difficulty in designing internationally-binding legal instruments to promote sustainable uses of the earth's resources, and effective enforcement of regulations."[111]

Public/Private Forest Ownership

Roughly 25 percent of Brazil's forests are in public ownership. The remaining 75 percent are privately owned, or otherwise "unallocated."[112] Article 44 of the *Forest Code* of the Unified Environmental Law in Brazil requires public *and* private property owners to leave intact 80 percent of Amazonian rainforest areas.[113] These efforts, however, have been largely unsuccessful at addressing private forest destruction. Though the national government has the constitutional authority to avoid the issues faced by the United States in implementing federal policy on private and state-owned lands, entrenched and "archaic" views of private property rights in Brazil still affect the ability of the national government to enforce forest regulation. As noted by one scholar,

> [i]ntervention of public authorities in what goes on inside a legally titled property is opposed by the elites who control very large properties, and by others who aspire to someday have them. Even though the Constitution links the right to private property to its 'social function,' this linkage has remained vague in legal terms and unapplied to destruction of vast areas within the private domain of individuals or corporations.[114]

Thus, the high proportion of private forest ownership, as in the United States, affects implementation of forest policy at the national level—it does so, however, due to lack of enforcement, not due to lack of recognized constitutional authority as in the United States. Ultimately, because the national government in Brazil maintains the constitutional authority to regulate both private and public forests, the division of forest ownership between private and public entities does not *legally* constrain the national government in international climate negotiations.

Canada

Constitutional Primacy, National Sharing, and Institutional Enforcement

Like the Brazilian Constitution—and unlike the U.S. and Australian Constitutions—the Canadian Constitution Act of 1867 explicitly allocates forest management regulatory authority between the federal government and the provinces.[115] Though a more thorough review of these provisions will take place in Chapter 8, an introduction is necessary here for comparison purposes. Section 92A of the Canadian Constitution delegates responsibility for non-federally owned forest regulation and overall management *exclusively* to the provincial governments.[116] In other words, the Canadian Constitution does not allow concurrent jurisdiction over forests,[117] as do the constitutions of many other federal systems. This explicit grant of authority has significant implications for Canada's ability to both maintain a national forest policy, and to negotiate an international climate treaty that includes forests, because 84 percent of Canada's forests are non-federally owned (7 percent are privately owned and 77 percent are provincially owned).[118] This is an even higher proportion of forests under subnational control than in the United States, where state governments are responsible for regulating the 60 percent of forests that are privately owned and the 5 percent of forests that are state-owned.[119]

Passage of Section 92 of the Constitution Act of 1982 reinforced provincial authority over subnational forest management by declaring that provinces maintain exclusive control over property rights.[120] Canadian courts have broadly construed this constitutional provision to include land use and natural resources management.[121] These amendments to Canada's Constitution place it "beyond dispute that the provinces are primarily responsible for forest management."[122] As a result, Canadian forest policy is "extremely decentralized," with national authority over forests being "particularly weak."[123] Even the national government itself has come to eschew attempts to form a national policy on forest management, declaring that "[f]orest management is a matter of provincial jurisdiction. Each province and territory has its own set of legislation, policies and regulations to govern the management of its forests."[124] Indeed, the Canadian national government has consistently refused to apply national environmental laws, forest policies, or international forest management agreements to the provinces.[125]

Despite explicit provincial constitutional authority over forest management, Section 91 of the Canadian Constitution does grant the national government exclusive authority over "trade and commerce" as well as "peace, order, and good government."[126] The Canadian Supreme Court has construed this provision as including the implementation of treaties concerning trade and commerce and other matters of "national concern."[127] Certainly climate change would seem to affect both commerce and trade in Canadian forest products, and it is clearly a matter of national and global concern. Yet the Canadian national government has not attempted to invoke this constitutional power to justify the implementation of international climate and forest agreements, and "[t]he Canadian federal government has so far adopted the position that, under the Canadian Constitution, its hands are tied."[128] Indeed, scholars have noted that the "ambiguous nature of the federal role in … forest policy" formation has resulted in "a variety of idiosyncratic organizational" mechanisms geared toward greater federal input into Canadian forest policy, and "[t]he need for governments at both levels [to maintain] greater administrative capacity in order to better coordinate increasingly sophisticated policy regimes ... [as is] evident in efforts made at the intergovernmental level to develop more effective forest policy structures."[129] This is especially so since Canada has been "aggressive" in signing on to various international treaties related to forest management, including climate change, even though "implementation remains the responsibility of the provinces."[130] As a result, scholars have recognized "the need for greater coordination of these increasingly sophisticated policy regimes"[131] or Canada's forest practices will continue to come under international scrutiny. Similarly, scholars have recognized that Canada must play a role in shaping international relations on forests by "vigorously participat[ing] and be[ing] proactive in international discussions."[132]

Despite the Canadian national government's desire to act "aggressively" regarding international environmental agreements, the Canadian Provinces' exclusive control over direct forest management has in the past contributed to Canada's lack of formal participation in a variety of international agreements[133] and has resulted in "constant tensions between the provinces and the federal government over sharing of power" over forests.[134] It appears that the presence of explicit constitutional provisions regarding forests actually causes federalism to be far more of a problem in the forest context than in the context of other types of resource management, such as fisheries and agriculture. In those areas, the federal and provincial governments have resolved management conflicts with "cooperative federalism" arrangements, whereby political and fiscal pressures by the national government achieved provincial compliance with national policy[135]—an approach that might better be called *uncooperative federalism*. These results have yet to be achieved regarding forest management, even though scholars have argued that similar avenues exist for greater federal involvement in nonfederal forest policy.[136]

Ultimately, the lack of national constitutional primacy (element 1) adversely impacts not only the Canadian federal government's ability to formulate a national forest policy, but also the interplay between Canadian federalism and international agreements concerning forests, since the Canadian national government is constrained by provincially reserved powers in exercising its treaty power.[137] Limitations on the Canadian treaty power became Canadian constitutional precedent in the *Labor Conventions* case,[138] where the Privy Council established that the Canadian federal government does not have the authority to implement treaties via enacting legislation that interferes with matters constitutionally reserved to the provinces. In other words, "in Canada, the federal government lacks legislative competence to implement treaties whose subject matter falls within provincial jurisdiction"[139]—a constitutional state of affairs similar to the situation in the United States, if not more problematic. The U.S. Supreme Court's narrow ruling in *Missouri v. Holland* did not give such definitive treatment to the question of the relationship between the treaty power and federalism principles,[140] and it remains to be seen whether the U.S. Congress has the power, pursuant to an international treaty, to intrude upon the regulatory role of the states over subnational forest policy.

The explicit constitutional grant of regulatory authority over forests to the provinces, coupled with the fact that Canadian courts have definitively declared the treaty power to be restricted by reserved provincial powers, makes it clear that Canada is currently even more restricted in international negotiations regarding forests than the United States. Indeed, "[w]hile the United States Constitution actually contemplates a system that values the importance of the nation's being able to implement its treaties, the Canadian constitutional framework appears to subordinate international concerns to domestic separation of legislative competence."[141] Furthermore, and unlike U.S. courts, "Canadian courts have consistently extended rather than diminished provincial power."[142]

This review demonstrates that the Canadian national government, though maintaining institutional enforcement capacity (element 3) as a general matter,[143] currently does not maintain constitutional primacy over forest management (element 1). As a result, the government necessarily cannot maintain any resulting national sharing of constitutional forest policy authority (element 2). Thus, subnational constitutional primacy over forests, combined with the vast subnational ownership of forests, constrains the national government from utilizing certain forms of global forest governance to address climate change—a constraint equal to, if not greater than, that placed on the U.S. federal government by the states.

Public/Private Forest Ownership

Ninety-three percent of Canada's forests are publicly owned, with provincial governments responsible for regulating both the 7 percent of privately owned forests and the 77 percent of forests in provincial ownership.[144] As a result, the national government only maintains constitutional authority to regulate the 16 percent of public forests in national ownership. Because the provinces are in charge of regulating both private and subnational public forests, as in the United States, forest ownership may affect the shape of an international climate treaty that includes forests. In Canada, however, it is subnational *public* ownership rather than private ownership that constrains the Canadian national government in treaty negotiations. Subnational constitutional primacy over forests combined with the vast provincial ownership of forests likely means the national government would be legally prohibited from implementing certain potential international forest management obligations on a vast majority of forests within its borders.

India

Constitutional Primacy, National Sharing, and Institutional Enforcement

Like the Canadian and Brazilian Constitutions, the Indian Constitution explicitly addresses forest protection, with Article 48A declaring that the government "shall endeavor to protect and improve the environment and to safeguard the forests and wildlife of the country."[145] Article 51-A(g) states that "[i]t shall be the duty of every citizen of India to protect and improve the natural environment including forests."[146] The central government's role over forests has increased over time, and in 1972 the 42nd amendment to the Constitution granted concurrent oversight over forests to the national and state governments, further "empowering the central government to have decisive decision-making authority over management of the nation's forests."[147] In the event that national and state legislation clash, as in Brazil, "the Union enjoys a primacy over States in that its legislation in the Union and the Concurrent List prevails over State legislations."[148] The Union capitalized on this recentralization of forest authority by passing the Forest Conservation Act of 1980,[149] which further "increased centralized control by making it mandatory to obtain permission from the central government for converting forest land to non-forest uses."[150] Indeed, the National Forest Policy of 1988[151] "is driven by top-down targets, with the national government setting clear objectives" with the goal of achieving forest cover on one-third of the total land area.[152] Thus, it is clear that in India the national government has constitutional primacy over forests (element 1) to act as a fail-safe for forest management.

Despite this strong national constitutional authority, however, India's Constitution also incorporates a decentralized approach to forest management—at least on paper—granting a great degree of regulatory authority to its 35 state governments. Like Australia, India's governance structure can thus be characterized as the national government purposefully ceding authority via decentralization as a policy choice for improved forest management—thus establishing a framework for national sharing of constitutional forest policy authority (element 2). In fact, India has actually taken its national sharing of constitutional forest authority further than simply decentralizing to the state government level. The seventy-third and seventy-fourth amendments to the Constitution require states to decentralize forest regulatory authority to even lower levels of government—local governmental units known as "panchayats."[153] The national fail-safe authority operates concurrently with this local authority, as federal agencies continue to mandate policy at the subnational level in areas such as forest fire control and long-term forest management planning.[154]

Ultimately, India's constitutional structure establishes both national constitutional primacy (element 1) and national sharing of constitutional forest policy authority (element 2). The effects of these elements are evident specifically in the context of international treaty-making. International agreements have had a direct impact on the forest sector planning process in India—again, at least on paper—signifying that national government adoption of international protocols is not hampered by subnational government interference.[155]

Like Brazil, however, India is missing the key element of institutional enforcement capacity (element 3). Enforcement capabilities are hampered by the budgetary constraints of a developing country and "[i]nadequate resources seriously constrain the implementation of the National Forest Policy."[156] India also ranks low on rule of law and environmental regulatory regime indices, as it struggles with corruption and lack of enforcement.[157] So even though India has a "well-articulated forest policy, its translation into a feasible strategy has been slow."[158] As a result, "[i]nstitutional reform in forestry needs to be pursued with great vigour."[159]

Public/Private Forest Ownership

Ninety-seven percent of all forests in India are publicly owned, and roughly 85 percent of forests are managed by the state governments.[160] Government forests "are managed either directly by state institutions or granted in usufruct to private entities or to communities under a variety of arrangements."[161] Ultimately, due to the high proportion of publicly owned forests and the national government's constitutional authority to direct management on state-owned forests, the public/private forest ownership divide does not limit India's options in entering into and implementing an international treaty that includes forest management.

Russia

Constitutional Primacy, National Sharing, and Institutional Enforcement

Russia alone accounts for more than 25 percent of the standing forests worldwide.[162] The Russian Federation Constitution[163] establishes a hierarchy of legal authorities, with the Constitution being the supreme legal authority.[164] Treaties to which the Russian Federation agrees are incorporated into this supreme authority, as Article 15.4 of the Constitution declares that "norms of international law and international treaties and agreements of the Russian Federation shall be a component part of its legal system. If an international treaty of the Russian Federation establishes other rules than those stipulated by the law, *the rules of the international treaty shall apply.*"[165] So not only does the national government maintain broad authority to negotiate and implement treaties, but treaties are also constitutionally declared to trump domestic legislation in the event that the two conflict—setting a firm *legal* foundation for an unconstrained national government in treaty negotiations.[166]

The Russian Constitution establishes areas of sole national jurisdiction and areas of joint jurisdiction between the national and subnational governments (known as "subjects").[167] Article 72 declares that areas of concurrent jurisdiction include "issues of possession, use and disposal of land, subsoil, water and other natural resources … land, water, and forest legislation."[168] The Russian Federation's stance on forest policy, however, is that though subject governments may have their own forest legislation, it must not conflict with national forest legislation.[169] This policy, combined with the broad treaty power, clearly establishes national constitutional primacy over forest management (element 1), especially in the context of international agreements. Indeed, the Russian Constitution, distinct from other constitutions here reviewed, "confirms the current trend in Russian practice of giving a prominent place to international legal standards in the domestic legal setting."[170]

The primary forest legislation in Russia is the Russian Forest Code of 2007.[171] The Code has been credited as a direct attempt by the national government to decentralize Russian forest policy, demonstrating national sharing of constitutional forest policy authority (element 2).[172] Yet it is clear that the Code leaves in place ultimate national control over both public and private forest regulation, as the national government delegates some forest regulatory tasks to the subject governments, but explicitly reserves for itself final authority over forest standard setting.[173] Article 83 of the Forest Code states that the

> authorised federal executive body shall have the right to issue enactments on exercising the powers delegated to the public authorities of the Subjects of the Russian Federation, as well as mandatory guidelines and instructions on exercising such powers by the executive authorities of the Subjects of the Russian Federation.[174]

The national government must approve the methods by which a subject utilizes delegated authority and must also approve the appointment of subject executive heads exercising delegated powers. The national government also oversees legislation passed by subject governments pursuant to their delegated powers, retaining the right to "issue mandatory prescriptions to invalidate enactments of Subjects of the Russian Federation or to amend them," and even maintains the power to "prepare proposals on withdrawal of respective powers from the public authorities of the Subjects" and to have those powers revoked.[175] Areas of forest regulation that in the United States are the role of state and local governments, such as zoning for forestry activities and regulation of clear-cutting, are ultimately administered by federal agencies in Russia. For example, the national government can go so far as to prohibit clear-cutting altogether.[176] Thus, governance of forests in Russia has been described as remaining "*de facto* quite centralized"[177] under its broad national constitutional primacy (element 1), even though it has established the legal framework for decentralized sharing of national constitutional authority (element 2).

Similar to Brazil and India, however, Russia lacks adequate institutional enforcement capacity (element 3), inhibiting the national government's ability to utilize the great degree of *legal* authority it maintains over forest management.[178] This lack is because the "division of powers between the center and subjects is still unclear … and administrative competencies are not well defined."[179] Specifically in the forest sector, an "[u]nclear hierarchy of laws, division of powers, and contradicting laws affect the credibility" of forest legislation and further complicates implementation of legislation.[180] Overlapping jurisdictions have led to conflicts between national and subject governments, as some subjects "claim that their own constitution is superior to the federal constitution" and that certain areas constitutionally designated as joint jurisdiction are in fact areas of exclusive subject jurisdiction, resulting in inconsistencies in local forest laws and national legislation.[181]

Scholars have recognized that in countries where the central government owns most forest resources, like Russia, central agency control and overall governance of forests is weak, whereas governance is stronger in countries where subnational governments own the resource, like Canada.[182] A causal link between which level of government owns the resource and the quality of management is not necessary to explain that descriptive result, however, as whether the national government maintains institutional enforcement capacity regardless of ownership may be of greater importance. Russia does not maintain such capacity, as its young federation is still battling elements of corruption, unclear constitutional balance and separation of powers, and a weak judiciary. Indeed, the Forest Code of 2007 "appears to undermine Russia's capacity to realise its international legal commitments and agreements" since it is "convoluted, vague and frequently in contradiction to the sincere efforts by many to realise sustainable forest legal mechanisms for the 21st century."[183] Like Brazil and India, Russia maintains elements 1 and 2, and therefore maintains much of what would otherwise provide a sufficient constitutional framework for participating in international climate and forest negotiations as well as retaining the benefits of decentralized forest governance. Yet lack of element 3 inhibits enforcement of the Russian Federation's constitutional authority.

Public/Private Forest Ownership

An overwhelming majority of Russian forests are owned by the national government.[184] Article 9 of the Constitution gives the Russian Federation the power to protect land and natural resources "as the basis of the life and activity of the people living in corresponding territories."[185] Whereas the U.S. Supreme Court has ruled that direct land use regulation is a "quintessential state and local power,"[186] Article 36 of the Russian Constitution explicitly grants land use regulatory authority to the national government in the area of the environment, stating that private property owners have the right to "possess, utilize, and dispose of land and other natural resources provided that this does not damage the environment and does not violate the rights and legitimate interests of others."[187]

The current Russian Constitution no longer places restrictions on private ownership of property, as it had done in the past, and Article 9 allows land and other natural resources to be in private, state, municipal, and other forms of ownership. Similarly, the 2007 Forest Code now allows for privatization of forest resources.[188] At the time of the 1997 Forest Code, private forest ownership was actually illegal, as was subject regulation of private property owners' management of forest resources.[189] The privatization of other forms of property, however, has occurred much more quickly than forest privatization, and though the current forest code allows for privatization, the national government still controls virtually all of the country's forests.[190] Because the national government remains both the primary owner of forests *and* the primary regulator of public and private forest management, forest ownership distribution in Russia is not an impediment to the Russian Federation's ability to enter into and implement a climate treaty aimed at forest management.

Survey Summary and Situating Federal Constitutional Orders within the Policy Formulation/Implementation Matrix

The foregoing comparative constitutional analysis, as depicted in Table 7.1 and Figure 7.3, demonstrates that only Australia, within its constitutional structure, maintains all three elements that most readily facilitate federal nation-state agreement on the widest range of international negotiations on forests, successful treaty implementation, *and* the preservation of decentralized forest policymaking authority.

To summarize, Australia maintains national constitutional primacy (element 1) over both publicly and privately owned forests through its "external affairs" power, yet it shares this authority with the states and territories, as evidenced by the Inter-Governmental Agreement on the Environment, the National Forest Policy Statement, and various RFAs, in order to achieve optimum forest management on local scales (element 2). Australia also

Figure 7.3 Status of elements of constitutional structure conducive for effective forest governance across scales within select federal systems

maintains sufficient institutional enforcement capacity (element 3), since Australia is not plagued by inadequate legal and enforcement institutions. The Australian national government's control over *all* subnationally owned forests via its "external affairs" power means that the public/private forest ownership divide depicted in Figure 7.2 does not operate as a significant legal obstacle for international climate and forest negotiations.

Brazil, India, and Russia, meanwhile, maintain only two key elements. Brazil's Constitution explicitly establishes national constitutional primacy (element 1) over all subnational forest management through its provisions allowing the "supervenience" of national laws over contrary state laws and the general constitutional deference afforded the national government by Brazilian courts. New laws aimed at transferring approval and enforcement of forest management plans to state environmental agencies, increased focus on greater subnational involvement in forest regulation at both the national and subnational levels, and explicit constitutional concurrence over forest policy also demonstrate a framework of national sharing of forest policy authority (element 2). Brazil, however, is missing the crucial element of institutional enforcement capacity (element 3) because prosecutorial apathy, a weak judiciary, general corruption, deficient legal structures, severe budgetary constraints, and other institutional problems hamper enforcement. In addition, the high proportion of private ownership of forests in Brazil, as in the United States, affects implementation of forest policy at the national level. This effect, however, is due solely to a lack of enforcement, rather than a lack of national government legal authority over private lands, as is the case in the United States. Thus, the constitutional framework is in place for the Brazilian national government to prevent Brazil's high degree of private forest ownership from limiting the range of options in international climate and forest negotiations.

Amendments to the Indian Constitution allowing concurrent oversight over forests and legislative acts passed pursuant to that authority—the Forest Conservation Act of 1980 and the National Forest Policy of 1988—have resulted in national constitutional primacy over forest management (element 1). India also maintains national sharing of constitutional authority (element 2), as its Constitution mandates that regional (state) governments must decentralize forest policymaking to even lower levels of government. Even so, budgetary constraints, corruption, and other regulatory enforcement issues cause a lack of institutional enforcement capacity in India (element 3). Due to the high proportion of public ownership of forests and the national government's authority to direct management on state and other subnationally owned forests, however, the public/private ownership divide does not negatively affect India's legal capacity to enter into and implement an international climate treaty that includes direct forest management standards.

Russia also maintains national constitutional primacy (element 1), as subject government legislation on forests must not conflict with national mandates, and the Russian Federation has a sweeping treaty power. The Russian Forest

Code of 2007 also encapsulates a national sharing of constitutional authority (element 2). Due to a confusing hierarchy of laws, unclear division of powers, and contradictory national and subnational laws, however, Russia lacks adequate institutional enforcement capacity (element 3)—even though national ownership of an overwhelming majority of the forests in Russia causes the public/private forest ownership divide not to be an impediment to the Russian national government during international negotiations.

Canada, like the United States, only maintains one key element: institutional enforcement capacity (element 3). Various provisions of the Canadian Constitution provide *subnational* constitutional primacy over forests; and the Canadian national government, like the U.S. government, has refused to attempt an extension of its other constitutional powers over nonfederal forests. Subnational primacy over forest policy, combined with the vast subnational ownership of forests, means that the public/private ownership divide in Canada, as in the United States, places a limit on the national government's options during international negotiations, as the national government would be constrained in implementing international obligations on a vast majority of forests within its borders.

The preceding review demonstrates that the public/private forest ownership divide presented in Figure 7.2 only legally constrains the United States and Canada in international negotiations on forests. Even then, the constraint is *a result of* the other axis of analysis shown in Figure 7.2—that is, the constraint results from the split in national and subnational constitutional authority over forests. Subnational governments maintain constitutional primacy for regulating the majority of U.S. forests, which are privately owned. Similarly, the Canadian Provinces, the regulator with constitutional primacy over all subnationally owned forests in Canada, actually own a majority of the nation's forests. This indicates that the national/subnational primacy divide over decentralized forest governance has the greatest impact on international negotiations of the two axes (see Figure 7.2).

Recall the four components of policy formulation and implementation described in Chapter 2 (Figure 2.5). The global forest policy/decentralized forest governance elements, though useful descriptors of federal forest-management governance structures, are more properly categorized as subsidiary elements of this new, broader theory of policy design and success.[191] This framework facilitates a more focused study of the drivers of policy failure and the areas of domestic governance upon which attention should be concentrated to improve the policymaking process, including a focus not only on political will, but also on the legal institutions that facilitate policy formulation, such as federal constitutions. Though a great amount of research has been performed on the policymaking process, including the linear progression of agenda setting, policy formation, decision-making, implementation, and policy evaluation,[192] scant attention has been given to the overarching framework in which this linear process operates. In other words, a requisite level of institutional and political capacity must be maintained by systems of government before they can engage in linear policy formation that begins with an idea for policy and ends with its successful implementation and evaluation. As you will recall, the requisite level of institutional and political capacity necessary for successful policy formulation and implementation can be represented by a Venn matrix (Figure 7.3) containing four intersecting components: (1) the government's institutional capacity to formulate policy, (2) the government's political will to formulate policy, (3) the government's institutional capacity to enforce policy, and (4) the government's political will to enforce policy.

As the above review demonstrates, governmental systems can contain any combination of these components, but the presence of all four components provides the necessary framework for successful policymaking. As seen in Figure 2.5, at the intersection of institutional capacity to formulate and to enforce, we can say a sufficient policymaking institution exists. At the intersection of political will to formulate and to enforce, we can say that sufficient policymaking political will exists. Similarly, a governmental system may have both institutional capacity and political will to formulate policy, leading to successful policy formulation, or both institutional capacity and political will to enforce, leading to successful policy implementation. When all four are present, the government has achieved a successful policy.[193]

So where does the study undertaken in this chapter fall within this matrix? If we define the "institution" for these purposes as constitutional authority at the national level to formulate forest policy, then component 1 of Figure 2.5 is our focus. Indeed, component 1 of the matrix subsumes element 1 of the global forest governance/decentralized forest policy balance (national constitutional primacy). Without the national government first maintaining the institution of constitutional authority, institutional capacity to enforce, political will to formulate, and political will to implement policy are irrelevant.[194] It is also this component which has the potential to legally entrench the commons dynamic across governance scales.

The domestic forest policies here reviewed provide a case study of how federal systems can maintain different combinations of policy formulation/implementation components, leading to divergent outcomes regarding a national government's ability to formulate policy as a resource management fail-safe in the event that subnational governments do not adequately manage the resource, for both domestic and global policy objectives. As demonstrated above, the Brazilian, Indian, and Russian Constitutions all maintain explicit constitutional provisions related to forest protection, with Brazil in particular maintaining some of the most stringent national-level forest protection mandates in any federal constitution.[195] Thus, each of these systems maintains component 1 (institutional capacity to formulate forest management policy). In addition, each of these federal systems maintains component 2 because each has politically capitalized on its institutional capacity by formulating national forest policy legislation.

Even so, each nation is missing crucial components of policy implementation and enforcement (components 3 and 4, which effectively subsume element 3 in the global forest governance/decentralized forest policy balance). These national governments are unable to enforce legislation passed pursuant to their broad constitutional powers over forests because each is plagued by some implementation/enforcement malady, such as a weak judiciary, lack of financial resources, lack of enforcement culture, corruption, unclear division of powers between different levels of government, and unclear separation of powers between branches of government. National policies will not be successful without these crucial components of policy implementation and enforcement.

The U.S. and Canadian federal systems, on the other hand, present quite the opposite scenario regarding national-level forest policymaking, as each maintain sufficient enforcement and implementation capabilities (components 3 and 4), but neither maintains institutional capacity to formulate policy (component 1)—a scenario arising directly out of their chosen forms of constitutional federalism. In the future, the U.S. and Canadian national governments may very well gain the political will to formulate a national forest policy applicable to privately, state, and provincially owned forests (component 2), and may also maintain both the institutional capacity (component 3) and political will (component 4) to enforce such a policy. Yet, the presence of those three components is irrelevant if the constitution does not grant the national government legal authority to formulate policy in the first instance (component 1). Thus, the policy will either never be formulated, or even if it is formulated—and regardless of whether it actually succeeds on the ground—it may be challenged and later held unconstitutional by the courts.

It is lack of institutional capacity to formulate policy—arising out of constitutional structure—that affects not only the ability of federal systems like those of the United States and Canada to formulate national domestic forest policies, but also prevents their participation in the full range of global forest governance approaches to addressing climate change. It is important to situate the U.S. and Canadian constitutional orders within this policy formulation/implementation matrix so that scholars can undertake a clearer and more focused study of the drivers of law and policy failure, and understand how those drivers may be adjusted to achieve success and resolve commons dilemmas—which is the goal of Chapters 8 and 9.

Conclusion

Ultimately, we see that in the context of international forest negotiations, the concept that "[f]ederalism and a spirited foreign policy go ill together"[196] need not apply, in a *legal* sense, to countries with all three key elements, like Australia. Countries with the Australian model of constitutional structure maintain the ability, via national constitutional primacy, to enter into an international agreement on forests without concern over potential subnational legal interference. They also have adequate institutional enforcement capacity to ensure implementation, and they voluntarily share forest authority with subnational governments to preserve the benefits of decentralized forest management. This is true within a *legal* sense because whether such countries politically choose to allow federalism to bode ill for their foreign policy is a separate question from whether the legal institution that facilitates political will (the constitution) allows conformation to foreign policy objectives.

Similarly, Brazil, India, and Russia maintain the institutional framework for both national constitutional primacy and national sharing of constitutional authority, but they do not have institutional enforcement capacity. Lack of this element hampers their ability to implement an international agreement and thus may give rise to apathy at the negotiating table and political interference with legal objectives. It also prevents the benefits of decentralized forest governance from being realized.

Without national constitutional primacy over all forests, the United States and Canada will have difficulties engaging fully in global climate change governance and entering into certain types of binding treaties that include forest management, especially ones that mandate particular forms of prescriptive or minimum standard setting regulation. Furthermore, without the sharing of constitutional authority that can flow from national constitutional primacy, the U.S. and Canadian national governments may not effectively balance the benefits of centralized forest management *planning* with decentralized *management* domestically.

Scholars have adequately assessed, and are currently exploring, the implications of weak constitutional structure, apathetic judiciaries, corruption, and other institutional problems in countries like Brazil, India, and Russia—governance characteristics that lead to a lack of institutional enforcement capacity on forest policy (element 3). Scholars, however, have failed to assess how the domestic constitutional orders of countries like the United States and Canada might be adjusted to leave all of the legal and policy response tools on the table for global climate and forest governance. Chapters 8 and 9 undertake that endeavor and explore both the implications of, and solutions to, the absence of elements 1 and 2 in the United States and Canada. If the U.S. and Canada place value on international treaty-making and global governance to address climate change via utilization of the world's forests, then these solutions will be crucial. Most federal constitutions provide a "treaty power" in one form or another. As a result, these countries already—at least on paper—value global governance to a certain degree, having provided a constitutional tool authorizing the national government to participate in international agreements. Given that federal systems controlling important forest resources maintain constitutional structures that allow subnational governments to constrain international climate change negotiations, the need for creative constitutional methods facilitating effective global environmental governance has never been more apparent. Though regulation of land use activities like private forest management may have historically been the "quintessential" state and local government role, climate change is now the "quintessential" global challenge. Forging national level fail-safes within the constitutional orders of forested federal systems will allow the ultimate source of legal authority in these countries, the constitution, to recognize that which science already does—that local forests, despite privatization or government regulation, remain global commons resources, having impacts beyond subnational and national political boundaries and which are felt on the other side of the globe.

Notes

1 The material constituting significant portions of this chapter originated in Blake Hudson, Federal Constitutions, Global Governance, and the Role of Forests in Regulating Climate Change, 87 *Ind. L.J.* 1455 (2012).
2 Edward T. Swaine, Does Federalism Constrain the Treaty Power? 103 *Colum. L. Rev.* 403, 461–62 (2003).
3 K.C. Wheare, Federal Government 196 (1953).
4 Held at Yale University on September 17–19, 2010, and sponsored by the United Nations Institute for Training and Research, available at http://conference.unitar.org/yale/democratic-institutions-and-environmental-sustainability.
5 Conference papers are available online. Unitar, at http://conference.unitar.org/yale/conference-papers.
6 See Swaine, supra note 2.
7 See Wheare, supra note 3.
8 U.N. Env't Programme, Global Environment Outlook 3: Past, Present and Future Perspectives 110 (2002), available at http://www.unep.org/geo/GEO3/english/pdf.htm (follow "Forests" hyperlink).
9 Wahjudi Wardojo, Foreword, in *The Politics of Decentralization: Forests, People and Power* ix (Carol J. Pierce Colfer and Doris Capistrano eds, 2005).
10 See Hans M. Gregersen et al., Forest Governance in Federal Systems: An Overview of Experiences and Implications for Decentralization, in *The Politics Of Decentralization: Forests, Power And People*, id., at 15; Ian Ferguson and Cherukat Chandrasekharan, Paths and Pitfalls of Decentralization for Sustainable Forest Management: Experiences of the Asia Pacific Region, in *The Politics of Decentralization: Forests, Power and People*, id., at 63, 65.
11 Arnoldo Contreras-Hermosilla, Hans M. Gregersen, and Andy White, *Forest Governance in Countries with Federal Systems of Government: Lessons for Decentralization*, Center for International Forestry Research Governance Brief 1, (January 2008, Number 39), available at http://www.cifor.cgiar.org/publications/pdf_files/GovBrief/GovBrief0739E.pdf. There are approximately 167 unitary systems of government, while there are only 26 federal systems of government. *Federalism by Country*, F. of Federations, available at http://www.forumfed.org/en/federalism/by_country/index.php.
12 These may include bilateral or multilateral arrangements between groups of nations or nongovernmental organizations. Scholars have highlighted a recent trend toward bottom-up and flexible transnational approaches to engaging in global environmental governance in the absence of a centralized, legally binding international arrangement. See Kenneth Abbott, The Transnational Regime Complex for Climate Change, 30 *Envtl. & Plan. C: Gov't & Pol'y* 571 (2012); Daniel Bodansky, A Tale of Two Architectures: The Once and Future U.N. Climate Change Regime, 43 *Ariz. St. L.J.* 697 (2011).
13 Of the world's approximately 4 billion hectares of forest, Australia maintains 165 million hectares; Brazil, 493 million hectares; Canada, 310 million hectares; Russia, 809 million hectares; and the United States, 302 million hectares. Jacek P. Siry, Frederick W. Cubbage, and David H. Newman, XIII World Forestry Cong., *Global Forest Ownership: Implications for Forest Production, Management, and Protection* 3 (2009), available at http://www.pefc.org/images/stories/documents/external/global_forest_ownership_FD.pdf. India

maintains 77 million hectares. Indian Inst. of Forest Mgmt., National Forest Policy Review: India 111, available at ftp://ftp.fao.org/docrep/fao/005/AC921E/AC921E04.pdf.

14 Jesse C. Ribot, Choosing Representation: Institutions and Powers for Decentralized Natural Resources Management, in *The Politics of Decentralization: Forests, Power and People*, supra note 9, at 86, 98.

15 As a general matter, scholars maintain mixed views on the value of forest policy decentralization, and the means by which it occurs, with some arguing

> for slowing the pace [of decentralization] in order to give governments and citizens a chance to adapt to the new features of a decentralized approach; others suggest that local governments and citizens will become adept at dealing with their new powers only by using them. Although [scholars] see the potential value of decentralization, some favour a stronger central role and others a stronger local role, in the balance of power. Some show more faith in communities' management abilities, some have less.

Jürgen Blaser et al., Introduction, in *The Politics of Decentralization: Forests, Power and People*, id., at 1, 5.

16 See Gregersen et al., supra note 10, at 27–28.

17 Hans Gregersen et al., Ctr. For Int'l Forestry Res., *Forest Governance In Federal Systems: An Overview Of Experiences And Implications For Decentralization* 8–9 (2004), available at http://www.cifor.cgiar.org/publications/pdf_files/interlaken/interlaken_pre-paper.pdf.

18 Gregersen et al., supra note 10, at 29.

19 Id. at 15.

20 Id. at 28–29.

21 Doris Capistrano and Carol J. Pierce Colfer, Decentralization: Issues, Lessons and Reflections, in *The Politics of Decentralization: Forests, Power and People*, supra note 9, at 296, 311.

22 Anne M. Larson, Democratic Decentralization in the Forestry Sector: Lessons Learned from Africa, Asia and Latin America, in *The Politics of Decentralization: Forests, Power and People*, supra note 9, at 32, 36. Some scholars have noted that "[t]he role of national government is to ensure that the many micro-level management decisions of local community governments aggregate into a coherent policy, not to mandate a policy in ways that disrupt and marginalize the community members who ultimately form the state/forest interface." Craig Segall, Note, The Forestry Crisis as a Crisis of the Rule of Law, 58 *Stan. L. Rev.* 1539, 1549 (2006).

23 See Larson, supra note 22, at 36. Scholars have noted that "[e]lected forest councils in Kumaon, India, have historically operated under such an arrangement. They have an important autonomous decision-making space within rules and limits established by the central government. ... The upward, as well as downward, accountability of the councils has been important to their success." Id.

24 Id. at 43.

25 Ribot, supra note 14, at 89–90.

26 Segall, supra note 22, at 1556.

27 Ribot, supra note 14, at 98.

28 Contreras-Hermosilla et al., supra note 11, at 7.

29 Id. This is because "[u]ncoordinated decisions on forest management taken at subnational levels of government may weaken national policy coherence." Arnoldo Contreras-Hermosilla, Hans M. Gregersen, and Andy White, *Forest Governance in Countries with Federal Systems of Government: Lessons and Implications for Decentralization*, Ctr. for Int'l Forestry Res., Forests and Governance Programme 2008, at 12, available at http://www.cifor.cgiar.org/publications/pdf_files/Books/BContreras-Hermosilla0701.pdf.

30 Contreras-Hermosilla et al., supra note 11, at 4.

31 Constance L. McDermott et al., *Global Environmental Forest Policies: An International Comparison* 21 (2010).

32 "Capacity" is here defined as "the ability of ... governments to carry out their mandates." Larson, supra note 22, at 50.

33 Contreras-Hermosilla et al., supra note 29, at 22.

34 James Rasband, James Salzman, and Mark Squillace, *Natural Resources Law and Policy* 171 (2nd ed. 2009).

35 Id. at 172.

36 Commonwealth of Austl., National Forest Policy Statement: A New Focus for Australia's Forests 1 (1995), available at http://www.daff.gov.au/ – data/assets/pdf_file/0019/37612/nat_nfps.pdf; see also Ferguson and Chandrasekharan, supra note 10, at 75 (stating that "[u]nder Australia's constitution, administration of all matters of land management, including forestry, were delegated to the provinces").

37 Unlike the U.S. Constitution, the Australian Constitution is silent regarding whether the federal and state governments have shared, or whether either has exclusive, authority to negotiate and implement treaties. See Brian R. Opeskin and Donald R. Rothwell, The Impact of Treaties on Australian Federalism, 27 *Case W. Res. J. Int'l L.* 1, 2 (1995). For a discussion of the implications of this constitutional difference, see Cyril Robert Emery, Treaty Solutions from the Land Down Under: Reconciling American Federalism and International Law, 24 *Penn St. Int'l L. Rev.* 115, 125 (2005); Julia Yoo, Note, Participation in the Making of Legislative Treaties: The United States and Other Federal Systems, 41 *Colum. J. Transnat'l L.* 455, 487 (2003).

38 (1983) 158 CLR 1 (Austl.).

39 Marcus B. Lane, Regional Forest Agreements: Resolving Resource Conflicts or Managing Resource Politics? 37 *Austl. Geographical Stud.* 142, 144 (1999) (citing Koowarta v Bjelke-Petersen (1982) 153 CLR 168 (Austl.)).

40 Australian Constitution s 51(xxix).

41 Opeskin and Rothwell, supra note 37, at 31.

42 Id. at 12 (emphasis added).

43 Marcus B. Lane, Decentralization or Privatization of Environmental Governance? Forest Conflict and Bioregional Assessment in Australia, 19 *J. Rural Stud.* 283, 287 (2003) (citation omitted). Also noting that the High Court has consistently upheld Commonwealth involvement in forest policy as "in keeping with its constitutional powers for trade and foreign affairs." Id.

44 Some have argued that "[t]he U.S. legal environment is substantially different from that in Australia. While the Australian High Court has consistently favored the federal government's ability to make and implement treaties, the [U.S.] Supreme Court has applied limits to the U.S. federal government's power in a variety of areas." Emery, supra note 37, at 151.

45 Ian S. Ferguson, Australian Forest Services: Institutions of Change or Changing Institutions? 75 *Commonwealth Forestry Rev.* 136 (1996). Scholars have noted that "[i]ncreasingly, the national government has used its powers to influence outcomes at a provincial or district level." Ferguson and Chandrasekharan, supra note 10, at 76.

46 Lane, supra note 43, at 287.

47 Id. (citation omitted).

48 See, e.g., *Richardson v Forestry Commission* (1988) 164 CLR 261 (Austl.); *Queensland v Commonwealth* (1985) 159 CLR 192 (Austl.). Scholars note that these High Court cases "further expanded the scope of the external affairs power" and "had substantial implications for Australian federalism because the Commonwealth Parliament had never before been able to legislate comprehensively in respect of state properties in reliance on an international treaty. The Commonwealth Parliament also gained expanded powers over the environment." Opeskin and Rothwell, supra note 37, at 30–31. For further discussion of these cases, see id. at 33–42.

49 Opeskin and Rothwell, supra note 37, at 10, 31.

50 Id. at 42. Scholars have asserted that

> the current position is that irrespective of whether or not a treaty is representative of international concern or that it contains an international obligation upon State Parties, the mere acceptance of the treaty by Australia is a sufficient basis for the Commonwealth to rely on the terms of the treaty to enact implementing legislation.

Id.

51 Lane, supra note 39, at 145. Australia's 1995 National Forest Policy Statement acknowledges this federal authority, citing international agreements and acts of Parliament requiring federal government involvement in land use decision-making regarding forests. See National Forest Policy Statement, supra note 36, at 19–20.

52 Lane, supra note 39, at 145 (citation omitted); see also id. at 287; National Forest Policy Statement, supra note 36, at 19–20.

53 Lane, supra note 39, at 144.

54 Id. at 145 (emphasis in original). Again, this is distinct from the United States, where the federal government has never claimed, nor been judicially conferred, land use and forest management regulatory authority.

55 Environment Protection and Biodiversity Conservation Act 1999, (Cth) (Austl.).

56 Kah Low and Sinniah Mahendrarajah, Future Directions for the Australian Forest Industry, *Issues Insights*, Mar. 2010, at 13, available at http://daff.gov.au/–data/assets/pdf_file/0010/1894168/a1.pdf.

57 Id.

58 Inter-governmental Agreement on the Environment, May 14, 1992 (Austl.).

59 Lane, supra note 39, at 145.

60 Id.

61 National Forest Policy Statement, supra note 36, at 19–20.

62 The Commonwealth's role in resource management is "restricted" to "[r]epresenting the national interest ... [e]nsuring Australia's international obligations are met ... [a]ssisting in the resolution of transboundary issues ... [p]romoting co-operative approaches to assessment and standard setting," and "[c]oncern for its own environmental responsibilities arising from Commonwealth actions and decisions." Lane, supra note 39, at 145 (citation omitted).

63 Id.

64 Opeskin and Rothwell, supra note 37, at 2. Some have argued that this has "bound the Commonwealth politically, if not legally, to consensus-based outcomes." Phillip Toyne, *The Reluctant Nation: Environment, Law and Politics in Australia* 14 (1994). For a criticism of this approach, see Gary Musselwhite and Gamini Herath, Australia's Regional Forest Agreement Process: Analysis of the Potential and Problems, 7 *Forest Pol'y & Econ.* 579, 580 (2005).

65 National Forest Policy Statement, supra note 36.

66 Id. at 4.

67 Lane, supra note 39, at 146 (citation omitted).

68 National Forest Policy Statement, supra note 36, at 1.

69 Id.

70 Lane, supra note 39, at 143.

71 Lane, supra note 43, at 288.

72 Lane, supra note 39, at 151.

73 Musselwhite and Herath, supra note 64, at 581 (citation omitted).

74 Ferguson, supra note 45, at 140.

75 Musselwhite and Herath, supra note 64, at 585 (citation omitted).

76 Opeskin and Rothwell, supra note 37, at 56–57. Even so, this approach has not been without its complications, as scholars note that this cooperative approach has caused delays in fulfilling international obligations, a lack of uniformity in implementing laws,

and legal issues arising out of coordination between the federal and state governments and by the fact that a state has the potential to place the federal government in breach of its international duties. Id. at 57.

77 The World Justice Project Rule of Law Index rates Australia eighth out of 97 countries studied for the absence of corruption, and fifth out of 97 for regulatory enforcement. Mark D. Agrast, Juan C. Botero, Joel Martinez, Alejandro Ponce, and Christine S. Pratt, *The World Justice Project, Rule of Law Index 2012–13* [hereinafter World Justice Project], available at http://worldjusticeproject.org/sites/default/files/WJP_Index_Report_2012.pdf. Australia also has a positive score on the Environmental Regulatory Regimes Index developed by Yale and Columbia Universities, which "integrates assessment of the stringency of environmental pollution standards, the extent of subsidization of natural resources, the strictness of enforcement and the quality of environmental institutions." McDermott, et al., supra note 31, at 43.

78 Low and Mahendrarajah, supra note 56, at 5.

79 National Forest Policy Statement, supra note 36, at 11.

80 Lane, supra note 43, at 287. Despite the high proportion of public ownership, 44 percent of public forestland is privately managed, placing the percentage of privately-managed land in Australia at approximately 70 percent. Low and Mahendrarajah, supra note 56, at 5.

81 Sofia R. Hirakuri, *Can Law Save the Forest? Lessons from Finland and Brazil* 19 (2003), available at http://www.cifor.cgiar.org/publications/pdf_files/Books/Law.pdf.

82 Lei No. 4.771, de 15 de setembro de 1965, Codigo Florestal [C. Flor.] [Forestry Code], D.O.U. de 28.09.65 (Braz.), reprinted in 5 Coleçao das Leis 157 (1965), amended by Provisional Measure N° 1.511 of 25 July 1996.

83 Simone Bauch et al., Forest Policy Reform in Brazil, 107 *J. Forestry* 132, 134 (2009) (citation omitted), available at http://www.fs.fed.us/global/iitf/pubs/ja_iitf_2009_bauch001.pdf.

84 Article 225 begins by stating: "All have the right to an ecologically balanced environment, which is an asset of common use and essential to a healthy quality of life, and both the Government and the community shall have the duty to defend and preserve it for present and future generations." Constituição Federal [C.F.] [Constitution] art. 225 (Braz.).

85 Constituição Federal [C.F.] [Constitution] art. 24 (Braz.).

86 Id.

87 Janelle E. Kellman, The Brazilian Legal Tradition and Environmental Protection: Friend or Foe, 25 *Hastings Int'l & Comp. L. Rev.* 145, 153 (2002). Provisional Measure No. 1511 of July 1996, which was meant to increase forest reserves as well as restrict clear-cutting, is one such example. Provisional Measure N° 1.511 of 25 July 1996. The federal government actually establishes, through the forest code, that clear-cutting is restricted to 20 to 80 percent of a parcel of land. Hirakuri, supra note 81, at 21. This is very different from the United States, where such regulations are currently the role of state governments.

88 Hirakuri, supra note 81, at 19.

89 See Bauch et al., supra note 83, at 135. For example, IBAMA previously required all forest owners to have an approved forest management plan (Plande Manejo Florestal Sustentavel (PMFS)) before harvesting timber, and all harvested timber was required to have a transport authorization to demonstrate that it came from an area with an approved forest management plan. Id.

90 See Hirakuri, supra note 81, at 20.

91 Id. (citation omitted).

92 Keith S. Rosenn, Federalism in Brazil, 43 *Duq. L. Rev.* 577, 584–85 (2005).

93 Id. at 585.

94 Id.

95 Gregersen et al., supra note 17, at 33; Bauch et al., supra note 83, at 135.

96 Bauch et al., supra note 83, at 135.

97 Id. at 134.

98 See Kellman, supra note 87, at 159. The World Justice Project Rule of Law Index rates Brazil thirty-eighth out of 97 countries studied for the absence of corruption, and thirty-seventh out of 97 for regulatory enforcement. See World Justice Project, supra note 77. Brazil also has a negative score on the Environmental Regulatory Regimes Index developed by Yale and Columbia Universities. McDermott et al., supra note 31, at 43.

99 Emilio F. Moran, The Law, Politics, and Economics of Amazonian Deforestation, 1 *Ind. J. Global Legal Stud.* 397, 397 (1994).

100 Benjamin J. Richardson, Environmental Law in Postcolonial Societies: Straddling the Local-Global Institutional Spectrum, 11 *Colo. J. Int'l Envtl. L. & Pol'y* 1, 26 (2000).

101 Constituição Federal [C.F.] [Consitution] art. 26 (Braz.).

102 Moran, supra note 99, at 401.

103 Hirakuri, supra note 81, at 2.

104 Id. at 78 (citation omitted).

105 It has been argued that "the Brazilian Constitution ha[s] affirmed the rights of all their citizens to a healthy, stable environment. But these are constitutional provisions dis-associated from the funding required for their implementation and can be interpreted as efforts to satisfy international pressure without requiring any practical steps to bring them into action." Moran, supra note 99, at 406.

106 Hirakuri, supra note 81, at 51.

107 Id. at 29, 56; Kellman, supra note 87, at 159–60; Moran, supra note 99, at 401. Scholars have noted that:

> Environmentalists had hoped that the Constitution would mark a great advance for environmental protection in Brazil by making environmental concerns a national priority, at least on paper. The Brazilian Constitution attempts to provide a comprehensive approach to environmental protection. Perhaps most importantly, at least rhetorically, is its guarantee of a healthy and stable environment to all Brazilian citizens. The truth, however, is that the "promise of the amendments" contained in the Constitution has been 'illusory.'

Kellman, supra note 87, at 152 (citing Armin Rosenkranz et al., Rio Plus Five: Environmental Protection and Free Trade in Latin America, 9 *Geo. Int'l Envtl. L. Rev.* 527, 567 (1997)). A report issued by the Brazilian Institute of Agriculture Research demonstrated that the federal government has failed to enforce forest management regulations, and has thus failed to implement forestry laws. Hirakuri, supra note 81, at 2. The federal government itself, in 1996, recognized that it had not adequately implemented forest management laws. Id. at 29. Government audits in Brazil in 1996 found the compliance rate with forest laws to be just 30 percent. Id. at 78. Compare this with a 96 percent rate of compliance among Finnish timber interests in 1997. Id. Some scholars believe that the lack of enforcement is caused "more by lack of human and financial resources and institutional capacity than by lack of adequate legislation." Lila Katz de Barrera-Hernandez and Alastair R. Lucas, Environmental Law in Latin America and the Caribbean: Overview and Assessment, 12 *Geo. Int'l Envtl. L. Rev.* 207, 231 (1999). It has also been noted that in Brazil, "it is implementation, rather than policy, that is the problem. … [L]ow compliance with existing forest management laws, rather than lack of laws, is often a leading cause of unsustainable forestry practices." Hirakuri, supra note 81, at 2. Yet other scholars have argued that "Brazilian environmental agencies tend to be among the least powerful agencies in the government. They have difficulty defending policies and administrative actions that run contrary to the priorities of political leaders and other governmental agencies." Lesley K. McAllister, *Making Law Matter: Environmental Protection and Legal Institutions in Brazil* 41 (2008).

108 McAllister, supra note 107, at 55–56. As a further example, scholars have noted that Provisional Measure No. 1511, passed in July 1996 in order to increase forest reserves and restrict clear-cutting, "impose[s] stricter requirements on paper, [but] are not routinely

enforced and represent merely temporary measures rather than long-standing environmental change." Kellman, supra note 87, at 156. For further discussion on how judicial deficiencies, lack of education and training for the citizenry, financial, and other societal constraints hamstring enforcement of environmental laws in Brazil, see id. at 160–64.

109 Keith S. Rosenn, Judicial Review in Brazil: Developments Under the 1988 Constitution, 7 *Sw J. L. & Trade Am.* 291, 318 (2000).

110 Id. at 318 (citing *Carta ao Leitor*, Veja, Feb. 1989, at 23 (original in Portuguese)).

111 Moran, supra note 99, at 406.

112 Hirakuri, supra note 81, at 54.

113 Lei N° 4.771, art. 44, de 15 de setembro de 1965, Codigo Florestal [C. Flor.] [Forestry Code], D.O.U. de 28.09.65 (Braz.), reprinted in 5 Coleçao das Leis 157 (1965), amended by Provisional Measure N° 1.511 of 25 July 1996. This is an increase from the 50 percent required in the original 1965 Forest Code. Hirakuri, supra note 81, at 11.

114 Moran, supra note 99, at 401.

115 Constitution Act, 1867, 30 & 31 Vict., c. 3 (U.K.), §§ 92–92A, reprinted in R.S.C. 1985, app. II, no. 5 (Can.).

116 Id. § 92A.

117 Paul Stanton Kibel, Canada's International Forest Protection Obligations: A Case of Promises Forgotten in British Columbia and Alberta, 6 *Fordham Envtl. L. Rev.* 231, 247 (1995).

118 See Canadian Counsel of Forest Ministers, *Sustainable Forest Management in Canada* 4 (2010).

119 See Global Environment Outlook, supra note 8, at 110.

120 Constitution Act, 1982, c. 11 (U.K.), § 92(13), reprinted in R.S.C. 1985, app. II, no. 44 (Can.).

121 Kibel, supra note 117, at 247.

122 David R. Boyd, *Unnatural Law: Rethinking Canadian Environmental Law and Policy* 133 (2003). Under the Canadian Constitution, however, the federal government does retain the role of participating in international negotiations "related to the conservation and use of forests." Id. at 132.

123 Michael Howlett and Jeremy Rayner, Globalization and Governance Capacity: Explaining Divergence in National Forest Programs as Instances of 'Next-Generation' Regulation in Canada and Europe, 19 *Governance: An Int'l J. of Pol'y, Admin., & Institutions* 251, 265 (2006).

124 Kibel, supra note 117, at 246 (quoting Canadian Forest Serv., The State of Canada's Forests 1993 8 (1994)).

125 Kibel, supra note 117, at 246.

126 Id. at 248.

127 Id.

128 Id.

129 Michael Howlett, Introduction: Policy Regimes and Policy Change in the Canadian Forest Sector, in *Canadian Forest Policy* 3, 11 (Michael Howlett ed., 2001).

130 Michael Howlett and Jeremy Rayner, The Business and Government Nexus: Principal Elements and Dynamics of the Canadian Forest Policy Regime, in *Canadian Forest Policy*, supra note 129, at 23, 36–37.

131 Id. at 37.

132 Steven Bernstein and Benjamin Cashore, The International-Domestic Nexus: The Effects of International Trade and Environmental Politics on the Canadian Forest Sector, in *Canadian Forest Policy*, supra note 129, at 65, 85.

133 Howlett and Rayner, supra note 123, at 268.

134 Gregersen et al., supra note 17, at 37.

135 Kibel, supra note 117, at 250.

136 Id. at 249.

137 Curtis A. Bradley, The Treaty Power and American Federalism (pts. 1 & 2), 97 *Mich. L. Rev.* 390, 456 (1998).

138 Canada (Att'y Gen.) v. Ontario (Att'y Gen.), [1937] 1 D.L.R. 673 (Can.).

139 Jeffrey L. Friesen, The Distribution of Treaty-Implementing Powers in Constitutional Federations: Thoughts on the American and Canadian Models, 94 *Colum. L. Rev.* 1415, 1416 (1994). This state of affairs arises from the Labor Conventions case where the Privy Council established that the Canadian federal government may not implement treaties via implementing legislation that intrudes into matters constitutionally reserved to the provinces. Canada (Att'y Gen.) v. Ontario (Att'y Gen.), [1937] 1 D.L.R. 673 (Can.).

140 Missouri v. Holland, 252 U.S. 416, 431–35 (1920).

141 Friesen, supra note 139, at 1433.

142 Id. at 1439. Additionally, "proposed constitutional amendments, particularly since 1982, have uniformly sought to vest more power in the provinces at the expense of the central government." Id.

143 The World Justice Project Rule of Law Index rates Canada twelfth out of 97 countries studied for both the absence of corruption and for regulatory enforcement. World Justice Project, supra note 77, at 108, 110. Canada also has a positive score on the Environmental Regulatory Regimes Index developed by Yale and Columbia Universities. McDermott, supra note 31, at 43 fig.2.5.

144 Canadian Counsel of Forest Ministers, supra note 118, at 4–5.

145 India Const. art. 48A.

146 India Const. art. 51A(g).

147 Gregersen et al., supra note 17, at 55. Article 246 of the Indian Constitution grants concurrent oversight over items listed in "List III" of the Indian Constitution, including forests. India Const. art. 246(2).

148 SJVN Ltd., Environmental Regulations and Legal Framework in India § 1.2, available at www.sjvn.nic.in/projects/environmental-regulations.pdf.

149 Forest (Conservation) Act, 1980, no. 69, Acts of Parliament, 1980 (India).

150 Gregersen et al., supra note 17, at 55; see Ministry of Env't & Forests, National Forest Policy Resolution § 4.3.2 (1988) (India).

151 Ministry of Env't & Forests, supra note 150.

152 Alon Tal and Jessica A. Cohen, Bringing 'Top-Down' to 'Bottom-Up': A New Role for Environmental Legislation in Combating Desertification, 31 *Harv. Envtl. L. Rev.* 163, 203–4 (2007).

153 Gregersen et al., supra note 17, at 54. In fact, the greater tension in Indian forest regulatory authority seems to be between the state and local governments, rather than between the state and federal governments. See id. at 57. It is unclear just how effective this level of decentralization is, due to a lack of institutional enforcement capacity, and it is also unclear exactly how much authority decentralized governments and groups actually maintain.

154 Indian Inst. of Forest Mgmt., *National Forest Policy Review* 120 (2010), available at ftp://ftp.fao.org/docrep/fao/005/AC921E/AC921E04.pdf.

155 Id. at 115.

156 Id. at 128.

157 The World Justice Project Rule of Law Index rates India eighty-third out of 97 countries studied for the absence of corruption, and seventy-ninth out of 97 for regulatory enforcement. World Justice Project, supra note 77. India also has a negative score on the Environmental Regulatory Regimes Index developed by Yale and Columbia Universities. McDermott et al., supra note 31, at 43.

158 Indian Inst. of Forest Mgmt., supra note 154, at 129.

159 Id. at 113.

160 Gregersen et al., supra note 17, at 54.

161 Id.

162 Natalia V. Malysheva, Main Features of Russia's Forest Management System, in *The Politics of Decentralization: Forests, People and Power*, supra note 9, at 229, 230.

163 Konstitutsiia Rossiiskoi Federatsii [Konst. RF] [Constitution] (Russ.).

164 Minna Pappila, Int'l Inst. for App. Sys., IR-99-058, *The Russian Forest Sector and Legislation in Transition* 2–3 (1999).
165 Konstitutsiia Rossiiskoi Federatsii [Konst. RF] [Constitution] art. 15.4 (Russ.) (emphasis added).
166 Gennady M. Danilenko, The New Russian Constitution and International Law, 88 *Am. J. Int'l L.* 451, 453, 465–66 (1994).
167 There are 83 sub-national units of government in Russia, called "subjects."
168 Konstitutsiia Rossiiskoi Federatsii [Konst. RF] [Constitution] art. 72 (Russ.).
169 Pappila, supra note 164, at 21.
170 Danilenko, supra note 166, at 464.
171 Lesnoi Kodeks Rossiikoi Federatsii [LK RF] (Forestry Code) [hereinafter Forest Code], available at http://www.iiasa.ac.at/Research/FOR/forest_cdrom/downloads/Forest_code/ForestCode-3rdReading-061108-eng.pdf.
172 Contreras-Hermosilla et al., supra note 11, at 10.
173 The federal government maintains primary regulatory authority for various forest activities, such as restrictions on clear-cutting (Article 17), forest uses (Article 27), reforestation (Article 62), development of forest management planning procedures (Article 67), and at least 50 other forest management activities (Articles 81 and 82). Forest Code, supra note 171, arts. 17, 27, 62, 67.
174 Id. at arts. 83–88.
175 Id. at arts. 83–89.
176 Id. at arts. 15, 17–6.
177 Contreras-Hermosilla et al., supra note 11, at 3.
178 The World Justice Project Rule of Law Index rates Russia seventy-first out of 97 countries studied for the absence of corruption and sixty-eighth out of 97 for regulatory enforcement. World Justice Project, supra note 77. Russia also has a negative score on the Environmental Regulatory Regimes Index developed by Yale and Columbia Universities. McDermott et al., supra note 31, at 43.
179 Pappila, supra note 164, at 5. Also noting that "[t]here are doubts whether Russian federalism really works" and "whether the law-making powers are really clear in Russia." Id. at 2.
180 Id. at 2.
181 Id. at 5. Scholars have noted that "[t]he federal government has no means of prior surveillance of local legislation in order to avoid inconsistencies. The only way to control that regional law does not contradict the Russian Constitution or federal laws is to appeal to the Constitutional Court, which takes approximately five years." Id. In some situations the federal government has given powers granted to it exclusively by the Constitution to subject governments. Id at 6.
182 Gregersen et al., supra note 17, at 6.
183 Taiga Rescue Network, Comments on the New Russian Forest Code, Briefing Note, Taiga Rescue Network, Jokkmokk, Sweden, January 2007, 3.
184 Gregersen et al., supra note 17, at 41.
185 Konstitutsiia Rossiiskoi Federatsii [Konst. RF] [Constitution] art. 9 (Russ.).
186 Rapanos v. United States, 547 U.S. 715, 738 (2006).
187 Pappila, supra note 164, at 7.
188 Taiga Rescue Network, supra note 183, at 1.
189 See Pappila, supra note 164, at 8.
190 Id. at 7–8.
191 See generally Pearl Eliandis, Margaret M. Hill, and Michael Howlett, *Designing Government: From Instruments to Governance* (2005); Michael Howlett, *Designing Public Policies: Principles and Instruments* (2011); Allan McConnell, *Understanding Policy Success: Rethinking Public Policy* (2010); David Marsh and Allan McConnell, Towards a Framework for Establishing Policy Success, 88 *J. Pub. Admin.* 564 (2010); Allan McConnell, Policy Success, Policy Failure and Grey Areas In-Between, 30 *J. Pub. Pol'y* 345 (2010).

192 See Michael Howlett, M. Ramesh, and Anthony Perl, *Studying Public Policy: Policy Cycles & Policy Subsystems* (2009).

193 Of course, whether the policy that "succeeds" is qualitatively "good" or "bad" and whether it fairly represents the will of the entire corpus of civil society rather than merely interest groups or the politically elite is a separate question from whether the fundamental ingredients exist for actual formulation and implementation of a particular policy. Questions of civil society inputs are affected by broader democratic processes and design of governmental structure.

194 At first blush one might consider the Policy Formulation and Implementation matrix also to be a linear process. It may appear that components 3 and 4 cannot exist unless components 1 and 2 first exist. In other words, how can a government enforce and implement a policy that does not yet exist? The resolution of constitutional law questions, however, is quite often nonlinear. Governments may maintain the political will to formulate policy (component 2), believing they have sufficient institutional (constitutional) capacity to formulate it (component 1). They may even set up institutions to administer and enforce the policy (components 3 and 4). Even so, sometime later the legislation may be challenged in the courts as unconstitutional. If it is found to be so, then the "retroactive" absence of component 1 renders policymaking unsuccessful. Examples are the statutes at issue in the *Lopez* (United States v. Lopez, 514 U.S. 549 (1995)) and *Morrison* cases (United States v. Morrison, 529 U.S. 598 (2000)) where the court struck down as unconstitutional statutes already passed by Congress and already put into implementation.

195 See Constituição Federal [C.F.] [Consitution] arts. 23, 24, 225 (Braz.).

196 Wheare, supra note 3, at 196.

8 Keying on Federal Systems with Weak Keystone Constitutions

The Role of Private Versus Public Forest Ownership in U.S. and Canadian Law and Policy[1]

Climate change is perhaps the most important environmental issue of our time, and is clearly the largest quintessential commons problem faced globally. Yet it is also one of the most complex commons challenges ever faced by humans. While it is difficult to craft a regulatory solution or a cooperative response among nations for most global governance issues, it is especially challenging in the case of climate change. Scientific uncertainty regarding climate change's potential impacts, the difficulties in measuring and predicting changing climatic conditions, the global scale of the problem, the innumerable sources of greenhouse gases (GHGs), the role of those sources in forming the very carbon-constructed foundation upon which society operates, and the political and jurisdictional complexities arising out of these factors make climate change an exceptionally difficult environmental and global governance challenge. The global nature of the problem requires that each nation be able to successfully utilize mechanisms of domestic governance to forge a collaborative international response, and that nations act "irrationally" under the Hardin paradigm in order to overcome the collective action problems that have contributed to the accelerated rise of carbon concentrations in the atmosphere. Chapter 7 described the United States and Canada as two nations in particular that maintain constitutional orders that pose a challenge to international negotiations because regulatory authority over treaty subject matter may be constitutionally decentralized (or non-centralized) and divided in an exclusive manner between the national and subnational governments. As a result, U.S. states and Canadian provinces may legally constrain national governments during international negotiations by resisting domestic treaty implementation as outside the scope of the national government's constitutional authority. The complications presented by federal systems like the U.S. and Canada for international negotiations have critical implications for global climate governance—at least to the extent that countries wish to preserve a legally binding treaty as one mechanism for addressing climate change.

The role of the United States and Canada in climate change and global forest management negotiations provides a compelling case study of the potential impact of federal systems on global governance via international treaty, as "realization of the significance of climate change impacts of greenhouse gas (GHG) emissions from deforestation and forest degradation has brought renewed impetus to efforts to conserve and better manage forests globally."[2] Recall from Chapter 5 that forest destruction is not only a substantial *source* of atmospheric carbon, but that one-third of global carbon emissions are absorbed by forests each year, making forests the most significant terrestrial carbon *sink* on the planet.[3] Thus, protecting important global forest resources—70–80 percent of which are found in federal systems—can both halt significant carbon releases and can absorb additional carbon from other sources.

The United States and Canada alone account for over 13 percent of the world's land base,[4] over 15 percent of the world's forests,[5] and maintain two of the top ten world economies as measured by annual gross domestic product[6]—carbon-based economies to be certain. With these two nations controlling such a significant amount of the world's natural and financial capital, full and unconstrained participation by the United States and Canada in international climate negotiations is of crucial importance if that route of response is ultimately chosen.

As noted in Chapter 5, despite arguments over the merits of dual federalism in the U.S. or Canada, legal perception is political reality, as governments politically refuse to act both domestically and internationally at least in part based upon perceived constitutional constraints. The consequences of this constitutional state of affairs for U.S. and Canadian forests are substantial, with grave threats to domestic forest resources in both countries. Under current understandings of constitutional law in both countries, a prescriptive regulatory response at national or international levels may be an unavailable mechanism for avoiding these dramatic losses of forest cover and the carbon sequestration and other ecosystem service benefits forests provide. The U.S. stands to lose 23 million acres, or 13 percent, of forests in the southeast alone over the next 50 years, as described in Chapter 5. Similarly, the lack of national or international input into Canadian forest practices also has implications for preserving the full slate of climate change solutions. While Canadian boreal forests store a great deal of carbon—an estimated 67 billion tons (equal to 303 years of the country's 2002 carbon emissions)—deforestation of nearly 230,000 acres of forest a year due to cropland conversion and urbanization is a significant source of emissions.[7] At this rate, over 11 million acres of Canadian forest will be lost over the next 50 years. This is in addition to logging activities that remove an average of 122 megatons of carbon dioxide equivalent forest carbon a year, an amount that if released into the atmosphere would equal 16 percent of Canada's total yearly GHG emissions.[8] Without greater coordination of forest policies, either among the provinces or provided by some higher governmental authority, destruction of forests in the name of economic development may proceed apace as provinces jockey for economic growth and development.

In the final assessment, if utilization of full treaty-making authority is to be preserved in the context of climate change, federal systems like the United

States and Canada will need to overcome the holistic resource management problems posed by federalism. In other words, mechanisms for forging "Fail-safe Federalism" will need to be established in the event that U.S. states or Canadian provinces do not unilaterally act to protect their respective forests in ways consistent with the needs of a robust global climate change response. Such mechanisms would allow these countries' federal governments to have the constitutional authority to act as a fail-safe by participating in the establishment of national forest objectives based upon minimum forest protection standards—standards that may need to be coordinated on a global scale to effectively address climate change. In order to provide context for Chapter 9's analysis of the various mechanisms that may be utilized to facilitate Fail-safe Federalism in the context of global forest governance and climate change in the U.S. and Canada, this chapter digs deeper into the drivers that shape U.S. and Canadian forest policy and the implications of these drivers for the suggested mechanisms of Fail-safe Federalism discussed in Chapter 9.

Summary of U.S. and Canadian Constitutional Impacts on Global Climate and Forest Governance

As detailed in Chapter 7, the three elements of federal systems that best facilitate the "global forest governance/decentralized forest policy" balance and that can avoid the legal entrenchment of the commons dynamic in federal systems are (1) national constitutional primacy over both national and subnational forest policy; (2) national sharing of constitutional authority over forest policy with subnational governments; (3) forest policy institutional enforcement capacity. The United States and Canada each only maintain one element, institutional enforcement capacity.

In the U.S., the lack of national constitutional primacy and national sharing of that constitutional authority with subnational governments results largely from the fact that the federal government has yet to test the waters of its authority over subnational forest management. But again, it is exceedingly difficult to determine if this is because the federal government perceives legal constraints so that it politically refuses to act or it does not want to act politically and so fails to do so under the guise of legal constraints. The legal constraint, or threat of legal constraint, however, matters a great deal, because even if the national government politically chose to act, it would only take one private property owner or one state government combined with the right mix of U.S. Supreme Court Justices to have national action blocked by a constitutional challenge. Regardless, in the U.S. the lack of these elements is open to argument and interpretation, which means the status quo is potentially easier to adjust over time.

There are two means by which the U.S. federal government could attempt to exert constitutional authority over subnational forest management. First, Congress could attempt to pass domestic legislation asserting direct control over subnational forest management under one of its other enumerated powers, such as the Commerce Clause. To date, this route has not been taken by the federal government, and U.S. courts have not had an opportunity to assess the constitutionality of federal private forest legislation. Second, notwithstanding Commerce Clause authority, the United States might enter into a legally binding international treaty requiring Congress to pass implementing legislation mandating that certain forest management directives be carried out on subnationally owned forests. This scenario would implicate the question analyzed in Chapter 6 regarding whether the federal government's treaty power trumps the states' reserved power under the Tenth Amendment to regulate subnational forest management.

In Canada, the explicit constitutional allocation of forest management regulatory authority between the federal government and provinces is a more intractable scenario than U.S. federalism on forests. As noted in Chapter 7, this explicit grant of authority has significant implications for Canada's ability both to maintain a national forest policy, and to negotiate an international climate treaty that includes forests, because 84 percent of Canada's forests are non-federally owned (7 percent are privately owned and 77 percent are provincially owned).[9] Other amendments to Canada's Constitution provide provincial control over property rights, including land use impacting natural resource management, and leading to Canada's "extremely decentralized" forest federalism and the "particularly weak" authority of the Canadian national government over forests.[10] As a result, the federal government has all but given up on crafting inputs into subnational forest management[11] or even applying national environmental laws, forest policies, or international forest management agreements to the provinces.[12] As noted in Chapter 7, "[w]hile the United States Constitution actually contemplates a system that values the importance of the nation's being able to implement its treaties, the Canadian constitutional framework appears to subordinate international concerns to domestic separation of legislative competence."[13]

The U.S. and Canadian federal systems' lack of the necessary elements required to fully balance global governance of forests with effective decentralized forest policy must be addressed. Mechanisms for doing so are discussed in Chapter 9. First, however, the remainder of this chapter explains that even though the U.S. and Canadian brands of federalism impact global governance of forests in similar ways, their respective subnationally established domestic forest policy frameworks are quite different—a difference driven largely by the fact that subnational governments own a vast majority of forests in Canada, whereas private property owners maintain control over a majority of forests in the United States. These differences, combined with the distinct constitutional structure of each country in the context of forest policy, give rise to contrasting recommended approaches for forging Fail-safe Federalism in the event that subnational governments do not address the increasing threats to domestic forests and the international community seeks to aggressively harness domestic forestry to combat climate change via a legally binding international treaty. These distinctions also provide a glimpse into how certain nested governance scales can reach across all others to affect scales much farther up the spectrum—private property owners on the local commons scale, for example, affecting U.S. federal authority to effectively engage in crafting solutions on the global commons scale.

U.S. and Canadian Domestic Forest Governance: Divergent Approaches, Disparate Implications for Fail-safe Federalism

The primary differences in the U.S. and Canadian domestic forest governance structure arise because a vast majority of Canada's forests are provincially owned (77 percent)—in stark contrast to the 60 percent of U.S. forests that are privately owned.[14] As a result, Canada's subnational governments tend to maintain forest management standards that are both more consistent across the nation and more rigorous in setting minimum standards for a variety of forest management policies. The provinces also seem to respond more readily to external demands for heightened forest management standards, such as those raised by environmental, scientific, or other members of civil society, than do U.S. state governments. This is likely due to the fact that a government will more readily respond to the demands of civil society regarding the management of its own lands than the management of private lands. In addition, the provincial electorate's constituent members have no legally vested private property rights in public forestlands. Rather, their interests are likely to be focused on the benefits that forests can provide the subnational government's citizenry as a whole. In the United States, on the other hand, where 60 percent of forests are privately owned, a higher proportion of civil society consists of the very private forest owners who would be regulated, and who are, therefore, more resistant to government interference. Provincial governments are simply freer to adjust the management of their own policies in response to the electorate's demands than are state governments in the United States. As explained below, it is true that the provinces may face countervailing pressure from the forest industry, but provincial interaction with the "one face" of this relatively unified industry is a different matter altogether from U.S. state governments, who interact with innumerable private property owners, any one of whom may constitutionally challenge regulatory action as infringing on private property rights.

Despite the more responsive nature of Canadian provincial forest management, however, it remains that the Canadian federal government is more constitutionally restricted from asserting any measure of authority over forest management than is the U.S. federal government. This state of affairs creates a curious scenario in Canada, where—from a *strictly domestic* perspective—constitutional prescriptive (and even sometimes cooperative) national involvement in forest policy is exceedingly difficult to achieve, but it may also be less necessary from an environmental protection standpoint. Canadian subnational domestic forest policy, at least from a statutory point of view, is simply more rigorous and of a higher quality across the board than that of U.S. subnational governments. This assertion is made from a *strictly domestic* perspective, because if the international community seeks robust mechanisms to utilize forests as carbon sinks to regulate carbon via a legally binding treaty, then a "good" Canadian forest policy today may not be viewed as "good" tomorrow. In other words, Canadian forests may currently be subject to strong, fundamental forest management standards such as protecting riparian watersheds, limiting clear-cut sizes, or regulating the number and extent of roads built during foresting operations; but if the goal is to keep fewer trees from hitting the ground, then the Canadian national government remains limited in institutional capacity to formulate such a policy consistent with the needs and requirements of the global community. Correspondingly, while U.S. subnational forest standards may not be as robust, the U.S. Constitution appears to allow more opportunity for the U.S. federal government to achieve inputs into subnational policy, whether those inputs are prescriptive or cooperative in nature. So an understanding of U.S. and Canadian domestic forest policies provides insights into the most appropriate methods of forging Fail-safe Federalism to facilitate global climate governance related to forests.

Explaining the United States–Canada Forest Policy Gap: Private Versus Public Forest Ownership

The methodology for determining national and subnational forest policy stringency presented in Chapter 5 demonstrates stark differences between subnational forest policies in the U.S. and Canada. To recap, the Canadian provinces of Alberta, British Columbia, and New Brunswick, the U.S. state of California, and the U.S. Forest Service (which manages federally owned forests) each score a "9" on the scale, maintaining very high forest policy standards.[15] The Canadian provinces of Ontario and Quebec and the U.S. state of Washington score a high "8" on the scale. The U.S. state of Oregon scores a "7" while Idaho scores a "5," and Alaska scores a "4." Lowest on the scale are the states of Montana with a "2.5," Louisiana and Virginia with a "2," and the rest of the southeastern United States—Alabama, Arkansas, Georgia, Mississippi, North Carolina, South Carolina, and Texas with a score of "1." To put the southeastern U.S. states' legal standards for forest policy in perspective, consider that developing countries average a "6.7" on the scale while nine southeastern U.S. states average a "1.2," maintaining entirely voluntary "guidelines" or no standards at all. The implications of these lax standards in the southeastern United States for domestic forest health are profound and provide just one of the many compelling justifications for forging Fail-safe Federalism, not only to facilitate the international community's efforts to utilize forests to mitigate the effects of climate change, but also for the benefit of domestic forests.

The gap between Canadian provincial forest policy—the uniformity of which *somewhat* approximates a national forest policy (though one driven solely by subnational interests)—and the widely divergent forest policies of the U.S. states is in large part explained by the respective splits in forest ownership in the two countries. As described below, the vast majority of Canadian forests being provincially owned facilitates greater uniformity, stringency, and adaptability of Canadian provincial forest policy. In contrast, the majority private ownership of U.S. forests thwarts uniformity across, as well as stringency and adaptability among, U.S. states. A variety of domestic governance nuances arise out of the private versus public forest ownership split in the United States and Canada, driving distinctions in subnational forest policy in the respective nations. For example, the nature of forest industry leaseholds in Canada is a key driver of the uniformity across provincial jurisdictions. In addition, a more stable regulatory environment in Canada, as well as a public forest management "spillover effect" in the western United States not seen in eastern states, each feed into the stringency of subnational forest policy in the two countries, as well as into the adaptability of subnational governments to respond to needed changes in forest policy.

A Formula for Uniformity: The Canadian Private-Industry/Provincial Interface as Quasi-corporatist Negotiations

The relative uniformity of high forest policy standards across subnational governments in Canada is a result of a fairly basic formula—a handful of provincial governments are negotiating with a relatively uniform industrial base for the management and extraction of forest resources. The Canadian forest sector is governed by 11 major provincial jurisdictions and historically has been Canada's largest industry and employer.[16] Due to 77 percent of Canadian forests being owned by the provinces, scholars describe the current Canadian forest policy regime as one of "public forest management for private timber harvesting."[17] The Canadian provinces allocate harvesting rights on government-owned forests through large-scale, long-term licenses. These licenses require the development of management plans that "align with strategic regional land use plans overseen by the province."[18]

Even though Canadian forest policy is extremely decentralized with complete, independent control maintained by each province, similar management challenges in the forest sector have led to "similar legislative and regulatory responses across the country."[19] This results from the corresponding uniformity and small number of forest owners controlling a vast majority of forests (the 11 provinces), as well as the uniformity of the industrial profession operating on provincially owned forests. Forest industry professionals, though spread across various jurisdictions, "brought with them similar approaches to and ideas about appropriate solutions to common forest policy problems."[20] Consequently, there is a measure of continuity and a resulting institutional inertia for both the regulator/owner of the forests and the parties being regulated/using the forests, leading to a "tendency towards enacting similar policies in different jurisdictions."[21] These similar policies have led to "extensive management responsibilities" and "increasingly intensive government regulation of company harvesting practices" to both ensure timber supply and protect other environmental values of forests.[22]

Because of the intertwined nature of the regulator and the regulated, the process by which forest policy is formulated in Canada is typically one of private negotiation in a "quasi-corporatist" style, whereby the government readily establishes prescriptions for forest management, but with input from the regulated industry.[23] Though this negotiative process might give rise to concerns of a type of institutionalized agency capture, and though some have been critical of the industry's maintenance of "a strong bargaining position,"[24] vast government ownership of forests actually gives the provinces "a special place over and above the usual roles available to a legitimate government"[25] in directing forest policy standards in the face of industrial inputs.

The symbiotic relationship between the Canadian provinces and the forest industry also relieves provincial administrative burdens by providing a direct line of technical and professional forest management expertise.[26] Indeed, as administration of forest policies has become increasingly burdensome, the provincial governments have moved toward including basic forest management standards in the terms of timber licenses, which has caused "a gradual shift of responsibilities from overworked provincial forestry services to large corporations with their own professional forest staff."[27] Though this does give rise to concerns about the monitoring of licensees to ensure compliance, at the very least the standards are in place. In addition, in recent years academics and consultants acceptable to environmental groups have become integrated into forest policy design committees, whereas in the past only industry and the provinces were represented at the negotiating table. Furthermore, where once "carrots" were the preferred mechanism for attempts at achieving compliance, increased use of fines and stronger mechanisms of enforcement demonstrate that "the regulatory 'stick' has been wielded more frequently."[28]

Though the quasi-corporatist nature of the Canadian forest policy framework certainly leaves much to be desired regarding the protection of the full suite of forest resources and ecosystem services[29]—especially the carbon sequestration value of forests—at a minimum it has helped forge fundamental, fairly uniform, and legally enforceable forest management standards across the Canadian provinces. These standards relate to buffer zones in forested watersheds, stand density requirements, clear-cutting regulations, forest road regulations, and afforestation or reforestation requirements. This scenario is very much unlike the situation in the United States, where major industrial players are largely not negotiating with the government regarding the extraction of the government's own resources (except, of course, on federal and state-owned forestlands). Rather, those industries and a vast array of non-industrial private forest owners are managing their own private lands, oftentimes without any inputs from governments hesitant to place restrictions on private property rights. Thus, each state government in the United States manages, or fails to manage, forest practices in their own way—setting the stage for a tragedy of the commons in the forest policy arena, as state governments maximize their own citizens' use of forest resources in their jurisdictions to the detriment of a forest base defined more broadly by national boundaries and which takes into account the value of forests across and beyond subnational boundaries. The large number of private property owners hamstrings the formulation of higher forest management standards, while the forest policy disparity across U.S. state jurisdictions makes anything resembling a national forest policy simply non-existent. As a result, it is also important to understand the nuances of the public–private forest ownership divide in Canada and the United States that give rise to different levels of stringency and adaptability among subnational governments in the two countries.

A Formula for Stringency and Adaptability: Greater Public Forest Ownership Leads to a More Stable Regulatory Environment and a Public Forest Policy "Spillover Effect" on Private Lands

McDermott et al. found a stark difference in the stringency of policy prescriptions on public forestlands versus private forestlands, not only in the United States and Canada, but among all of the developed countries reviewed. Indeed, whether forests are publicly or privately owned is a strong predictor of policy prescriptiveness, especially in North America, where "private property rights, including the requirement to compensate forest owners once a regulation has been deemed by the courts to infringe upon such rights, make it much more difficult for governments to regulate private rather than public forests."[30] Thus there is a marked difference in the stringency of forest policy on public versus private forestlands in Canadian provinces and U.S. states, though these differences are of far less consequence in Canada given the small amount of privately owned forests.[31]

Correspondingly, when governments own most of the forest resource base, as in Canada, they are more likely to adapt to pressure to increase the stringency of forest policy standards, as "[g]overnments in developed countries respond to pressure from environmental activists and the community for high forest management standards by developing high levels of policy prescriptiveness, and high performance thresholds, for public forestlands."[32] Indeed, given the provincial status as to what is effectively a "landlord" over forest resources, "provincial governments can set the terms for access to Crown forest resources, impose more onerous restrictions on harvesting activities, and use more intrusive policy instruments for regulation than would be tolerated if private forest lands were involved."[33] This is a situation very different than in the United States, where private property owners control 60 percent of forests and where there is a wide range of variability in subnational forest management policies. Nonetheless, McDermott et al. noted that even subnational governments with voluntary BMPs (best management practices) in the southeastern United States maintain monitoring procedures on state-owned forestlands that are well developed and "subject to greater scrutiny and perhaps higher performance expectations"[34] than are private forests, which, of course, do not legally require monitoring since there are no procedural or substantive requirements with which to comply. As described below, this public–private divide has many nuances, two of which play a role in explaining the stringency and adaptability gap in subnational forest management standards between the United States and Canada—a more stable regulatory environment in Canada and the public forest management "spillover effect."

More stable regulatory environment in Canada

In the United States, the vast array of forest owners combined with 50 different state governments regulating (or not regulating) mostly privately owned forests creates a very volatile regulatory environment—more rational herders on the commons presents greater regulatory difficulty. In contrast, Canada's regulatory environment is far more stable. Provincial ownership of Canadian forests establishes continuity and stability regarding both the owner of forest resources and the primary regulated entity, the commercial forest industry in this case. As demonstrated in the earlier discussion in this chapter of Canada's quasi-corporatist negotiations, it seems easier to construct and maintain similar regulatory approaches across subnational governments when there are relatively few forest owners (11 provinces) and relatively few major industrial forest players. This is quite a contrast to the United States, where private ownership not only makes crafting regulatory standards more difficult due to constitutional concerns (such as Fifth Amendment Takings claims), but also makes it harder to establish consistent, responsive forest policies due to volatility in forest ownership.

In the southeastern United States, large commercial interests have rapidly divested their holdings over the last few years, resulting in smaller private forest properties that are "subject to new dynamic forces that encourage parcelization and fragmentation."[35] Commercial forest owner divestiture of forestland between 1998 and 2010 is "the most substantial transition in forest ownership of the last century," as industry divested itself of nearly three-quarters of its forest holdings.[36] Much of the land has ended up in the hands of real estate investment trusts, which not only represent a voting block whose interests are diametrically opposed to high forest management/preservation standards, but whose ownership also only exacerbates the concerns regarding urbanization and reduction of forest cover over the next 50 years.[37] Indeed, the Southern Forest Futures Project highlighted the truism that "[p]rivate owners continue to control forest futures" in the southeastern United States.[38]

If then, as in Canada, large commercial forest interests negotiating with governments owning forest resources generally leads to higher and more consistent forest management standards across a nation—due to economies of scale in industry expertise and interactions with government regulators—then increased fragmentation of ownership in the United States may result in further negative consequences for forest management practices in general, not to mention forest loss by urbanization and land development activities. Indeed, 86 percent of southern forests are privately owned, and while 60 percent of privately owned forests are 100 acres or more, 59 percent of all private forest owners own fewer than 9 acres of forestland. Family forest holdings in the region average only 29 acres in size.[39] The result is a large number of individuals who may choose to act rationally regarding the appropriation of forest resources, maximizing personal gain to the detriment of the subnational, national, and global resource base—either through poor forest management practices or through replacement of forest resources with human-made capital in the form of urbanization.

In the end, the Canadian provinces have a far more stable regulatory environment within which to operate than do U.S. states, facilitated by more continuity in both the entities owning most of the forest resource base as well as with regard to the actors being regulated. As a result, the government may more readily adopt heightened and adaptable forest management standards applicable to the "known quantity" that is the Canadian forest industry. Even so, and as next described, public ownership of forests in the United States is not without effect, as it can actually help "ratchet up" forest management standards on private lands, providing further insights into the difficulty of crafting any discernible national forest policy in the United States via subnational government volition alone.[40]

Southeast to Northwest Disparity Among U.S. States: Public Forest Management Spillover Effect

Notably, McDermott et al. also found that a forest management spillover effect may occur whereby heightened standards on public lands can lead to higher regulatory standards on nearby private lands. This could be one factor explaining why more prescriptive forest regulations exist in western states in the United States—even on private forestlands—since there are far more public forests in the West than in the East. For example, California, Washington, Oregon, Idaho, and Alaska maintain an average 67 percent of forests in public ownership[41] and also maintain far more stringent forest policy standards for both public and private forests (a "6.7" average) than do states in the southeastern United States (a "1.2" average), where 86 percent of forests are privately owned.[42] In other words, "[w]here there are substantial public and private lands within a given jurisdiction, greater regulation of public lands may, over time, result in increased pressures from civil society and environmental groups for greater regulation on private lands."[43]

In fact, the United States Forest Service's "9" score on the forest policy ranking does seem to have spilled over into western forest policy in a way not seen in the southeast—perhaps no surprise since 92 percent of federally owned land is located in the western United States whereas less than 5 percent is located in the South.[44] Though this spillover effect is important and can improve forest policy standards on private lands in states with large public forest holdings, its implications for U.S. subnational forest policy only provides another example of the arguable need for national-level inputs into that policy. The southeastern United States simply does not maintain the critical mass of publicly owned forests that would help facilitate a spillover effect, as again, 86 percent of forests are privately owned. Though other factors, such as overall governance culture and the limited administrative capacity of southeastern governments, may also contribute to the region's lax standards, it seems that the lack of a spillover effect further exacerbates continuation of the status quo.

Indeed, in a federal system of government without a national forest policy, a rise in standards in one area of the country is not without consequence for resource management in other areas. For example, heightened regulatory standards for forest management policies on U.S. federal lands in recent decades reduced timber harvests in western states while shifting demand to southern forests,[45] no doubt in part due to a spillover effect of public standards on private forestlands near federal forests. Timber production in the South, where federal forests are virtually non-existent, increased from 40 percent of the national total in 1952 to almost 60 percent in 1996.[46] This again reflects how policy change may be more readily achieved for forests owned by the government than when the government must regulate private property owners to achieve those same results.

To be clear, this is not to say that enhanced regulatory standards on public lands or those spilling over onto private lands necessarily means less timber production in those jurisdictions. Indeed, a race-to-the-bottom may partially explain the shift to southeastern forests as forest interests likely moved to an area that imposed fewer monetary and regulatory costs on forest operations. In this way, sudden changes in publically owned forest policy can not only spill over to private forestlands in the form of heightened forest management standards, but can also shift resource extraction to another area of the country with less stringent standards. It is certainly true that this market shift to southeastern forests resulted in increased economic growth and prosperity for the region—a region in need of jobs and increased revenues. Even so, the region remains one with some of the weakest forest management standards in the United States, and indeed in the world. It also, not coincidentally, is the region projected to experience potentially precipitous drops in forest cover over the next 50 years due to that same push toward economic growth and development. In the end, this spillover effect demonstrates an increased likelihood of higher forest policy standards wherever the public forests are—and public forests are decidedly in short supply in the most intensively managed part of the United States, the southeastern United States.

Ultimately, the public–private forest divide in the United States and Canada affects the stringency and adaptability of subnational forest policy in the two countries, due primarily to: (1) governments being able to set more stringent standards on their own lands; (2) governments adapting more readily to pressure from civil society; (3) a more stable regulatory environment and the public forest spillover effect. In addition, the quasi-corporatist nature of Canadian forest policy gives rise to greater uniformity across subnational jurisdictions. These distinctions in uniformity, stringency, and adaptability of subnational forest policy in the United States and Canada contribute to the different suggested mechanisms for forging Fail-safe Federalism in the two countries presented in Chapter 9.

Implications of the Private–Public Forest Ownership Divide for Suggested Mechanisms of Fail-safe Federalism

To summarize this chapter, the United States and Canada are in very different positions with respect to fundamental forest management policies at the domestic level—such as those related to riparian buffer zones in forested watersheds, forestland roads, clear-cutting, reforestation, and annual allowable cut limits. Canadian provinces maintain high legal standards for these types of policies on the vast majority of Canada's forests. The vast public ownership of Canadian forests gives rise to a great degree of uniformity across provincial forest policies as well as more stringent standards and the ability to adapt to newly recognized mechanisms for achieving sustainable forest management. U.S. states, on the other hand, maintain a wide range of legal standards for forest management, from high standards in some states to standards in southeastern states less stringent than those in developing countries.

Though the United States and Canada are in different positions domestically, they face a similar challenge internationally, as their constitutional structures do not currently allow significant or direct, national-level regulatory inputs into domestic forest policy on a majority of the forestland within their borders. More specifically, these nations' federal governments would be limited from participating in any forest preservation/carbon sequestration mandates arising out of international efforts to harness the power of forests to combat climate change. For example, if an international treaty were to require the United States to curb the projected destruction of 23 million acres, or approximately 13 percent, of all forestland in the South over the next 50 years, or require Canada to halt the destruction of over 11 million acres of boreal forest during the same time period, then these countries' national governments would be unable to ensure compliance. It would be up to individual states and provinces to preserve those forestlands. Yet these subnational governments face incentives diametrically opposed to preserving their forests in the form of urbanization driven by economic development and growth.

As a result, the U.S. and Canadian national governments need to either adjust the constitutional status quo or work with subnational governments to develop fail-safes for their particular forms of federalism that trigger in the absence of subnational climate policies related to forests—*if* they are to effectively participate in the full suite of options available to the international community to effectively address climate change. In Canada, such fail-safes are needed mostly to allow the Canadian national government greater flexibility in participating in international negotiations related to climate change and forests, though clearly the national government may also need to develop inputs into domestic forest policy to curb projected losses of provincial forests due to urban sprawl and agricultural growth. The United States, on the other hand, needs a fail-safe not only to allow greater flexibility in international negotiations, but perhaps more fundamentally to improve the overall quality of the highly variable and often inadequate domestic subnational forest management standards in the United States.

Based upon this review, however, different mechanisms for developing federal fail-safes may be more appropriate as between the two countries. As detailed in Chapter 9, the greater constitutional powers afforded the United States federal government as a general matter and the greater amount of forests in *federal* ownership in the United States make forging Fail-safe Federalism out of constitutionally validated top-down and bilateral mechanisms, or by horizontal arrangements among the states, far more efficacious. Correspondingly, the vast public forest ownership in Canada, the far more limited constitutional power at the federal level, and the resulting limitations on civil society's procedural rights at the federal level render a federal fail-safe in Canada far more likely to arise out of transnational pressures from civil society.

Most importantly, the fail-safes discussed in Chapter 9 can have a ripple effect down the chain of nested governance commons scales. Once forged, a fail-safe that allows the global nested governance commons dilemma to be overcome can also resolve the natural capital commons dilemma at the national, state/provincial, and local levels. Though the solutions presented in Chapter 9 are not exhaustive, with regard to either the countries to which they might apply or the actual substantive solutions available, they do constitute examples of mechanisms needed to uproot the legally entrenched commons dynamic created by certain federal systems of government.

Notes

1 The material constituting significant portions of this chapter originated in Blake Hudson, Fail-safe Federalism and Climate Change: The Case of U.S. and Canadian Forest Policy, 44 *Conn. L. Rev.* 925 (2012).

2 Constance L. McDermott et al., *Global Environmental Forest Policies: An International Comparison* 4 (2010).

3 News Release, USDA Forest Service, US Forest Service Finds Global Forests Absorb One-Third of Carbon Emissions Annually (July 14, 2011), available at http://www.fs.fed.us/news/2011/releases/07/carbon.shtml.

4 See *Countries of the World Ordered by Land Area*, *List of the Countries of the World*, available at http://www.listofcountriesoftheworld.com/area-land.html.

5 Of the world's approximately four billion hectares of forest, Canada maintains 310 million hectares and the United States 302 million hectares. Jacek P. Siry et al., *XIII World Forestry Congress*, *Global Forest Ownership: Implications for Forest Production, Management, and Protection* 3 tbl.1 (2009), available at http://www.pefc.org/images/stories/documents/external/global_forest_ownership_FD.pdf.

6 World Economic Outlook Database, Int'l Monetary Fund (Sept. 2011), available at http://www.imf.org/external/pubs/ft/weo/2011/01/weodata/index.aspx.

7 World Wildlife Fed'n, *Canada's Boreal Forests*, available at assets.panda.org/downloads/canada_forest_cc_final_13nov07_lr_1.pdf.

8 ForestEthics, *Robbing the Carbon Bank: Global Warming & Ontario's Boreal Forest* 3 n.2, available at http://forestethics.org/downloads/globalwarming_2.pdf.

9 See Canadian Counsel of Forest Ministers, *Sustainable Forest Management in Canada* 4 (2010).

10 Michael Howlett and Jeremy Rayner, Globalization and Governance Capacity: Explaining Divergence in National Forest Programs as Instances of 'Next-Generation' Regulation in Canada and Europe, 19 *Governance: An Int'l J. of Pol'y, Admin., & Institutions* 251, 265 (2006).

11 Paul Stanton Kibel, Canada's International Forest Protection Obligations: A Case of Promises Forgotten in British Columbia and Alberta, 6 *Fordham Envtl. L. Rev.* 231, 246 (1995).

12 Id. at 246.

13 Jeffrey L. Friesen, The Distribution of Treaty-Implementing Powers in Constitutional Federations: Thoughts on the American and Canadian Models, 94 *Colum. L. Rev.* 1415, 1433 (1994).

14 Can. Counsel of Forest Ministers, supra note 9, at 4.

15 McDermott et al., supra note 2, at 327 tbl.10.7.

16 Michael Howlett, Introduction: Policy Regimes and Policy Change in the Canadian Forest Sector, in *Canadian Forest Policy* 3 (Michael Howlett ed., 2001).

17 Id. at 8.

18 McDermott et al., supra note 2, at 76.

19 Michael Howlett and Jeremy Rayner, The Business and Government Nexus: Principal Elements and Dynamics of the Canadian Forest Policy Regime, in *Canadian Forest Policy,* supra note 16, at 30.

20 Id.

21 Id.

22 Id. at 31.

23 Id. at 32.

24 Id. at 33, 43.

25 Id. at 32–33.

26 Id. at 33.

27 Id. at 42–43.

28 Id.

29 Scholars argue that "[t]he industrial-governmental interests constitute the principal promoters and users of Crown lands, and their dual goal is to extract as much fibre from the forest as possible while viewing other forest uses as mere constraints on extraction." Jamie Lawson et al., Perpetual Revenues and the Delights of the Primitive': Change, Continuity, and Forest Policy Regimes in Ontario, in *Canadian Forest Policy,* supra note 16, at 279, 281.

30 McDermott et al., supra note 2, at 346.

31 Similar to the United States, Canadian forest scholars note that "[b]oth legal and political considerations have discouraged provincial governments from aggressively regulating private forest lands." Peter Clancy, Atlantic Canada: The Politics of Private and Public Forestry, in *Canadian Forest Policy,* supra note 16, at 205, 207.

32 McDermott et al., supra note 2, at 346. An example arose in the United States in the context of biodiversity protection, but directly implicated forests—the case of the Northern Spotted Owl in the states of Washington and Oregon. After the Endangered Species Act (ESA) was utilized to protect the owl in the early 1990s, timber harvest on private lands remained relatively steady, whereas harvest on public lands dropped precipitously. Id. at 92–93, 93 fig.3.4. The government was more willing to respond with

regulatory standard setting, was also more willing to enforce those standards on its own property than on private property, and was therefore able to adjust course more readily.

33 Howlett and Rayner, supra note 19, at 33.

34 McDermott et al., supra note 2, at 110–11.

35 David N. Wear and John G. Greis, *U.S. Forest Serv., The Southern Forest Futures Project: Summary Report* 58 (2011), available at http://www.srs.fs.usda.gov/futures/reports/draft/summary_report.pdf.

36 Id. at 60, 62.

37 Id. at 60.

38 Id. at 4–5.

39 Id. at 62.

40 See McDermott et al., supra note 2, at 346–47 (discussing hypotheses that may account for differences in public and private forestland regulation and why and how higher prescriptions on private lands emerge).

41 See id. at 80 tbl.3.3.

42 Wear and Greis, supra note 35, at 58. The 86 percent of forests in the south that are privately owned account for almost the entire amount of timber harvested in the south. Id.

43 McDermott et al., supra note 2, at 347.

44 Wear and Greis, supra note 35, at 71.

45 Id. at 5.

46 Id. at 17.

Part V

Fortification of Commons Constitutions

9 Forging Fail-safe Federalism by Strengthening Keystone Constitutions[1]

Parts I–IV of this book identified the ways in which a federal system of government's constitutional order may legally entrench a commons from local to global scales, which poses a number of complications for holistic management of natural resources. This part looks at what may be done to remedy the legal deficiency in the allocation of governance authority among levels of government in certain federal systems, and uses the case study of U.S. and Canadian forest policy to do so.

Scholars have noted that a global treaty aimed at forest management activities would necessarily "mandate some degree of harmonization of forestry practices."[2] If, as seen in Chapters 6–8, a binding treaty provided prescriptive forest management directives at the national level, it necessarily would involve potentially unconstitutional regulation of private lands in the United States due to the large private ownership of forests, and in Canada due to the large provincial ownership of forests. The Intergovernmental Panel on Climate Change (IPCC) has highlighted several forest management goals that could be achieved through a prescriptive, "traditional governance" framework,[3] including "maintaining or increasing the forest area" and "maintaining or increasing stand-level carbon density."[4] Though these goals can be accomplished by voluntary, market-based programs, the IPCC leaves the mechanism of implementation unanswered. Thus, it is feasible that an international treaty could require signatory nations to increase and maintain forest area by prescribing mandatory maintenance of partial forest cover on all forested lands, implementation of soil erosion reduction programs, or limitation of fertilizer use. For example, a global governance scenario that required that "within x number of years, treaty participants must increase and maintain forest area by 25 percent and implement active carbon sequestration projects on 50 percent of their forested lands" may not be viable under the U.S. or Canadian federal systems, because the federal governments in those systems arguably would be unable to ensure compliance with the mandate on even a majority of forested lands within their borders.[5]

Of course, before discussing mechanisms for fortifying the constitutional structures of these federal systems to allow such inputs it is appropriate to first highlight mechanisms of resource management that do not implicate constitutional questions—namely, voluntary and market-based mechanisms. This book, as you will recall from Chapter 1, does not intend to suggest that prescriptive, top-down regulations are the only or necessarily the optimal approaches for natural capital management. Rather, the book's primary focus is to highlight one aspect of the problem—in the absence of successful voluntary, market-based, or other management mechanisms, regulatory inputs may be needed but may be legally thwarted, thus entrenching the commons dynamic across governance scales. Yet the easiest way to avoid constitutional complications is to circumvent questions of legal authority by utilizing non-prescriptive mechanisms. That is, to utilize voluntary or market-based mechanisms that make domestic treaty implementation complications disappear.[6]

Indeed, such voluntary mechanisms have arisen directly out of failed past forest negotiations as governments "[u]nable to conclude treaties cementing traditional 'command and control' regulation in binding conventions … searched for new mixes of policy instruments" to achieve global forest governance.[7] And today we see a new round of voluntary and transnational approaches to managing climate change, again resulting from the continuing failure of the international community to negotiate a legally binding climate treaty.[8] Provision of such voluntary instruments releases a federal government from forcing private landowners or state/provincial governments to manage forests in a prescribed manner, which in turn frees the federal systems from potential federalism complications as they implement the treaty. These mechanisms might take the form of forest offsets available under a carbon emissions trading scheme, forest certification,[9] REDD,[10] ecosystem service,[11] or a variety of other programs aimed at voluntary, market-based protection of natural capital.

Regardless of the availability of voluntary, market-based approaches within the policy toolkit, the precipitous decline in global natural capital indicates that voluntary mechanisms are not currently enough, and should be balanced with other policy tools. Herder rationality counsels against voluntarily restraining one's own appropriation of natural capital because you are simply leaving more for others. As a result, this chapter will look at a variety of mechanisms that may be utilized to allow federal systems that present legal impediments to effective natural capital management to maintain robust management regimes based upon strong legal structures at local and national scales, and so that they can fully participate in resource governance on the global scale. The U.S. and Canada provide a good case study for exploring these mechanisms, since they are the two federal systems reviewed in this book that have been identified as currently having a dual federalist structure in the area of forest management.

Fortification from Within: Top-Down, Bilateral, and Horizontal Governance

A variety of mechanisms are available to the U.S. and Canadian governments for adjusting their respective constitutional structures to allow a national government fail-safe in the event subnational governments fail to act on forests and climate change. As discussed in Chapter 2, these mechanisms are aimed at fortifying the "keystone constitutions" guiding these federal systems. These constitutions provide governance stability on many levels, and

> stability is protected in many nations, especially those with federal structures, by a special status for the constitution that makes it of a higher order than other laws and subject to more rigid rules for change than any statute. A constitution should not be easy to change.[12]

Even though the difficulty of amending constitutions is important for providing stability in the social construct of governance, when stability becomes rigidity in the face of a changing environment and the resultant changing needs of society, reassessment of constitutional structure is warranted. This is especially the case when society also depends upon the stability of non-social constructs for its success, such as the "natural" construct of a stable environment—stability that is the antithesis of an abruptly changing climate and other modern environmental challenges. In this way, keystone constitutions in federal governments lie at the very center of an arch of resource governance, as seen in Figure 2.1 in Chapter 2. The constitution in federal systems acts as a keystone in this arch, providing the governance framework that dictates the rules for resource management on both the subnational and global levels. If these keystone constitutions allow dynamic regulatory inputs across scales—such as national level inputs into resource management on subnational scales, that in turn allows unfettered national involvement in resource management on global scales—then they maintain a stable arch of resource governance that can adequately facilitate resource management solutions across scales. If keystone constitutions do not allow national level inputs into subnational resource management, and consequently allow subnational governments to constrain national involvement in global resource governance, then they contribute to a weak and vulnerable arch of resource governance that is likely to crumble due to the legal entrenchment of a resource commons not only within national boundaries but also internationally.

As a result, fortification of the U.S. and Canadian constitutional structures is needed in the context of forestry. As discussed below, some of the mechanisms for doing so arise directly out of national or subnational initiative and utilize existing constitutional processes. Other mechanisms arise from pressures civil society places on governments to take action or adjust constitutional structure. Importantly, certain of these mechanisms are more viable in the United States than in Canada, and vice versa—a circumstance driven largely by the differences in domestic constitutional structure and the split of forest ownership in the two countries discussed in Chapter 8.

Top-down

The first mechanism for forging Fail-safe Federalism is a "top-down" approach, whereby the national government in a federal system attempts to use its current constitutional powers to gain legal inputs into subnational forest policy. The top-down approach would require either a direct amendment to a country's constitution allowing the national government constitutional authority, or would necessitate expanded judicial interpretation of current constitutional provisions granting the national government such authority.

Constitutional Amendment

A variety of scholars have assessed both the need for, and the effectiveness of, amending the U.S. Constitution to either provide citizens with a fundamental constitutional right to environmental protection, or allow the federal government to constitutionally regulate the environment with greater scope than it currently employs.[13] Far less has been written about the viability of amending the Canadian Constitution, primarily for two reasons, discussed in greater detail below. First, Canada's ability to amend its own constitution only recently became a reality, as Great Britain granted exclusive amendment rights to the Canadian government only 30 years ago.[14] One consequence is that Canada's procedures for amending its constitution are arguably unsettled, with some scholars raising doubts about their efficacy.[15] Second, and related to the amending procedures themselves, amending the Canadian Constitution in a way that ensures provincial adherence is exceedingly difficult and is so unlikely in areas of explicit constitutional grants of exclusive provincial regulatory authority that scholars have simply ignored the question in the forest management context. Ultimately, for the reasons discussed below, this mechanism of forging a fail-safe on forest policy is not the most viable in either the United States or Canada.

There have been over 10,000 proposed amendments to the United States Constitution,[16] and only a few have passed—no doubt due to the difficulties of passing an amendment via the Article V process.[17] Professor Ruhl has provided an analytical tool for assessing the efficacy and desirability of amending the U.S. Constitution with an "environmental quality amendment" (EQA). The calls for such an amendment have been on the rise in recent decades.[18] Proposed EQAs tend to be aspirational and generalized, as Ruhl describes, including language such as: "[t]he natural resources of the nation are the heritage of present and future generations. The right of each person to clean and healthful air and water, and to the protection of other natural resources of the nation, shall not be infringed by any person."[19]

Ruhl developed a matrix to assess the viability of proposed constitutional amendments along two axes: a function axis and a target axis. The function axis describes the institutional purpose of the amendment, such as whether it: (1) alters the operational rules of government; (2) prohibits specified government action; (3) creates or affirms individual rights; (4) expresses aspirational goals.[20] The target axis describes the societal interaction adjusted by the functional change, such as: (1) intra- and intergovernmental relations; (2) relations between the government and its citizens; (3) relations between citizens.[21] EQAs tend to fall into a category that no existing amendment to the Constitution does—that of an amendment establishing aspirational goals (function 4) for citizen–citizen relations (target 3). Ruhl believes the Constitution is not meant to include these types of aspirational dictates,[22] largely because they must necessarily be drafted either ambiguously or so narrowly as to make implementation nearly impossible.

The amendment that would allow U.S. federal government inputs into subnational forest policy,[23] however, would fall into a category far more likely to be efficacious according to Ruhl's matrix, assuming it could be passed in the first instance. Such an amendment might simply declare: "The federal government of the United States maintains the authority to regulate the management of the nation's forest resources; federally-owned, state-owned, and privately-owned." This amendment would function to alter the operational rules of government (function 1) in order to adjust the target of intergovernmental relations (target 1). In fact, nine amendments currently fall under this category of the matrix.[24] If United States federal and subnational governments one day agreed to change the operational rules of government and the current status of intergovernmental relations by rebalancing federal-state roles in regulating forest management via amendment, it would fall into the category described by Ruhl as far more likely to be viable than aspirational/citizen–citizen relation amendments. Furthermore, though the legislative process is preferable to constitutional amendment a vast majority of the time, lest the U.S. Constitution become diluted and take the form of a legislative instrument, society may be unable to achieve some policies in the absence of an amendment. Ruhl argues that:

> The question of need, therefore, is whether there is any institutional barrier to fulfilling the fundamental, widely accepted social policy through routine legislative and judicial forums. … [S]ome amendments have forced an intransigent minority of states to come into line with the rest of the nation on fundamental social policy issues associated with matters traditionally (or constitutionally) left to state jurisdiction. Where federal legislation cannot impose the policy over state resistance and the courts cannot mold the existing constitutional text to handle the stubborn states, an amendment is the only alternative. These are examples of institutional necessity, where an amendment, and only an amendment, can allow the widely accepted social policy to move forward in society.[25]

There is arguably an institutional barrier to certain federal regulatory inputs into subnational forest policy—a barrier in the form of current understandings of U.S. constitutional law. Furthermore, the absence of responsible state government management of forest resources, as illustrated by the current lack of management standards for the highly threatened forests of the southeastern United States, confirms that an amendment remedying exclusive state regulatory authority over subnational forest policy *could* be a last resort to overcoming that barrier with the most effective social policy.

Other scholars have also argued for constitutional amendments that rebalance the relationship between the U.S. federal government and the states to allow greater federal inputs into environmental policymaking in the absence of state action.[26] These types of amendments would be "purely structural," unlike a substantive constitutional amendment providing a fundamental right to a clean and healthy environment, and would simply "empower[] Congress to legislate regarding the environment"[27] if it chose to do so. In other words, nothing would compel the federal government to legislate pursuant to its authority nor would any new fundamental constitutional rights be created for U.S. citizens. At the very least, this type of amendment would remedy the frequent awkwardness of justifying federal environmental regulation under the Commerce Clause.

The likelihood of an amendment being effective, however, is a different question from whether such an amendment is likely to be passed in the first place. The U.S. Congress has never attempted to harness *current* constitutional powers, such as the Commerce Clause, to address subnational forest policy, much less placed a constitutional amendment on its agenda. So even though this type of structural amendment may be of the kind most likely to be workable if enacted, and remains an option that should certainly continue to be studied, it remains perhaps the least viable mechanism for forging Fail-safe Federalism in the United States on forest policy—especially given the difficulty of convincing three-quarters of the states to ratify an amendment that intrudes on state regulatory powers and given that any kind of "constitutional environmental amendment is unlikely in the current political climate."[28]

A similar state of affairs exists in Canada. The Canadian Constitution has only been amended ten times since Canada officially received the power to amend its own constitution from the British in 1982[29]—and most of the amendments that have been passed are province-specific.[30] Though Canada has a formal amendment procedure,[31] it was not unanimously agreed to by the provinces—Quebec voiced resistance to its legitimacy.[32] In fact, the rules governing constitutional amendment in Canada have been described by at least one scholar as a "failure."[33] Fears regarding the perceived illegitimacy of these amending procedures have caused courts to actually ignore their interpretation, and even their existence, on some constitutional questions[34]—lending evidence regarding not only the difficulty of amending the Canadian Constitution but also the legitimacy of such amendments in their own right.

Even if the amending procedures are accepted as legitimate, it is exceedingly difficult to pass an amendment that effectively binds the provinces, once again demonstrating the far more robust constitutional decentralization presented by the Canadian brand of federalism relative to that in the United States, at least in the context of forest policy. The amending procedure that would be relevant to a forest policy amendment would require two-thirds of the provinces, including at least 50 percent of the population, to approve the amendment.[35] Once passed, however, provinces may opt out merely by passing a resolution opposing the amendment within one year.[36] In addition, an amendment fails altogether if the amendment procedures are not finalized within three years of the beginning of the process.[37] Some have criticized this lengthy time limit as allowing ever-shifting changes in political will, increasing opposition, and election-driven changes in the provinces' political make-up to lead to amendment failures.[38] Indeed, the failure of one such amendment in the late 1980s was "particularly distressing" because at the time the proposed amendment died it

> had the support of resolutions of the House of Commons and of eight provincial legislatures representing approximately ninety-four percent of the national population. That an amendment could fail in such a situation, with such widespread support from popularly elected legislatures, does suggest a problem with the amending formula.[39]

Ultimately, the questions surrounding the soundness of Canada's amending procedures, coupled with the fact that provinces can simply opt out of any amendment that sought greater federal involvement in subnational forest policy, renders this mechanism for forging Fail-safe Federalism unpromising. In addition, politics in Canada regarding constitutional amendment has trended in the opposite direction from granting greater federal power, as "proposed constitutional amendments, particularly since 1982, have uniformly sought to vest more power in the provinces at the expense of the central government."[40] Not only would it be politically difficult to persuade the provinces to divest their current, explicit constitutional authority over forest policy on 84 percent of Canada's forests, but it would, potentially, also be legally insufficient if some provinces opted out. This legal insufficiency would fail to change the status quo regarding the Canadian federal government's inability to ensure that international obligations related to subnational forest management are met or to craft its own domestic subnational forest policies. An amendment, however, is not the only top-down mechanism available to the United States or Canada. Current constitutional provisions may provide the respective federal governments authority over subnational forest policy that they have not yet claimed or that has not yet been validated by courts interpreting their respective constitutions.

Constitutional Interpretation

A more viable mechanism for top-down forging of Fail-safe Federalism on forest policy, at least in the United States, is expanded interpretation of current constitutional provisions. While the United States currently maintains constitutional provisions that may be well-suited for allowing federal inputs into subnational forest policy, Canada's options are not only more limited, but the *explicit* constitutional grant of forest policymaking authority to the provinces makes expanded constitutional interpretation of federal powers virtually unattainable.

In the United States, Congress could certainly pass a "Carbon Sequestration and Forest Management Act" that tests the waters of judicial interpretation regarding the scope of Congress's authority under the Commerce Clause and that establishes mechanisms for utilizing forests to sequester carbon to combat climate change. To that end, the act could establish a variety of forest management standards, such as riparian buffer zone requirements, restrictions on clear-cutting, afforestation and reforestation requirements, annual allowable cut, and stand density requirements, among a variety of other standards. If such an act were found constitutional, then the federal government would no longer be constrained by subnational governments in international negotiations related to climate and forests (not to mention that local, state, and national forest commons issues could be addressed more effectively). Even though private forest management has long been the constitutional purview of state governments, there is a distinct possibility that such an act would be found constitutional as part of the federal government's suite of Commerce Clause powers.

The interstate markets into which timber resources directly flow are quite robust. As noted in Chapter 5, timber production in the South alone, which happens to be the region containing the highest proportion of private forestland subject predominantly to state jurisdiction, contributed more than one million jobs and $51 billion of employee compensation in 2009.[41] Southeastern forests are "the most intensively managed forests in the United States,"[42] and a majority of the United States' lumber is harvested from southeastern forests.[43] Furthermore, 89 percent of U.S. timber is harvested from private lands[44] subject to state governments' land use regulatory authority. In other natural resource contexts, private lands may be reached by federal regulation of resources appropriated in a way that has substantial effects on interstate commerce. A variety of federal statutes regulating natural resources have been upheld under this test,[45] as discussed in Chapter 4, including the Endangered Species Act (ESA)—held valid even for the regulation of entirely intrastate species with arguably tenuous connections to interstate commerce.[46] How much more so, then, might a robust industry like the timber industry be found to substantially affect interstate commerce? Unlike endangered species, after all, timber is a commodity that is exchanged on the open market.

The commons analysis presented in Chapter 4 demonstrates that the federal government maintains constitutional authority to regulate two categories of environmental resources that have substantial effects on interstate commerce: (1) natural resources contained on land (wetlands, endangered species, or other natural capital) that are appropriated by economic development (retail, housing, industrial, agricultural, etc.); (2) resources appropriated by individuals and tied to an interstate market (wheat, marijuana, or other natural capital commodities). Timber commodities clearly fall into this latter category. Though it seems clear that timber production on private lands can be constitutionally regulated by the federal government under this second category, federal *preservation* of forests threatened by urbanization—such as the forests in the southeast—may even be constitutionally viable under the first category. Any time commercial development replaces forest resources, there is an appropriator of the resource tied to interstate markets (the developer) and a resource that is being appropriated (the forest). These are the constituent components of a commons, and it is the act of "appropriation" by the developer of the forest resource that substantially affects interstate commerce and that gives the federal government constitutional authority over resource management.

Either way, if the federal government sought input into subnational forest policy pursuant to its Commerce Clause power, there are strong arguments that it may do so—either to provide standards for timber production or to preserve forests and their corresponding carbon sequestration/climate change mitigation values in the face of threatening urbanization. This mechanism is not without complication, however. While subnational forest management may more readily be considered to have a substantial effect on interstate commerce than, say, endangered species protection, it also falls more squarely within the category of a direct land use activity traditionally regulated by state and local governments. This is because regulation of endangered species may only indirectly impact land use activities otherwise subject to state regulatory authority. As a result, passage of federal private forest legislation is more difficult as a political matter, especially given the current political climate. The federal government may perceive that it is just as limited in enacting private forest legislation as it would be invoking zoning authority to establish growth boundaries around major U.S. cities. Therefore, legal perception becomes political reality once again, as the government politically views its hands as tied due to perceived legal constraints. In addition, such an act, even if passed, would be subject to other legal protections afforded to private forest owners, such as the Fifth Amendment Takings Clause.[47] Even so, it certainly seems that regulation requiring a minimum level of carbon density on forested lands could be crafted to avoid such constitutional complications and could further be structured to maintain the benefits provided by decentralized forest governance. Ultimately, the constitutionality of federal subnational forest management legislation has yet to be tested by the U.S. Congress or within U.S. courts—despite the fact that there are good arguments supporting its legitimacy. As a result, a top-down, expanded constitutional interpretation mechanism may be a viable option for forging Fail-safe Federalism on subnational forestlands in the United States.

Canada, on the other hand, maintains a far less firm foundation of federal constitutional authority upon which to potentially expand. While the Canadian Constitution grants exclusive regulatory authority over forest management to the provinces, Section 91 of the Canadian Constitution allows the national government exclusive regulatory authority over "trade and commerce" and residually over "peace, order and good government" (POGG). The Canadian Supreme Court has construed these provisions as including the implementation of treaties concerning trade and commerce and other matters of "national concern."[48] As asserted in Chapter 8, it would seem that climate change would affect both trade and commerce in Canadian forest products, and it is certainly a matter of national and global concern. The Canadian national government, however, has not yet invoked these constitutional powers to justify the implementation of international climate and forest agreements.[49]

Scholars have debated the efficacy of utilizing the trade and commerce and POGG clauses to allow greater federal inputs into provincial environmental policy.[50] The trade and commerce power operates quite differently in Canada than does the Commerce Clause in the United States, and "[w]hile American courts have had no trouble reading into their federal interstate commerce power the power to regulate the environment, Canadian courts have read Canada's federal trade and commerce power restrictively,"[51] thus limiting its application to environmental law. The POGG clause, in turn, has been described as "the poor Canadian cousin of the American Commerce Clause,"[52] has historically been controversial, and "its full extent is a matter of considerable dispute."[53] The clause was "reduced during the middle years of constitutional interpretation to little more than a basis for federal action in national emergencies"[54] and as an occasional basis of federal authority over matters of "national concern."[55] Over time, "the Supreme Court has continued to seek limits on the national concern branch of the POGG power,"[56] and national concern has been subsumed by the doctrine of "provincial inability."[57] Though two cases in the late 1980s and early 1990s narrowly applied the doctrines to allow federal intrusion into arguably provincial matters,[58] more recently the Canadian Supreme Court "seems to have purposely turned away from POGG justifications for federal jurisdiction ... [and] has preferred to channel justifications into other enumerated powers ... [B]y ignoring POGG justifications almost entirely, the Court is clearly expressing some reservation about working under the national concern heading."[59]

Indeed, as a textual matter, the POGG clause is qualified by a subsequent clause stating that the federal government may regulate "in relation to all [m]atters not coming within the [c]lasses of [s]ubjects ... assigned exclusively to the [l]egislatures of the [p]rovinces."[60] Given that the clause is meant to bridge gaps between federal and provincial constitutional authority where a matter of national concern cannot be addressed by the provinces,[61] the *exclusive* grant of authority to the provinces over forest policy could very well lead to a view that there is no "gap" in forest policy at all. The question would likely turn on whether global concerns over climate change trigger a strong enough national concern that the provinces alone would be unable to adequately address—a potentially difficult argument to make given the weakness of the POGG clause.

Even so, some scholars have argued that the POGG clause could be utilized to justify federal regulation of resources over which the provinces typically maintain exclusive authority, such as wildlife resources, and "on problems having such unique significance for the nation as a whole that they cannot appropriately be dealt with at the provincial level"[62]—as is arguably the case with ensuring Canada's forest resources are adequately utilized to combat climate change. Yet it remains that in order to invoke the POGG power, "the issue in question must have some 'ascertainable and reasonable limits,' so as not to impair provincial constitutional jurisdiction unreasonably."[63] Ultimately, the Canadian constitutional provisions that would be looked to for expanded federal authority over subnational forest policy are exceedingly weak, and their interpretation has been purposefully narrowed by Canadian courts over time. As a result, a top-down, expanded constitutional interpretation mechanism for forging Fail-safe Federalism in Canada is not nearly as promising as it is in the United States.

Though a top-down approach for achieving federal inputs into subnational forest policy via constitutional amendment is equally difficult in the United States and Canada, it appears doing so via expanded interpretation of current constitutional provisions is far more likely in the United States than in Canada. Even so, a top-down approach for forging Fail-safe Federalism is not a necessary or inevitably preferable mechanism. While top-down inputs can certainly be crafted in a way that preserves decentralized forest governance and the role of subnational governments in crafting either their own policies or policies supplemental to federal policy, top-down approaches are not without risk. Improperly crafted top-down prescriptive regulation

> often leads to an increasing spiral of tightening regulations, which progressively jeopardise the viability of forest management systems through excessive bureaucratic processes. Such processes impose considerable costs on both industry and government, and often result in systems that achieve only the minimum standards necessary to avoid penalties, rather than the pursuit of excellence.[64]

As such, bilateral and horizontal mechanisms should also be considered.

Bilateral

A bilateral approach to forging Fail-safe Federalism involves the federal government incentivizing subnational governments to take action on climate policies related to forest management, which can be accomplished in two basic ways. The first is a cooperative federalism approach, whereby the national government passes an act establishing minimum forest management standards to which subnational governments can voluntarily bind themselves, while at the same time receiving "carrots" in the form of financial payments or authority to dictate policy over matters that might otherwise be the purview of the federal government. The second approach is one of "uncooperative federalism," whereby the federal government uses other constitutional "sticks" at its disposal, such as spending power, by refusing to fund projects within subnational jurisdictions or refusing to provide some other economic entitlement subnational governments normally receive.

Under either approach, the national government "encourages" the states or provinces to develop minimum forest management standards aimed at capturing forests' climate change mitigating potential. Once accomplished, the federal government would be free to commit to those standards on an international level. Unlike the top-down approaches discussed in the previous section, which are dependent on the respective and distinct constitutional orders of the United States and Canada, the bilateral mechanisms discussed here are political or legislative in nature and thus would operate very much the same in both the United States and Canada.

Cooperative Federalism

Under a cooperative federalism approach, the U.S. or Canadian federal governments can pass a "Carbon Sequestration and Forest Management Act" (CSFMA) that establishes the forest management standards outlined above to combat climate change, such as restrictions on clear-cutting, afforestation and reforestation requirements, annual allowable cut, and stand density requirements, among a variety of other standards. The states and provinces would develop their own forest carbon sequestration plans and would voluntarily opt into the program based upon a variety of financial, political, and legal incentives. Not only might subnational governments receive funds to implement the program on state/provincially and privately owned forests, but they might also gain a degree of authority over the actions of both the federal government and adjacent subnational governments—to ensure that those actions are consistent with the state/provincial plan. Once a state or province voluntarily opted in, however, their forest management policy would be subject to the federal standards established in the act. Finally, subnational governments refusing to opt into the act might be induced to do so based upon a variety of disincentives, such as pulling federal funds for projects within the jurisdiction if they do not opt in within a certain time frame.

The CSFMA could operate like a combination of the proposed National Land Use Policy Act (NLUPA), which the U.S. Senate passed twice in the early 1970s but which was never enacted, and the more narrow but ultimately (and relatively) successful Coastal Zone Management Act (CZMA).

The purpose of the NLUPA was to establish

> a national policy to encourage and assist the several States to more effectively exercise their constitutional responsibilities for the planning, management, and administration of the Nation's land resources through the development and implementation of comprehensive "Statewide Environmental, Recreational and Industrial Land Use Plans" … and management programs designed to achieve an ecologically and environmentally sound use of the Nation's land resources.[65]

NLUPA would have provided economic support to states for the development of land use management plans in accordance with federal standards and would have further provided data to assist in developing such plans. Furthermore, the NLUPA would have established a federal agency to ensure that all other federal agencies were complying with state plans.[66] State plans, in turn, were to designate areas of conservation and areas of development.[67] States with approved plans would have been required to establish management standards for five types of land-use activities that were of "more than local concern:"[68]

1 all development in areas of "critical environmental concern," e.g., beaches, wetlands, important wildlife habitats, and historic sites;
2 key facilities, such as major airports, highway interchanges, and recreational facilities;
3 large scale developments, such as industrial parks, shopping centers, and major subdivisions;
4 regional public or private facilities, such as solid waste disposal or sewerage systems that significantly affect surrounding land uses;
5 major recreational or second-home development of rural land.[69]

The NLUPA was intended to "establish[] a clear role for each level of government and insure[] that their activities would be coordinated."[70] Perhaps most importantly, "[i]t would have integrated local, state and federal systems."[71] John Nolon has argued that "had such a law been adopted before the complex structure of environmental law was cobbled together, the cost, complexity and confusion of the current system could have been lessened."[72] The voluntary approach of NLUPA, which "favored incentives to cooperate over mandates to conform to rigid standards," was intended to "lessen the 'needless and costly conflicts between agencies and departments of the Federal Governments, between State and Federal Government, and between State and local government.'"[73] In other words, this approach could alleviate the problems created by an overly zealous top-down approach, though it might also have less bite in achieving results, since there is no legal mechanism to ensure the standards are put into place.

Though the NLUPA was never passed, the United States has already succeeded in establishing a bilateral approach in the land use context with its CZMA, passed to gain greater federal inputs into the protection of the coastal zone.[74] Many had hoped the CZMA would be part of a larger land use management act, such as the NLUPA,[75] but the CZMA succeeded where the NLUPA failed in part "due to the fact that it both aided development while preserving the environment"[76]—at least a balance of these arguably contradictory tasks was the CZMA's aspirational goal.

The CZMA program is voluntary, but federal incentives induce states to opt in. The first incentive is simply funding the program's implementation, the aims of which are:

> to preserve or restore specific areas of the state because of their conservation, recreational, ecological, or aesthetic values, or contain one or more resources of national significance; to redevelop a deteriorating or underutilized urban waterfront[] or port[]; to provide public access to public beaches, coastal waters and areas of recreational, historical, aesthetic, ecological or cultural significance; or to develop a coordinated process for regulating permits for aquaculture facilities.[77]

The second incentive is perhaps more enticing from a state or provincial point of view. Subnational governments effectively gain authority over the actions of both the federal government and other subnational governments that it otherwise would not have. After the federal government has approved a state plan, it cannot undertake any action or issue any permits for action within the state's coastal zone unless those actions are found by the state to be "consistent" with the state's plan.[78] So, for example, if the U.S. Coast Guard wants to build a new facility within a state's coastal zone, though the agency previously had the authority to do so at its discretion, it now must obtain approval from the state in which the facility is to be located that siting of the facility will be consistent with the state's CZMA implementation plan. The same holds true for federal actions in adjacent states in the coastal zone—there is a reciprocal responsibility for federal agency action or permitting in adjacent states to be consistent with neighboring state plans.[79] Currently 34 states and U.S. territories maintain federally approved management plans implementing the CZMA.[80]

Though Congress failed to enact the NLUPA, and the CZMA has been criticized as inconsistent[81] and lacks the "bite" that it perhaps could have, these examples of bilateral approaches to forging Fail-safe Federalism provide models for how a similar act might be structured for forests and climate regulation in the United States and Canada. Though these bilateral mechanisms would operate similarly in the United States and Canada, emanating from a legislative act by their respective national legislative bodies, it is important to note that the probability of achieving bilateral mechanisms in the United States and Canada is not the same. While the United States seriously considered the NLUPA and currently maintains one such successful program, the CZMA, Canada has had a more difficult time even attempting to craft bilateral approaches, especially in the forest context.

The Canadian federal government established a Model Forests Program (MFP) that, while not a holistic bilateral approach—since it operates on a project-by-project basis—is nonetheless a multi-stakeholder mechanism of forest policy formation that attempts to encourage the Canadian forest sector to "shift the management of Canada's forests from sustained yield to sustainable development."[82] The program's purposes are to further "create, by national competition, working-scale model management areas where a partnership of stakeholders would put ecological forestry into practice, develop integrated resource management tools to help commercial forestry coexist with other natural resources, conduct research, and apply the most advanced forest management practices."[83] Given the historically closed nature of the private-industry/provincial quasi-corporatist negotiations, the MFP is aimed at opening up the forest policymaking process to parties other than the provinces and the forest industry.

MFPs, however, have been met with varying success,[84] with provinces maintaining low enthusiasm for the program, in part "because of the federal nature of the model forest project and its potential threat to provincial authority."[85] Indeed, provinces have been described as "reluctant" to participate in the programs.[86] Any absence of the policymaking branch of government from negotiations understandably renders those projects ineffectual, and "[a]lmost certainly the federal nature of the model forest initiative is to blame."[87] As a result, "the experience of the Model Forest Program gives little reason to believe that such partnerships, just because they are based in the consensus process, are much more than advisory."[88] Even so, "[w]hile the Model Forest Program has not led to fundamental regime change, it does underwrite innovative experiments which, however incremental in impact, may provide examples of how to govern future forest management."[89] Despite the MFP being a creative attempt by the federal government to gain inputs into case-by-case forest projects, it seems clear that "[i]f long-term solutions are wanted ... then process reform will need to be embedded in structural reform,"[90] such as a change in Canada's constitutional structure that facilitates more viable inputs by the federal government into Canadian forest policy.

Importantly, the MFP is emblematic of federal-provincial tensions in the area of forest policy as a general matter. The history of provincial pushback on federal involvement in subnational forest policy, even through non-regulatory bilateral arrangements, is quite deep. When the Canadian federal government commenced a "National Forest Congress" under the oversight of the federal Department of Forests in 1966, it "failed to secure provincial approval of federal leadership in the formulation of national forest policy ... [and the] government had to acknowledge the limited direct role of the federal government in regulating an industry dependent on the exploitation of provincially owned resources."[91] The provinces even resisted conditional grant programs that would have funneled federal money their way in exchange for adjustments in forest policy.[92] This resistance coupled with "an inability to overcome constitutional barriers to an increased direct federal role in forest regulation" resulted in the federal government ultimately dissolving the Department of Forestry.[93]

Provincial resistance to even bilateral attempts by the federal government to gain a foothold in provincial forest policy has resulted in the aforementioned efforts by the federal government either to harness international trade, or to utilize a number of international environmental agreements to gain a foothold, but these initiatives, of course, "have had a limited impact on actual forestry practices in Canada."[94] In the end, "the new role of the [Canadian] federal government as an agent of international and intergovernmental coordinator represents a significant decline from earlier eras," and "the federal government has lost its ability to affect most aspects of Canadian forest policy and practices."[95] Given the limited nature of the Canadian federal government's influence on forest policy, this information is not surprising. Considering, however, that these statements are made in the context of attempts by the federal government to make *bilateral* inroads into forest policy, they indicate that even these types of voluntary mechanisms are not nearly as efficacious as they might be in the United States. Once again, we see how certain federal systems may be more likely than others to legally entrench the natural capital commons dynamic depending upon the resource in question as well as the type of policy tool sought to rectify the commons dilemma.

Uncooperative Federalism

Uncooperative federalism is the "mostly stick" end of the bilateral spectrum. Rather than the federal government providing "carrots" in the form of positive incentives for cooperation, it provides disincentives through the threat of withholding federal funds from states or provinces. The federal government may withhold federal highway funds, for instance, as the United States Federal Government has successfully done in other contexts,[96] or it could withhold funds that it normally funnels to the states to implement other federal statutes, such as the Clean Water Act in the United States.[97]

To be most effective, an uncooperative federalism arrangement would most likely need to be tied to a cooperative bilateral statute. Interestingly, though the NLUPA was designed as a voluntary program, it had bite in the sense that it blended cooperative and uncooperative federalism approaches. For instance, if a state failed to adopt a land use plan within four years after the act was passed it would no longer receive funding for other federal programs, such as highway construction or other public works. Such funding would be reduced by 20 percent a year until the state developed a land use plan comporting with NLUPA standards.[98] Later amendments to the bill strengthened sanctions even further, providing that if a state did not submit a statewide plan within five years, then "no federal agency was permitted to undertake any new action or financially support any state action that may have a substantially adverse environmental impact."[99] In the United States, for example, such a provision would grind commercial development in certain wetland areas to a halt if states did not pass a state plan, since the United States Army Corps of Engineers must permit the filling of certain wetlands for development.[100]

Canada has successfully utilized this approach in the context of fisheries and agriculture, where "constitutional conflicts over environmental jurisdiction have been resolved" by subnational governments utilizing "political and fiscal pressures to bring provincial practices in line with federal laws."[101] These pressures have "enabled the federal Canadian government to make significant jurisdictional in-roads into areas that were previously provincial. These developments suggest that Canada has been moving increasingly toward a de facto, if not a de jure, policy of concurrent jurisdiction in the environmental field"[102]—though this is clearly not yet the case for forest policy, again due to the explicit nature of the constitutional provisions related to forestry. Indeed, though the Canadian federal government has attempted to utilize its spending powers to promote reforestation and other practices on provincial forest lands, its ability to utilize the spending power to affect subnational forest policy has been relatively inconsequential.[103]

As seems to be a pattern with the other "fortification from within" options discussed above, an uncooperative federalism approach might be a more viable option in the United States, especially when coupled with a cooperative federalism statute, than it would in Canada. In Canada, such approaches have failed to influence forest policy in any significant way due to persistent provincial opposition to federal involvement. To be clear, in the United States the federal government has not yet aimed cooperative or uncooperative mechanisms at subnational forest policy. But given that the U.S. Congress seriously considered such an approach in the land use context with NLUPA and has succeeded in a "soft" approach with the CZMA in the environmental and land use context without state resistance—and indeed with broad state participation—a bilateral statute aimed at subnational climate policy on forests might in fact be a particularly viable mechanism available for forging Fail-safe Federalism in the United States if crafted properly. This is especially so if a top-down, expanded constitutional interpretation approach does not prove viable.

Horizontal

A horizontal approach to forging Fail-safe Federalism would result if subnational governments agreed with other subnational governments to take collective action to address the role of forest management in climate change regulation—even in the absence of a top-down mandate or voluntary bilateral program. This would be the (non-tragic) NT-2 scenario first outlined in Chapter 2 (Figure 2.4). In this way, subnational governments might avoid constraining national action on global climate governance related to forests. For example, states or provinces could create regional forest management plans whereby each agreed to legislate minimum forest management standards related to carbon sequestration and climate change, such as clear-cutting, afforestation and reforestation requirements, annual allowable cut, and stand density requirements. Such plans could conceivably create a de facto national forest policy. This would give the national government more flexibility during international negotiations related to forests, since subnational governments would voluntarily bind themselves to a position that does not restrain the national government in international negotiations, but that rather reinforces the goals of the global governance regime.

If a top-down approach is a compulsory mechanism for federal governments to forge Fail-safe Federalism, and a bilateral approach operates by federal provision of incentives for Fail-safe Federalism, then horizontal approaches rely almost entirely on the volition of subnational governments (though horizontal approaches may themselves be induced by federal incentives). This is the same volition, notably, that currently facilitates a great degree of subnational government *inaction* on crafting fundamental forest management standards in the United States. In this way, horizontal approaches in either the United States or Canada are likely low on the list of options for forging Fail-safe Federalism. This is because the U.S. and Canadian federal governments would have to "wait and see" if subnational governments forged horizontal forest policy arrangements before they could assure the international community that any global standards related to forest carbon sequestration standards would be implemented. Ultimately, it is unclear why subnational governments that individually fail to maintain standards related to forest carbon sequestration would band together to craft standards with a group of other states or provinces. Even so, this approach should be briefly discussed, as it is not without precedent, and the regional carbon trading schemes discussed below demonstrate that states concerned about climate change do seem willing to enter into these types of arrangements under at least some circumstances.

There are a few reasons why states might band together to create "Regional Forest Management and Carbon Sequestration Standards," whereby individual states would agree to establish standards that increase the carbon sequestration potential of private and state-owned forests. The first is simply federal inaction—which has spurred the creation of a number of carbon cap-and-trade initiatives aimed at curbing carbon emissions in the absence of a federal program. These have included over the last decade: the Regional Greenhouse Gas Initiative, including the states of Connecticut, Delaware, Maine, Maryland, Massachusetts, New Hampshire, New York, Rhode Island, and Vermont; the Midwestern Regional GHG Reduction Accord, including the states of Illinois, Iowa, Kansas, Michigan, Minnesota, and Wisconsin, and the Canadian province of Manitoba; and the Western Climate Initiative (WCI), including the states of Arizona, California, Montana, New Mexico, Oregon, Utah, and Washington, and the Canadian provinces of British Columbia, Manitoba, Ontario, and Quebec.[104] To be clear, the governments in the Midwestern Regional GHG Reduction Accord are no longer participating in the program, and participation in the WCI has waned. Even so, states or provinces may be motivated to tie forest offsets to any similar future carbon trading schemes which may arise in a way that fundamentally alters forest management standards in order to take account of carbon sequestration potential. Importantly, no regional arrangement on carbon has appeared in certain regions, such as the U.S. South, indicating that the initiative to forge these arrangements is still likely to vary across the United States in the same way that current forest management standards do.

Additionally, if states or provinces are truly concerned with federal inaction on climate change, as evidenced by the formation of these regional cap-and-trade schemes, then presumably they would be interested in the significant loss of forest carbon sequestration capabilities that rapid urbanization is projected to cause in regions such as the southeastern United States and parts of the boreal forest in Canada. After all, it seems that preserving forests in order to sequester carbon may potentially be less politically contentious than reducing industrial emissions—though certainly there are private property rights to consider in the United States, as well as the forest sector lobby in Canada. Even so, if states and provinces get serious about the threats to forests from urbanization, then there are strong incentives to create regional forest preservation compacts in order to head off concerns of a race-to-the-bottom, whereby urban development interests might flee to other jurisdictions due to forest carbon preservation statutes in the jurisdiction in which they wish to develop. By developing regional forest policy agreements, individual states and provinces may be able to preserve their own individual economic growth interests without losing out to other jurisdictions while also tackling climate change via forest carbon sequestration.

There is little precedent in the United States or Canada for subnational horizontal approaches to issues related to land uses, especially in the forest context. As a result, the availability of horizontal approaches provides little assurance to the U.S. and Canadian federal governments that they can commit to international standards. The drivers for such arrangements, however, are certainly in place, especially if states and provinces that are facing similar threats to forests from urbanization decide to take more robust action on carbon policies in the future.[105]

The United States and Canada face similar difficulties in relying on top-down amendment of their respective constitutions and on horizontal approaches to ensuring Fail-safe Federalism on climate and forests. It seems that expanded constitutional interpretation and bilateral approaches, whether cooperative or uncooperative, are far less viable in Canada than in the United States, where such approaches would seem to be viable and to have a relatively good chance of success if the United States Congress can garner the requisite political will to pass legislation. The next section, Pathways of Transnational Impacts, discusses a mechanism for forging Fail-safe Federalism that does not arise from current, internal volition to adjust constitutional structure, but rather that is created due to external forces arising from civil society. These are mechanisms by which the commoners on the lowest scale, that of individual herders, might overcome collective action problems to change the very structure and functioning of their governmental systems, rather than trying to elicit change from within the existing framework.

Fortification in Response to External Forces: Pathways of Transnational Impacts on Domestic Governance

This section will build entirely off Bernstein and Cashore's framework for assessing various "pathways" by which civil society can influence domestic and global forest policy via external pressures when governments refuse to take initiative from within current governmental systems and processes.[106] Specifically, these pathways arise from increasing international pressures on domestic policies that have global implications, like forest management, as "[t]ransnational actors and international institutions influence policies by bringing norms generated or promoted in the international sphere into the domestic political arena."[107] Bernstein and Cashore identify four pathways by which international pressures shape and change domestic policy. These include: (1) market dependence; (2) international rules; (3) international normative discourse; (4) infiltration of the domestic policymaking process.[108]

Pathway 1, "market dependence," is when transnational actors "use global markets to force policy responses."[109] The most common example is boycott campaigns, where "a company or government faces market loss and economic hardship if it does not bow to demands of consumers in other countries."[110] This pathway may directly bypass domestic politics since consumers drive the government's choice to change its policies. In other words, though "domestic politics influence the specifics of the policy response, the relationship among the state, business and nonbusiness interests (the policy network) is relatively unimportant for success because the coercive force of the market dependence path affects business interests as much as the state."[111] The emergence of market-driven institutions, like forest certification schemes, has also created economic pressures in favor of more stringent forest management standards[112] and has "effectively bypass[ed] domestic regulatory and land-use policies"[113] inconsistent with those standards.

Pathway 2, "international rules," includes the legally binding treaties that are the focus of this book, as well as trade agreements or other policies crafted by international organizations such as the International Monetary Fund and the World Bank—which might require countries receiving funds to adopt environmental standards as a condition of the loan.[114] Non-governmental organizations (NGOs) or other non-governmental institutions like forest certification systems too can influence the international rules pathway.[115] International rules often affect domestic policy, of course, when "rules and regulations commit signatory countries to change their domestic regulations."[116] As a result, of all the pathways raised by Bernstein and Cashore, this is the one most likely to be adversely impacted by constitutional federalism since "[d]omestic policy-making structures are also important when states require domestic ratification of international agreements or implementing legislation."[117] Nonetheless, despite domestic governance structures that may limit direct participation at the federal level, assuming these agreements are legitimately negotiated and arranged at the international level, they may create a "pull toward compliance" by subnational governments.[118] In fact, though a variety of international negotiations have failed to result in a legally binding global forest treaty, these forums have indeed provided a "pull toward compliance" with heightened forest management standards, as have a variety of non-forest-specific agreements, such as the Convention on Biological Diversity.[119]

Pathway 3, "international normative discourse," effectively involves transnational actors engaging in symbolic or information campaigns at the international level for the sole purpose of changing domestic governance.[120] An example would be increased international focus on the inclusion of aboriginal rights in forest policy creating pressure for domestic change. Such norms, "even when they are not binding on states, can alter state identities and interests" and "even if an institution appears weak along one dimension, such as providing binding rules, it may still play a powerful normative role … primarily through moral suasion and communicative action rather than coercion or enforcement."[121] The problem with this pathway for the United States and Canada, however, is that it depends on the "moral vulnerability" of the target state[122] and its domestic ideology and culture. Countries most reachable by this pathway are those that "aspire to belong to a normative community of nations."[123] Oftentimes the culture of powerful federal nations is somewhat self-fulfilling in this regard, in that the domestic ideology of federalism may trump other moral pressures as the values of federalism are seen as moral imperatives in their own right. Even so, one of the most prominent examples of successful norm influence on domestic policy is sustainable forest management (SFM), which has been widely accepted (at least on paper) by governments globally, and includes protection of indigenous rights and protection from illegal logging.[124] Another example is the direct impact international norms have had on forest policy reform in Brazil, as international interest in the Amazon and its global value have directed pressure on Brazil's domestic forest policies.[125]

Pathway 4 is the "infiltration of the domestic policy-making process" by transnational actors, which "internaliz[es] the external influence[s]" of civil society.[126] This is basically a scenario where the policymaking process is open to a broad swath of civil society, rather than just, say, business interests. When the process accommodates new and additional organizations within deliberations, governing officials are autonomous and free to consider a wide variety of societal needs, and the government can successfully implement policy choices, this pathway may lead to domestic change through *direct* participation of transnational actors. These actors can "provide resources, knowledge, training and financing to existing domestic groups, or help organize or finance new domestic-based groups or coalitions."[127]

These four pathways of transnational influence have had direct impacts on subnational forest policy in Canada, with British Columbia (B.C.) providing a compelling case study. For example, logging of old-growth forests in B.C. created a public and media backlash both in Canada and abroad and, coupled with international pressure concerning the status of the world's forests, contributed to a shift toward heightened forest management standards in B.C. Indeed, the high legal standards discussed in Chapter 8 for clear-cutting, riparian buffer zones, and annual allowable cut limits arose in part out of these pathways,[128] which further had a hand in shifting provincial management to an ecosystem-based approach for particular forests of interest to civil society.[129] Boycott campaigns were successfully utilized along the "market dependence" pathway and were especially vigorous in targeting clear-cutting policies (or the lack thereof). B.C. was effectively branded by environmental groups as the "Brazil of the North" on forest policy.[130] In the United States, legislation was proposed in the state of California to ban B.C. forest products and the *New York Times* was under pressure to stop printing on paper from B.C. forests.[131] In fact, due to the United States accounting for 59 percent of B.C.'s forest products export market, the influence of U.S. transnational actors was significant.[132] Similar pressure arose from other countries abroad, ultimately contributing not only to heightened standards for subnational forests, but also to the strict protection between 1999 and 2005 of over 38 million hectares of boreal forest.[133] Millions more hectares have been protected since that time, resulting in a truce of sorts between groups boycotting provincial forest products and the forest sector.[134] Ultimately, because of the market dependence pathway, "[p]rovincial governments and industry have been forced to consider new forest management issues and values such as biodiversity, landscape scale management, wildlife, recreation, subsistence, aesthetic and watershed management, recycling, and climate change."[135]

Trade laws were utilized along the "international rules" pathway, though the effects of this pathway on B.C. forest policy are less clear.[136] In addition, the possibility, however unlikely, of a global forest convention provides another potentially powerful mechanism along this pathway, and international negotiations on global forest standards may have created a "pull toward compliance" on the B.C. government. Transnational actors utilized the "international normative discourse" pathway to inject new concerns over biodiversity, ecosystem management, aboriginal rights, and tropical deforestation into B.C. forest policy.[137] Finally, along pathway 4, transnational actors were able to infiltrate the domestic policymaking pathway through a variety of resource-sharing and coalition-building efforts among numerous environmental groups—including those established specifically for the purpose of engaging in domestic forest policymaking.[138] Some of these groups had a direct role in the establishment of more stringent riparian buffer zone requirements.[139] This pathway has "arguably had the biggest impact on domestic policymaking" in B.C.[140]

To be clear, Bernstein and Cashore note that durable and lasting policy change requires more than just one pathway, as the market dependence pathway alone, for example, will only result in change as long as market pressures remain in place.[141] Thus, synergies among pathways are of utmost importance. In addition, a variety of other factors drive specific policy outcomes, and pathways of transnational pressure is just one such set of factors.[142] Even so, the case of B.C. demonstrates that pathways can be a significant contributor to domestic forest policy change at the federal or provincial level, or both.[143]

The pathways approach has proven to be a valuable mechanism for changing subnational forest policy in Canada, and if appropriately utilized, would seemingly be a viable approach for facilitating subnational climate policies related to the preservation of forest carbon sequestration values. These changes at the subnational level may allow the federal government to assure the international community that binding global standards will be honored by subnational governments already engaged in such standard-setting; or pathways may be utilized to rebalance federalism related to Canadian forest policy in a way that allows the federal government to directly implement international standards. In fact, this cursory overview of mechanisms for forging Fail-safe Federalism in Canada indicates that the severely limited nature, if not the effective non-existence of federal government constitutional authority over subnational forest policy, leaves a pathways approach as perhaps the only viable mechanism for forging climate policies related to forest carbon sequestration in Canada—a mechanism initially arising not from the constitutional authority of the federal government or the benevolent volition of subnational government legislatures, but rather from external forces that necessarily synergize to create pressures that contribute to domestic policy change.

Interestingly, one of the facilitators of transnational pathways affecting subnational forest policy in Canada arose out of successful efforts by U.S. environmental groups in the early 1990s in the Pacific Northwest to increase forest preservation and management standards.[144] This once again indicates how civil society's influence on *public* forest management standards, through the wielding of procedural rights such as citizen suits under the ESA, can have immediate and significant impacts—a far more difficult task on private forestlands like those in the southeastern United States. Indeed, U.S. environmental groups successfully shifting focus from the Pacific Northwest, with its high proportion of government-owned forests, to Canada, with its exceedingly high proportion of provincially owned forests, and having a direct role in increasing the stringency of provincial forest standards, provides further evidence that such pressures are more efficacious when the government is the owner of the resource—further illustrating the importance of the private–public forest ownership divide explored in Chapter 8.[145] These groups have yet to successfully target forest policy in the southeastern United States, with its exceedingly high proportion of private forests.

Even so, in the United States a pathways approach might also be a viable mechanism for forging Fail-safe Federalism for forest policy. In the western United States, pathways might succeed for similar reasons as they would in Canada—as the high proportion of government-owned forests may allow for more sudden policy change with a resulting spillover effect for private forests. Indeed, for the reasons discussed in Part III, all four of the pathways seem likely to more readily impact forest policy on government-owned forestlands, as governments are more responsive to each of the pressures/inputs presented by each pathway. Similarly, in the southeastern United States, where pathways 2 through 4 are far less likely to be efficacious in spurring stringent private forest management standards, pathway 1, market dependence, could result in a shift in subnational forest policy. The huge economic importance of the forest industry to southeastern U.S. states makes subnational governments and citizens in the region far more susceptible to market pressures, which, if properly focused, could theoretically drive climate policies aimed at preserving forests' carbon sequestration values. Even so, given the greater amount of constitutional power available to the U.S. federal government relative to the Canadian federal government, a pathways approach is more appropriately left as a reserve option in the United States. Pathways are more of a "wait-and-see" option in the absence of fortification from within. While a pathways approach may be a necessity in Canada due to the lack of any other realistically viable mechanisms for forging Fail-safe Federalism, the U.S. government maintains other tools it should first attempt to utilize.

Conclusion

Both the U.S. and Canadian constitutions allot treaty-making authority to the federal government for the specific purpose of allowing these countries to arrange their international obligations. When the U.S. Constitution was drafted, for example, it was designed to allow the federal government supreme authority in all international treaty matters because "state interference in foreign affairs had nearly driven the country to war under the Articles of Confederation."[146] The U.S. and Canadian constitutions, however, also provide federalism protections by reserving certain powers, such as subnational forest policymaking authority, exclusively to the states and provinces in order to gain the benefits of decentralized policy formulation. Though federalism principles are valuable, they arguably place a disproportionate burden on the treaty power of the U.S. and Canadian federal governments when and if those governments garner the political will to address climate change by fully utilizing each nation's forests. They also entrench legal protections that perpetuate a natural capital (forest) commons across local, state/provincial, national, and global scales.

As a result, mechanisms for forging Fail-safe Federalism should be developed to allow greater federal inputs into subnational forest policy so that federal governments can more freely arrange their international affairs and can preserve all of the legal and policy tools needed to combat climate change. Importantly, the United States and Canada maintain very different domestic forest governance systems, due primarily to disparities in the entities owning most of the forest resources in the respective jurisdictions and far less constitutional authority at the federal level in Canada than in the United States. Accordingly, the top-down approach of expanded interpretation of existing constitutional provisions and a bilateral cooperative/uncooperative federalism approach to forging Fail-safe Federalism would be most effective in the United States, whereas the external influences of transnational pathways would be most effective at spurring Fail-safe Federalism formation in Canada.

Fail-safe Federalism is not intended to completely supersede the benefits provided by subnational regulatory authority over forest policy. Nor should that policy be completely controlled by the federal government. Instead, to the extent that constitutional grants of treaty authority are valued as a means of federal governments arranging their international affairs to combat climate change, approaches to forging Fail-safe Federalism should be pursued. In other words, federal systems like those of the United States and Canada must adjust constitutional structure if they are to most effectively and flexibly participate in global governance related to forests and climate or develop more stringent domestic policies. The ability of federal nations to overcome commons dilemmas to address the most important global environmental issues of our time should not be hampered by otherwise valuable principles of federalism.

Notes

1 The material constituting significant portions of this chapter originated in Blake Hudson, Fail-safe Federalism and Climate Change: The Case of U.S. and Canadian Forest Policy, 44 *Conn. L. Rev.* 925 (2012) and Blake Hudson, Reconstituting Land Use Federalism to Address Transitory and Perpetual Disasters: The Bimodal Federalism Framework, 2011 *BYU L. Rev.* 1991 (2011).

2 Ronnie D. Lipschutz, Why is There No International Forestry Law? An Examination of International Forestry Regulation, Both Public and Private, 19 *UCLA J. Envtl. L. & Pol'y* 153, 159 (2001).

3 Though climate negotiations are primarily concerned with forest carbon only, the Intergovernmental Panel on Climate Change (IPCC)'s findings are relevant to future UNFF negotiations, as the UNFF has also recognized the role of forest carbon in addressing climate change.

4 Gert J. Nabuurs et al., 9: Forestry, in *Climate Change 2007: Mitigation, Contribution of Working Group III to the Fourth Assessment Report of the Intergovernmental Panel on Climate Change* 549 (Bert Mertz et al. eds, 2007) available at http://www.ipcc.ch/ipccreports/ar4-wg3.htm (follow "Chapter 9: Forestry" hyperlink).

5 U.N. Env't Programme, *Global Environment Outlook 3: Past, Present and Future Perspectives* 110 (2002), available at http://www.unep.org/geo/GEO3/english/pdf.htm (follow "Forests" hyperlink).

6 For a discussion of a hybrid market-based/regulatory treaty solution, based upon a global system of tradable forest conservation obligations or, rather, a system of "beneficiaries pay" financing of forest conservation, see Jonathan Wiener, Making Markets for Global Forest Conservation, in *Painting the White House Green: Rationalizing Environmental Policy Inside the Executive Office of the President* 119 (Randall Lutter and Jason F. Shogren eds, 2004).

7 Michael Howlett and Jeremy Rayner, Globalization and Governance Capacity: Explaining Divergence in National Forest Programs as Instances of 'Next-Generation' Regulation in Canada and Europe, 19 *Governance: An Int'l J. of Pol'y, Admin., & Institutions* 251, 256 (2006).

8 See Kenneth Abbott, The Transnational Regime Complex for Climate Change, 30 *Envtl. & Plan. C: Gov't & Pol'y* 571 (2012); Daniel Bodansky, A Tale of Two Architectures: The Once and Future U.N. Climate Change Regime, 43 *Ariz. St. L.J.* 697 (2011).

9 Lars H. Gulbrandsen, Overlapping Public and Private Governance: Can Forest Certification Fill the Gaps in the Global Forest Regime? 4 *Global Envtl. Pol.* 75, 81 (2004); Graeme Auld, Ben Cashore, and Deanna Newsom, Perspectives on Forest Certification: A Survey Examining Differences Among the U.S. Forest Sectors' Views of Their Forest Certification Alternatives, in *Forest Policy for Private Forestry* (Benjamin Cashore, Lawrence Teeter, and Daowei Zhang eds, 2003).

10 The IPCC found that "[r]educed deforestation and degradation is the forest mitigation option with the largest and most immediate carbon stock impact in the short term …

because large carbon stocks ... are not emitted when deforestation is prevented." Nabuurs et al., supra note 4, at 550. One study found that forest carbon, sequestered primarily through REDD activities, could "cut the global cost of climate change policies in half and reduce the price of carbon by 40 percent." See Erin C. Myers, *Policies to Reduce Emissions from Deforestation and Degradation (REDD) in Tropical Forests: An Examination of the Issues Facing the Incorporation of REDD into Market-Based Climate Policies* 25 (2007), available at http://www.rff.org/documents/RFF-DP-07-50.pdf.

11 James Rasband, James Salzman, and Mark Squillace, *Natural Resources Law and Policy* 1206–7 (2nd ed. 2009).

12 Katherine Swinton, Amending the Canadian Constitution: Lessons From Meech Lake, 42 *U. Toronto L.J.* 139, 145 (1992).

13 See Robin Kundis Craig, Should There Be a Constitutional Right to a Clean/Healthy Environment? 34 *Envtl. L. Rep.* 11013, 11014 (2004) (questioning the effectiveness of courts taking on environmental issues in the absence of a constitutional amendment); Dan L. Gildor, Preserving The Priceless: A Constitutional Amendment to Empower Congress to Preserve, Protect, and Promote The Environment, 32 *Ecology L.Q.* 821, 846–47 (2005) (advocating amending the Constitution to promote environmental goals); Rodger Schlickeisen, Protecting Biodiversity for Future Generations: An Argument for a Constitutional Amendment, 8 *Tul. Envtl. L.J.* 181, 206 (1994) ("Only an amendment ... will be able to resolve all doubt about the standing of a citizen to enjoin government actions that endanger those resources."); Pamela B. Schmaltz, Is It Time for an Environmental Amendment? 38 *Loy. L. Rev.* 451, 461–62 (1992) (discussing the ineffectiveness of statutory environmental initiatives). But see J.B. Ruhl, The Metrics of Constitutional Amendments: And Why Proposed Environmental Quality Amendments Don't Measure Up, 74 *Notre Dame L. Rev.* 245, 250–51 (1999) (arguing that environmentally focused constitutional amendments have been ineffective).

14 William C. Hodge, Patriation of the Canadian Constitution: Comparative Federalism in a New Context, 60 *Wash. L. Rev.* 585, 585 (1985).

15 See, e.g., Sujit Choudhry, Ackerman's Higher Lawmaking in Comparative Constitutional Perspective: Constitutional Moments as Constitutional Failures? 6 *Int'l J. of Const. L.* 193, 225 (2008) (describing the amendment procedure as a "failure").

16 See Richard B. Bernstein and Jerome Agel, *Amending America: If We Love the Constitution So Much, Why Do We Keep Trying to Change It?* 169 (1993) (discussing the likelihood of an amendment to the United States Constitution being ratified); John R. Vile, *Encyclopedia of Constitutional Amendments, Proposed Amendments, and Amending Issues*, 1789–1995, xi, 363–80 (1996) (collating proposals by year); Ruth B. Ginsburg, On Amending the Constitution: A Plea for Patience, 12 *U. Ark. Little Rock L.J.* 677, 679 (1990).

17 An amendment must be proposed by either two-thirds of both houses or two-thirds of state governments and ratified by three-quarters of state governments. U.S. *Const.* art. V.

18 Ruhl, supra note 13, at 248–49.

19 Id. at 248.

20 Id. at 253.

21 Id.

22 Ruhl states that "*any* EQA (Environmental Quality Amendment) attempting to capture a normative statement about the environment and plug it into the United States Constitution is simply a bad idea." Id. at 252. Furthermore, "amendments purporting to express aspirational values or regulate civil relations, or do both, should set off bells and whistles in the political evaluation process." Id. at 260.

23 The same would also be true for an amendment that sought to allow federal involvement in land-use policymaking generally.

24 Ruhl, supra note 13, at 261 fig.1.

25 Id. at 271.

26 See, e.g., Craig, supra note 13, at 11018. Professor Craig argues that "a constitutional amendment could allow Congress to reenact the federal environmental statutes pursuant

to that amendment's grant of legislative authority, freeing them of any lingering Commerce Clause limitations and leaving Congress free to reach the last federally unregulated impediments to environmental quality—such as nonpoint source pollution—currently deemed to be outside the federal regulatory sphere." Id. at 11019–20.

27 Gildor, supra note 13, at 823.

28 Craig, supra note 13, at 11018.

29 The Supreme Court of Canada held in the *Patriation Reference* case that the Canadian federal government could gain exclusive authority to amend the Canadian Constitution, though it could only do so with a "substantial degree" of provincial support. The federal government was able to do so in December of 1981. Kevin Sneesby, National Separation: Canada in Context-Legal Perspective, 53 *La. L. Rev.* 1357, 1366 (1993).

30 Constitution Act, 1867, 30 & 31 Vict., c. 3 (U.K.).

31 Constitution Act, 1982, pt. V, *being* Schedule B to the Canada Act, 1982, c.11 (U.K.) (requiring different procedures for different types of amendments, such as those relating to the composition of the Supreme Court of Canada or that are province specific).

32 Choudhry, supra note 15, at 222.

33 Id. at 225.

34 Id. at 227.

35 Constitution Act, 1982, § 38(1), *being* Schedule B to the Canada Act, 1982, c.11 (U.K).

36 Id. § 38(3).

37 Id. § 38(2).

38 See, e.g., Swinton, supra note 12, at 144–45.

39 Id. at 145.

40 Jeffrey L. Friesen, The Distribution of Treaty-Implementing Powers in Constitutional Federations: Thoughts on the American and Canadian Models, 94 *Colum. L Rev.* 1415, 1439 (1994).

41 David N. Wear and John G. Greis, *U.S. Forest Serv., The Southern Forest Futures Project: Summary Report* 17 (2011), available at http://www.srs.fs.usda.gov/futures/reports/draft/summary_report.pdf.

42 Id. at 29.

43 Id. at 5.

44 U.S.D.A., *U.S. Forest Facts and Historical Trends* 7 (Sept. 2001), available at http://fia.fs.fed.us/library/briefings-summaries-overviews/docs/ForestFactsMetric.pdf. Carbon flux, or the net difference between carbon removal and carbon addition to the atmosphere, is 50 percent greater on public forestlands in the United States than on private forestlands, most likely resulting "from greater land use conversions and disturbance (including timber harvest) on private forests relative to public forests." Eric M. White and Ralph J. Alig, Public and Private Forest Ownership in the Context of Carbon Sequestration and Bioenergy Feedstock Production—A Briefing Paper on Existing Research and Research Needs 9–10 (Mar. 2010), available at http://www.fsl.orst.edu/lulcd/Publicationsalpha_files/White_Public_Private_Briefing.pdf.

45 Gonzales v. Raich, 545 U.S. 1, 22 (2005) (upholding the federal regulation of marijuana); Hodel v. Ind., 452 U.S. 314, 326 (1981) (upholding the federal regulation of minerals); Hodel v. Va. Surface Mining & Reclamation Ass'n, Inc., 452 U.S. 264, 281 (1981) (same); United States v. Riverside Bayview Homes, 474 U.S. 121, 133 (1985) (upholding the regulation of wetlands by the federal government); Wickard v. Filburn, 317 U.S. 111, 128–29 (1942) (upholding the federal regulation of wheat); see also Babbitt v. Sweet Home Chapt. Comms. for Ore., 515 U.S. 687, 708 (1995) (noting that Congress has exercised its delegated powers in crafting the Endangered Species Act); TVA v. Hill, 437 U.S. 153, 194 (1978) (stating that Congress not only has the power to create legislation, but also to determine the relative priority for the country).

46 Rancho Viejo v. Norton, 334 F.3d 1158, 1158 (D.C. Cir. 2003) (Sentelle, J., dissenting); id. at 1160 (Roberts, J., dissenting).

47 U.S. Const. amend. V, cl. 4 ("[N]or shall private property be taken for public use, without just compensation.").

48 Paul Stanton Kibel, Canada's International Forest Protection Obligations: A Case of Promises Forgotten in British Columbia and Alberta, 6 *Fordham Envtl. L. Rev.* 231, 248 (1995).

49 It is true that exclusive federal power in the areas of trade, commerce, and taxation has "limited the thrust of provincial constitutional supremacy in many resource matters," especially given the great number of natural resources that enter interprovincial or international markets. Michael Howlett and Jeremy Rayner, The Business and Government Nexus: Principal Elements and Dynamics of the Canadian Forest Policy Regime, in *Canadian Forest Policy* (Michael Howlett ed., 2001) at 23, 39. This was noted above with regard to agriculture and fisheries. Even though forest products certainly enter into those same markets, they remain separate and apart from these other natural resources—due primarily to the explicit nature of the constitutional forest mandates—and the federal government's use of constitutional powers in the forest context has largely been limited to mitigating forest management impacts on fisheries or agriculture. Id. at 40. For example, the forest practice standards along the British Columbia coast have been governed by the *British Columbia Coastal Fisheries Forestry Guidelines*, which "were established in a classic bargaining process between the federal Department of Fisheries and Oceans, the B.C. Ministry of Forests, the B.C. Ministry of Environment, and the industry trade group, the Council on Forest Industries." George Hoberg, The British Columbia Forest Practices Code: Formalization and Its Effects, in *Canadian Forest Policy* (Michael Howlett ed., 2001), at 354. These guidelines established standards for maximum cut and watershed buffer zones in coastal forested areas, though they were non-binding. See id. (discussing specifications in the British Columbia Coastal Fisheries Forestry Guidelines).

50 See Vincent P. Fiore, Federal Wetlands Regulation in Canada and the United States: Suggestions for Canada in Light of Crown Zellerbach and the Peace, Order and Good Government Clause of the Canadian Constitution, 27 *Geo. Wash. J. Int'll L. & Econ.* 139, 159–60 (1993) (discussing the inadequacy of the criminal law power and trade and commerce power to effectively support environmental legislation); Rodney Northey, Federalism and Comprehensive Environmental Reform: Seeing Beyond the Murky Medium, 29 *Osgoode Hall L.J.* 127, 136–39 (1991) (discussing the limits on federal powers, particularly through criminal law and trade and commerce powers).

51 Northey, supra note 50, at 139; *accord* Fiore, supra note 50, at 160.

52 Gerald Baier, New Judicial Thinking on Sovereignty and Federalism: American and Canadian Comparisons, 23 *Just. Sys. J.* 1, 12 (2002).

53 Dale Gibson, Constitutional Jurisdiction Over Environmental Management in Canada, 23 *U. Toronto L.J.* 54, 62 (1973).

54 Id.

55 Baier, supra note 52, at 12.

56 Id.

57 Id. For a thorough discussion of this test, see id. at 13, and Fiore, supra note 50, at 161–62.

58 Ontario Hydro v. Ontario (Labour Relations Board), [1993] 3 S.C.R. 327, 379–80 (Can.) (holding that the production, use, and application of atomic energy constitutes a matter of national concern and properly falls under the power of the Parliament of Canada); R. v. Crown Zellerbach Canada Ltd., [1988] 1 S.C.R. 401, 436–38 (Can.) (holding the Ocean Dumping Control Act as a constitutionally valid exercise of power by the Parliament of Canada). See also Baier, supra note 52, at 13–16 (discussing the *Crown Zellerbach* case and the effect of its decision).

59 Baier, supra note 52, at 15.

60 Constitution Act, 1867, 30 & 31 Vict., c.6, § 91 (U.K.) (consolidated with amendments).

61 Fiore, supra note 50, at 164.

62 Gibson, supra note 53, at 62, 65.

63 Fiore, supra note 50, at 164; see also Peter W. Hogg, Canada: From Privy Council to Supreme Court, in *Interpreting Constitutions: A Comparative Study* 55, 63 (Jeffrey Goldsworthy ed., 2006) (noting that early court interpretations of the POGG (peace, order, and good government) clause demonstrated a "relentless refusal to give significant content to the federal peace, order, and good government power whenever it came into potential conflict with the provincial power over property and civil rights.").

64 Graham R. Wilkinson, Codes of Forest Practice as Regulatory Tools for Sustainable Forest Management 2–3 (Paper Presented to the 18th Biennial Conference of the Institute of Foresters of Australia [Hobart, Tasmania, 3rd–8th October, 1999]) (noting that, "[i]n contrast, a self-regulatory approach can avoid unnecessary bureaucratic costs and provide greater flexibility and autonomy for industry, in return for improved environmental performance").

65 S. 3354, The National Land Use Policy Act of 1970, 116 *Cong. Rec.* 1760, 1761.

66 1 Patricia E. Salkin, *American Law of Zoning* § 3:2 (5th ed. 2011).

67 John R. Nolon, Fusing Economic and Environmental Policy: The Need for Framework Laws in the United States and Argentina, 13 *Pace Envtl. L. Rev.* 685, 719 (1996).

68 John H. Davidson, Ecosystem Management in the Smaller Watershed, *2 Great Plains Nat. Resources J.* 68, 76 (1997).

69 2.

70 Nolon, supra note 67, at 724.

71 Id.

72 Id. at 718.

73 Id. at 724–25 (quoting Senator Henry Jackson introducing S. 3354, The National Land Use Policy Act of 1970, 116 *Cong. Rec.* 1757, 1759 (1970)).

74 See 1 Salkin, supra note 66, § 3:3 (discussing how the National Land Use Policy Act (NLUPA) failed and the Coastal Zone Management Act (CZMA) succeeded in providing the federal government the opportunity to protect the coastal zone with increased state involvement).

75 Marc R. Poirier, Environmental Justice and the Beach Access Movements of the 1970s in Connecticut and New Jersey: Stories of Property and Civil Rights, 28 *Conn. L. Rev.* 719, 751 (1996).

76 1 Salkin, supra note 66, § 3:3.

77 Id.

78 Id.

79 Kristen M. Fletcher, Managing Coastal Development, in *Ocean and Coastal Law and Policy* 147, 159–60 (Donald C. Baur et al. eds, 2008).

80 1 Salkin, supra note 66, § 3.3.

81 Bradley C. Karkkainen, Biodiversity and Land, 83 *Cornell L. Rev.* 1, 81 (1997).

82 Joanna M. Beyers, Model Forests as Process Reform: Alternative Dispute Resolution and Multistakeholder Planning, in *Canadian Forest Policy,* supra note 49, at 172, 177.

83 Id.

84 See id. at 178 (discussing the non-compliance of partners in the original MFP and the inability of two to fulfill their mandate).

85 Id. at 180.

86 Id. at 184.

87 Id.

88 Id. at 193.

89 Evert Lindquist and Adam Wellstead, Making Sense of Complexity: Advances and Gaps in Comprehending the Canadian Forest Policy Process, in *Canadian Forest Policy,* supra note 49, at 419, 425.

90 Beyers, supra note 82, at 194.

91 Michael Howlett, The Federal Role in Canadian Forest Policy: From Territorial Landowner to International and Intergovernmental Co-ordinating Agent, in *Canadian Forest Policy,* supra note 49, at 378, 387.

92 See id. at 397 (discussing the dissolution of the Department of Forestry in the face of provincial opposition to federal conditional grant programs).
93 Id.
94 Id. at 399.
95 Id.
96 See, e.g., Lynn A. Baker and Mitchell N. Berman, Getting off the Dole: Why the Court Should Abandon Its Spending Doctrine, and How a Too-Clever Congress Could Provoke It to Do So, 78 *Ind. L.J.* 459, 462–64 (2003) (discussing the litigation surrounding the federal government's withholding of highway funds from those states that had not raised their minimum legal drinking age to at least 21 years of age).
97 See Clean Water Act of 1977, 33 U.S.C. § 1251 (2006).
98 Jayne E. Daly, A Glimpse of the Past—A Vision for the Future: Senator Henry M. Jackson and National Land-Use Legislation, 28 *Urb. Law.* 7, 12 (1996) (citing S. 3354, 91st Cong., § 407(1)–(2) (1970)).
99 Id. at 18.
100 See 33 U.S.C. § 1344(a), (d).
101 Kibel, supra note 48, at 250–51.
102 Id.
103 Howlett, supra note 49, at 40.
104 See *North American Cap-and-Trade Initiatives*, *Pew Ctr. on Global Climate Change*, available at http://www.pewclimate.org/what_s_being_done/in_the_states/NA-capandtrade.
105 Id.
106 See generally Steven Bernstein et al., Examination of the Influences of Global Forest Governance Arrangements at the Domestic Level, in 28 *Embracing Complexity: Meeting the Challenges of International Forest Governance 111* (Jeremy Rayner et al. eds, 2010), available at www.iufro.org/download/file/6572/5017/ws28-ch07.pdf/; Steven Bernstein and Benjamin Cashore, Globalization, Four Paths of Internationalization and Domestic Policy Change: The Case of EcoForestry in British Columbia, Canada, 33 *Can. J. Pol. Sci.* 67 (2000).
107 Bernstein and Cashore, supra note 106, at 71.
108 Id. at 75.
109 Id. at 76.
110 Id.
111 Id. at 77.
112 Bernstein et al., supra note 106, at 113.
113 Id. at 121.
114 Bernstein and Cashore, supra note 106, at 79.
115 Bernstein et al., supra note 106, at 112.
116 Bernstein and Cashore, supra note 106, at 79.
117 Id. at 80.
118 Id.
119 Bernstein et al., supra note 106, at 114. In addition, Bernstein et al. note that REDD programs are "likely to lead, eventually, to one of the first sets of rules in international forest governance to have a binding impact on domestic practices such as land-use change and logging." Id.
120 Bernstein and Cashore, supra note 106, at 81.
121 Id. at 82–83.
122 Id. at 83.
123 Id. at 81–82.
124 Bernstein et al., supra note 106, at 119.
125 Id. at 120. Whether Brazil's domestic forest policies are successfully implemented is another matter. See Chapter 7.
126 Bernstein and Cashore, supra note 106, at 83.
127 Id. at 85.

128 Id. at 87–88.
129 Id. at 88.
130 Hoberg, supra note 49, at 357.
131 Bernstein and Cashore, supra note 106, at 89.
132 Bernstein et al., supra note 106, at 121.
133 Id.
134 Id. at 122.
135 Lindquist and Wellstead, supra note 89, at 427–28.
136 Bernstein and Cashore, supra note 106, at 91.
137 Id. at 92.
138 Id. at 96–97.
139 Id. at 97.
140 Bernstein et al., supra note 106, at 126.
141 Bernstein and Cashore, supra note 106, at 90.
142 Id. at 98.
143 Of course, one of the greatest ironies of transnational impacts on domestic governance is the circular nature of their interaction with binding legal standards on national and global scales. The lack of binding global governance has been one of the primary causes of increased transnational approaches to governance formation, yet these transnational approaches may have impacts on domestic governance in a way that actually makes binding global governance more likely. In other words, global treaty-making is complicated by domestic federalism and other legal and political conflicts, giving rise to action by transnational actors, which in turn actually effect change within federal nations that may remedy the very federalism constraints that were previously prohibiting full interaction by federal systems in global governance.
144 Bernstein and Cashore, supra note 106, at 86, 97.
145 Id. at 97–98.
146 Cyril Robert Emery, Treaty Solutions from the Land Down Under: Reconciling American Federalism and International Law, 24 *Penn St. Int'l L. Rev.* 115, 127 (2005).

Conclusion

Overcentralization of resource management within nations has long been associated with resource management tragedies. Developing world rainforests where locals have little to no control over resource appropriation, and therefore no incentive to preserve the resource, has received great attention in the literature. By contrast, in some federal systems of government, local citizens have a phenomenal degree of control over resource appropriation. This gives them a stakeholder interest in the democratic process that would be the envy of a vast majority of citizens the world over. And yet, with this great degree of control comes a great degree of responsibility—responsibility that is being largely abdicated as citizens utilize the democratic process to provide themselves with short-term economic gains despite the high degree of environmental losses that will be suffered by future generations. As with Hardin's herders, these citizens externalize these harms because they will negatively affect someone else, most likely in the future. The resource tragedies associated with this over-decentralization of management has largely been overlooked in the literature. While political overcentralization or over-decentralization can result in any governmental system, what makes federal systems particularly challenging is the legal entrenchment of rules mandating over-decentralized environmental management, such that even if a central authority wanted to prevent resource tragedies by enacting minimum standards policies nationwide it would be prevented from doing so absent a wholesale augmentation of constitutional structure.

National governments in federal systems of government have the ability, *if* granted constitutional authority, to address the nested governance commons problems described in this book. National governments that have regulatory authority to address land use issues related to urban development or private forest management can spur subnational governments to craft rules for natural capital appropriation by private entities, or can do so directly in the absence of state action to protect the natural capital of the nation as a whole. In turn, national governments unconstrained by lower level commons are freer, from a legal perspective, to enter into international treaties or other governance regimes addressing the global natural capital commons. Though these federal systems may be politically bounded by their own rationality regarding whether to coordinate internationally to manage the global commons, since there is no global hegemonic entity to direct them in the same way that they may direct subnational governments, they are no longer *legally* bound to rational commons outcomes.

A variety of federal systems maintains an adequate allocation of legal authority across levels of government to have dynamic resource management inputs, but rather face resource management challenges due to a variety of political, enforcement, corruption, or other deficiencies. Yet others, like the U.S. and Canada, may not have sufficient legal authority across levels of government to maintain regulatory inputs that can avoid natural capital commons tragedies, thus entrenching all scales of the nested governance commons with regard to certain types of natural capital. This book only undertakes a cursory review of a handful of federal systems and their attributes to identify the potential of federal systems to legally entrench the commons dynamic. Hopefully this review will give rise to future, more comprehensive study of federal systems on the whole, and study which may strengthen both the commons and the governance literature.

Understanding the crucial role of federal governments along the nested commons continuum is crucial to establishing sufficient legal frameworks for managing natural capital across scales, from local, to national, to global. Federal constitutions act as keystones to these management scales, either allowing or legally denying coordinated efforts.

In the final assessment, analysis of constitutionally entrenched natural capital commons created by federal systems of government allows us to better understand how keystone constitutions can be fortified to address natural capital commons tragedies across scales. Advanced understandings of new commons, like federal nested commons, "put[s] us into a better position to facilitate the development of commons institutions in the future," because "in the absence of appropriate institutions, it is in the individual's best interest to take as much as possible as soon as possible, damaging the resource further in his or her greed and haste."[1] Federal systems and their constitutions are institutional mechanisms for managing natural capital commons, and so their study will result in increased understandings of how governmental systems do not "become the commons," but rather how they can operate in balance with private property rights and successful collective action arrangements.

Note

1 Joanna Burger et al., Common-Pool Resources and Commons Institutions, in *Protecting the Commons* 1, 2 (Joanna Burger et al. eds, 2001).

Index

Index of Legal Cases

For Product Safety Concerns and Information please contact our EU representative GPSR@taylorandfrancis.com Taylor & Francis Verlag GmbH, Kaufingerstraße 24, 80331 München, Germany